MAKING
A
DIFFERENCE

MAKING A DIFFERENCE:
The Management and Governance of Nonprofit Enterprises©

Howard Berman

Robert Thompson

Melanie Phillips

To order additional books, access electronic sections of the book and the appendices, or
to read additional content on the book's topic, go to www.ccepublications.org. Some
content that appears in print may not be available in an electronic format.
Printed in the United States of America
THIRD EDITION – 2021
SECOND EDITION – 2015
FIRST EDITION – 2010

Publisher/Marketing Contact: Kevin P. Kane, kevin.kane@excellus.com
Third Edition:
ISBN-10: 978-1-7923-6239-2
ISBN-13:
DOI #
Library of Congress Control Number:

CONTENTS

APPENDICES*

*Appendices also available at www.ccepublications.org

ACKNOWLEDGMENTS

The weaknesses and shortcomings of the resulting product are entirely ours. The strengths are due to the help received from a number of people who struggled through the earlier manuscripts. In particular, we want to thank Robert Sigmond, Tom Toole, Irwin Flack, Arnie Gissin, Gerardo Cahn-Hidalgo, Diane Howard, Ron Ambrosetti, Peter Carpino, Karyl Mammano, Lisa Moore, and Flynn Leo. Steve Cleary deserves special thanks for his endurance in going through the entire manuscript, a page at a time.

Two other people must be recognized for all that they have done to make this book possible: Elia Marcus and Catherine Ciardi (and the document services team). Elia's fingers touched every word of this manuscript. Without her, there would be just blank pages. Catherine Ciardi and the document services team have brought concept into reality.

To all these people, we publicly offer our thanks and appreciation. They deserve the credit for any value this book brings to the management and governance of nonprofit enterprises.

PROLOGUE

Market-based economies have demonstrated their ability to accomplish great things, creating wealth while simultaneously improving the overall standard of living. At the same time, they have also made clear their inherent harshness. The market, while offering the promise of great benefits, can also be unforgiving and even punishing, ignoring fundamental human needs and allowing "gaps" in the production of goods and services to go unaddressed. As a result, society has created a third sector, a component of the economy that (unlike government) is privately owned, but created for purposes (unlike commercial business) other than profits.

Nonprofit enterprises are certainly not the heart of the American economy. They are, however, its soul.

Nonprofit enterprises provide society with the means for both achieving its highest aspirations and satisfying its most valued beliefs. They provide the vehicles for individuals to meet their responsibilities not just to themselves, but to one and other and to the community—both large and small. Therefore, it is vital that they be well managed.

Managing nonprofit organizations, however, is arguably difficult. In fact, it is perhaps the most difficult of all contemporary management challenges. This is because they have all the operational and human resource problems of any market economy enterprise, but none of the profit making and capital generating decision making and financial advantages. The consequence is that sustainability, let alone survival, is problematic.

The only way to mitigate this reality is through good governance and management. The following text is dedicated to providing a road map for achieving this end. Its goal is to describe how nonprofit enterprises:
- Should be governed and managed—to achieve performance that recognizes a level of responsibility "beyond self"
- Can be successful—as measured not just by traditional structural and financial metrics, but also by the value they provide to their community.

Its target audience is primarily practitioners as well as current and prospective board members. Students, however, will also find it helpful as a detailed introduction to the nonprofit sector. Its goal is to describe who these organizations are, how they come about, how they fit into contemporary society, and how they must be governed and managed to fulfill their potential to "Make a Difference."

PART I
FOUNDATION

Nonprofit enterprises:
Who are they?
Why and how did they come about?

To begin a discussion of the management of nonprofit enterprises, the starting point must be the development of basic industry knowledge. That is, why they exist, as well as who they are and how they fit into contemporary society and the overall economy. The following chapters answer these questions. They also set the foundation for the organizational mechanism needed to enable nonprofit enterprises to productively pursue their mission—the corporation.

Chapter 1:

INTRODUCTION

Nonprofit enterprises are extraordinary organizations accomplishing both what business will not do and what society does not want government to do. While not unique to America, privately-owned, public benefit organizations (i.e., voluntary community enterprises, nonprofit companies), hold a special place in American society. In some form, they have been with us from before the birth of the nation, providing a catalyst for that birth by giving citizens a forum for representing themselves, as well as offering communities a way to tend to their common needs.

Today, they provide a voice for the voiceless, a safety net for those who have fallen, a means for preserving and promoting our arts and culture, and the vehicle for teaching our traditions and values. In addition, they are a provider of education, health care, and human and social welfare services.

> ### ROOTED IN THE AMERICAN EXPERIENCE*
>
> The late Daniel Patrick Moynihan once observed: "A distinguishing feature of American society is the singular degree to which we maintain an independent sector—private institutions in the public service. This is no longer so in most of the democratic world; it never was so in the rest. It is a treasure..."
>
> This distinctive feature of the American experience was documented by Alexis De Toqueville in the early 19th century when he observed:
>
> - *Americans of all ages, all conditions, and all dispositions constantly form associations.*
>
> - *The Americans make associations to give entertainments, to found seminaries, to build inns, to construct churches..., to send missionaries to the Antipodes; in this manner they found hospitals, prisons and schools.*
>
> The civic impulse that led our forebears to band together to hire a teacher for their one-room schoolhouses, to participate in barn raisings with their neighbors, and to establish volunteer fire departments and hospitals, continues today in myriad ways. The emergence and persistence over more than two and a half centuries of a strong voluntary sphere reflects a societal judgment that there are limits to what the commercial and government sectors can or should do. It is within this voluntary sphere that nonprofit enterprises have developed.
>
> *William J. Cox, Alliance Catholic Health Care, "Nonprofit Health Care, Making a Distinctive Contribution to Patients, Families and Communities," March 2007.

Nonprofit organizations are clearly not the economic engine of the economy. Though a small part of the nation's gross domestic product, nonprofit enterprises are the soul of our democratic society. Without them we could not be who we are, have accomplished all that we have achieved, or look forward to the future with optimism.

Put simply, nonprofit enterprises are vital to our individual and collective well-being. Therefore, it is important that these special organizations be well managed, efficient in their operation, and effective in their performance.

A RESOURCE

Recognizing this need, the purpose of this text is to provide an introduction to the governance and management of nonprofit organizations. It has been written primarily to serve as a resource guide for board and management leaders of medium and large nonprofit organizations. To this end, a detailed index has been included to make searching for information and ideas about a particular subject easier.

Its perspective is primarily operational management; therefore, it arguably suffers more from pragmatism than theory. Also, its focus is on the governance and management of social enterprises, those nonprofit organizations that provide products and/or services to their communities, sometimes in competition with other firms—both for-profit and/or nonprofit—and always in a circumstance of limited resources.

For purpose of this discussion, medium and large organizations are defined as the almost one-third (1/3) of reporting public charities, 501(c)3 organizations that have charitable purposes (assisting the poor and underprivileged, advancing religion, education, health, science, art, or culture, protecting the environment, or other purposes beneficial to the community), that have annual expenses of $500,000 or more. While these firms are the minority of nonprofit enterprises in terms of the number of entities, they represent almost 98% of the sector's expenses.[1] Importantly, in terms of organizational life cycle, these are organizations that have matured beyond the initial founding stages (concept and start up) and are faced with the challenges and demands that confront all ongoing business concerns, i.e., continuous improvement, growth, adaptation, and regeneration.[2,3]

SMALL AND STABLE

Some enterprises can remain both small and stable. Certainly these firms represent a nominal percentage of the total.

To be able to be both small and stable, an enterprise must, as a matter of strategy, decide to remain small and, as a matter of operating facts, have a committed group of volunteers and friends who provide both financial and human resource capital for the work of the organization.

As long as the financial and human capital is available, these enterprises can survive from generation to generation. However, while they are able to continue to operate, they will also continually face the same issues and challenges—of finding adequate continuing sources of volunteers to act as the staff, and friends to provide financial capital.

Smaller nonprofit enterprises certainly face governance and management problems—often more daunting than those confronting their larger brethren. For the most part, these smaller enterprises must either grow, through internal means or mergers, dissolve, or be acquired.

Anything else typically leaves them at the wrong economic and operational size, constantly struggling to find capital, both financial and human (i.e., management), and worrying more about money, for the organization's continuing survival, than mission—the reason to survive.

Hopefully, the following discussion will also have relevance to smaller organizations, helping to show them how to manage themselves in order to achieve growth.

Typically, these enterprises are passionately focused on service and view management and administrative activities as distractions—albeit necessary evils whose time commitments should be minimized. Being small, however, is not a justification for either lack of management or bad management.

In fact, smaller organizations need better management than their larger counterparts because they have less financial, human resource, and goodwill reserves to protect them during hard times. The simple facts are that while the depth and detail of activities and processes must be tailored to the size and capacity of the enterprise, the management and governance tools and tasks discussed in the following chapters apply to all nonprofit organizations, regardless of size or organizational maturity.

That said, even if an organization falls short in terms of reaching a self-sustaining size, dissolution is not the option of choice. Enterprises that are unable to grow to a point of sustainability should look to partnering with a mission-consistent, sister/brother organization. Consolidating with another like-minded/valued organization to sustain the enterprise's ability to pursue its founding mission is a positive strategic decision and initiative—not a defeat.

As a primer, its goal is to guide readers along a path that will enable them to help an organization achieve its mission. By design, it avoids formulas and fixed approaches, while attempting to explain the ends being sought and the pieces of the puzzle that have to be matched to get there.

Admittedly, from time to time the discussion will also touch on economics, history, politics, etc. However, readers wanting an in-depth understanding of the historical, political, or the theoretical roots of nonprofit enterprises should delve into the rich and growing literature of the nonprofit field. Similarly, readers interested in technical issues will want to supplement the framework laid out here with details from the appropriate accounting, tax, finance, operations management, human resources, philanthropic, etc., literature.

Every organization has a different history and tradition, as well as varying capacities and capabilities. The reality of these factors must shape the details of the policies adopted and the processes employed by the enterprise. The details, however, must always be built on a foundation of basic concepts. It is hoped that these basic concepts are presented in an understandable and memorable way in the following pages.

To help achieve this understanding, as demonstrated above, the text will be supplemented by "commentary" set off in a box. Sometimes these comments amplify the point being made. At other times they provide a contrary point of view or simply a related observation. They are intended to draw the reader's attention to a relevant point—at the relevant time.

PARTS

While the overall perspective is managerial, and the concentration is on providing management skills and tools, **Part I "Foundation"** starts by examining the place and character of nonprofit enterprises in both the structure of the American economy and the context of contemporary society. As part of creating common ground, it also looks at the corporation both as an innovative concept, necessary for society to marshal the resources required to grow and prosper, and as an operational mechanism for transforming those resources into goods and services.

Part II "Governance" examines governance as the conscience of the corporation, responsible both for assuring the enterprise's focus on its mission and for enhancing the public's trust in the enterprise. Governance, through the enterprise's board of directors, serves as an agent of the organization's stakeholders and beneficiaries, and as the steward of its assets and resources. The obligations and structure of the board, and the importance of governance leadership to an effective, continuously improving governance process are also examined.

Part III "Management Planning and Execution" looks at what has to be done to accomplish results—achieve mission, steward assets, serve the community, and earn the public's trust. The emphasis is on business planning and execution. The section begins by examining strategy, what it is, and how it is developed. It then moves on to consider how to convert strategy into measurable and meaningful results.

Part IV "Management and Governance Challenges" looks broadly at the unique challenges of nonprofit organizations. It examines capital formation, volunteers, succession management, chief executive transition, and the challenge of enhancing the public's trust.

Finally, a number of appendices are provided to address various topics and issues in more detail. These materials differ from the text's "boxes" in that they are designed to provide subject matter depth and/or mechanical detail, without breaking up the flow of the discussions.

LEADERSHIP

Before looking at any of these topics, it is useful to step back and consider the question of managerial leadership. It may seem unusual to begin a primer on nonprofit management by first looking at the matter of leadership. The reality is that no discussion of management concepts, techniques, or mechanics can have practical meaning without understanding that ideas and initiatives must be implemented—and implementation requires leadership.

Quite simply, without leadership, results cannot be accomplished. Without leadership, nothing can or will happen. With it, almost magical things can be achieved.[4]

Much has been written about leadership and how an individual can become an effective business leader. It would be a fool's task to try to capture this body of literature in a few pages. Instead, the discussion that follows is focused on providing a perspective on the personal attributes and techniques needed to lead a nonprofit enterprise—either in whole, or just a part of it.

From a pragmatic perspective, everyone knows what it takes to be a good leader. This is so because each of us has had the experience of being a follower. As followers, we have seen good leaders and bad leaders. The challenge is to distinguish between the two and then adopt the practices of those leaders who were able to make us willing followers.

History demonstrates that leadership opportunities, like political popularity, are fickle.

Even so, opportunities will occur and individuals, if they wish, can capture them and become successful leaders if they are willing to:

- work hard

- exhibit personal courage—the courage to take action, even if that action is simply stepping forward and saying, "I'll take that on."

- learn leadership techniques and even arguably, some tricks.

> **DIRECTION VS. LEADERSHIP**
>
> Leadership does not rely on compulsion. One cannot lead by just the power of his or her position or resources. One can direct by compulsion, making, for example, a gift/contribution conditional upon the enterprise following a particular path. Similarly, people in positions of power/authority can use their position to force others to do as they direct—or incur the personal costs and penalties of not complying.
>
> However, to successfully lead, there must be people willing to voluntarily follow. There must also be a continued willingness on the part of followers—to keep following.

Managerial leadership is influencing people to voluntarily work toward the accomplishment of common objectives. It is energizing and unifying the efforts of people to achieve commonly understood goals and objectives.

Recognizing that leadership requires voluntary followership, the central question is—how does a potential leader begin to generate this level of commitment? The starting point is recognizing that one leads through knowledge.

TRAITS

Competence is the key to leadership, and knowledge is the root of competence. Frankly, no one wants to follow a fool, someone who does not know how to solve the problem being faced. *Leadership, first and foremost, requires the ability both to conceive the path that will lead to the goal, and to share that vision in an understandable and compelling manner.*

This does not mean that leaders always have to be at the head of the line. Remember, no one wants to follow a fool—and quite simply, no one can "know it all." A self-proclaimed expert on all things, who always wants to take charge, will fail as a leader because people will realize that they are actually being asked to follow a fool—and no one will voluntarily do so for long.

Second, leaders must exhibit the courage to take action. They must have a bias for action.

A bias for action means that leaders must be decisive. It is often said that leaders can be right, they can be wrong, but they can never be unsure. Leaders must be decisive, but not stubborn. When events demand a change in course, leaders must have the self-confidence to recognize their error and be willing to take the required action to put the enterprise on a new path.

Third, leaders must subordinate themselves to the tasks to be accomplished. The effort is not about the leader, it is about the goals and objectives of the enterprise. As a rule of thumb, the only time leaders should use the pronoun "I," is when they are taking the responsibility for failure.

Fourth, leaders must be comfortable with themselves. They must have the self-confidence to be willing to trust the strength of their organization to achieve success, admit mistakes, and make changes to either the overall plan and/or the tactical approach and be humble.

Finally, leaders must establish a bond of trust with those that they hope to lead. Followers must come to accept the potential leader as their actual leader. To do this, they must trust the person who wishes to lead them. One can only begin to lead through knowledge and continue to lead through trust.

TRUST

The obvious question then is, "How does one create trust?" Part of trust is honesty. However, real trust involves more than just honesty. It requires that the people who one hopes to lead believe that the potential leader can get them successfully to the common end and will do it in a manner that protects them, enhances them professionally and personally, respects their skills and abilities, and honors their accomplishments. In a word, trust requires unflinching personal integrity.

Integrity is the product of personal decisions and consequent actions. In the context of leadership, integrity must be translated into a belief by those who are to be led that their leader will always do the right thing with respect to how he or she relates to them. Obviously, no one can be infallible. Infallibility is not the criteria. Rather, it is a belief by those who are to be led that their interests will always have their leader's priority. This belief can only exist if there is first a foundation of trust.

To achieve this level of trust, leaders must develop certain basic skills.

Leaders must be good listeners. Listening requires more than the discipline of not interrupting when someone else is speaking. It is an active skill, requiring the ability to draw people out and understand what they are trying to say, as well as helping them to better understand the meaning and implications of what they are saying.

They must also be able to communicate clearly. A leader must be able to express ideas that are easily understood, evoke a positive reaction, and also are memorable. This requires face-to-face interaction so that the speaker can see if the message is being understood and accepted. Email may be efficient, but it does not assure that communication is actually taking place.

Leaders must have the insight to anticipate possible crises. Reality does not always cooperate with the enterprise's plans. Leaders cannot prevent these kinds of variations. They can, however, plan for matters to "fail-safe"—so that people will feel both protected and confident that their leader can successfully get them to the common end.

Crises might not be able to be averted, but leaders plan for the actions that will be taken when things do not proceed as planned/hoped.[5]

TRICKS

In addition to the above, there are certain actions that leaders take, that at first blush, may seem to fall more in the category of tricks than skills.

The most important of these "tricks," is to always hire good people. This may seem obvious, but insecure leaders are often afraid to hire people who may be able to do their particular job better than the leader can do that job. Over the long run, no enterprise can achieve sustainable success if the people in leadership positions avoid building strong staffs. To be successful, leaders must hire good people, commit to them, nurture them by offering opportunities to grow and develop skills, and then trust them to do the work—driving decisions down to the lowest actionable level.

Leaders must also be predictable in both word and action. If people know how the leader will react in any given situation, then they will be more willing to take action and make decisions on their own. Key to this is people knowing that they will be supported in their decision making, even if it turns out that a poor decision was made.

As a corollary to predictability, people must have confidence that their leaders also do what they say they are going to do, when they say they are going to do it.

Leaders must encourage critical debate, understanding that dissent is not disloyalty. To encourage critical debate, leaders must allow themselves to be swayed in their decision making by the debate, so that people know that their opinions matter and that their arguments can make a difference. In terms of "tricks," for critical debate to work, leaders should plan, on occasion, to lose an argument.

Leaders must be flexible. Everyone has their own interpersonal style. For example, some people prefer one-to-one relationships. Others like to work in groups. Some prefer to talk things through, while others would rather rely on written documentation. Learning styles also vary, with some people learning best visually while others prefer verbal explanations or open-ended questions that enable them to explore alternatives. No style is better or worse; they are just different. The problem is not the differences, but rather the mismatches.

LEGISLATIVE & EXECUTIVE LEADERSHIP

A discussion of leadership in the context of nonprofit organizations must also recognize that nonprofit entities require a mix of both legislative and executive leadership. Legislative leadership is found most clearly in government where leaders must build consensus, molding and reshaping positions and programs to engage a broad constituency. Legislative leadership may not be an efficient process but it is effective in that decisions, once made, will be supported—because people have broadly been engaged in, and have become part of, the process.

In contrast, executive leadership is the hallmark of business (and the military) where command and control dominates and decisions are made from the top down.

Legislative leadership is horizontal in character. Executive leadership is vertical.

In the nonprofit enterprise, leaders must use a mix of both styles. The challenge is to be able to vary the mix, on the margin, to the issue and the structure so that decisions will be voluntarily supported and people willingly follow.

To enable people to function to their potential, leaders must recognize these differences and adapt to them, relating to each individual within the context of their style. It is the leader who, within limits, must adapt because it is the leader who has the most freedom to make changes.

Essentially, leaders must meet people where they are, in a way that is comfortable to them, and then take them on a path of guided discovery to the common end.

Leaders must also be a bit of a character, creating a "human side," that people can believe in. Leaders must create a persona that people can tell stories about and relate to—so that they can psychologically commit to the leader in the same fashion as the leader commits to them.

Being a character does not require outlandish behavior. Rather, it may involve as little as simple things like: walking around the organization and telling personal stories, as well as listening to personal stories, supporting the candy sale—but not taking the candy, dressing casually on "dress-down days," wearing the organizational logo at public events, etc.

As a leader, how does one test oneself to assure that he or she is exhibiting and enhancing these traits? The simple answer is that objective self-evaluation is very difficult. A better approach is to explicitly include a review of leadership performance as an element of managerial performance assessment. As a complement to this ongoing evaluation, exit interviews can also be used to explore leadership performance.

ACHIEVING SUCCESS

Emerging research suggests that high performing nonprofit organizations share some common characteristics.[6] Outstanding nonprofits demonstrate the following features:

- a focus on mission

- an openness to feedback—new ideas and criticism

- a commitment to continuous performance improvement

- an accountability for results—at all levels

- a commitment to their employees.

These values produce successful organizations. The following chapters will examine how to make these values come alive, becoming part of the enterprise's governance and management fabric. The first step, however, is leadership by both management and the board.

In today's society, with growing demands on nonprofit organizations and relatively shrinking available resources, the difficulties of achieving success and the consequences of failure have never been greater. To manage these enterprises well is a challenge worthy of society's best and brightest leaders.

Welcome to the beginning of solving the most interesting management problems in contemporary American life.

CHAPTER 1

Takeaways and Questions for Consideration and Discussion:

TAKEAWAYS

1. American society is unique in terms of the degree to which it relies upon an independent, nonprofit sector—private institutions dedicated to public service.

2. The nonprofit sector is economically dominated by about 5% of its entities that count for almost 86% of its size (expenses). In contrast, almost two-thirds (2/3) of its reporting enterprises have annual expenses of $500,000 or less.

3. Good management and governance is required of all nonprofit enterprises, regardless of size.

QUESTIONS

1. Do you need trust to lead?

2. How does competence of both the board and management relate to leadership?

3. How do boards and senior management teams build the foundation for ethical business and behaviors?

Chapter 2:
MEETING
COMMUNITY NEEDS

Nonprofit entities are society's safety net, entrusted by the community not just with assuring its health, education and welfare, but also protecting and advancing its arts, culture, and human values. Nonprofit enterprises create and enhance our quality of life, affecting every community in the nation and, ultimately, each person's life.

How do these organizations fit into both contemporary society and the overall economy? How do they relate to government (the public sector); to business (the for–profit sector); to each other, and how have they come to exist at all?

WHAT IS A COMMUNITY?

A community is often thought of in only geographic terms [i.e., a city, neighborhood or even a city block].

Certainly, these are all communities because they are bound together by location and the common concerns, problems, and opportunities that face that location.

A community can also be thought of in a larger, non-geographical sense, defined as a community of interest [i.e., people concerned about the environment, or preventing drunk driving, improving education or health, etc.]. Geographic communities and communities of interest can overlap or be separate. Regardless, all are communities, created to focus on the achievement of specific goals.

THE NONPROFIT SECTOR

To begin it is useful to recognize that the nonprofit sector is a bit of a "catch all" for organizations that do not fit neatly into other categories. What binds the entities of the nonprofit sector are two threads. One, they all involve the dedication of private resources for community purposes, as opposed to the purpose of making a profit. And two, they all have some sort of tax avoidance preference (i.e., depending on the organization, they are exempt from paying either sales taxes, local property taxes, and, in almost all cases, income taxes).

Also, it should be understood that in trying to describe the sector, the reported data does not include all the economic activity that takes place within it. This is because some nonprofit efforts are not incorporated, or, if incorporated, are not registered with the Internal Revenue Service (IRS).

In addition, as is common in many large databases that draw from independent sources, there are definitional and classification conflicts that make it difficult to make definitive statistical statements. Nevertheless, with these caveats in mind, the nonprofit sector can be described in managerially workable terms.

In 2013, nearly 1.5+ million nonprofit enterprises were registered with the IRS.[1,2,3] This number includes a heterogeneous mixture of charitable (about two-thirds of registered organizations are public charities and private foundations) and non-charitable enterprises (e.g., mutual insurance companies, social and recreational clubs, employee-beneficiary associations, credit unions, advocacy organizations, etc.). It includes organizations ranging in size from billion dollar plus medical centers and universities to small social service organizations. Interestingly, it does not include religious organizations and their auxiliaries or small organizations, with gross annual revenue of less than $50,000+.[4]

> ### WHAT IT ISN'T, WHAT IT IS.*
>
> The nonprofit sector is diverse. Nonprofit organizations encourage civic participation, allow for the expression of religious, social and artistic values, provide basic social and human services and strengthen communities. These organizations have different board and management styles, capacities, and needs. Recognizing the differences between organizations in the nonprofit sector makes it easier to define the sector by what it is not. It is not part of government, nor is it part of the business sector. What it is, is a resource for those in need as well as the voluntary foundation of a civil society.
>
> * The Nonprofit Almanac, Ninth Edition, page 2.

If these other categories were included it is estimated that the number of nonprofit enterprises would be more than 2 million.

Even at this larger estimate, nonprofit enterprises represent a small fraction of all private organizations in the United States. This is reflected in the estimate that the nonprofit sector accounts for only about 5.4% of the nation's gross domestic product (GDP). The sector's economic footprint, however, may in fact be larger with the sector accounting for almost 9% of the paid workforce. If economic wage value is also estimated for the nonprofit sector's volunteer workforce, the sector's economic size would be above 10%.

If measured by either expenses or assets, the largest components of the public charities portion of the nonprofit sector are providers of health services and education institutions. Though representing only about 18% of the organizations reporting to the IRS (education = 12.8% and health providers = 4.9%), they account for approximately 60% of expenses (education = 13.3%, health = 47.7%) and 48% of assets (education = 19.6%, health = 28%).

Public charities with $10 million or more in expenses account for over 85% of total public charity expenses. However, they only represent about 5% of the total number of public charities. In contrast, 77% of public charities account for only 8% of total expenses.

Exhibit 2-1 provides a quantitative description of the relative size of major components of the sector that report to the IRS. As a result, it only provides a limited view of the total sector. Even so, it is clear that the sector is economically dominated by its health and education enterprises and numerically dominated by small organizations having annual expenses of less than $1 million.

It is also clear that the sector is marked by great diversity. The homeless shelter and the art museum are both encompassed by it, as are universities and preschools; the nursing home and the childcare center; and the research medical center and the free street clinic. To understand how this disparate mix of enterprises fits into the contemporary socio-economic environment, it is helpful to first address the question, "Why are there nonprofit enterprises?" To answer this question, it is useful to begin by building an analytical framework consisting of a bit of economics, some political science and sociology, and a realistic view of human nature.

Exhibit 2-1*

NONPROFIT SECTOR ORGANIZATIONS REPORTING TO THE IRS				
Major Components	Number	Percent of Orgs Reporting	Percent of Expenses	Percent of Assets
Arts, Cultural, & Humanities	35,813	6.8	1.6	2.5
Animal-Related	8,740	1.65	0.4	0.4
Community Improvement & Capacity Building	48,387	9.1	1.9	2.3
Education	67,879	12.8	13.3	19.6
Health Services	25,643	4.9	47.7	28
Housing & Shelter	20,428	3.9	1.2	1.8
Human Services	40,880	7.7	6.2	3.7
Medical Research	2,203	1.6	0.4	0.2
Mutual/Membership Benefit Organizations	15,712	3.0	7.2	6.6
Philanthropy, Voluntarism, & Grant-Making Foundations	84,338	15.9	4.3	15.5
Public Safety & Disaster Preparedness	10,857	2.0	0.2	0.2
Recreation, Sports, Leisure, & Athletics	43,987	8.3	1.6	1.1
TOTAL	529,154			

* The Nonprofit Almanac Ninth Edition, The Urban Institute. Percentages are only for the major listed portions of the sector and therefore do not sum to 100%.

BUSINESS

Business and government are generally thought of as the basic organizational building blocks of the American economy. In reality, the economy involves a blending of sectors, not individual, discrete blocks or components. However, for purposes of initial discussion, the sectors can be considered to be distinct, with business and government each anchoring one end of an economic continuum. (See Exhibit 2-2.)

Exhibit 2-2

ECONOMIC CONTINUUM

Business   Government

PROFITABILITY BOUNDARY AND CORPORATE RESPONSIBILITY

Most business leaders would argue that their primary, if not exclusive, role is to make money. Therefore the full energies of the enterprise should be focused on generating profit. If profits can be achieved, employees can be paid and the wealth of the owners increased. Employees and owners—not the business itself—then can use their resources, income, and wealth as they see fit. One use can be the support of charitable activities.

In all fairness, this argument has some theoretical attractiveness. It also offers some pragmatic convenience, enabling the private sector to focus on what it is supposed to do, while leaving the support of the community sector to the self-regulated control of the independent decisions of individuals. It is essentially the application of the market model to determine the flow of funds from one sector to another.

This argument, however, ignores the realities of an economically and socially intertwined society. It also sidesteps recognition of the responsiblity of business, both to society at large and to the specific communities in which a firm operates. This notion of both a larger obligation and an obligation that goes beyond the personal to the firm as a whole represents a second perspective. It is known as corporate social responsibility and is the economic justification for the private sector's support of the community sector.

Business has come to understand that just as stable government is a precursor to success, a stable society also is necessary. To achieve a stable society, myriad social welfare needs must be met. While business may recognize these needs, it also understands both that it cannot fully meet them by just its own hand and that it must participate in the solutions. In fact, the further each sector stretches to interact with the others, the better the total result for society.

Business is the wheel horse of the economy. Whether measured in terms of the number of firms, assets, or earnings, it is the largest segment of the nation's economic system. It is composed of millions of independently owned organizations ranging in size from the one-person, non-incorporated sidewalk vendor to Walmart with its thousands of employees and shareholders. Regardless of individual firm size or structure, the goal of business is to enable private interests (i.e., individual people, whether employee or owner—investor as well as proprietor) to do well, as measured in monetary terms of income and/or accumulated wealth. In theory, business operates under the belief that the ethical pursuit of individual self-interest and gain will result in common gain.

This construct of self-interest yielding common benefit has produced remarkable results. However, it is not without limits.

Business, by its very nature, will not respond to societal needs unless those needs can be expressed in terms of both consumer willingness to pay for the desired goods or services and to pay at a rate that offers an adequate profit opportunity.[5] Consequently, certain needs (goods and services), regardless of their intrinsic merit or community benefit, will not be naturally/ automatically addressed by business.

The "working" of this economic reality is easily seen, for example, in services for low-income populations. Soup kitchens, food pantries, low-income housing, etc. certainly have merit and demand. However, they cannot be operated as market-guided, for-profit businesses. The income potential for an adequate profit simply does not exist and therefore they are not of direct interest to the business sector.

Less clear is the situation where individual consumer actions do not realistically translate into demand, price, or need. The goods and services in this category are known as public or collective goods (e.g. clean water, national defense, well-regulated markets, etc.). Public goods, while benefiting individuals in the aggregate, are not amenable to being allocated, by the consumer market, on an individually dictated basis. As a result, in spite of their value, business will not automatically meet the need for public or collective goods.

This seeming "failure of the market" is less a market shortfall than an example of the efficient workings of the market as expressed through the filter of human nature. The market has proven itself to be effective at providing goods and services whose demand and consumption are the results of individually determined and expressed spending decisions. Goods and services that are collective in character such as: safe neighborhoods and clean air, involve a "free rider" problem, since individuals cannot be excluded from the consumption of such commodities. That is, once the product is produced, everyone benefits from its availability and/or use, regardless of whether they directly pay for it. This creates the opportunity for so-called "free riders," people who consume the collective product, but who do not pay for it or who do not pay their full share of its cost. The result is that, if left to just the workings of the market, fewer of these collective goods than society really needs will be produced.[6]

In terms of the simple linear continuum found in Exhibit 2-2, two additional points should be recognized.

First, the necessity of adequate profitability produces a natural economic constraint on the activities that business will voluntarily pursue (i.e., the Profitability Boundary). Unless coerced or responding to pressures of social responsibility, business will not do things that knowingly will not result in profitability. Therefore, unless government steps in, or some other factor is introduced, an internal boundary in the business/government continuum can—and will—occur.

Second, the business component of the economy is fundamentally a private sector. Business sector, private sector, and private for-profit sector are used interchangeably to identify the for-profit business component of the economy. Both the business sector and the community sector are composed of private entities. Therefore, just using the term private sector may be considered by some as not providing adequate precision. While business entities can take a variety of legal forms (e.g., sole proprietorships, partnerships, closely held or publicly-traded corporations); common to all is the fact of private ownership. (Publicly-traded companies, regardless of the breadth of their stock ownership, are private entities, ultimately owned by private individuals who place their private interests in the forefront—expecting a positive monetary benefit from their investment of either sweat and/or financial equity.)

The previously described continuum should therefore be redrawn. As illustrated below, it is anchored on one end by the private sector, with the Profitability Boundary defining the limits of the business sector's activities. (See Exhibit 2-3.)

Exhibit 2-3

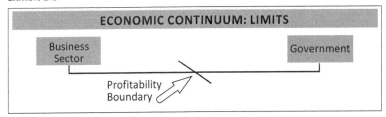

It should also be recognized that the exact location of the Profitability Boundary is constantly shifting, as private enterprises attempt to find the edges or the margins of the market. Innovation and dreams, along with the desire to increase profit and profitability, pushes the boundary to the right, as, at least in the short run, hope triumphs over fact (e.g., day care, for-profit primary and secondary schools). In counterpoint, the rational workings of the market push the boundary back (to the left), as reality triumphs over wishfulness and experience (e.g., Medicare HMO risk contracting). Regardless of the specific location, the concept of a boundary-limiting activity cannot be ignored.

GOVERNMENT

In contrast, government is a publicly owned enterprise, with its benefits ultimately inuring to public interests. Regardless of their geographical boundaries or specific purpose, all governmental units, whether special purpose districts (e.g., fire districts, sidewalk snowplowing districts, forest preserves, etc.), villages, towns, cities, states, or nations, are the result of public decisions as translated through a political process. Similarly, government's operational limits and performance results are established and judged by the same public political process.

Government is the "public sector" of the economy. Its role, through the redistribution of resources, is to maintain order, assure the public safety, and either directly or indirectly provide agreed-upon collective (public) goods and services.

The extent of government's share of the continuum can vary. With the power to both motivate and/or coerce behavior through taxation and law, government could finance, mandate, or otherwise encourage the production of goods and services that are not of intrinsic profitability interest to the private sector. It could even provide the services itself.[7] Government could play this latter role if such action was the agreed upon preference of the overall citizenry.

The services that government provides, either directly or indirectly, are the result of an overarching public consensus about its general role in the nation's activities, combined with shifting individual preferences regarding specific programs and activities. The latter is expressed through either elected or appointed representatives or directly through both the ballot box, and (as observed by de Tocqueville in his 19th century book, *Democracy In America*[8]) the voluntary, collective association (e.g., neighborhood associations, parent and teacher school organizations, ballot referendum, etc.).[9]

Voluntary association and collective action are fundamental mechanisms for protecting democracy.[10] They provide individual citizens with a means of expressing their opinions with regard to the nature and extent of government activities.[11] However, the more disagreement and diversity of opinion, the less government will be likely and able to do. Thus, while government, in theory, can prevent any gap in the private/public continuum, in practice, its actions are limited by the reality of what the public can politically and fiscally agree upon and, therefore, allow government to do. The product of this limiting process can be conceptualized as the public sector's Consensus Boundary. (See Exhibit 2-4.)

Exhibit 2-4

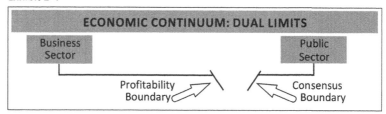

PROTECTIONISM*

In the latter part of the 19th century another set of forces both paved the way for, and shaped the emergence of, the American community sector.

The development of both the business corporation and the nonprofit corporation was a tortuous political and legal process. However, with the growth of corporations came two unsurprising consequences. First, the nature of wealth and economic power changed from agrarian and land-focused to industrial and monetary based. In the process, the focus of economic power also became more concentrated. Second, the public became increasingly resentful of both this unavoidable economic result of a capitalistic, free market and its implications for their living conditions and opportunities.

To address this circumstance and its risks to their positions of wealth and power, business leaders began to promote the notion of the equality of opportunity as a substitute for the ideal of equality of condition. This idea arguably flows not only from self-interest but also a Darwinian view that these self-made successful capitalists are examples of the triumph of the fittest and providing the equality of opportunity nurtures the ability of the best to economically succeed. To this end they began to use a portion of their personal wealth to establish programs that could enhance opportunities for the general population.

The practical problem they faced in pursuing this strategy was the lack of workable organizational vehicles for implementation. The solution was the creation of the charitable foundation and the organizational restructuring of private universities. Together these initiatives provided the means for both offering the promise of unlimited personal opportunity and training the personnel required to operate and lead the nation's growing industrial enterprises. They also produced, by design or not, a set of institutions providing the organizational models and underlying structure for important elements of today's community sector.

* Peter Dobkin Hall, *Inventing the Nonprofit Sector*, (Baltimore: Johns Hopkins University Press, 1992), Introduction and Chapter 1.

While real in a behavioral context, the Consensus Boundary, like the Profitability Boundary, reflects complex and changing relationships. Americans tend to be skeptical of government. This perspective acts, even in times of crisis, to push the Consensus Boundary back, narrowing the role of government. However, at the same time, government provides to the private sector substantial direct (e.g., grants and contracts), and indirect (e.g., tax credits, vouchers, and tax-exempt bonds), funding to support the provision of goods and services that may not hold intrinsic profit potential. These actions effectively push the Consensus Boundary to the left. The "real" effect of these political mechanisms is to extend the role of government without extending its day to day, direct operational involvement in the lives of its citizenry. As a consequence of these forces, the location of the boundary continually moves. Nevertheless, the Consensus Boundary, together with the Profitability Boundary, set the stage for two results.

First, because each sector's role is realistically limited, a gap occurs in the continuum. (See Exhibit 2-4.) Second, society (i.e., the community), reflecting its self-preserving nature, will reach out to fill the gap.

Just as nature will not tolerate a vacuum, communities will not allow either their collective needs or their unprofitable but necessary human service needs to be ignored. However, to fill the vacuum another organizational mechanism is required; one that falls neither completely within the public nor private sectors, yet has some of the attributes of both, but is not as limited as either. These requirements create the basis for another sector, an economic domain designed specifically to support and/or benefit stakeholder communities, whether those communities are defined by interest, need, or geography.

This conclusion is not a leap of faith. Rather, it is the unavoidable product of the combination of economic, political, and sociological pragmatism in a democratic society. Similarly, how this third sector takes shape and performs is a product of the same pragmatic alchemy.

THE COMMUNITY SECTOR

In some sense, the roots of this third or community sector reach back centuries. In sixteenth century England, voluntary private philanthropies (charities) provided funds for a wide range of activities (e.g., schools, hospitals, firefighting equipment, libraries, etc.).[12,13] In the United States, it has also existed for hundreds of years, predating both the founding of the republic or the invention of the tax code.[14] The historical genesis and the details of the mixture of private motivation and political need that produced the community sector may be subject to argument. What is clear, however, is that it has become society's solution for filling the gap between the needs of various communities and the aggregate of what the public sector is enabled to do plus what the private sector is willing to do. (See Exhibit 2-5.)[15]

Exhibit 2-5

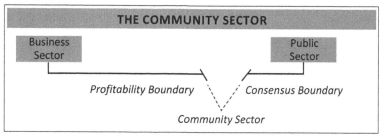

The community sector is able to fill the gap because it provides the means for private resources, in the form of contributions of time and money, to be used for community benefit, for purposes other than profits (e.g., free concerts, food pantries, scholarships, museums, colleges and universities, day care, legal aid services, etc.). The catalyst relaxing the profit requirement associated with private assets and the consensus constraint of the public sector is community ownership of the enterprise.[16] It is important to remember that community is not defined simply as a matter of geography, but rather as a congregation of interests, voluntarily self-identified by stakeholders who have a common concern, passion, goal, etc.[17]

Community ownership, along with the voluntary participation of people in the financing and operation of the enterprise, is really nothing more than a reflection of the fundamental working of the marketplace. Like any market phenomena, the community sector is the result of people voting with their feet, hands, and wallets. In fact, the ingredient that gives the community sector its energy is the voluntary commitment of financial and human resources.

It is also important to remember that community sector enterprises are private organizations, albeit owned by the community—as contrasted with private individuals. In fact, the nation's universe of economic activity can be fully described as being either in the public or private spheres. From this perspective, the community sector, because of ownership, could be viewed as a subset of the private sphere, effectively subdividing the sphere into two sections: individual and community. In this context, the community sector, in fact, would be the third largest element of the private sector, following retail and wholesale trade, and ahead of construction and banking.[18]

A two-sector characterization has a certain attractiveness. However, it also begs the pragmatic question of, *what does not fit?* Is a third *all other* sector needed? In this instance, what does not fit are organizations that utilize private resources for community/non-individual benefit purposes. These community benefit organizations, enterprises focused on benefits to particular stakeholders' communities, form a unique grouping of entities, a third sector—a community sector.

Similarly, a focus on core economic goals yields the same three sector structure (i.e., for-profit, no profit (government), and nonprofit). The private sector and the for-profit sectors are the same. The same can be said about the no-profit and public sectors and the nonprofit and community sectors. The distinction to be recognized is that one view looks at results, (i.e., who benefits), and the other looks at the mechanics of pursuing those results.

Being either for-profit or nonprofit has certain tax implications. Tax implications do not, however, define a sector. The actual generation of profits or surpluses also does not define a sector. From time to time governmental bodies might generate a surplus and either spend it or create a rainy-day fund. For-profit firms will also from time to time generate a loss. The reality and vicissitudes of actual performance should not be confused with the fiscal goal of the organization.

Similar to for-profit firms, nonprofit enterprises must strive over the long run to generate a profit/surplus. The important difference is that a nonprofit enterprise's profits cannot be used for private benefit. They must be used to benefit the particular stakeholder community.

The community sector is a separate sector because it has both a unique beneficiary group (i.e., community stakeholders) and a unique economic goal (i.e., private resources for community benefit).[19] The two concepts come together in that the first defines the boundaries of the sector and the second identifies the enterprises that populate it.[20]

SHAPE SHIFTING

While a linear depiction of the economic continuum (see Exhibit 2-5) explains the emergence of and the need for the community sector, it does not address another basic reality, sector interaction (i.e., interdependence and overlap). To recognize these phenomena the continuum must first be bent from a straight line into a circular, interdependent form. Then the sectors must be understood as overlapping with one another, as opposed to having impenetrable borders. (See Exhibit 2-6.)

Exhibit 2-6

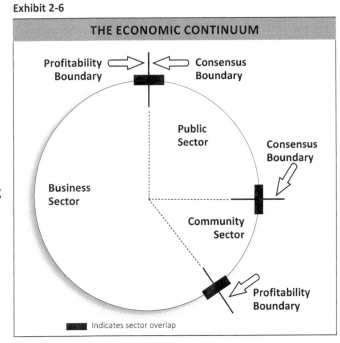

THE ECONOMIC CONTINUUM

Profitability Boundary

Consensus Boundary

Public Sector

Consensus Boundary

Business Sector

Community Sector

Profitability Boundary

Indicates sector overlap

How does this shift in economic geometry happen? The reality is that because of the complexity of the economy, both in depth and breadth, organizations from each sector, for reasons of efficiency, effectiveness, and political pragmatism must interact to succeed. To reflect this fact, the model must be adapted to allow each sector to "touch" the other. This is accomplished by bending the continuum into a circle.

A linear model is simply a discussion starting point. Its usefulness lies in establishing a conceptual base, not depicting operating interactions. Sectors are not islands of economic independence with inviolate shores. The reality is that there is inter-sector reliance. To reflect this, the continuum must be reshaped.

Examples of sector interaction can be seen in the public sector contracting with the private sector for goods and services that are unique to protecting the common good (e.g., military equipment). Similarly, the private sector contracts with the community sector for research (e.g., drug companies contract with medical schools for drug effectiveness and safety studies) and make contributions/donations to support various social welfare and cultural programs (e.g., art exhibits, concerts, adopting a public school). The public sector contracts with the community sector for health care services (e.g., hospital and nursing home care), and research (e.g., high energy physics). The public sector also contracts with the private sector for human services (e.g., hospital and nursing home care and child day care). Additionally, the public sector in some instances provides these same services through its own operations (e.g. county nursing homes, city and county hospitals). These examples demonstrate the interrelationship and interdependence of the sectors. The last examples, however, hint at another important reality.

> ### MORE SHIFTING/COST SHIFTING
>
> Why would the public sector contract with the community sector? The fact that the public sector has the funds to contract is evidence that the activity is within the consensus boundary. Why then not do it, itself?
>
> The answer is that it is cheaper to outsource to the community sector than to produce the services internally. The public sector's labor and production costs are generally higher than those of the community sector. The public sector, for a variety of historical reasons, simply pays more for labor than the private and community sectors. Therefore, by "buying" instead of "making," the public sector is able to obtain more services for the same level of expenditure.
>
> Arguably, this is good economics for the public sector. Is it good business for the community sector? The risk is that elements of the community sector become low cost substitutes for government, not only limiting what they are able to pay their employees, but also becoming increasingly dependent on government—as government payments support greater portions of overhead and indirect costs. This is not a sound strategy for building a robust community sector.

Inter-sector interaction can also result in the duplication of effort as well as tension between sectors. For example, the public sector often contracts with both the private and the community sectors for the same services (e.g., nursing home care, hospital care, childcare). In the same vein, higher education is provided by all three sectors. The question is simply, why do two or three sectors provide the same services? Why is there an inter-sector overlap of activity? If a product or service can be provided profitably, won't the private sector produce it on its own initiative, eliminating the need for other sector involvement? If the public sector is providing a service, why would either the private or community sector do the same thing?

The answer to these questions lies in returning to the understanding that sector boundaries are not fixed lines like national borders. Rather, the boundaries between sectors are porous. The result is sector blending and service overlap (i.e., two or more sectors providing the same service). Examples of this can be seen in: public schools and community-based charter schools; private universities and public universities; museum retail shops and privately owned gift stores; investor owned hospitals and community owned hospitals; for-profit and nonprofit health insurers, and private sector health clubs and the YMCA or hospital offered health clubs.

Again, these examples are meant to be only illustrative. They do, however, demonstrate examples of overlap in economic activity and therefore, competition. They also evidence that the flow is not in just one direction. Sometimes it is the private sector seeing a profit opportunity in an area that has been traditionally left to the community sector, in effect pushing out the *profitability boundary* (e.g., health care, childcare, exercise facilities, etc.).

Sometimes it is just the opposite, with the community sector seeing a mission-related opportunity to generate incremental revenue (e.g., gift stores, mail order catalog or Internet sales, travel tours, counseling services, etc.).

Even so, why does this overlap and resulting competition happen?

Notwithstanding the traditional barriers to market entry (e.g., capital requirements, market structure, product alternatives and innovation cycles, regulatory hurdles, etc.), the answer is as varied as the points of competition. Sometimes it is nothing more than hubris, people feeling that if they organize and operate in one way versus another, they can produce a better result. Community-based charter schools versus public schools might be an example of this. Private for-profit colleges versus public universities is another.

Sometimes the reason is more egalitarian. An example of this might be state-sponsored, public universities (e.g., University of Michigan), versus community owned (private, nonprofit) universities (e.g., Harvard University).

At other times the driving force may be the need for additional revenue and/or simply opportunism. Museums creating gift catalogs (mail and/or Internet), opening gift shops, either on or off site, to capture retail sales illustrates direct private sector versus community sector competition for consumer dollars. The growth of private health clubs, invading the market space previously held almost entirely by YMCAs and similar organizations, is an example of the same phenomena, except from the opposite perspective. The same can be seen in the targeted growth of for-profit health care enterprises.

Finally, part of the reason for a competitive overlap may simply be the reflection of trust or the lack of trust. The market may not trust the motives or the priorities of either the public or the private, for-profit business sectors to fairly meet its needs. Therefore, it looks to an alternative to provide the same services. Examples of this can be seen not only in health and childcare but also in personal care for the elderly and health care insurance/payment.

Regardless of the cause, the simple reality is that overlap and resulting competition exist.

Exhibit 2-7 illustrates the same point, but from a different perspective. Here, the sectors are depicted as independent spheres that both interconnect and overlap. In this view, the limits of the private and public sectors, or the genesis of the community sector, are less important than the reality of there being three sectors and that they interact with one another and compete (see shaded area).

> **CONTRACT FAILURE AND COMPETITIVE OVERLAP**
>
> From a more micro perspective, it can be argued that the community sector, or at least some elements of it, is the consequence of "contract failure."
>
> Contract failure is the notion that a principal may not feel that his or her agent is acting in the principal's best interest because they are placing a higher priority on some other result (e.g., profits). This idea can be seen in particular where it is difficult for the principal to measure either quality or results and the consequences of shortfalls are significant. For example, will care provided in a for-profit healthcare institution be as good as that provided in a nonprofit entity or will corners be cut, to increase profits? Hopefully, the answer is that the care decisions will be the same. However, human nature being what it is, one cannot always be sure. As a result, it is argued that nonprofit enterprises should be created, as an alternative to for-profit firms, to better align principal and agent interests.

Exhibit 2-7

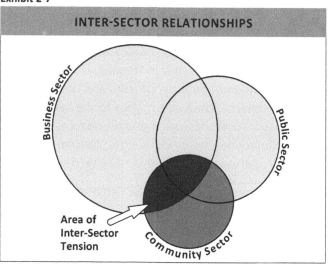

SECTOR EQUITY

Sector overlap and inter-sector competition reflect the working of the marketplace. Though competition can provide some benefit (see box), it also produces an increase in both inter-sector tension and public confusion concerning the appropriate role of the community sector.

COMMENTARY: COMPETITION AND COLLABORATION

The consequences of inter-sector competition and overlap are not all negative. For example, the presence of for-profit hospitals (market share of 10% or less), in markets dominated by nonprofit hospitals, results in nonprofit hospital efficiency increasing. Similarly, the presence of nonprofit hospitals (20% to 30% of the market), in markets dominated by for-profit hospitals, yields overall improvements in trustworthiness.*

The introduction of nonprofit nursing homes into markets dominated by for-profit homes is also shown to increase overall community benefit.**

Inter-sector competition may arguably be a community benefit. *** In counter-point, collaboration must also be recognized as providing a vehicle for community benefit.

The power of intra- and inter-sector collaboration is easy to imagine. Intra-sector collaboration takes place at a variety of levels. It can be seen in inter- governmental commissions and state/federal project funding. In the private sector, trade and professional associations provide the vehicles for collaboration as do joint operating agreements (for newspapers) and joint ventures. The community sector also has examples of intra-sector collaboration (e.g., regional health and hospital councils and back office operating consortia).

Inter-sector collaboration reaches beyond inter-dependence to active pursuit of cooperative efforts intended to produce community benefits, or more precisely, greater community benefits. Examples of these kinds of initiatives can be seen in business support of cultural and arts events and business and government scholarship support of undergraduate education.

More problematic is the realization that if collaboration could be encouraged, the results might be profound. The dilemma is how to do this. While competition may be instinctive, collaboration has to be learned and continually reinforced. Importantly, it is not a Hobson's Choice. Collaboration and competition can take place simultaneously, each adding value to the community.

* Bradford Gray and Mark Schlesinger, "Four Views on Nonprofit Healthcare Performance, Public Accountability and Tax Exemption," *Health Affairs*.

** Rexford E. Santerre and John A. Vernon, "Ownership Form and Consumer Welfare: Evidence from the Nursing Home Industry," *Inquiry*, Winter 2007/2008, 381-399.

*** Philip Betbeze, "The Benefits of Nonprofit/For-Profit Competition," HealthLeaders.com, July 20, 2005.

Because competition may, in effect, be hard coded into society's DNA and the economy's structure, inter–sector tension is arguably unavoidable. (See Exhibit 2–7, shaded area.) The matters of public confusion and inter–sector equity, however, are different matters. Sector equity goes to the heart of democratic society's sense of fairness. Public confusion creates ongoing operational management and legislative/ regulatory challenges. Neither have easy answers. Both, however, must be addressed, if society is to be well served.

Part of the answer to assuring equity lies in the community sector being willing to make adjustments to its regulatory treatment. For example, the fact that most of the nation's BlueCross and BlueShield plans remained nonprofit even after they lost their federal income tax exemption, demonstrates that being a nonprofit enterprise is first a matter of philosophy and operational strategy and only second an issue of tax status. If federal income tax exemption is a flash point, then consideration should be given to relinquishing it in favor of simultaneously leveling other areas of inter–sector regulation. Loss of an exemption on profits clearly can have an effect on building internal capital. Just as clearly, it can also act as a catalyst for promoting more benefits and services.[21]

Part of the answer also lies in achieving a clear public understanding of the role, character and benefits of the community sector. Here the community sector must simply do a better job of telling its story, putting as much effort into "friend" raising as it does "fund" raising.

CONCLUSION

Before closing, it is important to reiterate four fundamental points:

- A three-sector model is a useful descriptive device for conceptualizing the economy. However, its usefulness is limited, and care must be taken not to view it too literally.

- The three economic sectors are not only interdependent but also synergistic.

- The three sectors are not in conflict with one another over which is better. None is better or worse than the other. Each, however, is different, with one better suited than the other for the achievement of particular goals.[22]

- Finally, in characterizing the components of the economy, the foregoing has taken a benefit focus, recognizing as a result three sectors: business, public, and community. Often the sectors are called by different names: private, government, and nonprofit. These latter labels are rhetorical synonyms and can be useful in providing enhanced public understanding. Therefore, it is not uncommon, or inappropriate, to use them interchangeably.

CHAPTER 2

Takeaways and Questions for Consideration and Discussion:

TAKEAWAYS

1. Nonprofit enterprises are a small part of the national economy, as measured by either GDP (5+%) or paid workforce (9%).

2. Nonprofit enterprises exist simply because there is a gap between what communities and society need and what the public does not trust government to do, or cannot agree that government should do (lack of consensus), and what business will do because of a lack of profit potential.

3. The nonprofit sector is diverse, dominated economically by health and educational enterprises, and numerically by small enterprises addressing all sorts of community needs. However, what all have in common is that they are private organizations, owned by stakeholders (not shareholders), and dedicated to community benefit.

QUESTIONS

1. What is the weakness of a single sector economy? Does your answer change if the single sector is government? If it is business?

2. How does the pursuit of self-interest produce enhancement to the common interest?

3. Is inter-sector competition inevitable? Is it preventable? Would it be beneficial to prevent it?

Chapter 3:
THE COMMUNITY SECTOR

T he idea of private resources dedicated to community purposes is a business model that on first glance seems counterintuitive, if not nonsensical. However, the power of the idea is apparent just by considering the community sector's growth and accomplishments.

The community owned sector is society's pragmatic invention for meeting its special interest and heterogeneous needs. Though pragmatic and voluntary, the sector has not always been an acclaimed socioeconomic innovation. In fact, while de Tocqueville was observing the importance of the collective association as a major feature of American democracy, state legislatures were both denying charitable institutions the right to incorporate and forbidding courts from assuming the enforcement powers needed to make charitable endowments feasible.[1]

STATISTICS—STATISTICS*

As noted in the previous chapter, accurately measuring the community sector's size is a more difficult challenge than one would expect. Measuring its composition is equally challenging, due to the fact that many of the entities in the sector are small and/or unincorporated and therefore do not report to the IRS. Also, some organizations seemingly come and go, becoming dormant/defunct during difficult economic times only to reemerge later.

According to 2015 IRS data, there are about 1.55 million registered tax-exempt enterprises. The largest number of these organizations is in the (Section 501 (c) (3)) religious, charitable and

similar enterprise category. Within this category there are about 1.076 million public charities and more than 103,000 private foundations. The largest public charities subsector is Education, with almost 68,000 reporting entities.

For those really curious about nonprofit data, The Nonprofit Almanac has over 200 pages of statistical charts and tables describing the sector from a variety of perspectives, including sources of revenue.

*The Nonprofit Almanac Ninth Edition, (Washington DC: The Urban Institute)and Inventing the Nonprofit Sector (Baltimore: Johns Hopkins Press).

GROWTH

In spite of these and other hurdles, the community sector is a social and economic movement that has taken hold, particularly in the later part of the 20th century. While the data are not precise, because religious and small organizations are not required to register with or report to the Internal Revenue Service (IRS) (see Chapter 2), in 1940 there were only about 12,500 secular, nonprofit organizations in the United States. By 2015, there were 1.5 million plus (1,549,264) entities registered with the IRS. From 2010 to 2015, the number of reporting organizations declined from almost 1.6 million to 1.55 million. The decline was a consequence of the Great Recession and as to be expected, impacted small organizations. From 2000 to 2015, the number of reporting public charities increased by over 40% and the number of employees in the nonprofit sector increased by almost 23% to 14.4 million (as of 2013).

Looking at just public charities, from 2000 to 2010 the assets of reporting public charities increased by 80% to $2,708,905, with net assets growing to $1,598,057. The simple facts are that the community sector is growing and that it is growing faster than either the public sector or the private for-profit (business) sector.[2]

It is not hard to speculate as to why the community sector has grown and is continuing to grow.

Society's needs for education, health care, social welfare, human, and cultural services, have increased. At the same time, the nation has become ideologically more divided, making it increasingly difficult to reach political consensus, not only on what new programs and services government should provide/support, but more importantly, what current activities should be continued. This dual reality pulls the consensus boundary back, shifting increasing demands onto the community sector.[3]

At the same time that government's role may in real terms be shifting, if not shrinking, the ability of some segments of society to become engaged in voluntary and community service work is expanding.

Personal wealth, while becoming more concentrated, has also increased. As a result, a substantial resource base can be tapped to support the community sector.

COMMENTARY: PUSH VERSUS PULL*

The community sector is generally viewed as being a response to unmet collective needs (i.e., demand pull).

Alternatively, it can be considered as the consequence of the supply of resources, both financial and human, pushing the pursuit of specific initiatives (i.e., supply push).

The importance of supply push forces bringing energy and direction to the community sector should not be ignored. The supply side perspective argues that the community sector is really about the people with resources and commitment who support both nonprofit enterprises and voluntary social action.

Instead of starting with the demands of clients or members, the supply side perspective recognizes the way various forms of entrepreneurship drive innovation. In the supply side model, the entrepreneur/donor and volunteer take on a much greater role—as they are the supplier of the new ideas, contributions, and volunteer time.

In reality, the sector is the result of the interplay of both supply and demand forces. A supply side perspective, however, makes clear two points:

1. Entrepreneurism has an innovative role in the community sector, just as it does in the private sector; and

2. The interests and values of those who contribute their time and/or money to support the maintenance, growth and innovation of the sector must be recognized and nurtured.

* Peter Frumkin, On Being Nonprofit, (Cambridge: Harvard University Press, 2002), 21 and 22.

Simultaneously, the time that individuals, particularly the growing retiree population, can make available for working in and supporting community sector activities has also increased. The net effect is that, in spite of the loss of volunteer time due to the growth of two-worker families, more financial and human resources are becoming available to encourage, stimulate, and support the work and expansion of the community sector of the economy.

> **FOUNDATIONS[4]**
>
> As a reflection of the growth in personal wealth, the number of foundations increased from 2001 to 2013 by over 25,000 to a total of 87,142. The increase has been concentrated in independent (private) foundations. These have grown by over 24,000 entities. Assets of all reporting foundations in 2001 were $472,820,000. By 2013, assets had grown to $798,176,000, with independent foundations having assets of $654,309,000—up from $403,541,000 in 2001.

The sector's growth is also the result of human nature—protectionism, compassion, passion, distrust, and hubris. In some instances, individuals with financial means have taken it upon themselves to promote, and then aggressively support particular interests (e.g., public health issues in poor countries, foundations to support public schools, venture capital, philanthropy, etc.). Some of these efforts have had a narrow focus, in effect, by making available funding resources, creating a supply side impetus, or economic push, for the growth of the sector. Others have focused on protecting the larger economic system, by making available the means to provide the promise of equality of opportunity as an alternative to pressures for equality of condition. The majority of financial initiatives and contributions, however, have had a social welfare perspective, demonstrating insight and wisdom. Regardless of either their scope or motivation, all have in common the dedication of private resources to public purposes and common benefit.

In other circumstances people with only modest, or even no discretionary income, have taken it upon themselves, out of a sense of social obligation and/or compassion, the responsibility to become engaged in community-serving organizations, primarily volunteering their skills and time instead of, or in addition to, contributing money.

Like the initiatives of their wealthier brethren, all of these efforts have in common the fundamental value of individual effort directed to the betterment of the common good.

As the community sector has grown, its visibility has also increased. Not surprisingly, more attention and scrutiny has been focused by both government and the general public on how the sector is structured and how it operates. To some degree this attention is justified. To some degree, it is a distraction, the result of misunderstanding and confusion about what it means to be a nonprofit enterprise.

CONFUSION

Probably the most frequent misunderstanding is the assumption that while being nonprofit is a universal characteristic of community sector firms, **nonprofit does not mean no profit**. In fact, the opposite is, and must be, the case.

If an organization is to survive, it must, at least over the long run, make a profit (i.e., have total revenues greater than total expenses). Anything else dooms the organization to eventual failure. This lesson is obvious from the experience of the private sector. Certainly, in some years, a particular business enterprise might lose money.

However, if over the long run that firm does not have aggregate revenues in excess of its total real expenses, it will ultimately fail, and go out of business. The same natural economic law applies to nonprofit organizations. Over the long run they must make a profit to survive, let alone succeed.

Recognizing this reality, it is a small step to understand that while being nonprofit is a unifying and guiding feature of all community sector organizations, "nonprofitness" is, at its core, nothing more than a strategic and operating business decision. It is a business policy choice borne out of an understanding that the profit motive will both distort the organization's decision making and reduce its ability to maximize its service impact, and achieve its mission.

> ### COMMENTARY: TO PROFIT OR NOT
>
> If the work of the enterprise could be done profitably, it would, in theory, be done by the private business sector. Therefore, adequate profit opportunity either does not exist or when the activity was initiated did not exist. However, even if it did, the decision to operate as a nonprofit enterprise reflects an understanding that requiring an economic rent in the form of a monetary profit that can be used to pay a return to investors/contributors, is counter-productive to meeting the community's needs, limiting either output and/or creating an unnecessary barrier, through higher prices, to individuals and groups accessing services. Both of these consequences are contrary to the reasons for creating the enterprise. The conclusion is straightforward; profit maximization is in conflict with benefit maximization.
>
> Given the community's needs, profit maximization is not an option. Alternatively, profit minimization is a nonsensical goal, missing any real understanding of organizational purpose. Therefore, the remaining choice is to operate as a nonprofit enterprise.

Clearly, the business decision to be nonprofit is important. However, it can be justifiably argued, given the purposes for which community sector enterprises are created, that there is really no alternative. Community ownership of the enterprise and a nonprofit operating paradigm are inextricably linked. The linkage should not, however, mask the fact that community ownership (whether the community is defined geographically or in terms of stakeholders, donors, beneficiaries, the board of directors, corporate members or just interested parties) defines the character of the sector—who controls it and who benefits from its work—and being nonprofit defines its operations.

From a management perspective the key factor is not simply electing to be nonprofit. Rather, it is the resource allocation criteria embedded in the election. In making the strategic decision to be nonprofit, the enterprise is affirmatively deciding that any profits generated by it will be used to benefit its mission— not distributed either directly or indirectly to employees, board members, or contributors/donors to the organization.[5] This does not mean that employees cannot be paid reasonable compensation or that board members cannot be reimbursed for their legitimate expenses or paid a reasonable fee. What it does mean is that all of the resources and assets of the enterprise must be used to pursue its mission.[6]

Nonprofit is really just shorthand for *non-distribution of profits*. Like many shortcuts, it has unintended consequences. While it has the advantage of being memorable, it also creates public confusion, and potentially undermines public trust.

In this same vein, **nonprofit does not always mean non-taxable**. Certainly, the vast numbers of nonprofit enterprises are not subject to federal, state, or local taxation. However, some of the largest nonprofit enterprises (nonprofit Blue Cross and Blue Shield health insurers) are subject to federal taxation on their profits. Also, some charitable foundations are subject to a tax, albeit modest, on their investment income.[7]

Many nonprofit enterprises, while exempt from both income and local property taxes, make payments in lieu of taxes to their local government entities to help support needed, common local services. Similarly, some health care providers make payments in lieu of taxes to their local county to help support the county's portion of the Medicaid program.[8]

The overall matter of nonprofit taxation is a complicated issue. Tax law and tax accounting are technical fields, laced with subtleties and interlocking complexities. As a general principle, managers and boards having tax questions or undertaking activities that may have tax consequences should seek the guidance of qualified tax counsel.

Against this operating guideline, it should be recognized that the tax code is as much an expression of political policy as anything else. While society's political consensus defines the limit of what government can do by its own hand, the tax code allows government to figuratively "reach over the fence," encouraging certain activities through favorable tax treatment. A primary example of this is the personal income tax deduction allowed for contributions to charitable, 501(c)(3) organizations.

The importance of the "deductibility privilege" cannot be overestimated. The ability of donors to deduct contributions to 501(c)(3) enterprises, for purposes of calculating taxable income creates a major source of non-operating income and capital for nonprofit enterprises. Additionally, research suggests that the ability to take advantage of the itemized deduction tax preference results in increased levels of charitable contributions, regardless of income level.

In the same vein, it should also be understood that tax exemption is not a right that automatically goes with being nonprofit. It is a privilege that must be earned.

This reality was learned by the nation's Blue Cross and Blue Shield health insurers in the late 1980s, when they lost their tax exemption. Looking ahead, the loss of either federal and/or state tax exemption is a possibility that is being brought more clearly into focus for other nonprofit enterprises, particularly hospitals.

To be exempt from federal income taxation a nonprofit corporation must:
- apply to the Internal Revenue Service for an exemption;[9]

- meet the requirements set out in the Internal Revenue Code; and

- obtain the approval of the Internal Revenue Service.

Additionally, to maintain its exemption, an organization must refrain from committing and/or participating in, as defined by the Internal Revenue Code, any prohibited transaction.

Section 501(c) of the Internal Revenue Code is the portion of the law that addresses tax exemption eligibility for most nonprofit organizations. The section lists more than 30 types of organizations that can be exempt. An abridged extract of this section is presented in Appendix 1: "Excerpts: Internal Revenue Code."

A third source of confusion is the counter-intuitive reality that the sector is an amalgam of charitable and non-charitable organizations. It is a rich stew of the selfless and the self-serving. Based on data from the Ninth Edition of The Nonprofit Almanac, Exhibit 3-1 provides a structural depiction of the community sector from the perspective of each major functional category.

For purposes of this discussion, two points should be understood.
- The bulk of community-sector organizations, regardless of whether they are charitable or non-charitable, are social enterprises. That is, they are nonprofit businesses providing goods and/or services, often in competitive environments and always under conditions that require operational efficiency and managerial effectiveness. This means that charities must operate with the same operational, business discipline as non-charities—and even for-profit enterprises.

- The details of numbers are less important than an appreciation that the sector is a varied mix of organizations that fit together in an awkward mosaic.

Numerically and economically, charitable social enterprises are the most prominent element in the sector. Regardless of whether they are primarily commercial in character, where revenues come primarily from fees (hospitals and universities), or donatives (homeless shelters and food pantries) where support comes primarily from donations, social enterprises are hybrid business/social entities. They are enterprises operated for purposes other than profits. However, to survive they must operate with a business discipline similar to that of a for-profit enterprise. Yet, at the same time, if they are to make a difference, they must make choices with the conscience and ethos of a social welfare agency.[10]

Charitable social enterprises account for more than two-thirds of the sector's economic activity. As a group, they receive half of their income from fees and about a quarter from government.[11] Charitable social enterprises are arguably the heart of the community sector. At the same time, because of their competition as well as interdependence with the other sectors, the governance and management of these organizations presents the most interesting policy and operational performance challenges in contemporary society. Social enterprises have the same problems as any business, (i.e., product innovation, marketing, internal control, etc.), as well as the unique public policy and operating issues of the community sector.[12,13]

DOING GOOD AND DOING WELL: SOCIAL ENTERPRISES

It is in social enterprises that many of the nation's most interesting management and governance problems can be found.

There are many kinds of social enterprises. The limiting factor is one's imagination—as tempered by the tax code. Common to all, however, are four defining characteristics:

1. All social enterprises are organized legally as nonprofit entities (public benefit corporations, cooperatives, mutual companies, standard corporations, etc.).

2. They often compete in some significant way with for-profit firms, either in general as an industry (such as, the hospital field or HMOs) or with respect to specific components of their overall operations (the fitness facilities or daycare programs in YMCAs).

3. Irrespective of their competitive circumstance, to be successful they simultaneously must be managed with the same operating acumen and rigor as a for-profit venture and make business decisions with the conscience of a social service agency.

4. The performance litmus test of the business sector—increasing profitability—is not the sole measure of success.

It is the operational interplay and balancing of these factors that makes the management and governance of social enterprises so challenging.

FUNDING INTERMEDIARIES

Funding intermediaries (see Exhibit 3-1) are both separate from and a part of the social enterprise component of the community sector. Funding intermediaries are organizations that primarily provide financial support to other organizations. They can be viewed as falling into two broad categories—collective fundraisers and foundations.

Collective fundraisers can also be thought of as falling into two categories, either single purpose (cause focused) or multi-purpose (community focused) organizations. The March of Dimes, with its exclusive focus on eliminating birth defects, is an example of a special purpose, collective fundraiser. The United Way and Jewish Community Federation are examples of community focused collective fundraising entities that support a variety of different community sector enterprises.

Exhibit 3 -1 A

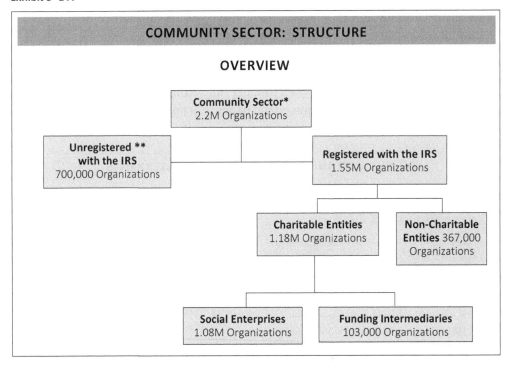

Exhibit 3 -1 B

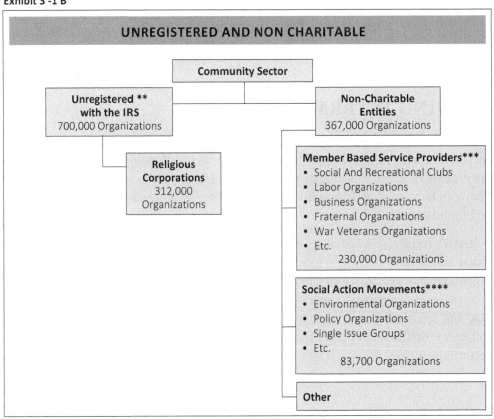

Exhibit 3 -1 C

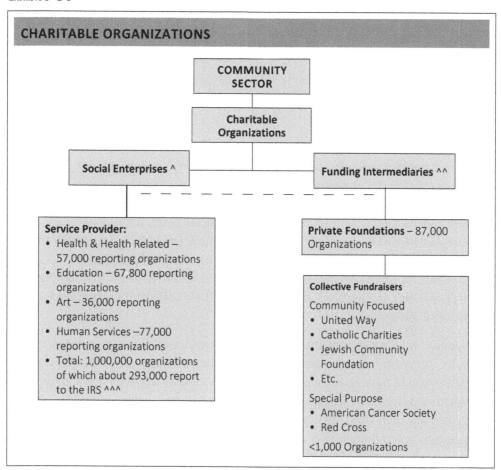

CHARITABLE ORGANIZATIONS

COMMUNITY SECTOR

Charitable Organizations

Social Enterprises ^

Funding Intermediaries ^^

Service Provider:
- Health & Health Related – 57,000 reporting organizations
- Education – 67,800 reporting organizations
- Art – 36,000 reporting organizations
- Human Services –77,000 reporting organizations
- Total: 1,000,000 organizations of which about 293,000 report to the IRS ^^^

Private Foundations – 87,000 Organizations

Collective Fundraisers

Community Focused
- United Way
- Catholic Charities
- Jewish Community Foundation
- Etc.

Special Purpose
- American Cancer Society
- Red Cross

<1,000 Organizations

*The purpose of the above taxonomy is to provide a sense of the shape of the community sector, not depict its structure or numbers in detail. Consistent with this goal, all data are approximations. Data are drawn from The New Nonprofit Almanac Ninth Edition, Urban Institute. All data are approximate, providing a relative order of magnitude.

**Organizations with less than $50,000 in gross receipts and religious organizations and congregations are not required to register with the IRS. It is estimated, however, that about half of religious congregations register. Many religious congregations, in addition to their spiritual/worship mission, are active fundraisers. Many are also service providers, particularly in the human services areas. Other unregistered organizations are small, grassroots efforts, sometimes unincorporated, of unknown numbers.

***Mission: Provide services to individuals and/or groups that have, by their own choice, decided to be affiliated with the organization. The organization's efforts are focused on primarily providing collective benefits to a self-identified/selected group. Member serving organizations can be either service provider entities and/or social movement entities.

****Organizations substantially engaged in political action and lobbying.

^ Mission: Provide benefits to the community as a whole. The organization's efforts are focused on promoting the general welfare of the stakeholder group regardless of personal affiliation action by any individual or group. The organization's focus is on the community of stakeholders as a whole, not the members of the organization.

^^ Mission: Primarily provide support for public serving social enterprises. If they did not exist, the enterprises would have to increase their own fundraising efforts.

^^^ These are estimated to be 529,000+ reporting entities—registered organizations with more than $50,000 annual revenue.

Regardless of whether they are single purpose or multi-purpose, collective fundraisers exist to provide support to other community sector enterprises. The tax code requires that the funds raised can only be contributed or in effect redistributed to qualified organizations (i.e., 501(c)(3) entities).

Foundations can also be structured in several ways. Regardless of their specific legal form, foundations are created to hold donated assets whose investment income, and in some instances principal, is to be used to support the pursuit of specific public benefit purposes/goals.

For the most part, foundations accomplish their objectives by providing support to other social enterprises. Certainly, some foundations actively pursue programs through their own operational initiatives and will both hire internal staff and contract with community and private sector firms for specific work. However, because of the tax code requiring, for most foundations, a minimum level of contributions (grants) each year (a percentage of the foundation's assets) and limiting the organizations that grants can be made to (i.e., only to 501(c)(3) entities), foundations effectively focus their support on community sector, social enterprises.[14]

Functionally, funding intermediaries are shared service entities that exist to assist donors in supporting social enterprises. If they did not exist, community sector enterprises would have to increase their internal fundraising efforts, incurring costs for themselves, and in aggregate, duplicative costs for the community. It is for this reason, their fundamental shared service role, that collective fundraising organizations, even though they are legally independent, private entities, can be thought of as being part of the social enterprise segment of the community sector.

This is not to suggest that funding intermediaries are not important entities, with unique management and public relations challenges.[15] Rather, it is a conclusion offered to provide a managerial context as to how these organizations can be viewed as fitting into the whole.

SOCIAL ACTION MOVEMENTS

The same codification conclusion cannot be made regarding the approximately 84,000 social/political action movement organizations.

Just as the community sector can be viewed as a residual economic category, political/social movement entities (i.e., special interest groups, like the Sierra Club, National Rifle Association, National Organization of Women, MoveOn. org, etc.), can be thought of as the residual within the community sector. These organizations are nonprofit, private, self-governing, and controlled by their stakeholders, not investors.[16] Therefore, they do not fit into either the for-profit business or the public sectors. At the same time, they are neither traditional direct service providers nor do they raise funds for anything other than their own needs.

Moreover, it is arguable if they provide a collective good or just pursue some self-defined narrow special interest. As a result, while generally classified as part of the community sector, they do not fit neatly into the community sector.

Reinforcing this conclusion is the unavoidable reality of their purpose. Social movement organizations exist to influence public opinion, public policy (i.e., government), and the decision and operating behavior of other organizations.

Certainly, the political lobbying role of special interest groups is well recognized. These organizations, however, also try to shape the policies and operating behavior of both private and community sector firms. Examples of this can be seen in the environmental arena with respect to plant location decisions and pollution control. It can also be seen in the health services area where the pressure that consumer groups bring on hospitals and health plans to lower costs, expand access, improve quality, etc. is constant.

> **SOCIAL ENTERPRISES**
>
> Social enterprises dominate the community sector both in number and economic footprint. They reflect an amalgam of two powerful ideas:
> - the need for efficiency (a business standard), and
> - the need for decision making guided by mission and community expectations (a charity standard).
>
> The point of equilibrium between the pressure to do well and the pressure to do good is not profit maximization, though sufficient long-term resources, for resilience and sustainability, are necessary. Equilibrium, rather, demands that:
> - money not be left on the table, either by paying too much or not capturing available revenue opportunities (income maximization) while simultaneously
> - program decisions be made to provide the greatest value added to the community (benefit maximization).

Given their purpose, social movement organizations generate significant emotional reaction among both their supporters and detractors. The facts of both their persistence and growth, however, evidence their effectiveness. Moreover, they can claim political legitimacy by pointing out that they are rooted in the voluntary, collective associations that are so much a part of America's philosophical and political character, as so impressed de Tocqueville. The question, however, is not about their genesis, evolution, or utility. Rather, it is about their fit or place in the system.

Recognizing that they do not produce traditional products and that their efforts are focused on influencing public opinion as well as the policy decisions and operational behavior of all sectors of the economy, they can be viewed as not being a natural part of any sector of the economy. At the same time, because of their private, self-governing, nonprofit character, they cannot be viewed as a separate sector. Given these realities, it is reasonable to think of them as being the equivalent of organizational satellites orbiting the entire political, social, and economic system, creating pressures (i.e., analogous to a political force field), intended simultaneously to influence public opinion—as well as all aspects of policy and operational behavior. (See Exhibit 3-2 on next page.)

Exhibit 3-2

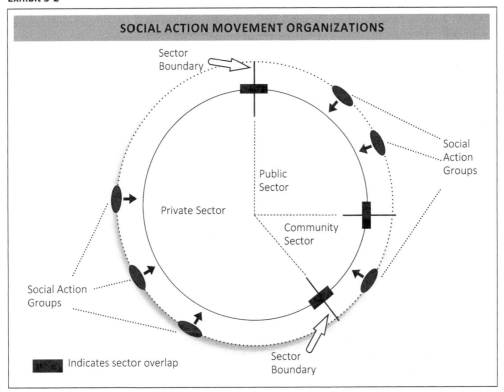

RELIGIOUS CONGREGATIONS

Religious congregations present a different set of issues. The importance of religious congregations to society cannot be overstated. They are powerful in their influence, pervasive in their reach, independent in their behavior, and complex in their operations.

In addition to worship and religious education work, they are often, through their social action ministries and faith-based initiatives, significant providers of services both to their members and to the larger community. At the same time, they are also fundraisers both for their internal operations and their social service humanitarian initiatives. Finally, they often actively engage in trying to influence public and social policy. Examples of this can be seen in the involvement of some religious congregations in anti-war, right-to-life, and anti-poverty movements.

Clearly, even within the idiosyncratic structure of the community sector, religious congregations are unique. They are simultaneously both a part of and apart from the sector, as well as the overall economy. As a consequence of this and the fundamental American principle of separating church and state, the Internal Revenue Service recognizes this unique status by not requiring religious congregations to register with it.

From a structural perspective, how then should one think about these organizations? The answer lies in not being doctrinaire.

To the extent that religious congregations engage in social action, fundraising, and/or public benefit service activities, they are no different than their mainstream community sector counterparts. In pursuing these kinds of activities, they face the same issues and challenges and must respond with the same operational discipline as any other community sector enterprise engaged in similar pursuits. However, to the extent they act in their worship and religious education role, they are structurally separate from the community sector and the rest of the economy. Accepting this perspective, it is reasonable to show religious congregations as a distinct component of the community sector, linked to it, but at the same time, apart from it. (See Exhibit 3–3.)

Exhibit 3-3

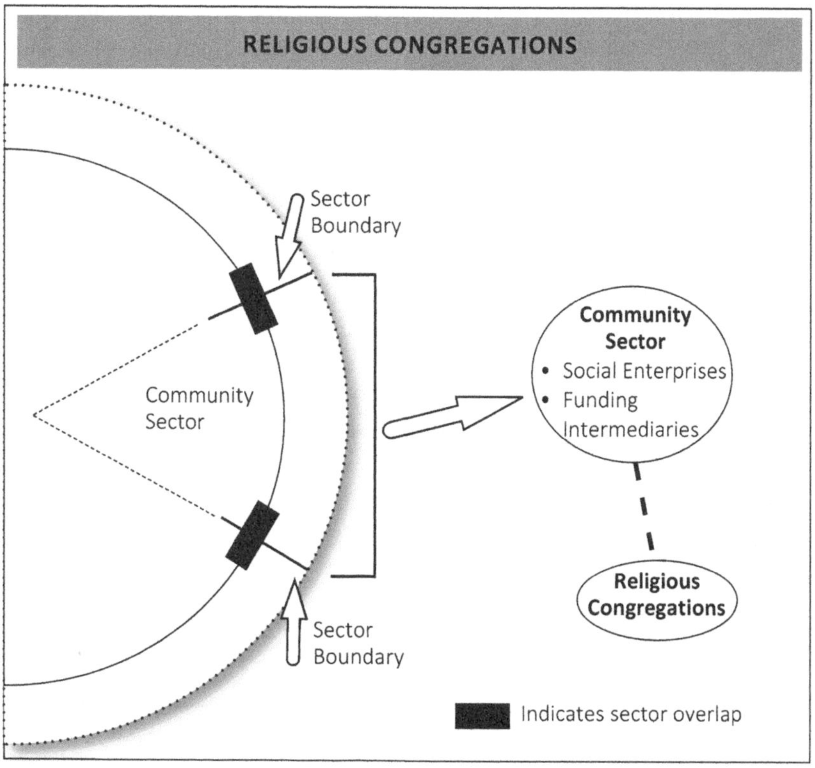

COMMONALITIES

What is clear is that the community sector is diverse. Each of its segments is unique, having its own operating requirements, performance standards, and organizational prerogatives. Each, however, also shares certain commonalities.

The two most obvious commonalities are: All community sector organizations are nonprofit entities. As noted earlier, they are nonprofit as a business and operating decision, not as a tax management and avoidance strategy. They are also all non-governmental organizations (i.e., privately owned), the result of private resources being dedicated to community purposes and, as a consequence, recognize that if their founding mission is to be best achieved, all efforts must be dedicated to that end—not increasing anyone's personal financial wealth.

A third commonality is the supremacy of mission. A business (private, for-profit) sector enterprise is created to make money for its owners. How it makes money is bound only by the moral, ethical, and legal limits of society. The enterprise may start, raise capital, and produce one product or service only to realize that it might do better by pursuing another. As long as it has sufficient resources, there is nothing to prevent it from changing its product or business purpose. Rhetoric and advertising slogans aside, for the private sector enterprise, mission is not product or service specific. Mission, rather, is simply an economic goal—increase owner's wealth.[17]

In contrast, community sector organizations are created to pursue specific missions (purposes)—not profits. An organization is established with a particular charitable, educational, scientific, civic, fraternal, political, etc., purpose. Contributions are made and/or fees are charged to fund the work needed to pursue and achieve that specific purpose. The organization may or may not be successful. However, regardless of result, it cannot, without the approval of the court, change its mission.[18]

Moreover, the enterprise cannot, in any material way, utilize its resources for anything other than the pursuit of the mission for which it was created.

A fourth major commonality is governance. Here the similarity is neither board size nor technical business issues. Rather, the glue is the complexity, beginning with the diversity of interests that must be captured by the board in its membership and deliberations and continuing through to the diversity of personal and professional goals that individuals bring to the board table.

COMMENTARY: WHERE IS THE EVIDENCE?

Good governance would seem to be a sustainable competitive advantage. The data supporting this intuitively reasonable conclusion are not overwhelming. Part of the problem lies in quantifying what is good governance. Part also lies in assessing comparative performance.

Bad governance is not an asset. By the same logic, good governance would not be a liability. The question then is a matter of cost and benefits. Does the cost of attention to good governance yield benefits, justifying the effort? The evidence-based answer suggests it does, but again the data are not robust.

A management perspective provides a stronger conclusion. An active, engaged board is a chief executive's best protection. A chief executive who is leading his or her organization will at some point find themselves in a difficult position. If the board knows of and has agreed to the enterprise's direction and actions, it will stand by its chief executive. If it does not, the chief executive may well be on his or her own.

The conclusion for the chief executive is clear. An engaged board and good governance may be a career saver.

Chief executives, who do not put personal priority on good governance, manage at their own peril.

Private sector corporate boards are generally small (typically 8–12 members) and intensely focused on achieving the singular financial performance purpose of the enterprise.

Community sector boards are generally larger (typically about 20–25 persons) and characterized both by diffuse reasons for people serving on the board, and within the boundaries of the organization's mission, by multiple business and social objectives. This circumstance is neither good nor bad. It is simply a reality that must be recognized for the governance and management challenges that it presents.

The net effect of this mixture of competing requirements is a complicated governance process. It is also a process that because of the need to harmonize various, and even at times contradictory, stakeholder interests, appears to be inefficient.

In reality, the governance of community sector organizations is as much a political as a business process, and like most political processes, efficiency is not the primary governance goal. However, when governance is done well, the results can seem almost magical. In contrast, when done poorly, stakeholders suffer, and board members are embarrassed. Therefore, there is a premium on getting governance right.

Community sector enterprises also share some common limitations. Because they lack the clear metric of *bottom line* financial performance, assessment of operational efficiency, and often even results themselves, is difficult.[19] Importantly, it also creates a particular challenge for maintaining the public's trust and confidence in the performance of the enterprise. Without the objective, quantified measures of both absolute and relative financial performance, the enterprise is always in a defensive position, having to use proxies to demonstrate that it is doing good works, competently accomplishing those results and that its profits are at publicly justifiable levels.

This latter challenge is perhaps the most difficult. For the for-profit firm, the level of profit is not a policy concern. The challenge is, over the long run, to maximize total profit. More is better. This clear guidepost is not available to the boards and managers of nonprofit enterprises. The more profits the enterprise generates, the less collective benefits it might be providing. Therefore, a balance is necessary, one that optimizes total benefits without jeopardizing survival and growth.

Survival is necessary, for if the enterprise fails, the generation of future benefits is lost. Implicit to survival is the dual need to operate efficiently and to generate the profits required to have the capital necessary to meet future needs. Given the limits of the objective, quantifiable metrics, where this balance lies can only be seen in the eyes of the public, as expressed through the enterprise's board.[20]

Capital generation can also be problematic. The traditional equity capital markets are not available to community sector enterprises. Instead, they must look to internally generated capital from operational performance, either to use immediately, accumulate as a reserve and/or use to acquire and service taxable or tax-exempt debt.[21] Also, as noted earlier, certain community sector organizations (501(c)(3) organizations) can generate capital through contributions from benefactors.[22]

CONCLUSION

The community sector is not the heart of the American economy. As a sector it is too small to be the driving engine of economic prosperity. It can, however, be said to be the soul of the nation.

As a sector it is a percolating cauldron of seeming inconsistency; private resources for public benefit; nonprofit not meaning no profit; taxable and tax-exempt organizations; part of the general economy and apart from it; competitive with and simultaneously dependent upon the public and private sectors, etc.

On the surface, the community sector makes little sense and would seem to offer little hope for success. The facts, however, belie this first impression. The community sector works. It protects values and cultural traditions, provides a safety net for those least able to care for themselves, educates the nation, teaches and protects democracy, and, perhaps most importantly, is the means for achieving goals that otherwise would only be unfulfilled dreams.

Recognizing all this, it is important that community sector organizations be well managed.

CHAPTER 3

Takeaways and Questions for Consideration and Discussion:

TAKEAWAYS

1. The Internal Revenue Code identifies over 30 different categories of tax-exempt organizations, making the community sector a mix of strange bedfellows – some of which even pay taxes.

2. The dominant element of the community sector is the 501(c)(3)—charitable, educational, scientific, religious, etc.—component representing more than two-thirds of all the organizations in the sector.

3. Within this component of the sector are hundreds of thousands of social enterprise organizations that provide food to the hungry, health to the sick, shelter to the homeless, education to society, and support to the needy.

4. It is these organizations that give society its soul. Therefore, they must be governed and managed better than commercial businesses—because the stakes are greater than simply profits.

QUESTIONS

1. What is the relationship between for-profit, nonprofit, and tax-exemption?

2. What makes social enterprises such an interesting management challenge?

3. Why is being nonprofit a strategic decision?

Chapter 4:
THE CORPORATION

Before going further, it is worthwhile to stop for a moment and recognize two assumptions that are implicit in the previous chapters. First, it is taken for granted that the corporation, as an entity for carrying out education, cultural, social, humanitarian, and other activities, exists. Second, it is within the organizational and legal structure of corporations that almost all nonprofit enterprises operate.

Given the ubiquity of the corporation in American life, these assumptions are not surprising. However, like many things that are taken for granted, the corporation had to be created (i.e., invented and accepted). Moreover, its growth was neither instantaneous nor without controversy. In fact, the corporation, as a form for carrying out business activities, emerged over a protracted period of time. It was shaped, obviously, by economic pragmatism. However, it was also tempered by society's social welfare needs and political ideology that both embraced and opposed it.

Today, corporations are taken for granted, easily established, and draw little public attention unless caught cheating their investors, the government, or their employees, or harming the public. This was not always the case. The invention of the corporation was initially a revolutionary idea whose birth was far more difficult than the casual observer might guess.

The corporation is an enabling technology. It enables financial capital and human effort to be efficiently gathered, concentrated, and deployed on a sustainable basis.

Usually innovations like the corporation, railroad timetables, or property loss insurance are not thought of as being technological breakthroughs. Certainly, they are not in the same class as discoveries like anti-viral drugs, jet engines, or computer chips. The fact that they are different from hard science or physical, technology breakthrough does not, however, make them any less creative or important.

> **PERSPECTIVE**
>
> The origins of the corporation are open to debate. However, as common to most important social and economic innovations, corporations are the product of the interaction of social, political, and economic forces over a period of time. As a consequence, their early stages cannot be easily detected out of the complex background of economic formant in which they were nourished.
>
> Similarly, it is difficult to detect in their early stages which economic innovations will become important. It was not until corporations obtained their present day significance that economic historians became interested in their origins.*
>
> * The Financial Policy of Corporations, Volume 1. Fifth Edition. Arthur Stone Dewing.

Where, for example, would society be without the computer chip? Life certainly would be different—and arguably, not for the better. But in the same vein, where would society be without the corporation to accumulate the capital and organize the resources needed to manufacture and distribute computer chips? Without the corporation, computer chips might have been invented in the laboratory, but their commercial utilization would, at best, be limited. With the corporation, their manufacture, distribution, and utilization have been pervasive. The corporation enables other technology to be implemented. By any measure this is an important contribution.

FORM, FUNCTION, AND NECESSITY

While there can be a myriad of variations, in general, the organizing form for the contemporary conduct of business falls into one of three broad groupings: individual (sole) proprietorships, partnerships, or corporations.

The virtue of the sole proprietorship business model is its simplicity—both to create and to operate—and its unambiguous, single-owner point of control.

Its primary drawbacks are its inability to focus on a sustained common purpose; the risks of business liability being transferred, without limit, to the individual owner, difficulties in raising capital, and the problems inherent in perpetuating or continuing the enterprise beyond the natural life of its owner. As a result, while individual proprietorships may be a reasonable "starting point" for structuring an economic or social pursuit, their long-run usefulness is limited.

Partnerships obviously have more capacity than individual proprietorships.

Partnerships are an old organizational concept. They are the product of an agreement between and among the involved parties (the "partners"). Like all agreements (regardless of how carefully and precisely drafted) partnerships are subject, over the course of time, to reinterpretation and misinterpretation.

The result of this normal confluence of human nature and the flow of time is, not surprisingly, the potential for interpersonal tension among partners. The risks to the continued existence of the venture are clear.

Like sole proprietorships, partnerships have benefits and liabilities. Ease of creation is clearly a positive feature. In contrast, unlimited individual-partner financial liability, and the restricted ability to raise capital are all intrinsic features that limit partnerships.

The solution to many of these structural, capital, and legal limitations lies in establishing the venture as a corporation.

In the same vein, a simple agrarian society, organized around individual efforts and personal production, does not require the human resource and financial capital structure of the corporation. But when the production of goods or the solution to a social problem requires division of labor and the combined and coordinated efforts of many – a sustainable organizing form and force is needed. Commonly this form and focus is the corporation. It is the preferred solution simply because it is a remarkable mechanism for aggregating human and financial capital, liability, and longevity in a mixture that has an acceptable degree of personal risk (i.e., investors can only, at a maximum, lose what they have invested).

THE BEGINNINGS

Historians suggest that the beginnings of the corporation can be traced back more than three thousand years. Ancient Mesopotamians had business arrangements that went beyond simple barter. Assyrians created partnerships. The Phoenicians spread the notion of involved business arrangements throughout their trading areas and the Athenians built on that model, adding rules of law to guide operations. The Romans created fundamental concepts of corporate law, particularly the idea that an association of people could have a collective identity.

With the fall of Rome, commercial life moved to other corners of the world.

The roots of the modern business corporation, however, came from more contemporary sources and economic needs.

The origins of today's business corporation stems from an evolutionary flow of the development of the borough, guild, chartered association, and joint stock company. Each of these approaches to organizing and directing resources is linked, building on one another and reflecting increasingly sophisticated solutions to growingly complex social and economic issues.

More important than its genealogy is the recognition that the contemporary corporation is the evolved organizational solution developed to meet society's changing economic needs. It is also important to understand that in America this happened within a political environment that was fearful of the creation of corporations.[1,2]

POLITICS AND ECONOMICS

On one side was Thomas Jefferson. On the other Alexander Hamilton.

Jefferson advocated a decentralized agrarian republic. His vision was that the United States would be a decentralized republic. The engine of the economy would be planters and farmers. Commerce, factories, and urban life would have only a small role. Corporations in his view were a threat to individual freedom and a government that was close to the people.

Hamilton sought strong central government acting in the interest of commerce and industry. Corporations, while at the time not central to this goal, were a necessary part of it.

Hamilton, as a Federalist, represented the urban mercantile interests, and as Treasury Secretary, planned and implemented a financial revolution in the United States, laying the enabling financial foundation for America's growth. Jefferson was an Anti-Federalist or Republican, believing that supporting manufacturing was not as important to the future as supporting the established agrarian economy.

Out of different economic perspectives and visions of the future emerged the two-party political system (at the time Federalists and Republicans). The Federalists dominated national government through the 18th century and on the coattails of this domination, the path was cleared for the emergence of corporations as the pragmatic mechanism for economic growth.

It is not difficult to understand why there would be political opposition to the development of the corporation. In theory, government can do everything for everyone. Moreover, with an arguably infinite life, government could do this forever.

To the extent that the citizenry wants to limit the reach of government and/ or private sector interests seek to provide goods and services, including human and social welfare services, a multi-sector economy emerges with a changed and diminished operating role for government. In the short run, the "economic pie" is essentially fixed in size. Therefore, what one sector gains another loses. Over the near and long term, the size of the total economy can certainly grow. However, while the absolute size of a particular sector can increase, relative size is diminished as economic influence is shared/spread.

Recognizing this essentially zero-sum economic geometry, it is understandable that government, particularly the newly-formed American experiment in democratic self-government, would not embrace, let alone trust, the notion of corporations as a development that could or would benefit society. Nevertheless, the demands of capital and commerce ultimately pushed the idea forward.

FEATURES

The real magic of the corporation lies in one overriding feature. The corporation allows, almost without restriction, for continuous efforts to be focused on the achievement of a single, commonly understood purpose. This is a feature that holds the potential for both great accomplishments, and if not properly guarded and harnessed, substantial abuse.

Whether the purpose is the production of a computer chip or the care of the sick, the core attribute is the same. Corporations provide the organizational vehicle for bringing together diverse sources of resources and energy for long enough periods of time to achieve a common purpose. In the case of nonprofit enterprises, the necessity and the power of the long-term fusing of both effort and capital to achieve a specific mission are clear.

While specific mission may provide the heart of the corporation, from a less poetic perspective, a corporation must have several practical features both to exist in a legal sense and to function as an economic entity.

Corporations are not creations of nature. They are political inventions of society. To exist they must be created by an act of government. This step—of legally establishing the existence of the corporation—is accomplished by the state's approval (or acceptance) of the corporation's proposed charter or articles of incorporation. (See Exhibit 4-1 at end of this chapter.) This document explicitly sets out the mission for which the corporation is being created. The state's approval creates the corporation as a legal entity.[3]

The state, in effect, provides the corporation with a franchise to operate. Not surprisingly, in exchange, the corporation has certain obligations to the state and society at large. Some of these are explicit, such as reporting requirements and compliance with regulatory requirements—both operating and disclosure. Others are more subtle, reflecting the corporation's role in maintaining a prosperous and stable society.

In addition to creating it, the state also gives the corporation certain properties (rights and features) that enable it to function as an economic entity. In effect, it gives the corporation a legal life and the ability to function within that legal existence as an economic being. In particular, it gives the corporation the right to own real property, to sue, and to be sued. It also establishes that the owners of the corporation have limited personal liability for the financial losses of the enterprise.

These features enable the corporation to transact its affairs and operate in a manner similar to that of an individual person conducting business.[4] Limited personal liability—part of the alchemy that makes it all work—provides the mechanism for controlling and managing the financial and personal risks involved in pursuing grand, imaginative efforts. It is the legal safety net for the owners of the enterprise, limiting their maximum potential losses and obligations to the amounts they have invested or contributed.[5]

If part of the alchemy comes from limited liability, the remainder comes from unlimited life. Together they transform the philosophical focus on a common purpose into a consequential mechanism for achieving significant business and social outcomes.

Unlimited life is obviously an overstatement. As the portfolios of many investors evidence, corporations come and go. More precisely, corporations are granted the ability to have a life span that while not necessarily infinite is also not subject to the biological limitations of a single human life. The importance and practicality of this requirement becomes clear when considering the vast amounts of capital that must be assembled to pursue certain goals. If this capital had to be disbursed and re-gathered every time the venture's leader died, the enterprise's ability to move forward (and also society's opportunity to benefit) would be impaired, if not entirely lost. The solution to this problem is straightforward: allow the corporation's existence to go beyond the bounds of human longevity.

The value of this attribute is just as important in the nonprofit setting. Imagine the difficulty of creating and sustaining today's hospitals or universities if the effort had to start over each time its leader changed jobs or died.

FORM TO SUBSTANCE

It is easy to accept that the state can create a legal entity that has business transaction abilities exceeding that of an individual. The more difficult understanding is the next step—translating the legal concept of the corporation into an operational enterprise. The answer lies in how the corporation is able to organize four key factors:

1. Capital (both human and financial)   3. The Board
2. Management   4. The Owners

Capital is the raw material of any enterprise. It is both financial and human— intellect as well as muscle. Without it, there can be nothing. Even with it, absent the skill of management, there may still be nothing. Management gives productive substance to raw capital. It organizes and then nurtures the application of capital to the achievement of the agreed-upon common purpose.

The board's contribution, in macro terms, is to select and oversee the leader of the management group; that is, to hire the chief executive and to provide the oversight necessary to ensure that everything and everyone stays focused on achieving the enterprise's purpose. It does this on behalf of the enterprise's owners. In theory, the board acts as the agent of the owners, having a stewardship responsibility for assuring that the capital provided to the corporation is used in the best interests of the owners.[6]

The owners, at a minimum, provide financial capital and select the board. They also arguably provide oversight of the board. In practice, they have traditionally been primarily just a source of capital. The growing activist stockholders' movement, however, may be changing this. Professional investors (i.e., mutual and pension fund managers), are making it clear that owners (stockholders) will punish, at least in terms of stock prices, management that does not meet performance expectations.

FOR-PROFIT VS. NONPROFIT

So far, the discussion has applied to both for-profit and nonprofit corporations. It is important to recognize that the statutory foundation and taxation of nonprofit corporations are not the same as those of for-profit or general business corporations.[7]

The flow and interactions from capital to management to the board and then to the owners are easy to visualize in the for-profit enterprise. For the nonprofit corporation, the relationships are both more subtle and more complex.

Nonprofit corporations do not have owners. However, if there are no "owners," what is the source of capital? And how is the board selected? The answer to the first question is the community, and the individual and corporate benefactors who are committed to the enterprise's purpose are the source of capital. The individuals and business corporations who endow university professorships and give hospitals money for new facilities and equipment clearly provide capital. However, by virtue of their gift or investment, they do not own the nonprofit enterprise. Similarly, community-wide contributions or government grants to nonprofit enterprises provide capital, but they do not establish ownership. For the nonprofit corporation, capital comes from those interested in furthering the enterprise's purpose—not from traditional financial investors.

NONPROFIT AS A STRATEGY

As the experience of many investors illustrates, for-profit enterprises can produce losses. Nonprofit corporations can, and often do, have profits; they generate surpluses by having revenues in excess of expenses. In fact, as noted earlier, they must do well (make a profit, or at least avoid sustained losses) to be able to do good (carry out their mission).

These surpluses, however, cannot be used to provide financial rewards to the benefit of the corporation's owners or other private individuals. Of equal importance, any surpluses generally are not subject to income taxation. As a result, more resources are available for the pursuit of the nonprofit enterprise's public purposes.

To many it is this last factor—exemption from income tax—that is the defining characteristic of a nonprofit organization. In reality, it is the converse. As a result of their defining characteristic, the dedication of private resources to community benefit, nonprofit enterprises are provided with tax preferences to encourage their efforts.

The answer to the second question is more involved. The board—or individual directors—of a nonprofit corporation may be selected in one of several ways.

They may be elected by the corporation's membership (if the corporation has a separate membership body[8] with voting rights); elected by the board itself (if the board is self-perpetuating and members simultaneously serve as board and corporate members), and/or appointed by another organization. The corporation's bylaws (as will be discussed later) typically determine which mechanism, or which combination of these approaches, is used.[9]

In all this, what should be appreciated is that in place of traditional owners (i.e., stockholders), nonprofit corporations have members. Unlike a for-profit enterprise where an owner, as a consequence of investment, effectively is a member of the corporation; members of nonprofit corporations—who they are and how they are selected—are typically regulated by the corporation's certificate of incorporation and/or bylaws.

Members, like stockholders, are at the top of the corporation's control hierarchy. In the nonprofit environment, they have the ultimate control over the corporation. They are expected to ensure that the enterprise pursues its purpose. Typically, they also must approve any sale, merger, or dissolution of the corporation. However, unlike owners, members cannot benefit financially from the performance of the enterprise or the sale or disposal of any of its assets.

A consistent theme winds through all this. Nonprofit corporations are created so that private assets can be used to pursue public purposes. The corporate form of a business organization is used because it provides benefits in terms of longevity and protection. But nonprofit incorporation also has constraints:
- it limits what can be done with any profits;

- it requires that all the efforts and assets of the enterprise be focused expressly on, and used for, the purpose for which the corporation was created.

THE STATE

In this latter regard government again plays a role. Just as government must act to create the enterprise—through the chartering process—it also serves as the ultimate protector of the public's interests.

Early in the history of charities, it was established that the state's attorney general spoke for the beneficiaries of a nonprofit enterprise. It is the office of the attorney general, in almost all states, which has the authority to call the members and directors to account.[10]

Historically, this authority has related to representing the public interest relative to protecting the assets (both funds and property) of the corporation. It also has involved assuring that the corporation's stated public purpose was being pursued.

These responsibilities endure to the present. Nonprofit corporations are subject to the oversight of the attorney general of their state of incorporation. They also potentially require the attorney general's approval if they wish to change the purpose for which their assets are used, alter their legal structure or tax status, merge or effect any other significant change.

The state, in effect, is supposed to serve as the public's safety net. It has the ultimate accountability for ensuring that the purpose for which the corporation was created, and for which the state's approval was granted, is actually, at least in broad terms, being pursued.

CORPORATIONS AND CONSCIENCE

America is a nation of corporations. Why the corporate form of organization? The reason is simple. The corporation provides an economic advantage, minimizing the transaction costs of coordinating any particular commercial activity. It enables the hand of management to be more efficient than the invisible hand of market forces.

The corporation is a legal entity, born out of a necessity.[11]

SHAREHOLDER VALUE

In the 1970s, it became generally accepted that a business corporation, through its board and management, had a singular goal–to increase shareholder value/wealth. This premise justified brutal capitalistic behavior, e.g., layoffs, plant closings, wage stagnation, etc., if it could be argued that such actions would increase shareholder wealth. In the last several years, this point of view has begun to erode.

A new understanding is emerging that argues that in addition to shareholders, corporations also have obligations to their employees and community. This evolution in thinking reflects a belief that shareholder long term goals are best served by a broader view of the board's and management's responsibility. Only time will tell if this view is accurate, let alone sustainable.

Whether for-profit or nonprofit, the corporation is a powerful organizational entity—one that has changed the face of the world.

At the same time, it is an organizational structure that can be abused and misused. Examples abound of how corporations have fouled the environment, ignored basic human rights, and put consumer health and safety at risk. Just as they have the ability to do great good, corporations also have the ability to do bad. The corporation is essentially a body without a soul, without a conscience. As discussed in Part II, governance—the board—both as a group and its individual members—offers the means for providing the corporation with a conscience.

Exhibit 4-1: SAMPLE CERTIFICATE OF INCORPORATION

New York State

CERTIFICATE OF INCORPORATION

OF

_____

(Insert Corporation Name)

Under Section 402 of the Not-for-Profit Corporation Law

FIRST: The name of the corporation is:

SECOND: The corporation is a corporation as defined in subparagraph (a)(5) of Section 102 (Definitions) of the Not-for-Profit Corporation Law.

THIRD: The purpose or purposes for which the corporation is formed are as follows (type or print clearly):

FOURTH: The corporation shall be a Type_____corporation pursuant to Section 201 of the Not-for-Profit Corporation Law.[1]

_____

Type of Corporation:
In drafting the purpose clause, state exactly what the organization plans to do. The purposes will dictate what type of not-for-profit corporation will be formed. Below is a description of the four types of corporations under New York law. (See N-PCL §201).

> **TYPE A**—formed for non-business purpose or purposes, including civic, patriotic, political, social, fraternal, athletic, agricultural, horticultural, animal husbandry, and for a professional, commercial, industrial, trade or service association.

> **TYPE B**—formed for one or more of the following non-business purposes: charitable, educational, religious, scientific, literary, cultural, or for the prevention of cruelty to children or animals.

> **TYPE C**—formed for any lawful business purpose to achieve a lawful public or quasi-public objective, for example local development corporations under N-PCL §1411.

> **TYPE D**—formed under two New York laws for any business or non-business or pecuniary or non-pecuniary purpose when such formation is authorized by any other corporate law of New York, for example corporations formed under the N-PCL and the Private Housing Finance Law.

Distinctions Among Type B, C, and D Corporations:
> **TYPE B CORPORATIONS** are limited to one or more of the following non-business purposes: charitable, educational, scientific, literary, cultural, or for the prevention of cruelty to children or animals (N-PCL §201b). Such corporations provide a benefit to the public or some segment of it. Organizations exempt from federal income taxation under Internal Revenue Code (the "Code") §501(c)(3) are generally Type B corporations.

> **TYPE C CORPORATIONS** may be organized for a purpose normally carried on by business corporations for profit. However, the purpose of a Type C corporation must be non-pecuniary; that is, it must be formed with an objective other than the making of money. Therefore, it is necessary to set forth, in a separate paragraph from the purposes, the lawful public or quasi- public objective which each business purpose will achieve (N-PCL §201).

> **TYPE D CORPORATIONS** are formed under the N-PCL and certain other laws. Such corporations are subject to all provisions of the N-PCL applicable to a Type B corporation and the other law under which they are created, such as the Private Housing Finance Law or Mental Health Law. Approval from the agency that administers the other law must be attached to the certificate of Incorporation.

Exhibit 4-1: SAMPLE CERTIFICATE OF INCORPORATION, continued

FIFTH: The office of the corporation is to be located in the County of   , State of New York.

SIXTH: The names and addresses of the initial directors of the corporation are (a minimum of three are required):

SEVENTH: The Secretary of State is designated as agent of the corporation upon whom process against it may be served. The address which the Secretary of State shall mail a copy of any process accepted on behalf of the corporation is:

EIGHTH: (Corporations seeking tax exempt status may include language required by the Internal Revenue Service in this paragraph. See instructions, paragraph eighth).

The incorporator or incorporators must sign the Certificate of Incorporation and type or print his/her name and address.

(Type or print name of incorporator)   (Signature)

(Address)

(Type or print name of incorporator)   (Signature)

(Address)

(Type or print name of incorporator)   (Signature)

(Address)

CHAPTER 4

Takeaways and Questions for Consideration and Discussion:

TAKEAWAYS

1. The corporation is a significant technological innovation, enabling the aggregation of capital for the pursuit of long-term economic and societal goals.

2. Nonprofit corporations enable private capital to be used for public purposes.

3. The corporation is such a powerful innovation because of the dual concepts of guaranteed limited liability and through the ability to use stock, the potential of unlimited gains.

4. The state gives the corporation a legal life, the board gives it a conscience.

QUESTIONS

1. Was the invention of the corporation inevitable?

2. Does limited liability encourage reckless behavior?

3. Why is the state's role greater concerning nonprofit corporations than for-profit entities?

PART II

GOVERNANCE

It is generally accepted that good governance results in better organizational performance. The data supporting this conclusion, however, is limited. Also, there are circumstances where good management overcomes bad governance, producing good results.

In contrast, as events of the past decades make clear, bad governance provides the gateway for bad performance—with its cost to both the community at large, the enterprise, and its stakeholders. Given this reality, is it worth the risk to allow bad governance?

Since good governance costs no more—and often less—than bad governance, the answer is obviously no. Good governance provides the corporation with a conscience, the enterprise with an economic soul, and the community with protection. These benefits make good governance a priority—both for the enterprise and the community.

Chapter 5:
GOVERNANCE

The corporation was a product of a political battle. It came into being out of economic need and because the state and the courts had given it license to do so, granting it the privilege to raise capital by issuing (selling) shares in itself, as well as limited investor liability, unlimited life, and the ability to own property, sue and be sued, and speak out on issues of policy and politics. The state had essentially created a body without a conscience. The question is how do you breathe the discipline of conscience into the body of the corporation? The answer lies in the concept of corporate governance.

FUNCTION

Governance is a function carried out by the enterprise's board through the actions of its board members. (See Exhibit 5-1.)

Exhibit 5-1

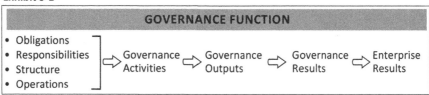

The purpose of governance is to assure that the enterprise works to achieve its mission. For many community sector organizations, mission is a journey without a realistically achievable end (i.e., eliminate hunger, care for the poor, etc.). Therefore, a more pragmatic starting point is to recognize that governance is a function whose purpose is to accomplish four tasks:

1. serve as an effective agent of the enterprise's stakeholders (i.e., at a minimum protecting their interests and ideally enhancing their condition)[1]

2. serve as an efficient steward of the enterprise's assets and resources (i.e., protect the assets)

WHY BOARDS?

Why do nonprofit enterprises either need or have boards?

The short answer is that the state laws that established for-profit corporations require it. Nonprofit corporations simply follow the for-profit model. Both the for-profit and nonprofit boards have a fiduciary responsibility. They both also have to harmonize agency issues between various interest groups and stakeholders. Nonprofit boards, however, also have to handle stewardship issues related to the enterprise's sources of capital.

The more complete answer is that while the law requires boards and they can be viewed as reflecting the need to establish a mechanism that provides limits on and direction for corporations, the real operational and economic impetus for boards is organizational longevity and complexity. Boards exist because organizations will generally exceed the natural lives and ability of their owners to provide hands on management.

3. increase public trust and confidence in the enterprise and its performance

4. assure sustainability.

Complex and/or large organizations and efforts require that one party engage another to perform work on their behalf, creating a principal/agent relationship. The principal is the enterprise's stakeholders and the initial agent is the enterprise's board and then its management and staff. The board is the agent of the stakeholders, and therefore, has an obligation to assure that the enterprise functions in a way that best serves the needs and goals of the stakeholders.

Simultaneously, governance involves a stewardship obligation that must assure not only that the assets placed in its trust are well utilized, but also that the work of the enterprise is done without waste. This stewardship responsibility focuses the board on striving to maximize the long-term impact of the enterprise's assets and efforts.

The board's third task is to enhance public trust in the enterprise. Success here requires an understanding of an outward perspective, presenting the work and accomplishments of the enterprise both to its stakeholders and to the public at large.

The fourth task, assuring sustainability, has a priority focus on mission—not organizational—sustainability. A collective responsibility of the board is to assure adequate human and financial resources. Hopefully, adequacy can be achieved through the enterprise's own efforts. If this is so, then organizational sustainability can be achieved. If not, the board must look to other means (e.g., partnerships, back office consolidations, mergers, fundraising, etc.), to assure the sustainability of the enterprise's ability to pursue mission.

As a function, governance is carried out by people acting in concert, as an organized group (i.e., the board as an entity, and its individual members as its component elements). It is driven by both board and board member obligations and responsibilities while simultaneously being guided by structural design and operational processes. This chapter focuses on obligations and responsibilities and the resulting required actions. The following two chapters address structure and operations—the manner by which people act in concert.

ORGANIZATION SUSTAINABILITY

Organizational sustainability, and its short-run first cousin resilience, is the measure of the organization's likelihood to survive in the face of unexpected catastrophic events. The key to both sustainability and resilience are cash—either in the form of cash reserves, investments that can be easily liquidated, assets which can be mortgaged, or an available credit facility—line of credit or long-term loan. Hurricanes, tornadoes, and other natural disasters have demonstrated how quickly earned revenue and philanthropy can shrink while demand for services explode.

Part of the board's oversight job is to understand this and assure that management includes sustainability and resilience considerations in its multi-year plans. The COVID-19 pandemic of 2020 emphasized both the imperative of doing this, and that sustainability planning should be grounded in trying to anticipate the unthinkable.

THE JOB

Governing a nonprofit enterprise is not a passive activity. It is a real job with real consequences associated with failure (i.e., the 2011 Penn State University experience).

Failure has a cost to the enterprise's clients and beneficiaries—who lose needed services—and to the enterprise's employees—who depend on it for their livelihoods. This reality and its cost must be understood by every board member.

Those looking at board service as an honorific position or as a way to just embellish their résumés should not apply!

DUTY OF OBEDIENCE

Corporate governance, while perhaps not conceptually difficult, is a multi-faceted process involving certain legal duties as well as common sense operational responsibilities. This is particularly true for community sector organizations because of:

- their various stakeholders with, at times, conflicting constituency goals and agendas

- the progressively evolving state of an enterprise's board from founding board (where members are often the staff of the enterprise), to developing board (where the organization begins to employ a critical mass of professional staff), to a mature, corporate board focused on strategy, policy, and oversight.

From a legal perspective, corporate directors have four personal duties. (See Exhibit 5-2.)[2] One, the duty of obedience, can be viewed as a stewardship concept, flowing from the obligation of a trustee to assure that the assets of the trust are only used for the purpose for which the trust was created. The duty of obedience is not a requirement for good behavior. Rather, it is an affirmative obligation to keep the enterprise focused on its intended mission, the purpose for which it was created and for which the assets were provided.

Exhibit 5-2

GOVERNANCE FUNCTION: OBLIGATIONS				
Obligations: ⇨ Accountabilities: • Agency • Stewardship	**Governance** ⇨ **Activities:**	**Governance** ⇨ **Outputs:**	**Governance** ⇨ **Results:**	**Enterprise** ⇨ **Results:**
Duties • Obedience • Care • Loyalty • Add Value	Agent of stakeholders Steward of assets Judgment • Preparation • Attendance • Participation Confidentiality No conflicts of interest Active participation Continuous improvement Ambassador to the community	Approved strategy Operating plan and budget Monitor performance against plan and budget and approve changes Approve independent audit Approve chief executive performance review and compensation Conduct annual governance assessment Approve succession plan: • Governance • Management Adequacy of resources	Sound stewardship of resources • Pursuit of mission Effective agent of stakeholders • Pursuit of mission Increased public trust Sustainability	Pursuit of mission Efficient operations Effective operations A caring enterprise Sustainability
Responsibilities				
Structure				
Operations				

The other two generally recognized legal duties are operational in character: the duty of care and the duty of loyalty. In addition, from a managerial perspective, directors have a fourth duty. This last duty, while not a traditional legal requirement, is as operationally important as any of the legal duties. Directors, both individually and as a group, have an affirmative (positive and active) obligation to add value to the enterprise. In the same vein, the board's obligation to provide active oversight of the enterprise's performance, both what is achieved and how it is done, is increasingly being viewed as an explicit, distinct duty. It can be argued that this obligation always existed, subsumed within the duties of obedience and care. This implicit understanding may be so. However, the fact that oversight is now being singled out, as an explicit obligation, may simply reflect the governance failures of recent years and the need now to make the implicit, explicit and the passive, active.

DUTY OF CARE

The duty of care sets a minimum standard for how directors must approach their job as board members. It requires that a director act in good faith, and with the level of diligence, care, and skill that a concerned person would apply in a similar circumstance. It does not require that decisions of either individual directors or the full board always be correct. In fact, experience shows that business decisions may not always prove to be correct or even wise. This reality, though unfortunate, does not mean that a director has breached the duty of care.

Wrong decisions—especially if there is a persistent pattern—may result in the replacement of management, as well as changes to board leadership and/or membership. However, because of a protective concept known as the "business judgment rule," wrong decisions—regardless of how bad they might be—do not automatically result in a director facing disciplinary action or personal liability.

The "business judgment rule" modifies the duty of care by protecting a director from the consequences of decisions, so long as those decisions are made in the best interests of the enterprise, in good faith (acting honestly), and on an informed basis with attention, common sense, and objectivity. The critical factor is neither the ultimate decision nor result, but rather the process by which the decision was made.

To have the protection of the "business judgment rule" directors must:
- attend meetings, both of the board and of any committees of which they are members

- receive the necessary information to make decisions (and if they do not receive it, request it)

- ask reasonable questions to satisfy themselves that the information provided is complete, objective, and sensible and that the actions proposed are consistent with the enterprise's mission and resources

- exercise independent, objective judgment.

In this last regard, while a director can depend on the information of management and the work of board committees, structure, process, and reliance on management cannot replace common sense and independent judgment.[3] If directors meet these criteria then they are protected from liability, but perhaps not criticism and embarrassment, regardless of the outcome of their decision.[4]

DUTY OF LOYALTY

If the duty of care concentrates on process (the way a director must go about doing the job of being a board member), then the duty of loyalty emphasizes focus. It requires that directors exercise their decision-making influence and authority in a manner that reflects the best interests of the enterprise. It prohibits a director from using his or her position of trust to further either his or her own private interests or the private interests of other persons or organizations.

While the business judgment rule may provide room for second-guessing without penalty, no such flexibility surrounds the duty of loyalty. Directors are expected to observe this duty scrupulously, not only through affirmative actions to protect the interests of the enterprise, but also by refraining from doing anything—either actively or passively—that would harm the corporation. The duty of loyalty requires an undivided and unselfish commitment to the enterprise and its mission. The duty of loyalty applies both to for-profit and nonprofit board members. The related issues of conflicts of interest and confidentiality of information are also the same in both settings.

Among active directors with multi-faceted lives, conflicts of interest are a nearly unavoidable fact of corporate life. Directors must always be aware of such conflicts, erring on the side of caution to even the appearance of conflicts; disclosing them immediately through a proper, transparent process. The existence of a real or potential conflict of interest is not, by itself, a fatal flaw, which would prohibit a director's board membership. The flaw becomes fatal if the director fails to fully disclose the conflict and/or fails to avoid participation in related deliberations.

If directors disclose their interests and recuse themselves from the board's handling of related deliberations, then they have not breached their duty of loyalty.[5] (See Appendix 2 for a sample Conflict of Interest Policy and Disclosure Statement.) While disclosure and abstinence from the deliberations are generally sufficient to prevent problems, one important exception should be noted. Self-dealing, that is the enterprise doing business directly with a director or an organization (or person) in which the director has a significant personal interest, should be explicitly forbidden. Simply put, the enterprise should not buy or sell, on anything other than an explicit "arm's length" relationship basis, goods or services from or to any of its board members—or from any organization in which a director has a meaningful financial, business, or professional stake.

Self-dealing, regardless of how innocent or even prudent, is always difficult to explain. It creates an unnecessary risk and should be avoided.[6] If it is impossible to avoid (as is the reality in some small communities, where the board member is the only local purveyor of the product, or in enterprises with limited resources and where boards and individual board members act in a management/staff as well as governance capacity) the relationship and transaction must be at arm's length and disclosed by both the corporation and the director. The goals of such disclosure should be not only to allow for comment and potentially a change in decision, but also to eliminate the possibility of anyone later thinking that they have "discovered" something inappropriate.

CONFIDENTIALITY

The guideline regarding confidentiality is straightforward. The rule is that, "What is said in the board or committee room remains in the room." Until there is public disclosure, all information that a board member receives must be held in confidence.

NO PARKING LOT MEETINGS

Often, after a board meeting, one can look out into the parking lot and see small groups of directors in discussion. Even directors who do not actively participate in the board's official deliberations are energetically engaged in these conversations. Certainly these board members may be discussing personal matters, making social plans, or providing commentary on world affairs. However, the more likely topic may be the just-completed board meeting and the affairs of the enterprise.

These meetings are inappropriate and individual board members should avoid them. If members have something to say, they should say it in and during the board meeting.

The converse, corollary to "what is said here stays here" is that "what should be said in the board room and meeting is only said there."

Strict adherence to the standard of confidentiality is particularly important for publicly-traded corporations. For these corporations the Securities and Exchange Commission is very concerned about "insider" information and the potential harm of such information, not only with respect to unfair profiteering, but also to undermining the public's confidence in the market.

While nonprofit corporations do not have an "insider trading" concern, they may have a different kind of loyalty issue. Often, nonprofit boards have members who obtain their board position as a consequence of the actions of another organization. A hospital, for example, might designate that the president of its medical staff—by virtue of his or her position—is automatically a member of the board. A zoo that receives funding from its city or county may, as a condition of the funding, have to allow the supporting governmental agency to appoint some number of board members. The important point is this: although such board members obtain their seats as the result of holding some other position, or through the actions of another organization, they are not representatives of that other organization.

Boards are not made up of *representatives*. They are made up of *members*, and members owe a singular duty of loyalty to the enterprise. Board members cannot serve two masters. Moreover, board members do not have a choice as to which master they serve. The duty of loyalty requires that they serve the enterprise—not the organization that recommended or nominated or appointed them to the board.

DUTY TO ADD VALUE

As noted earlier, it can also be said that board members have a fourth, albeit perhaps not a legal, duty. In practical terms this fourth duty is every bit as significant as the other three. Specifically, board members have a duty to add value to the performance and standing of the enterprise.

It is not enough for a board member, through exercise of the duty of care, to try to protect the corporation from making bad decisions. A board member must go beyond this safety-net role and act affirmatively to help the organization make good decisions—decisions that will result in the organization better achieving its mission.

The duty to add value does not mean that directors, as part of their governance role, should be involved in day-to-day operational management. Frankly, when directors inappropriately intrude into operations, the organization is more often than not on a path to serious, if not terminal, trouble. Instead it means that board members must engage fully in the work of the board. It also means the directors must understand the role that the enterprise plays in serving its community and not adopt a simplistic, parochial perspective. Directors must appreciate that if inter-organizational collaboration, or even consolidation, is the best way to add value, then their obligation is to encourage those alternatives.

> **ONE VOICE**
>
> Boardroom discussions may be vigorous and even contentious. Robust discussions are important and can be viewed as a sign of organizational health and vigor. Disagreement and debate are not signs of disloyalty or inability to work together.
>
> While debate may be healthy in terms of reaching sound decisions, once a decision is made the board must speak with one, unified voice. Even if the vote were 51/49, the public decision must be portrayed as unanimous. Members who cannot tolerate this should resign—not undermine the board and enterprise with minority reports.
>
> Governance is hard work. The obligations of loyalty, confidentiality, adding value, and finally speaking with one voice also make it difficult work.

Meeting preparation and attendance is not enough. For the organization to prosper, management needs the benefit of the board's collective wisdom and judgment. If board members do not express themselves at meetings, then neither their colleagues nor management can know what they are thinking, debate their ideas, or weave the board's diversity of experience, knowledge, and opinion into the fabric of success.

RESPONSIBILITIES

The duties of obedience, care, loyalty, and adding value are obligations focused on individuals and provide defining standards of behavior. In addition to these duties, board members also can be viewed as having six basic operational responsibilities.

Three of these are collective responsibilities, requiring the action of the board as a whole. Two are hybrids, requiring both individual and group action, and one is an individual obligation. Taken together these duties and responsibilities give substance to the board as a group—and direction to the actions and conduct of individual members.[7]

COLLECTIVE RESPONSIBILITIES

The principal collective operational responsibility of a board is to select and oversee the performance of the organization's chief executive officer. This responsibility has many facets. The single most important of these is hiring the chief executive. It is the key decision because a good selection will result in good governance and create the pathway for successful operational results. Perceptive chief executives recognize that effective governance is in their self-interest, providing support when difficult or risky decisions must be made and job protection when times are "rocky."[8]

While the hiring decision is the most important, the most time-consuming elements of this responsibility involve: coaching and counseling the chief executive so that he or she can learn from their experiences and be successful; evaluating performance, determining compensation, and ensuring seamless succession. The most difficult aspect of oversight is obviously the decision to fire the chief executive. Hopefully, this will be a rare event. The more engaged the board is in its oversight responsibilities, the less likely that this will involve firing.

The selection and supervision of the organization's chief executive is the board's ultimate operational responsibility. This responsibility cannot be delegated. It must be carried out by the board itself, through explicit processes and specific actions. If the board does this well, then the potential for success of the enterprise, while not guaranteed, is markedly enhanced.

A board's second collective operational responsibility is to ensure that the enterprise has a business plan (strategic plan, operating plan, and budget) in place and that management is effectively and efficiently implementing that plan. The first steps in this process are to require that:

- there is a planning system in place

- the system is operating in a reasonable way

- the result is presented to, discussed with, perhaps modified by, and finally approved by the full board.[9]

Reviewing and approving the business plan, however, is only part of the task. The board must also:

- monitor performance against the quantified goals and objectives of the plan;

- hold management accountable for taking appropriate action to enhance performance or, if appropriate, to modify the plan to meet the realities of a changing environment.

These latter two actions are as vital as developing and approving the plan. They give life and a dynamic reality to the planning process. Without them the plan is no more than an unsupported promise. (See Part III for a detailed discussion of business planning and implementation.)

The board has a third collective obligation to ensure that the enterprise has both the necessary human and financial resources. How this is accomplished will vary with the enterprise. Regardless of the mechanical specifics, the board, to ensure human resource capacities and capabilities, must require that management, as part of the overall business planning process, develop and utilize a human resource management process, a plan for managing both personal and professional skill and competency development, as well as a plan for guiding succession, assuring the seamless transition from one generation of management to the next. Just as the board monitors performance against the business plan, it must also monitor performance relative to the human resources plan.

> **GOVERNANCE AND PLANNING**
>
> The enterprise's business plan is the keystone for governance. Without a plan, the board has no systematic means of governing (i.e., assuring that resources are being effectively and efficiently used to pursue the enterprise's mission). Without a plan, the board cannot objectively assess either the enterprise or management's performance. The board must therefore assure that the enterprise has a planning process and that it:
> - produces a useful and used work product and,
> - it is actively engaged in that process—reviewing and approving the plan and budget and monitoring actual performance against that plan.

Without the right people, the enterprise will fail. Similarly, without adequate capital the enterprise will fail. At a minimum, capital must be sufficient to sustain the effort. More optimistically, it must be enough to support the proposed strategy and corresponding business plan. If it fails this second test, the plan must be revised and reviewed again by the board.

The adequacy of capital, in terms of enterprise sustainability, is one of the most difficult issues facing a board. If, in spite of reasonable business plans to create internal capital and/or generate external capital, resources are inadequate, the board must decide if the enterprise can continue as a stand-alone entity or if it can better pursue its mission by combining with another organization.

These are difficult choices. Hope for a turnaround or good fortune always carries heavy sway in these deliberations. The only guidepost that can be suggested is to use mission as the benchmark and pursue the course of action that provides the highest reasonable probability of success toward this end.

HYBRID RESPONSIBILITIES

A board also has a responsibility to continually improve its own performance. This responsibility falls both to the board in total and to the individual members. Just as the board must expect that the enterprise's performance continually improves, it also must demand similar improvement of itself.

Performance improvement does not happen by chance. It can be assured only through the design and implementation of a systematic mechanism for assessing actual performance, reviewing results, discussing actions needed for improvement, and then employing the discipline needed to implement those actions.

The philosophical leadership for this must come from the board's chair. The operational leadership must come from management and particularly the chief executive. The board cannot do this on its own. The chair must set the standard and the chief executive must make it happen.

The duality of the chief executive's role—as both servant to and staff leader of the board—should not be overlooked. If the organization is to be successful, the chief executive must, simultaneously lead the board and follow its leadership in a variety of situations.

Assessing the performance of the overall board is obviously less threatening than evaluating individual board member performance. A group perspective provides a degree of psychologically protective anonymity. It also provides the flexibility of being able to reach generalized conclusions, avoiding the possibility of potentially uncomfortable individual conversations. Nevertheless, both group and individual assessments must be done.

> **GETTING TOGETHER**
>
> Combining the efforts of one enterprise with those of a similar organization is not a sign of failure. In fact, it may be just the opposite, reflecting best practice governance and management.
>
> Combining efforts can take a variety of forms. At one extreme, it might be the transfer of assets to an endowment or another organization with the same mission. At the other, it might be the combination of two or more enterprises into a new corporation. Between these extremes the only limiting factors are the imagination of the participants and their willingness to act.

The simple reality is that if individual board members are not actively engaged and participating, then the total board cannot provide the full benefits and safeguards of its collective wisdom, judgment, and experience. (See Appendix 8.)

Commitment to ethics is also a hybrid obligation. It centers on the concept of a director's personal responsibility to:

- act both ethically and in compliance with the laws and regulations affecting the enterprise;

- demand, both as an individual and as part of the board as a whole, that the enterprise, its employees, and volunteers (if any) behave in the same ethical manner.

The argument for the absolute necessity of ethical conduct stands on its own.[10] The issue is not one of principle; rather, it is one of mechanics. The challenge is how, in the reality of an increasingly complex world, operational compliance can be assured.

In an environment where federal, state, and local regulations run to thousands of pages, assuring total compliance is a daunting task. Failure to achieve it can be understood. However, there can be no tolerance of failure to enact the necessary policies, and install the requisite systems, to strive for it. Like other complex processes, it can be dealt with successfully only through systematic planning, implementation, and monitoring mechanisms. It also requires unambiguous questioning by the board of those, both internal and external, who are responsible for assuring ethical conduct and operational compliance. Each director should know who those staff are (i.e., chief compliance officer, general counsel, director of corporate audit, independent auditor, etc.), how to contact them and how to engage them to answer concerns and resolve issues.

If the enterprise does not have sufficient staff capacity to have an assigned compliance officer and/or program, then this responsibility should be assigned to a board committee (i.e., audit or finance). Regardless of how it is accomplished, the board as a whole must demand that management has in place control systems to assure compliance and a board–approved compliance program that protects the interest of the enterprise. (See Appendix 3 for an example.)

INDIVIDUAL RESPONSIBILITY

The last operational responsibility is an individual matter for each board member. It involves the interaction of two concepts: knowledge and commitment.

Board members must know the business of the enterprise. This does not mean that they should either be involved in, or interfere with, day-to-day operations. Rather, it requires that they be knowledgeable about the basic mechanics and relationships of the business, including:

• the identity and goals of the stakeholders;

• demographic influences, political sensitivities and key governmental relationships;

• the flow of money.

It is difficult to see how the board as a whole could appropriately carry out the duties of care and adding value, as well as the responsibility to review and approve strategy, if individual board members do not know the underlying structure of the enterprise's business.

Working knowledge of the enterprise's environment and the structural relationships and mechanics of the business does not come either intuitively or by accident. Neither should it be assumed that because a board member is knowledgeable and successful in non-board activities, this ability will be able to automatically transfer to knowing the workings and subtleties of the enterprise.

Enterprise knowledge must be taught, and the board must demand a program for such teaching. The board should expect that opportunities and mechanisms be in place to provide not only basic information, but also continuous education. How this is done will vary with the history and culture of organizations and the preferences and style of management and the board. The fundamental point is that management must assume the responsibility for assuring that the board is provided with a systematic program of both basic and ongoing education.

The second concept of commitment encompasses both work ethic and attitude. Work ethic involves preparation for board and committee meetings and attendance at meetings. If a potential board member does not have the time to prepare for and attend meetings, then he or she should not agree to serve on the board. Similarly, the board, in considering potential members, should satisfy itself that candidates have the time for board work. Ignoring this seemingly obvious requirement creates the potential for future frustration and disappointment. Moreover, it may well lead to the difficult task of having to ask a member to step down or the embarrassment of not reappointing someone who otherwise remains eligible.[11]

All this can be avoided if potential board members realize that they have a responsibility to put in the time needed to meet their board duties and responsibilities and that if they are not able to provide the time, they should decline the opportunity to serve. The same notion applies to sitting board members. If circumstances change and they are no longer able to put in the necessary time, then they should voluntarily take the initiative to resign from the board.

The final element of attitude may seem a bit more complex. Clearly, from a measurement perspective, it is intangible. At its core, attitude is the operational translation of the duties of loyalty and adding value. Simply put, each board member must be absolutely committed to making the enterprise successful. Such a commitment does not assure that the enterprise will maximize its potential for achieving its purpose. Without it, however, it is certain that the organization will never accomplish all that it could.

If a board member is not prepared to make this kind of commitment, he or she should not serve.

RISKS AND REALITY

With legal duties and substantive obligations, unfortunately and unavoidably, comes some degree of exposure to legal and financial risk.[12] It would be misleading to persons considering board service to leave the impression that the risk of exposure to personal liability is great. In fact, it is just the opposite.

For liability to exist, the duties of either care and/or loyalty must be violated, resulting in either personal profit to the director, another person or organization, or the diversion of the enterprise's resources from their intended purpose. For such a violation to have occurred, the facts of the situation must clearly demonstrate that a director did not meet his or her legal obligations.

Regardless of its practical unlikelihood, risk does exist.[13] Both directors and the enterprise must recognize this reality and both act to manage it, as well as to provide the means and mechanisms for protecting directors.

In this vein, the risks faced in being a director fall into these three broad categories: time, embarrassment, and money.[14]

A monetary loss may seem, at first thought, to be the most punitive penalty. In reality, it is not. In fact, it is the least likely penalty actually to be incurred. Time is the most likely, and embarrassment the most troubling and costly.

In all instances, if a director has to deal with a challenge to his or her behavior or decisions, time will be required—regardless of the outcome of the challenge. Time is a limited and scarce resource. This is particularly so among directors with involved lives and multiple obligations. Moreover, it is a commodity that cannot be husbanded for future use. Having to spend time trying to defuse a threat, planning a legal defense, giving a deposition, or even testifying in court is a serious issue. In fact, it can dissuade a person from agreeing to serve as a director.

Embarrassment, however, is likely to be the costliest aspect of risk faced by directors. Directors accept board service out of a desire to do good. They bring pride to their board membership and a personal history of accomplishment and success. In the face of this reality, for a director to be publicly associated with an organization that has failed, or even behaved poorly, is a circumstance that people can neither readily tolerate nor accept. The thought of having to face peers, colleagues, and friends and explain what happened to them "on their watch" can exact a higher price from a director (e.g., embarrassment and damage to personal reputation), than monetary damages.

In this latter regard, it is helpful to first recognize the context in which nonprofit enterprise directors carry out their jobs. Most are unpaid volunteers. In fact, in some instances they even pay meeting expenses out of their own pockets and make annual gifts to the enterprise. For these directors, while charitable immunity no longer exists, personal liability is unlikely unless they have acted in a grossly negligent manner or in a way intended to cause harm to the person asserting liability. Paid directors obviously are held to a higher standard with regard to negligence and required oversight.[15] However, the business judgment rule provides substantial protection to all directors.

In addition to practical and statutory measures, protection can be provided through bylaw provisions, the purchase of liability insurance and/or the adoption of board resolutions that indemnify directors from both the cost of defending themselves and the amount of any penalty. How much and for what activities and costs a corporation can indemnify its directors will vary from state to state. Practically, it is also dependent on the financial worth of the enterprise. The advice of counsel should be sought to maximize, within the limits of a particular state's laws, the indemnity protection that can be afforded to directors. In addition to maximizing the amount of indemnification, the protection also should be contemporaneous. That is, it should cover legal and other expenses as they are incurred, not wait until the matter is resolved before payments are made. The latter approach would place an unfair burden on directors, requiring them, in effect, to fund their own defense.

Similarly, the counsel of an insurance risk manager or insurance consultant should be utilized with respect to the design and purchase of liability insurance for directors and officers. Such insurance policies are complex, involving numerous exclusions and subtleties. Expert advice is needed to assure that exclusionary pitfalls are avoided and that the coverage is as extensive as is economically practical.

CONSCIENCE

Collectively, and as individuals, board members influence the strategic direction and operational decisions of the enterprise through the execution of their obligations and responsibilities. (See Exhibit 5-3.) The board exerts its influence by advising management; giving management both the courage to take risks and permission to act; and serving as coach, counselor, and sounding board. Most importantly, the board, collectively and individually, also serves as the enterprise conscience—assuring that management stays focused on its mission and pursues that focus in an efficient, effective, and ethical manner.

Before moving on to examining board structure and operations, it is important to consider another aspect of conscience. The previous discussion of a board member's duty to add value approached the subject from the perspective of helping management to enable the enterprise to succeed. It argued that if the organization was to prosper, management needed the benefits of the board's collective wisdom. The tone of the discussion was appropriately optimistic, envisioning what must be done to be successful. However, when combined with conscience, adding value has another facet.

Board members, and boards as a whole, also have an obligation to prevent chronic enterprise underperformance. It is not enough for a board to assume that its operational performance responsibility is focused just on hiring, overseeing, and if need be, firing the chief executive. This view essentially takes the perspective that if the board hires the right person, all else will be well. If they make a mistake, the board simply corrects it by replacing the chief executive.

Exhibit 5-3

GOVERNANCE FUNCTION: RESPONSIBILITIES				
OBLIGATIONS Accountabilities • Agency • Stewardship Duties • Obedience • Care • Loyalty • Add Value				
RESPONSIBILITIES: ⇨ Collective • Oversee Chief Executive • Approve and Monitor Business Plan • Assure Adequacy of Resources Hybrid • Continuous Improvement • Ethical Operations Individual • Knowledge • Commitment	GOVERNANCE ACTIVITIES: ⇨ Collective Responsibilities • Hire and fire Chief Executive • Oversight ▸ Approval: Plan/Budget ▸ Monitoring ▸ Chief Executive Performance and Development • Ministerial • Approve necessary corporate policies and decisions/documents Hybrid & Individual Responsibilities • Ethical Standard • Time/Commitment • Continuous Improvement • Continuous Renewal • Chief Executive ▸ Support ▸ Coaching/Counseling • Ambassador to the Community/Stakeholders ▸ Sharing feedback re: community and stakeholders feelings and needs	GOVERNANCE OUTPUTS: ⇨ Approve Strategy, Operating Plan and Budget Monitor Performance against Plan & Budget and Approve Changes Approve Chief Executive Performance Review and Compensation Approve Independent Audit Conduct Annual Governance Assessment Approve Succession Plan • Governance • Management Adequacy of Resources	GOVERNANCE RESULTS: ⇨ Sound Stewardship of Resources • Pursuit of Mission Effective Stakeholder Agents • Pursuit of Mission Increased Public Trust Sustainability	ENTERPRISE RESULTS: ⇨ Pursuit of Mission Sustainability Efficient Operations Effective Operations A Caring Enterprise
Structure				
Operations				

WHAT BOARDS DO

By this point, there should be a sense of both the complexity and the subtlety of what individual board members (as well as the full board) do. There are many steps and much work both within and between each of the following activities. That said, the work of the board can be collapsed into the following four principle tasks:

1. Hire the CEO

2. Review and approve the enterprise's business plan

3. Exercise active oversight (monitoring) of actual performance against the expectations of the plan as well as the various regulatory and compliance requirements

4. Based on actual performance against the plan, reward or replace the CEO

Certainly, the board has these responsibilities. The board, however, must be more than a "cleanup crew." It has an active obligation to the enterprise's stakeholders to create a governance and management culture that expects successful performance. To do this, a board must not simply be reactive. In fact, the opposite is required. The board must be willing to independently assert itself, adding value by acting to protect stakeholder interests before they are damaged, not just after the fact. To accomplish this, individual directors must place independence over blind collegiality. They must assume a personal obligation to assure not only that management stays focused on mission and pursues that mission in an efficient, effective, and ethical manner, but that it also does so with a reasonable degree of success.

Recognizing the obligations and responsibilities of governance provides the foundation for operational success. While success can never be guaranteed, the approaches and processes discussed in the following chapters are all focused on helping managers and board members not just avoid continual underperformance, but more importantly, to lead and govern a high-performing enterprise.

CHAPTER 5

Takeaways and Questions for Consideration and Discussion:

TAKEAWAYS

1. Agreeing to serve on a board is a personal promise and commitment with obligations and responsibilities, and which requires time, talent, and passion (interest).

2. Failed governance provides the gateway to failed organizational performance.

3. Governance matters.

QUESTIONS

1. Why is governance more complicated for a nonprofit enterprise than it is for a for-profit entity?

2. Why is enhancing the public's trust in the enterprise a key task of the board?

3. How do you balance the duty to add value with the board's need to focus on oversight of operations—not the management of operations?

4. How do boards mitigate their exposure to legal and financial risk?

CHAPTER 6:
BOARD STRUCTURE AND OPERATIONS

The previous chapter looked at the obligations and responsibilities of an enterprise's board—both in the aggregate and with respect to individual board members. This chapter and the next will examine the board's structure and operations (i.e., the mechanisms that are used to enable board members to fulfill both their individual and collective requirements).

State law, regulations, and judicial decisions define corporate governance obligations and responsibilities. What varies, therefore, is not what must be done, but rather the details of how it is done and the resulting outcomes. Just as function should define form, what must be done should influence structure and operational processes. In practice, it does. While organizations will differ with respect to the specifics of the mechanisms they employ, common patterns emerge. (See Exhibit 6-1.) The elements, as well as the details of these patterns, can be seen in the enterprise's bylaws.

Exhibit 6-1

GOVERNANCE FUNCTION: STRUCTURE AND OPERATIONS				
Obligations				
Responsibilities				

Structure
Corporate Members
Size of the Board
Board Composition
Officer
• Job Description
 	
Standing Committees
• Committee Charters
 	
Amendment Process
Etc.
	Governance Activities: ⇨
	Examples
	• Meetings
	• Advise/Counsel
	• Action/Approval
	• Marketing/
	  Oversight
	• Ambassador/
	  Representative
		Governance Outputs: ⇨
		Examples
		• Approved Policies
		• Approved Plan &
		  Budget
		• Secure/Directed
		  Management
			Governance Results ⇨	**Enterprise Results**

Operations Number of Meetings Board Member • Terms/Tenure/ Termination • Job Descriptions Meeting Notice Rules Quorum Requirements Annual Meeting Voting and Proxies Attendance Etc.	**Bylaws**			

BYLAWS

Bylaws are the reflection of the decisions that the enterprise makes regarding its structure and operational processes. At the same time, bylaws provide a template for making these decisions, as well as a means for documenting them. Bylaws, in effect, are the board's structure and operational rule book.[1] Along with committee charters and board member and board officer job descriptions which supplement them, bylaws serve as the enterprise's governance operating manual. They codify how the enterprise and the board will operate, not only establishing corporate and board membership, but also documenting answers relating to a number of issues, i.e.:

- maximum and minimum number of board members

- corporate officers[2]

- structure and operation of the board

- limits on the terms of the board chair and other elected board positions

- responsibilities of standing committees

- prerogatives/authority of management, and

- protections afforded to directors and officers.

Appendix 4 provides an outline of the typical subject areas of a nonprofit corporation's bylaws. The outline is not exhaustive. Nevertheless, it provides a starting guide to identifying the issues that should be considered in drafting the enterprise's bylaws. Also included is an excerpted example of bylaws.

BYLAWS

Why are bylaws called bylaws? Why not just call them what they are—corporate guidelines and rules?

The word bylaws was first used to refer to the laws that applied to a town or locality. It suggests local laws. Specifically, the prefix "by" refers to local matters such as a by-election. The word law refers to legal terms and definitions.

Bylaws therefore are rules and ordinances made by an entity for its own governance. In this instance, the entity is the corporation.

While Appendix 4 provides guidance, it does not offer a recipe. This is intentional, to emphasize that bylaws memorialize—not determine—governance policy decisions.

Except for matters stipulated by law or regulation, governance and operational policies are set by the enterprise's members and directors. The bylaws reflect these decisions—they do not determine them.

It is also important to recognize that bylaws, once approved, are a legally controlling document. Therefore, the language and content either should be drafted or reviewed by counsel. As a corollary it should also be remembered that:

- as a controlling legal document, the bylaws establish rules that the corporation must follow;

- given their controlling power, bylaws should be designed so that they provide direction and guidance, without being so prescriptive that they frustrate pragmatism or create artificial inefficiency (i.e., unrealistic meeting notice requirements or super-majority voting standards for non-core governance or policy matters).

Finally, bylaws must be understood to be a living document, subject to regular review and amenable to efficient periodic revision. The amendment mechanism must be practical. It should provide a reasonable, thoughtful hurdle to change, without creating an unbreachable barrier to efficient and effective decision making.[3]

SIZE

Recognizing that much of what follows ultimately will be translated into bylaws, the initial step in actually building—and later maintaining—a board is to decide its membership. With respect to membership the first question is determining the board's size.

The question of size may seem like an unusual place to start. Simple logic suggests that function defines size, but simple logic fails to recognize that nonprofit boards are both political and operational creatures. It also fails to appreciate that the basic building blocks of boards are people. Therefore, while logic may argue to start with functions and committees, practicality demands size and composition as better starting points.

While there is generally no practical minimum required board size unless required by state law,[4] there is also no ideal size. Typically, for-profit boards are smaller than nonprofit boards, varying in size from eight to twelve members.[5] In contrast, nonprofit boards often have more than twenty members and average about fifteen members. This larger size reflects the range and needs of stakeholders in the community[6] and the fact that board seats are, in many instances, used as part of the payout in nonprofit mergers and acquisitions.[7]

Clearly, smaller boards can be more efficient. Smaller size enables a board to act more as a committee of the whole. It also makes it easier for board members to know each other and develop productive working relationships.

Larger boards hold the potential for inefficiency and the risk that individual board members can get lost in the crowd. They also carry a danger regarding their ability to hold management accountable for performance—because of the inherent difficulty in getting a large group to a common level of understanding and agreement.

SIZE MATTERS
Managing a large board is challenging

For a large board to function effectively, the chair and the enterprise's chief executive must work together to find means of productively engaging individual board members in the work of the board. Committees, because of their smaller size and subject matter focus, must be used. However, if committees are to be used, they must have active meeting schedules and regular, transparent reporting to the full board—through meeting minutes and/or reports. Also, every board member should typically be assigned to at least one committee, with committee assignments changing from time to time, to expose individual board members to the various aspects of the enterprise's operations.

Also, board and committee meeting agendas must be carefully designed to assure that they emphasize strategic and policy matters,

and meetings must be managed in a manner that invites robust dialogue. The chair of the committee or the board should meet with the chief executive, or other assigned committee management staff, and review each meeting's agenda before it is published.

Active individual board member involvement is more difficult—as the size of the board increases and human nature asserts itself. Here, the chair must consider how to get people to "speak to the issues." This can be accomplished by explicitly asking individuals to be reactors/commentators to reports, establishing discussion panels, asking the board pointed questions, etc. What works will depend on the traditions of the organization and the character of the board members. Regardless of the specifics, more effort will be needed to assure that a large board performs well.

When is a board too large? Like most organization structure questions, there is no single, simple answer. As a general guide, a board is too large if it is:

- difficult to schedule meetings

- difficult to make meaningful committee assignments for all members

- difficult to have productive conversations or make decisions, because so many people have to be heard before a matter can be brought to closure

- difficult to recruit members

- not noticed when one or more members is not at a meeting.

If a larger board is necessary or unavoidable, then management and the board chair must design and implement governance and meeting management techniques that both provide systems of accountability and assure active participation by all board members. This can be accomplished by how committees are used, agenda design, and meeting management techniques.

The unavoidable conclusion is simply that large boards, to be effective, require more work not only by management, but also by both board leadership and individual board members. The results will be worth the effort, engaging more members of the community in the work and accomplishments of the enterprise. Nevertheless, attention must be paid to board size and to assuring that the board size remains manageable.

COMPOSITION

The obvious follow-up question to board size is board composition. That is, in a global sense, what mix of people, qualities, and skills should be knit together to form, maintain, and refresh the board? Taking general quality as a given, two factors stand out in designing the mix of board membership. The first is diversity. The second is member luster.

Diversity is the "root" of credibility. The board of a nonprofit organization needs to reflect and represent the complexity and differences of its community of stakeholders. It must do this to have credibility with its constituency. Without diversity, the board will lack the basis for:

- being accepted by its community

- bonding with its community

- understanding the substantive needs of its community, and

- having the community believe in it, what it does, and how it does it.

Diversity is also important for another reason. A range of experiences and skill sets are needed if the board is to be able to provide management with the combined wisdom and the substantive judgment needed for success. The board cannot realistically offer credible guidance or make sound decisions if the matters that it must address are beyond its experience or knowledge.

Diversity should not be misconstrued. It requires a mix of gender, ethnicity, and age, as well as a balance of community interest, contacts, and life experience. It rests on a foundation of knowledge, skill, and interest.

Diversity cannot simply be judged cosmetically or numerically scored. It must be substantive, focused as much on what people bring to the board as on who they are. It is achieved not by limiting the pool of potential board members, but rather by expanding it. For example, members from outside of the enterprise's geographical area have the potential to bring a new perspective and a different kind of energy to the board. Similarly, by mixing member interests, the opportunity exists to construct the creative tension often necessary for breakthrough decisions and innovations.

Diversity is achieved by selecting board members one at a time, evaluating each as an individual against the enterprise's needs and the existing board membership. The goal is to fit the pieces together in a way that creates a "whole" greater than the sum of its parts.

Membership "luster" is a further consideration in selecting board members. Like diversity, it is not a simple idea but recognizes three key points. First, who is on the board should not be a negative factor. That is, people should not turn away from an invitation to serve on a board because of who is already on the board.

Second, who is not on the board should not be a negative factor. This is the converse of the previous point. Finally, the addition of each new member should add attractiveness to the board. Each addition to the board should make serving on the board increasingly of interest and desirable to potential future members. Luster, however, must also involve using the composition of the board to enhance the public's trust in the enterprise.

THE MATTER OF DIVERSITY

It is generally accepted that diversity in board composition avoids "blind spots" and produces better governance results. Diversity should not, however, be viewed as an end in itself. Rather, diversity is one of the contributing means to the end of successful mission pursuit and accomplishment.

Age, ethnicity, or consumer diversity should not be given priority over knowledge of the enterprise's business, governance understanding, and experience or ability and willingness to support the enterprise.

Clearly a board of all old, white men is problematic. Equally problematic is a board of more diverse demographics but composed of individuals with little expertise or experience. Ability and quality must be the guiding forces in selecting and retaining directors. Extra effort must be directed to sourcing potential directors from unlikely and atypical places in order to achieve diversity. However, youth, ethnicity, or being a consumer of the organization's services do not outweigh the substantive qualities needed for effective board service.

As a matter of perspective, according to BoardSource's 2017 publication "Leading With Intent," almost 60% of board chairs are satisfied or neutral regarding board diversity. In contrast, the score for chief executives was 36%. Until board leadership and management have the same perspective, progress regarding diversity will be slow at best.

The composition of the board, as measured by the reputations of the individuals that compose it, should serve as evidence that the enterprise is well run, and doing serious, important work. People should be able to judge, by simply looking at the membership of the board, that the involved individuals would not tolerate an inefficient or ineffective enterprise nor, because of their other obligations and workload, waste their time on insignificant community matters. The composition of the board must contribute public credibility to the organization.

QUALITIES

At the micro or individual level, building and maintaining the board requires that all board members have certain personal qualities and basic skills. The list of these qualities holds no real surprises:

- **INTEGRITY**—demonstrating a zero tolerance for unethical behavior, both for themselves and their colleagues;

- **INDEPENDENCE**—having no unique business, financial or personal (crony) relationships—or hoped-for-relationships—that create, or could create, even the perception of a conflict of interest;

- **MATURE CONFIDENCE**—speaking out and actively participating in board and committee deliberations;

- **CORPORATE MANNERS**—recognizing the difference between productively participating in discussions and counterproductively dominating deliberations through the volume or length of comments; not creating decision-making gridlock through an unwillingness to seek solutions and workable compromises;

- **A SENSE OF CONTEXT**—making relevant, informed comments focused on the specific aspect of the issue being considered, and neither diffusing the discussion, by moving from point to point, nor preventing closure or consensus being reached;

- **COURAGE**—willingness to do the right thing/make the right decision—even if it is difficult or unpopular (i.e., no "fence sitting");

- **COMMITMENT**—understanding that being an effective board member requires the time, the heart, and the standards to make the enterprise successful.[8]

The importance of this last factor should be highlighted. Board members must have an unremitting belief in the enterprise's purpose. They must also understand that board service is a real job, with real consequences, and requiring a real priority. Board service is rewarding. It can be gratifying, as well as fun. However, it is not a source of entertainment or amusement. Board members who are not willing to make available the necessary time and attention risk embarrassing both themselves and the organization. Similarly, board members who do not hold the enterprise to high performance standards risk not only mediocrity, but more importantly the failure to fulfill their responsibility to the community.

Unfortunately, there are no litmus tests that can be used to assess these qualities. They can be determined only through observation, shared experience that incumbent members may have had with potential new members, interviews, and reference checks. Implicit in this kind of "vetting" of candidates is the recognition that board member recruiting is not a one-time thing.

> **CONTRACTS**
>
> Some boards use the mechanism of a pseudo contract to elicit, document, and evaluate board member commitment and contribution. While there is no money involved, each year board members are asked to set out what they expect to accomplish/contribute over the coming year. This can then be used, both by the individual member and the board, to evaluate board member performance.
>
> Clearly the document is one sided, being crafted by the individual board member. This limitation is both its strength and weakness. While it may not go far enough, it does, because it is created by the members themselves, set a "floor" for involvement. If this "floor" is not achieved, it is reasonable to question commitment and interest in continued service.

To be effective it must be not only an ongoing activity, but a long-term program, potentially even requiring that candidates serve in committee and advisory council roles before they are considered for board membership.

THE UNSPOKEN CRITERION

Though not strictly a criterion for assessing potential board members, the realities of the increasing demand for services and the shrinking availability of resources require that another factor be added to the mix in considering possible board member candidates. Increasingly, nonprofit enterprises have to look to external fundraising not only to protect the organization's future, but also often to meet current operating expenses.

The leadership burden for addressing this fiscal reality falls on the board. Individual board members must recognize that in many nonprofit organizations they will be expected, as an unspoken (or at least not vigorously advertised) obligation of membership, to make personal gifts, as well as perhaps solicit gifts from others. The logic underlying the expectation of personal financial support is straightforward. How can anyone else in the community be asked to support the organization if its own board members, the people who know and understand its mission best, do not unanimously support it?

This creates an obvious potential conflict between creating a board based on credibility and governance ability versus building one designed to give and/or get money. In the past, the latter has too often been the dominating factor. The consequence in many instances has been poor governance and poor organizational performance. The realities of the day require that a better balance be found.

This does not mean that fundraising, either through personal giving or personal contacts, can be ignored. Board members must understand this and its implications. At the same time, the enterprise must find ways to make annual personal giving expectations realistic. The goal should be that all board members contribute, not that every board member contributes at the highest bracket or in the same amount. Moreover, what is expected financially of board members should be made clear as part of the candidate vetting process and not come as a "welcome to the board" surprise.

In the same vein, it should be recognized that being able to help the enterprise raise money from either personal giving or personal contacts is important work and that the best contribution that some board members can make to the enterprise is in the fundraising. Through either their own resources or their contacts, they may be

---

JOB DESCRIPTION

Board membership is serious work. It may, however, be the best job you ever pay to be able to do.

Board work will take time and money. Both subjects can be sensitive matters to discuss when trying to recruit a new member to the board.

One way to manage this sensitivity is to prepare a board member job description that is used as part of the recruiting process. The job description, in addition to outlining the duties and responsibilities of the board and individual board members, can be used to discuss committee assignments, expected meeting and preparation time requirements, and member financial contribution and fundraising expectations.

The value of the job description to the potential new board member is that it makes clear what the enterprise's expectations are. The value to the organization is that it forces it to address and clarify its positions on these important questions.

able to help assure the future of the organization. Therefore, they can play an important role and be a vital part of the board. The challenge is to keep this role in perspective and not confuse successful fundraising with good governance or allow fundraising potential to be the key prerequisite for board membership.

Even with as much clarity and financial pragmatism as possible, it would be naïve not to recognize the inherent potential for substantive and interpersonal conflict over personal responsibility for fundraising. Understanding this, many organizations have separated the responsibility for fundraising from the accountability for governing the enterprise. This is typically done by creating a separate supporting fundraising organization, that is, a supporting charitable foundation. This independent companion organization focuses solely on development and has its own separate board, fully dedicated to this goal. The criterion for foundation board membership is generally unambiguous; members must be able either to give or to get money. However, even with this structure, members of the operating entity's board should understand that while they might not be expected to go out and "get money," they will still be expected to personally "give" some amount to the supporting foundation. (See Exhibit 6-2.)

Exhibit 6-2

BOARD COMPOSITION*

An alternative to the view set out earlier in this chapter (see Composition), is to consider boards as being potentially composed of four broad types or groups of directors:
- Those who bring luster to the board, making it an attractive/desired board to serve on;
- Those who bring credibility to the board, increasing the public's trust in the work of the enterprise—both that:
  - it is doing important work; and
  - it is operating efficiently and effectively;
- Those who can generate external capital, either through their personal gifts and/or through their contacts with others; and

- Those who are focused on providing governance oversight to the enterprise.

These four categories are obviously not mutually exclusive. In fact, their very breadth invites overlap. Also, they ignore technical skill categories that the boards of small and/or new enterprises might set as priorities.

Nevertheless, they provide a framework for a taxonomy to be used in shaping the board member recruitment and solicitation process.

* Michael Klausner and Jonathan Small, "Failing to Govern," Stanford Social Innovation Review, 42-49.

SKILLS

Beyond personal and financial qualities, board members also must bring certain basic skills to the job. The need for a set of core skills leaves little room for debate. The question is, "What skills are needed?"

The first part of the answer lies in recognizing that there is a difference between core skills and technical subject matter expertise. Certainly, the individual board members may have legal, financial, marketing, construction, human resources, or other technical knowledge. Board members, however, unless there is no realistic alternative, should not be selected simply as a low cost means of acquiring technical skills for the enterprise. The enterprise can generally either purchase or acquire technical skills through work service programs, discounts, or pro bono arrangements. In fact, it is often better served by doing so. Board seats are too dear to spend them on something that can be obtained relatively easily in the marketplace. Conversely, technical or subject matter expertise, barring conflicts of interest, should not eliminate anyone from potential board membership.

When considering board member skills, the focus should be on the general skills necessary to meet the duties and responsibilities of a board member. Building on this perspective, perhaps it is useful not to think in terms of finite skills, but rather areas of literacy—of general knowledge or understanding. In this context, there are four fundamental areas of literacy that all board members should have:

1. **FINANCIAL LITERACY**—the ability to understand financial statements. Financial literacy does not mean financial or accounting expertise. It implies a comfort level with financial reports and an ability to understand their implications.

2. **COMMUNITY LITERACY**—the ability to decipher and empathize with the service needs of the enterprise's stakeholders. Community literacy does not mean that board members have to be sociologists, psychologists, or community organizers. They merely need to demonstrate a willingness to listen to and understand the current and changing needs and sensitivities of the constituent community—and then to be able to translate that understanding into the enterprise's work.

3. **POLITICAL LITERACY**—the ability to build coalitions by being able not only to lead, but by being able, when appropriate, to follow. Political literacy requires the skills to do both and the sensitivity to know when to do which. It also requires the ability to convince without badgering—and being able to disagree without being disagreeable.

4. **COMMUNICATIONS LITERACY**—the ability to convey a point of view or decision in a manner that is efficient, understandable, and contributes to the flow of the board's deliberations. The need is to be able to present a position without being insensitive to the comments of others—or boring. Since most board member communication is oral, this is really spoken literacy. The requirement is not, however, great public speaking skills. Rather, it is thoughtfulness, brevity, and the ability to stay focused.[9]

Board members should have two other general skills. One is judgment—an ability to absorb information, evaluate it against the enterprise's purpose and needs, and reach a succinct conclusion. The other is a willingness to learn.

Successful organizations often are referred to as "learning organizations." They are entities that are evolving continually, based on both their own experience and the changes—competitive and innovative—that are occurring in their environment. A learning organization begins with a "learning board"—a board that is willing to learn the business and grow intellectually, a board that refuses to allow itself to be caught in the trap and limits of "how we have always done it."

An important point should not be lost in all this. Industry knowledge has not been highlighted as a board membership prerequisite. Knowledge of the business, though, is important. However, it is a technical matter and can be learned. The amount of knowledge that is initially brought to the table is less important than a board member's willingness to learn and the enterprise's commitment to teach.

VACANCIES

Size and skills define the basic parameters of the board. Knowing what is needed in turn sets the targets for member recruitment. While occasionally an entire board must be built from the ground up (i.e., when the enterprise is founded, or perhaps, by a court order), most board member recruiting is done to fill small numbers of vacancies. This both simplifies and complicates the task. On the one hand, fewer candidates have to be found. Complicating the matter, however, is the need to be more careful about "fit"—assuring the "right" interpersonal chemistry between the new member(s) and the existing board. Board vacancies are the result of both planned and unplanned events.

UNPLANNED VACANCIES

Unplanned vacancies are due to unexpected voluntary resignations or board member deaths. Voluntary resignations can be the result of a recruiting error, where the member comes to realize that he or she is either unable to make available the necessary time or does not have the requisite level of skills. They can also be the consequence of a change in a member's personal or professional status (i.e., a prolonged illness, position relocation, change in professional position, retirement, etc.).

No unplanned vacancy is good news. Potentially more difficult, however, may be a member's change in status that does not result in an offer of resignation. In this situation the board faces two risks. One centers on assuring the board's continued relevance. Certainly, a board whose members once resided in the community, but now increasingly reside elsewhere, risks losing touch with its stakeholders. Similarly, a board whose membership increasingly is comprised of retirees risks losing currency in its business and political environments. On the other hand, demanding a member's resignation may have relationship risks with not only current and potential board members, but also with possible donors.

An approach to managing such a situation is for the board to require that when a member's status changes, the resignation of the member is deemed to have been automatically offered.[10] This may seem harsh. However, the board does not have to accept the resignation. The fact that it must be offered is the key that eliminates the politics and the potential for embarrassment and awkwardness. Importantly, it gives the board a real, pragmatic method and option for protecting itself.

The change-in-status resignation requirement should be specified in the corporation's bylaws. The bylaws should make clear what events trigger the requirement for resignation and whether the resignation must be accepted by a particular committee or by the full board.

Another common automatic resignation provision is an attendance policy. The notion here is straightforward. A member who does not attend board or committee meetings not only fails to meet fiduciary duties and responsibilities, but also prevents someone else from serving. The solution is to have an attendance standard requiring that a member attend a certain minimum number or percentage of meetings each year. Members who fail to meet this standard are considered to have resigned from the board.

This provision, like the change-in-status provision, should be defined in the corporation's bylaws. The bylaw language should make clear the number or percentage of meetings which must be attended and the time period to be covered. The provision also should give the board the flexibility, in extraordinary circumstances, to refuse or override the automatic resignation.

PLANNED VACANCIES, TERM LIMITS

Planned vacancies are the result of three potential events:
1. Term limits
2. Eligibility limits
3. Mandatory retirement age

All board members should be elected for a fixed term specified in the bylaws. Typically, terms are two or three years in length and are renewable. Occasionally, a member will be elected to a shorter term, either to fill an unplanned vacancy or to provide a test period.

The value of term limits is that they provide an automatic mechanism for considering board members' performance and evaluating whether they should be given the opportunity to continue to serve.[11]

It is a sensitive matter not to re-elect a member who has remaining board service eligibility. The establishment of term limits, nevertheless, provides the opportunity to raise the question of continuing service. If nothing else, it offers a convenient and graceful mechanism for members to leave the board if they no longer wish to serve.

ELIGIBILITY LIMITS

While there is generally little debate about term limits, eligibility or tenure limits are another matter. Eligibility limits typically define how many successive years an individual can serve on the board. Eligibility limits are found more often in nonprofit organizations than for-profit companies. Typically, eligibility limits are in the six- to ten-year range, with a required break in service, usually at least one year, before a former member can be reelected to the board.

For example, if the bylaws specify three-year terms and nine years of eligibility, a member could serve for three successive three-year terms, take a year off and then be eligible to serve again for up to nine more years. Like term limits, eligibility limits—both the maximum potential number of successive years of service and the minimum period of time off—should be specified explicitly in the bylaws.

Critics of eligibility limits argue that they are not needed in the presence of term limits. Their position is that term limits provide the means for removing unproductive board members by simply not re-electing them. Moreover, by just having term limits—and not eligibility limits—productive members are not forced to leave the board, sparing the organization the:
- burden of continuously recruiting new members; and

- cost of losing productive members—with institutional experience and memory.

There is merit to this point of view. Productive board members are assets that must be nurtured and retained. This takes time and obviously has a cost to the organization. To lose productive members is an organizational setback—a problem that can be avoided by not having eligibility limits.

The attractiveness of this argument, however, falls on the sword of pragmatism. Term limits do provide a theoretical means for pruning the board of members who are not meeting performance expectations. However, it is a politically flawed mechanism. To deny re-election to a board member who can continue to serve, is interested in serving and willing to serve, and who has a good attendance record is to brand that member's performance as a failure.

This may be an accurate evaluation. Regardless of reality, or how the message is presented and packaged, the result is likely to be the same—embarrassment and anger. Board members are proud individuals. They are accustomed to success and expect positive recognition. To not re-elect a member raises questions in other board members' minds about their own status. It also has the potential of making recruitment of new members more difficult.

All of this can be avoided through eligibility limits. Eligibility limits provide an automatic, non-controversial tool for refreshing the board. Moreover, by requiring only a relatively short break in service, they allow—if the former member is invited back and agrees to serve—the organization's investment in board member education and development to be recouped.

Without eligibility limits, boards face the risks of stagnation. More importantly, organizations face the risk of being captured by either fatigued members too proud to step aside and/or an entrenched clique of board members, set in their ways and pursuing an outdated agenda. Either of these circumstances foretells organizational failure.

The board must, from time to time, be refreshed. If it is not, it ultimately will fail to adapt and grow. Eligibility limits provide a politically pragmatic way of forcing managed board renewal.

MANDATORY RETIREMENT AGE

The third mechanism for managing vacancies and assuring board relevance is for the board to establish a mandatory member retirement age. Like term limits, the merits of this kind of bylaw provision seem straightforward. Unfortunately, like eligibility limits, mandatory retirement also engenders some controversy.

Members may retire from their jobs and, if the board rejects their automatic change-in-status resignation, continue to serve. Similarly, some members may not retire and continue to serve. Others may not be actively employed when they join the board. The consequence of these circumstances, until eligibility limits provide relief, is a gradual aging and fatiguing of the board. Mandatory retirement age requirements provide a way to offer some protection against this risk.

At the same time, it should be realized that as board members age, their board service often takes on a more important role in their lives. As a result, they may be reluctant to leave the board. In fact, some whose eligibility has expired may even, after their requisite break in service, campaign to be re-elected. Mandatory retirement age provisions solve these potential problems. They provide an assured mechanism for managing the realities of age and ego.[12]

Retirement or even mutually agreed-upon resignation from the legally responsible board does not mean that the organization must sever its ongoing relationship with an outgoing member. As noted in Appendix 5 there are honorary and emeritus membership possibilities—as well as other structure or title configurations that creative minds can imagine for maintaining a continuous relationship.

Like the other provisions, mandatory retirement age requirements should be explicitly described in the bylaws (i.e., members must leave the board on reaching age seventy-five, or at the next annual meeting following their seventy-fifth birthday, or at the end of their current term, following their seventy-fifth birthday). The possibility of honorary, emeritus, or advisory positions should also be explicitly specified in the bylaws. Such positions, while having no legal fiduciary authority or obligation, should be defined so that there is no confusion regarding their status and prerogatives.

RECRUITING

Regardless of the precipitating event, from time to time boards will have to fill vacancies in their membership. In considering how to go about doing this, it is important to begin by realizing that board member recruitment is an ongoing process. As noted earlier, to think otherwise—to view it as an ad hoc event—is to diminish the importance of the basic building block of the board, the member. It is also to leave to chance the opportunity to build and maintain a high-performance board.

In addition to recognizing that member recruitment is an ongoing process, it is helpful to understand that it is a process consisting of several elements. The first is the identification of potential candidates and the subsequent narrowing of the candidate pool to "first round choices." The second step is the pursuit of the "first round choices." The goal here is to create in the candidate not only a "good feeling" about the enterprise, but also both an interest in board membership and a willingness, if asked, to serve on the board. The last element is to close the "offer"—getting the candidate to say "yes," with enthusiasm and commitment. If the second part is done well, the third step is often merely a formality.[13]

Like any other management process, board member recruitment must be tended to, guided, and supported. As is discussed in more depth later, boards typically create a nominating committee or a committee on directors or corporate governance to handle member recruitment and nomination, as well as other governance matters. This committee, by whatever name or designation, should work continuously to identify potential board member candidates, evaluate the most promising and, from time to time, meet with them, either formally or informally, to express the enterprise's interest in them and to assess their interest in board membership.

The staff support for this effort should typically be the enterprise's chief executive officer. While the chief executive does not select board members, he or she works for the board and is provided oversight and guidance by the board. Therefore, a wise chief executive will do all that can be done to assure that the best possible candidates are pursued, recruited, trained, and retained.

A CLOSING WORD

The larger the board, the greater the recruiting needs. As discussed in the next chapter, the larger the board and the more complex the committee structure, the more time and attention is required by management, particularly the chief executive. Good governance requires work, not only of individual board members and the board as a whole, but also of management.

Good governance does not simply happen. It is the result of the time, attention, and support that the chief executive gives to the governance function—from recruiting, through onboarding, operations, and revitalizing the membership.

CHAPTER 6

Takeaways and Questions for Consideration and Discussion:

TAKEAWAYS

1. Bylaws are the organization's rules for governance. The board and management must respect and follow them.

2. Boards don't manage themselves. Management must invest time and resources to assure that boards are productive.

3. Boards are like any other human resource. They require ongoing education, skill development, and continuous improvement, as well as thoughtful succession planning.

4. Time, talent, and passion are the key requirements for the selection of board members.

QUESTIONS

1. How difficult should it be to modify the enterprise's bylaws? To modify its mission?

2. How does a board achieve real (as contrasted with simply cosmetic or visual) diversity?

3. How do the qualities required of board members support the accomplishment of the duties of board members?

4. How important is it to periodically refresh the board in a planned manner? What are the risks of doing this?

Chapter 7:
BOARD COMMITTEES

The board has been sized, recruited, and is ready to go to work. However, unless it is a small board that has made the decision to act "as a committee of the whole," another ingredient is necessary. To carry out its duties and responsibilities, the board must establish and document its own infrastructure in the bylaws. It must organize itself so that it can work effectively, as well as efficiently.[1]

As with many real-world questions there is no one right solution to the question of infrastructure. Organizational leadership and structure—that is, officers' and committees' decisions—must reflect the enterprise's traditions, political and operational needs, the size of the board, statutory, regulatory, and accreditation requirements, etc. It also should mirror the good experiences of similar organizations—and guard against the bad.

Design and structure choices can—and should—be changed as new demands are placed on the enterprise.[2] The goal, however, of both the initial design and any subsequent changes must be the same. The enterprise must structure itself in a way that enhances its ability to pursue its mission.

COMMITTEE STRUCTURE

While there are no absolutes with respect to committee structure,[3] there are several general points that offer useful guidelines.

First, committees should be used to make the full board more efficient, not replace it. Therefore, as a rule of thumb the number of committees should be kept to the productive minimum. The actual number obviously will differ from organization to organization, depending on the issues being faced and the size of the board. A small board will organize itself and work differently than a twenty-five person board. Both boards can, and ultimately will, develop solutions that are workable and acceptable.

Second, corporate law permits directors to rely, in terms of meeting their duties and responsibilities, on the work of board committees so long as the following requirements are met:
- The purpose, powers, procedures, and limitations of the committee are clearly defined in the corporation's bylaws or in an appropriate board resolution.

- The committee maintains and distributes minutes of its meetings and other records appropriate to its charge.
- The committee regularly reports its deliberations and work to the full board.
- The composition of the committee is appropriate to its task.
- The committee is meeting and addressing matters appropriate to its charge.

Third, the membership of any specific committee should be structured so as to assure that it reflects the full composition of the board. To this end, care must be taken to assure that there is neither the reality nor the perception of different classes of committees or committee members. To do otherwise is to open the full board to potential divisiveness. The most pragmatic way to avoid this is to assure that committee membership reflects the character and mix of the full board, particularly in terms of tenure and overall experience, and to make it clear that all board members are welcome to attend the regular meetings of any committee.

Fourth, board committees can be thought of as falling into one of two categories: either special committees or standing committees.

Special committees can have a variety of titles: working parties, task forces, ad hoc committees, and so on. They can also be advisory, with no power to bind the enterprise, or have limited powers specific to their purpose. Regardless of title they are all typically intended to have both a limited charge or purpose and a limited life. That is, they are created to address a specific or special purpose/issue, such as a building project, a merger offer, a fundraising initiative, or revising the bylaws. Once that task is completed, the committee's work is ended, and it is dissolved.

Special committees are useful devices. They provide the organization with a vehicle for addressing particular issues without creating governance overhead that can get in the way of board efficiency. To be effective, their charge or objectives and expected duration (life cycle) must be defined as precisely as possible.

The enterprise's bylaws should specify how special committees are established. They should make clear whether committees can be appointed by the chair of the board or if their creation requires the action of the full board. The bylaws also should specify whether special committee membership is to be limited only to current board members or if it can be composed of a mix of members and non-members. If non-board members are eligible to serve, special committees can provide a substantive and organizationally valuable way to keep past board members and friends of the organization involved in the affairs of the enterprise.[4] They can similarly also provide a way to introduce potential future board members to the enterprise—and evaluate their readiness, interest, and fit.

Ideally, the bylaws should be drafted to provide as much flexibility as is practical. The chair of the board should be able to appoint special committees and their chairs and committee members. Committee membership in turn—unless the committee is by design an advisory, non-member group—should allow for a mix of members, so long as the majority consists of current board members. Obviously, all actions of the board chair are subject to the review and ratification of the full board.[5]

In contrast to special committees, standing committees are the core of the corporation's infrastructure. Standing committees should be specified in the bylaws, including their charge, membership size and mix (i.e., if non-current board members can serve), as well as the committee's chair, identified by office or position (i.e., treasurer as chair of the audit committee). A standing committee continues to function until it is eliminated through a change to the bylaws.[6]

Except for stock exchange requirements that listed companies have audit committees composed of independent directors, a corporation is free to create as many or as few standing committees as it wishes.[7] Most for-profit corporations have one to five committees. Nonprofit enterprises typically have more, as they have larger boards and more stakeholders to accommodate.

Practice and practicality suggest that there are three basic standing committees (see Exhibit 7-1 and Appendix 6): audit, compensation, and governance.[8] The first two, audit and compensation, reflect the need to "follow the money." As is discussed below, the audit committee must assure that the enterprise's resources are being properly focused on pursuing its mission. The compensation committee is responsible for assuring that management is equitably paid—neither underpaid nor paid more than the market and actual performance fairly justify. The committee on governance's focus is on assuring that the board not only fulfills its duties and responsibilities, but also does so in a manner that results in continuously improving its own performance.

Exhibit 7-1

COMMITTEE STRUCTURE

Percentage of Companies Having:*

- Audit Committee 100%
- Compensation Committee 100%
- Committee on Governance/Nominating 84%
- Executive Committee 70%
- Finance 38%
- Corporate Responsibility 20%

*The original source for this exhibit is the American Society of Corporate Secretaries, Survey of Board Committee Practices, June 1998. While still dated, a 2003 survey by the American Hospital Association found that for hospitals and health systems: 89% of respondents had finance committees, (additionally 24% had separate audit committees) and 74% had executive committees. The 2012 Deloitte Board Practices Report found that 98% of the responding firms had a separate audit committee, 96% had a compensation committee, and 94% had a governance committee. Only 52% had an executive committee. The latter likely reflects the smaller size of for-profit enterprise boards (7-14 members) as contrasted with hospital and health system boards.

More recent data from the BoardSource 2017 publication "Leading With Intent," reports that for nonprofit organizations, 76% have executive committees, 76% have finance or finance/audit committees, 70% have governance committees, and 53% have fundraising committees. Urban Institute data from 2010 suggests that for organizations of $1 million or more in total expenses, about 90% have audit committees.

Survey data vary with the source of the survey and the response rate. Even so, regardless of source, the general pattern holds.

Beyond these core committees, the number and nature of additional standing committees are determined by the enterprise's traditions and business needs. For example, a hospital would be expected to have a quality assurance committee, a medical staff relations committee, and a community relations committee. A health insurer likely would have a finance or investment committee. A museum would have a development or major gifts committee and an acquisitions committee. The possibilities are nearly limitless. Nevertheless, as noted earlier, the number of committees should be limited to the productive minimum—not the imaginative maximum.

AUDIT COMMITTEE

In the wake of governance scandals at United Way of America, Red Cross of America, Enron, Global Crossing, WorldCom, and others, the audit committee may well be the most critical of all the board's committees. When things go well and there are no public financial disclosure problems, an audit committee's work attracts little attention. When matters go bad, and the community feels deceived, the performance of the audit committee and the actions of its individual members (and those of the full board) cannot sidestep the spotlight of public and potentially governmental/legal scrutiny.[9] To assure that things do not go bad, the audit committee must play a central role in corporate affairs, acting as the assertive guardian of the community's financial and philanthropic/ social welfare interests.

Operationally, the audit committee has two basic functions:
1. to oversee the corporation's financial reporting process and the resulting financial reports;
2. to oversee the corporation's internal control processes and systems.

The two functions are different in perspective—one looking outward, the other looking inward. They are similar, however, in that they have the common objectives of avoiding both the misuse of corporate resources and organizational embarrassment.

The committee's external role of assuring valid and reliable financial data is the accountability that is best known to the general public. Here the committee's goal is to protect the enterprise from accounting irregularities (i.e., financial accounting abuses that require the restatement of financial reports).

To carry out this accountability with public confidence, the committee first must be composed entirely of financially literate, independent directors. The standard of having only outside directors is generally not an issue for nonprofit enterprises. The question of independence is potentially, for both nonprofit and for-profit corporations, a more sensitive matter. Independence requires that a committee member neither be an employee of the enterprise nor have significant business, advisory, or consulting transactions with the enterprise.

Independence also requires, at a minimum, that the committee:

- have clear access to the enterprise's management, including financial and legal staff;

- have the authority, as necessary, to retain external advisors if their guidance is needed;

- select and engage the external auditor, assuring both competence and independence (i.e., have no business including consulting engagements with the firm that might be perceived as compromising or appearing to compromise the integrity of the audit[10]);

- meet with the auditors both in open and executive session to:
  - review and approve the scope of the audit and audit work plan;
  - review the results and findings of the audit;
  - review and approve the annual financial statements;
  - receive and follow up on the findings of the auditor's management letter;
  - assure that management is cooperating with and supporting the auditors;

- meet with the auditors in executive session to discuss:
  - the quality of the enterprise's accounting practices;
  - concerns or potential problem areas;
  - areas of disagreement with management.

A bit more should be said about the audit committee's exploring of "concerns or potential problem areas." While it might not be a traditional audit committee responsibility, somewhere in the enterprise, as noted in Chapter 5, an assessment needs to be made of the organization's ability to survive significant unexpected events that imperil operations and/or finances. It is a matter of assessing resilience and sustainability and managing risk.

Resilience is the ability to bounce back from a short-run problem. It can usually be handled by having sufficient cash reserves or by having access to credit. Sustainability is the more difficult issue and has no straightforward answers. Of course, cash or access to cash is a key factor. However, sustainability may require more. Strategic decisions may have to be made about sales of assets, use of endowment assets (if any are available), services provided, partnerships, or consolidation, etc. If these questions are not being asked, and risk assessments are not being done elsewhere, then the audit committee should address these matters.

In addition to its accountability for assuring the validity and reliability of the corporation's financial statements, the committee:

- serves as the final arbiter of any changes in the corporation's financial accounting practices and procedures for preparing and publishing financial statements;

- provides oversight to the corporation's code of conduct and other compliance programs.

This last responsibility deserves further comment. With increased scrutiny of corporate behavior, compliance programs and compliance monitoring have become mandatory activities. The enterprise must have in place a conflict of interest disclosure program and a code of conduct and compliance program. It also must have a designated compliance officer who is responsible for assuring that the programs are in place and being followed.[11]

The compliance effort and officer may, depending on the organization, be a stand-alone function or be included with other assignments. Regardless of how it is structured, the audit committee and the full board should, at least annually, receive a conflict of interest and compliance report. The compliance officer should also have the ability to meet directly, either in open or executive session, with the committee. Finally, the audit committee should periodically review the conflict of interest and compliance programs and satisfy itself that they are adequate and fully implemented.

In simplest terms, the audit committee is responsible for making sure that the community receives financial information that is truthful, comparable from year to year, and understandable. Assuring that financial data are prepared in accord with generally accepted accounting principles is necessary. However, by itself, it is not enough if the result creates a materially misleading impression of the firm's performance and financial condition. The committee must assure that the financial data, taken as a whole, portray the understandable truth.

TWO FOR ONE

Audit committees are now ubiquitous. Many organizations also have finance or finance and operations committees to oversee operational performance. Recognizing the limits of board member time and calendar conflicts, why not incorporate the audit function into the finance committee or the finance oversight function into the audit committee—and eliminate a committee?

Why not? Because it jeopardizes the checks and balances and internal controls necessary to protect against potential financial misbehavior. It is a fundamental error to have a committee oversee and certify its own work.

The audit committee must be independent, able to judge the financial condition of the enterprise without the conflict of having to justify or gloss over its own prior decisions. Combining the two committees violates the principles of unbiased oversight and creates an unnecessary organizational risk—well beyond any benefit.

The bottom line—keep the audit and finance committees separate and independent.

It would be disingenuous not to recognize that there is a degree of tension in this three-sided relationship of auditor, management, and board committee. The audit committee must recognize this and assert its accountability and subsequent authority. While the auditors are paid by the enterprise and work with management, they are responsible to the committee. The committee engages them and, if dissatisfied, can terminate them. The auditors are not retained to offer creative rationalizations for, or guarded opinions of, management's decisions and performance. They are retained to validate unequivocally, to the committee and the public, management's data and reports. Anything short of this is unacceptable.

The audit committee's inward-looking role is to oversee the enterprise's internal audit program. Small enterprises may not have the resources to support their own internal audit function. In such instances, the committee must rely on the external auditors for examining the adequacy of the internal control systems and assuring that neither blatant fraud nor abuse is going undetected.

If reliance on the external auditors is the approach that is taken, it should be included as part of a multiyear audit plan and, as appropriate, be addressed in the management letter provided by the independent auditor to the board. Obviously, this added work increases the cost of the audit. Therefore, it must be negotiated as part of the audit engagement—and because of the potential size of the expense, be judiciously handled. Frankly, complete internal control certainty is beyond the practical means of any active, complex enterprise.

Business judgment must be used to find the proper year-to-year cost and benefit.

Larger organizations should have an internal auditor as part of their staffs. Enterprises such as hospitals, health plans, and the United Way agencies should go even further. They should have an internal audit department.

From a governance perspective the internal audit function is responsible for assuring that the enterprise's financial control systems and its operational procedures are designed, implemented, and functioning efficiently and effectively. Given this, the internal auditor is responsible for making sure that resources are being used appropriately to pursue the enterprise's mission and are not being diverted due to inefficiency, bad judgment, or fraud.

The internal audit function must protect the enterprise, its board, and management from public embarrassment. The job of the audit committee is to provide the oversight and environment needed to allow this to happen. To this end it must be clear that the internal auditor has direct and unencumbered access to the committee. The committee should meet, at least annually, with the internal auditor to review the corporation's risk assessment and the resulting internal audit plan. The committee should also periodically meet in executive session with the internal auditor to assure that there is a candid and frank review of the enterprise's risks and performance. (See Appendix 6 for an example of Committee Charters.)

A point should be noted regarding unencumbered access. While both the compliance officer and the internal auditor must have the unfettered ability to meet directly with the committee, the committee must recognize its obligation to act once notified of an issue or even a potential issue.

The committee chair, when approached, must bring the matter to the committee and assure that the committee addresses the issue. For the chair either to try to resolve or deflect the issue alone, or for the committee to stonewall staff's concern, is a patent mistake—one that will never pass the test of public scrutiny.

The principal staff to the audit committee should be the chief financial officer (CFO). The internal auditor, like the compliance officer, should report to—not serve as staff to—the committee and should be independent of the CFO.

COMPENSATION COMMITTEE

The compensation committee is the second core committee. It is responsible for the approval and subsequent oversight of the enterprise's compensation program, benefit policies, and management development programs. The committee is also typically charged with: setting the chief executive's compensation and benefits, evaluating chief executive performance, providing oversight to the administration of the incentive compensation plan (if one exists), establishing board compensation (if the board is paid), and reviewing management's staff development and succession plans. (See Appendix 6 for example of Committee Charters.)

In terms of governance, the goals of a compensation committee are threefold:

1. assure that the policies and programs are in place to ensure that the enterprise's general levels of compensation and benefits reflect market rates and standards;

2. assure that policies and programs are in place to ensure that individual compensation reflects performance;

3. assure that policies and programs are in place to ensure that the enterprise has an adequate supply of qualified people.

To accomplish the first, the enterprise must periodically survey the relevant labor market (local, regional, or national) from which key jobs likely will be recruited and, as necessary, revise its pay ranges and/or benefit programs. To do the second, the committee must assure that the compensation system measures and rewards actual performance results. This requires that the enterprise have an operating plan that includes specific, quantified objectives. The third goal requires that the committee assure that a formal employee education/development program and a succession management process are in place.

The need for quantified operating objectives goes back to one of the board's principal functions—approval of the enterprise's strategy, and the resulting operating plan and quantified performance measures/objectives. The interlocking character of how the pieces fit together should begin to have more clarity: the enterprise's strategy drives its operating plan, which in turn defines performance objectives. Performance objectives (expected results/accomplishments) become the basis for measuring individual results and setting individual pay.

This is not the place for a discussion of compensation theory and practice. (See Chapter 13 for a more in-depth discussion of compensation.) The responsibility of the board, through the work of the compensation committee, is not to be technical compensation and benefit specialists.[12] Rather it is to assure that the enterprise has compensation, benefit, and personnel development policies and systems; that they are being used; and that they result in equitable employee compensation and a skilled, continuously improving workforce. Equitable compensation is pay and benefits that reflect both market forces and individual performance. A skilled, continuously improving work force is a management and staff group that is always learning and developing, enabling both the enterprise to meet its human resources needs, and individual employees to fulfill their personal potential and work goals.

To this end several principals should be recognized:
• General pay levels should always reflect what is happening in the appropriate labor market (the labor market from which a successor to the incumbent would be hired);
  ⬥ The enterprise should never allow itself to lose competent employees because they have been underpaid—just to then have to go out into the market and pay their successors what the incumbents were asking for, or even more.
  ⬥ To assure compensation "market relevance," the committee should periodically review labor market survey data, along with management's recommendations for necessary compensation structure adjustments.
  ⬥ Admittedly the numbers, particularly for senior management, may be high. Competent management, however, is an enterprise's "least cost" strategy. Underpaying employees is a false economy, resulting in higher turnover, leadership gaps, recruiting expenses—and, likely, higher eventual salaries.

• At least annually, all employees should have a formal performance review. The committee's obligation in this regard is generally twofold. First, it is to assure that the corporation's overall compensation system includes an annual, formal, written evaluation component. Second, it is to assure that the chief executive has an annual evaluation.

The chief executive's evaluation can be accomplished in a variety of ways. Some organizations rely on the chair of the board to do it. Others might assign the task to the executive committee, if one exists. No single solution is better than another. However, logic suggests that it be handled, or at least led, by the compensation committee.

Chief executive evaluations should typically include, in some form, three elements:
1. **COACHING AND COUNSELING**—an ongoing process where the chair of the board and/or the chair of the compensation committee provides real-time advice and counsel directed toward continuous performance improvement.

2. **FORMAL BOARD ASSESSMENT**—annual review by the full board of the chief executive's performance.

3. **QUANTIFIED PERFORMANCE REVIEW**—annual review of performance against the quantified objectives of the operating plan. While the full board should participate in some form of chief executive evaluation, quantified performance

review is objective and can be done by the committee or the board's chair:

- As a corollary to the above, the chief executive's performance should be evaluated on basically a pass/fail basis. If the chief executive, or for that matter any senior manager, can be motivated to work harder or better for more pay, then the enterprise needs a new chief executive. Conversely, to keep staff from leaving, pay must be based on market factors—so that staff does not feel that they are subsidizing the organization.
- The organization should have a formal professional development system for all employees, including senior management. An explicit, formal succession management system also should be in place for all key positions, along with plans to develop the identified staff. The committee should assure itself that the system is in place and working, and should periodically review the succession plan. (See Chapter 14 for a discussion of succession management.)

The committee's annual work cycle begins with approving the translation of the operating plan's quantified objectives into performance targets. It ends with converting actual performance, by assessing the quantified results that were achieved vs. the performance targets, into actual pay. Along the way it must:

- assure, through independent survey data, that compensation reflects market rates;

- meet regularly with the senior human resources officer to assure that performance measures are in place and operationally meaningful;

- provide the chief executive with ongoing performance feedback.

The committee also should meet at least annually, in executive session, with the full board to report on its activities and actions.

Both the committee and the board must recognize the public's sensitivity to compensation matters. Everyone has an opinion regarding someone else's compensation (and seldom is it believed to be too low). Therefore, the committee must be scrupulous in assuring that compensation is based on market rates and clearly reflects actual performance. Anything short of this leaves the enterprise vulnerable to criticism and potential public embarrassment.

The compensation committee, like the audit committee, should be comprised of independent directors. The principal staff to the committee should be the senior human resources officer.

COMMITTEE ON GOVERNANCE

The third core committee is the committee on governance. In the past, this committee often was called the nominating committee. Consistent with its name, the nominating committee's responsibilities were relatively narrow in focus: identifying and recruiting new board members and recommending a slate of directors for election. In the current environment, this role, while still necessary, is too limited. The community's expectations of board performance and accountability are constantly increasing. To meet these growing expectations, the board needs more than a nominating committee. It needs a committee that is also focused on assuring not only that the board and its individual members are carrying out their duties and responsibilities, but also that governance performance is continually improving. (See Appendix 6 for an example of Committee Charters.) This is the basic role of the committee on governance.

By whatever name, the committee is responsible for:
- assessing the needs of the board;
- succession planning through individual board member development and recommending a slate of directors and officers for election;
- evaluating individual director performance and providing appropriate coaching and counseling;
- assessing the general performance of the board as a whole;
- recommending actions to improve overall performance, including oversight of educational programs for individual board members, board committees, and the full board.

The committee on governance is the committee that makes sure that the board and governance system works. Given its responsibilities, the committee should be composed entirely of independent board members, with a majority having significant board experience. Additionally, if it is the practice of the enterprise board to have past chairs remain on the board, then either a past chair or the current chair of the board should serve as the committee's chair.[13] This choice of chair provides an advantage, because it adds both credibility to the committee's work, and provides leadership and insight into the background and the interpersonal chemistry needed for new board members—as well as the standards that the board's performance must meet.

Principal staff to this committee should be the chief executive. This is purely a pragmatic reality. The chief executive works for and reports to the board. If the chief executive is to have a great board, he or she must nurture and encourage its growth. The vehicle for accomplishing this is the committee on governance. The chief executive should therefore work with and directly support this committee.

While the audit committee may be the most visible and vulnerable when things go wrong, it is the compensation committee, through its evaluation function, and the

> **THE WORK**
>
> The governance committee's responsibilities require more than just meeting occasionally to renominate directors with remaining eligibility or to fill member or officer vacancies. It must be an active and planful committee:
> - Systematically identifying and addressing governance performance needs
> - Aggressively sourcing diverse potential board members
> - Assuring through active succession management, that the board's membership is continually refreshed, and its leadership revitalized so that it can meet the changing demands and opportunities of the enterprise.

committee on governance that are the keys to making sure that the pieces and processes are in place to prevent things from going wrong.

EXECUTIVE COMMITTEE

While perhaps not a core committee, the larger the size of the board the more likely it is to have an executive committee. Executive committees, though they may be a common feature of large boards, are more a device to enable the board to function efficiently than a standard element of governance infrastructure. They are different from other board committees because, within the parameters of any bylaws or legislative limits, they can act as the board. They also can address any matter not delegated to another committee. For example, the executive committee might be charged with handling operational performance oversight (i.e., performance against the operating plan), or non-policy ministerial functions (i.e., general salary line adjustments). It also can handle ad hoc assignments, such as chief executive transition and acquisition review.

Regardless of the specifics, because the executive committee has the ability to function as the board, it also has the potential to create tension between itself (and its members) and the full board (and the remaining members). Despite this risk, if properly managed, an executive committee can be a useful organizational device, particularly for an enterprise with a large board. However, it must not be allowed to supplant, either in appearance or reality, the powers and prerogatives of the full board. Board members must not feel that board discussions and actions are simply a formality—with the real decisions having been already made by the executive committee. To protect against this, the committee's role must not be allowed either to slip over into new policy decision making or approval of the organization's strategy and operating plan.

The membership of the executive committee should consist entirely of board members. The chair of the committee generally should be the chair of the board. This is necessary to assure both that the executive committee does not overreach in its actions and that decision making is consistent. The principal staff to the committee, as well as to the full board, should be the chief executive.

LEADERSHIP

As noted earlier, depending on the requirements of the enterprise, other committees may also be needed. Moreover, it is not unusual for some committees to do double duty (i.e., finance and audit, compensation and human resources).

While there is no limit as to how many committees can be created, three represent a core group. Two focus on money (audit and compensation). They are necessary to assure that the public has confidence in the enterprise. The third (governance) is necessary to make sure that the board and its committees not only work, but also continually improve.

The guiding principal is simply that structure (i.e., board size and composition, the number and charge of committees, and the detail of the bylaws) must follow function.

Structure is not the "end," rather it is the means to the "end"—an effective and efficient enterprise.

However, for structure to provide the mechanism to be able to accomplish this, one other factor must be added. The animating catalyst that turns structure into the achievement of purpose is leadership.

CHAPTER 7

Takeaways and Questions for Consideration and Discussion:

TAKEAWAYS

1. Every enterprise should have a committee structure that follows its bylaws and is designed to work for it. However, there are no absolute rules or fixed models as to what the structure should be.

2. Practice and practicality suggest that there are three fundamental functions that can be best served by having committees tend to them: audit, compensation, and governance. The first two follow the money. The last is the vehicle for continuous governance improvement.

3. Good governance takes time and resources. It is work. Therefore, to be most satisfying to directors, it should be designed to operate as efficiently as possible.

QUESTIONS

1. How often should board members have contact with the enterprise through either board or committee meetings?

2. If the enterprise has an executive committee, how should its role be defined and managed?

3. Do members of the audit committee face additional financial and legal risks because of their membership on that committee? If so, would the potential of these risks hinder committee membership recruitment? How can both perspective and reality of these risks be managed?

4. Should the full board know all the details, including compensation, of the chief executive's employment? What are the risks of full disclosure? Of managed disclosure?

Chapter 8:
BOARD LEADERSHIP

Board size, member composition, membership tenure, committees, etc. are elements of the enterprise's governance infrastructure. But the catalyst that energizes the enterprise's governance mechanism is leadership.

In the context of governance, leadership is an interesting phenomenon. As individuals, almost all board members are typically accomplished leaders. People seldom rise to the point where they are considered for board membership without having first demonstrated significant personal leadership ability.

Leadership—the ability to voluntarily energize and unify the efforts of people toward a common objective—is, as discussed in Chapter 1, a complex skill involving not only knowledge and wisdom but also personal confidence, judgment, interpersonal dynamics, and courage. While these matters are important, the purpose of this chapter is not to explore the development of personal leadership skills. The focus here is on the formal structure of the enterprise's organizational leadership and what is needed to make it productive.

Equally complex is the idea of "followership." Followership is not the opposite of leadership. It is the obverse, the counterpart that complements leadership. Leadership and followership are simply two sides of the same coin.

Being a follower is typically not held in high regard. In fact, it is generally argued that as a society our problem is that we do not have enough leaders. The true shortfall may be just the opposite; not the lack of leadership, but the lack of thoughtful followership. Frankly, it often takes more understanding and courage to be a follower than a leader.

The notion of followership relates both to the earlier discussion of political literacy and to the ability and need for individual board members to create productive compromises and establish working coalitions. Successful boards have members who are comfortable in both leadership and followership roles. Successful board members understand the unavoidable reality that leadership is impossible without followership, recognizing that if everyone always tries to lead, the collective wisdom of the board is lost.

Can you have an effective board without leadership? Clearly, the answer is no. Can you have a functional board without effective structures and processes? The answer again is no. Leadership can compensate for structural and procedural shortcomings, but it cannot overcome them. Similarly, sound structure and process can protect the enterprise from the risks of inadequate leadership. They cannot, however, overcome leadership shortfalls. Both are necessary to have an effective board.

TWO POSITIONS

Board leadership is centered formally in two positions: the chair of the board[1] and the chief executive officer (CEO).

The chair manages the board and the governance process, making benchmark corporate policy decisions (e.g., strategy and operating plan approval). (See Appendix 7 for examples of board chair job descriptions.) The chief executive manages the corporation and its day-to-day operations, executing the board's policy decisions. (See Appendix 18 for examples of chief executive job descriptions.) Taken together, the two positions shape and produce the enterprise's performance.[2]

In Canada and the United Kingdom, the chair and the chief executive positions are generally held by two different individuals. In the United States, for-profit firms, while maintaining two separate positions, generally assign both to a single person. In contrast, nonprofit enterprises usually have a separate person in each position. Recently some larger nonprofit corporations have begun to adopt the for-profit model of a single person holding both positions. These corporations, however, are the exceptions to the general pattern.

Whether or not the two positions should be held by one person is a matter of debate in the American business community. Tradition and many prominent business leaders argue that the two positions should be consolidated, with a single person occupying both. They claim that separating the chair's office from that of the chief executive can create confusion and blur accountability. Having one person hold both positions, they suggest, avoids ambiguity, making it clear who is really in charge. It is also argued that combining the two roles publicly evidences the board's unequivocal support for the chief executive.[3]

In counterpoint, is the unavoidable recognition that a reasonable system of checks and balances requires that the two positions be separated. While relatively small in number and involving only a minority of the thousands of publicly-traded corporations, certain newsworthy events have demonstrated the need for stronger institutional checks on corporate chief executives. Separating the two roles is a logical, primary way to accomplish this. It also offers a practical mechanism for dealing with any difficult issue that directly involves the chief executive, such as poor overall corporate performance, poor chief executive performance, and management succession.[4]

The simple facts are that:
- there are two roles and

- the roles are distinct, as well as hierarchical—with the chief executive reporting to the chair.

Equally true is the operational reality that if the enterprise is both to do good and do well, there are and should be two positions, each held by a different person. Though distinct, the two positions (and the two individuals holding them) are inextricably linked, united by mission and passion.

For historical and cultural reasons, nonprofit enterprises overwhelmingly have adopted the dual position/dual person model (one person as chair and another as chief executive). The governance results, while not perfect, have served society well. It is a lesson that should not be lost.

THE CHAIR

Of the two leadership positions, the chair's role is the more ambiguous.

The chair has the final responsibility for the performance of the enterprise. However, the position has no direct operating responsibility or line management authority. (See Exhibit 8-1.) This places the chair in a unique circumstance. He or she has accountability but must carry it out through "process" mechanisms and legislative leadership, as opposed to "command and control" powers.

Exhibit 8-1

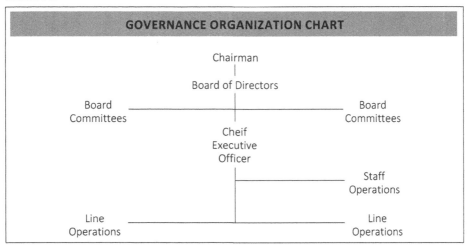

As will be discussed below, the most obvious role of the chair in this regard is chairing board meetings. This role is the end of the process, not the beginning. The chair manages the board, its agenda, and meeting processes. The chair also manages the corporate assessment processes of both the board (and its members), and of the chief executive. It is from these two roles that the chair is able to meet his or her accountability. Chairing the board meeting is but one facet of the chair's overall job.

Managing the board includes, as permitted by the corporation's bylaws, appointing committees and their chairs. More importantly, on an ongoing basis it involves working with the chief executive and committee chairs to develop appropriate board and committee work plans and supporting agendas. That is, agendas that build upon one another (e.g. topics from one meeting "set up" providing a context or exposure of an issue for a future meeting), and keep the board focused on: making policy, approving strategic and operating plans and monitoring resulting performance. All of this is done in preparation for the board meeting. At the meeting the chair must lead the board, guiding it and, if needed, mediating positions and points of view so that timely and appropriate decisions are made.

As with all management processes, continuous improvement requires continuous assessment. In this instance assessment occurs at three levels: the board as a whole, individual board members, and the chief executive—the board's agent for achieving operational results. The chair must assure that these assessments are done on a timely basis, appropriately shared and acted upon. It is this last element—acting on the results of the assessments, particularly that of the chief executive's performance—that both gives the chair corporate power and authority, and reinforces the importance of separating the chair's position from the chief executive's (see Appendix 7 for example board chair position descriptions and Appendix 18 for example chief executive position descriptions).

CHAIRMANSHIP: HOWARD'S RULES

While chairing a board or committee meeting may be the smallest part of a chair's role, it is the most visible, and for many, the source of the most anxiety. The following three rules provide a guide for both increasing the efficiency of meetings and effectively controlling the flow of the discussion and decision making.

1. Everyone will be heard—all board or committee members who wish to speak to a particular agenda item will be given the opportunity to do so. No one will be ignored. To assure this, the chair should keep a running list of those who wish to speak and the order that they will be called upon. From time to time, the chair should verbally review the order of the list. People who wish to interrupt the order should be reminded of the order and that they will have an opportunity to be heard.

2. When called upon to make a point, the speakers can say whatever it is that they wish. However, they can only say it once. Out of respect to the other members, they cannot try to dominate the conversation through repetition or harangue.

3. Speakers must stay on topic until the topic is completed, (i.e., a decision is made or other closure is reached). This is necessary to improve the efficiency of meetings and make sure that the discussion does not wander around. Speakers who wish to be recognized should be called upon in order of their request to speak. They should be asked if their comment is "on topic." If it is, they should proceed. If not, they should be deferred until the topic is resolved and then be called upon to make whatever comment they wish to make.

Finally, the chair and the chief executive, though having separate roles, are partners in accomplishing the enterprise's success. Their relationship sets the tone for the overall interaction between the board and the chief executive. Though the chief executive is responsible to the chair, the chair must support the chief executive—doing everything ethically and morally possible to assure the success of the chief executive and the enterprise. To do this there must be trust, respect, and good communications between the two positions.

QUALIFICATIONS

There are tens of thousands of nonprofit boards in the nation. Therefore, it is clear that people of ordinary backgrounds, skills, and experiences can and do successfully serve as a board chair. Even so, it is not a position for everyone. To leave the selection of the chair to chance is an error. To think that there is a clear prescription or fixed set of prerequisites for being a board chair is also an error.

The skills that a chair will need in any specific organization and at any point in the organization's history will change as the organization and its operating environment change. That said, there are still common attributes that all potential chair candidates should have.[5]

First is the time and the willingness to devote that time to the job. A successful board cannot be achieved with either an absentee chair or one who is not accessible both to the chief executive and to fellow board members. Time for the job, by itself, is not enough—but without time, nothing else matters.

Organizational and issue knowledge are key attributes as well. The chair must understand the nature of the enterprise's business, the character of its board and governance processes, and the interpersonal chemistry of both its senior management and individual board members. Such knowledge does not come by happenstance. It must be developed. A future board chair must be trained and groomed for the position—not expected to know things intuitively or learn them all on the job or by chance experiences.

The chair must bring objective decisiveness to his or her dealings with both board members and the management of board meetings. The chair must assure that the board is a forum for productive dialogue, not a debating society where outspoken members attempt to verbally bully their colleagues.

The chair also must instill in the board a determination to act and have the sensitivity to know when to ask it—or even force it—to act. This requires both subtle persuasiveness borne of continuous, gentle pressure, and constant monitoring to recognize when the board either has bogged down or coalesced around a position that moves the enterprise forward.

The chair also should have a degree of charm and style that acts to set a tone for the

---

DON'T FORGET

Two realities should be recognized by boards, board chairs and chief executives:

1. **Boards have chief executives; chief executives don't have boards.** A chief executive is hired and fired by his or her board. As a result, the chief executive is the servant, not the owner, of the board.

2. **A chief executive reports to the board's chair but is accountable to the board.** For the sake of organizational effectiveness, as well as morale and personal growth and development, a chief executive needs a single, primary reporting relationship. A chief executive, like anyone else, needs someone that he or she can go to for advice and counsel. Similarly, the organization needs a mechanism for providing the chief executive with guidance and constructive direction. The board chair fills these dual roles.

The board chair and the chief executive will have a close relationship. However, while at its core it is a superior/subordinate relationship, it is not a command and control or hire/fire relationship.

A chief executive is hired and fired by an act of his or her board—either directly or through explicit delegation.

board's behavior and deliberations. These are obviously personal characteristics that will vary from individual to individual. The goal and test is to create a meeting environment that is tolerant of disagreement, so long as people do not become disagreeable, and encourages debate.

With regard to style, the chair always should remember that the board is a group of peers and that while the chair leads it, he or she does not have command and authority over it. Therefore, the chair must employ a style that recognizes the limits of direct authority and the strength of the organizational pulpit. While the board is composed of peers, in electing the chair, it has selected one of its members as the first among equals. It will consequently defer, if not to the person, at least, to the position.

Finally, the chair must have the courage, or perhaps simply the self-confidence, to lead the board to fulfill its duties and responsibilities. He or she must have the commitment, and the personal will to energize that commitment, so as to assure that the board governs well.

THE CHIEF EXECUTIVE

While the chair has a governance-only role, the chief executive has both governance and operating responsibilities. The chief executive's management responsibilities are straightforward. He or she is responsible for managing operations. Like the chair's responsibility for chairing board meetings, this part of the chief executive's job, at least conceptually, is generally clearly understood.

With regard to governance, the chief executive has three distinct roles. These roles, while not in conflict with one another, are of markedly different character.

First, the chief executive must serve as the board's principal staff resource. The CEO must help to lead the board by continually challenging it with ideas and programs that enable both it and the enterprise to perform better.

Second, the chief executive, as the board's principal "line" resource, must also follow the board, implementing the decisions it makes. There is a certain amount of sensitivity and diplomacy required to be simultaneously a leader and follower. This dual role encapsulates the magic and the challenge of the chief executive's job. Chief executives who fail to understand that they must constantly work to harmonize these two roles place themselves in jeopardy.

Not only must chief executives recognize this duality, they also must remember that the board is not "theirs." They do not control it; they work for it and are accountable to it. Chief executives must always realize that the chair is his or her "boss," the person they are organizationally responsible to.

At the same time, the chief executive is generally a member of the board as well as the resource that the board looks to both for information and results when it wants to do something. The chief executive, in turn, is able to offer ideas and recommendations to the board, to substantively guide it with respect to the policy decisions it makes and the strategies and plans it approves. The price of being able to do this is the understanding that once the board acts, the chief executive has to apply the organization to carry out the board's wishes and directives.

The chief executive's third role, though intangible, is perhaps the most important.[6] The chief executive must want the governance process to work. He or she must believe that there is value in board member involvement in both shaping the direction of the corporation and in assuring accountability to the community. The chief executive must have the insight and confidence to understand that an ineffective board weakens, not strengthens, management and that a robust governance process—with an active board—is both management's best protection against making errors and its strongest ally when the going gets tough.

None of this means that the board should be involved in managing, or trying to manage, day-to-day operations. On the contrary, it emphasizes the importance of the board being a board and governing well.

MEETING MANAGMENT

Two additional matters require discussion: meeting management and continuous improvement.

The most visible role of the board chair is the management of the board meeting. For many board members, the style, preparation, and efficiency of board and committee meetings is their principal measure of how well the organization is organized and performing, because it is most often their most common interaction with the enterprise. Therefore, it is important that meetings be good.

Successful meetings all begin well before the gavel falls, calling the participants to order.

It is helpful to think of meeting management as involving three major interwoven parts: preparation, the event, and follow up.

Before exploring each of these elements and their interrelationships, two background comments should be noted. First, while the focus of this discussion is on board meetings, the same concepts apply to committee, advisory board, and other meetings. Second, while the following comments address a number of principles and techniques, they do not offer a prescription. Board chairmen and chief executive officers must find their own way, developing their own style and traditions.

Preparation

The meeting management process has an identifiable, ongoing cycle of activities and events. Meeting preparation, particularly board meeting preparation, is a continuing set of activities, paced by the calendar and the number of scheduled meetings per year and defined by the enterprise's operating needs.

Preparation is perhaps both the most basic and most important component of the meeting management process. The more attention and effort are invested in preparation, the greater the likelihood of meeting success.

The first step in preparation is the creation of the forward agenda. (See Exhibit 8-2.) The forward agenda is an organizational and meeting road map. It identifies the major recurring issues, events, and actions that the board must address throughout the year. It also specifies the time in the year that the board should expect to address those issues. Its value lies in that it sets forth a context and flow that all board members can see. It also serves as a reminder of both the breadth and depth of the work that the board must do and as the work plan for management to use in preparing for that work.

The second step in preparation is developing the actual agenda for the specific meeting. The forward agenda is the starting point, but it does not provide the entire agenda. An agenda must be planned not only for the meeting at hand, but also for future meetings. This requires that it be designed in a manner that makes the issues and discussion engaging and productive for the current meeting, while at the same time setting the stage for future meetings.

Agenda planning therefore involves anticipation. It necessitates management looking ahead to identify the nonrecurring issues (recurring issues being itemized in the forward agenda) that the board must address and then presenting them sufficiently in advance to avoid a sense of decision-making crisis. The agenda must allow the board adequate time to deliberate, in terms of discussion, and consider, in terms of contemplative reflection, an issue. How much time is adequate will vary with the history and culture of the board. As a general strategy, a topic should be introduced at one meeting, with a decision not needed until at least the next meeting.

Exhibit 8-2

SAMPLE FORWARD AGENDA		
Month	**Agenda Item**	**Action**
January	1. Legal Report	FYI
	2. Health Care Services Report	FYI
	3. Customer Satisfaction (3rd Qtr.)	FYI
	4. Finance Report	Approval
	5. Investment Report	Approval

Exhibit 8-2 continued on next page.

March	1. Customer Satisfaction (4th Qtr.)	FYI
	2. Governance Performance Review	FYI
	3. Community Investment Strategy (Strat. & Quant. Obj.)	FYI
	4. Recommendations for Board Member, Director, Officer elections	Approval
	5. Finance Report	Approval
	6. Investment Report	Approval
May	1. Conflict of Interest Report	Approval
	2. Fraud and Abuse Program	FYI
	3. Annual Internal Audit Report	FYI
	4. Environmental Assessment	Approval
	5. Finance Report	Approval
	6. Investment Report	Approval
July	1. Strategic and Operating Plan	Approval
	2. Customer Satisfaction (1st Qtr.)	FYI
	3. Finance Report	Approval
	4. Investment Report	Approval
September	1. Community Investment Policy (results for last 12 months)	FYI
	2. Customer Satisfaction (2nd Qtr.)	FYI
	3. Finance Report	Approval
	4. Investment Report	Approval
November	1. Budget Policy	Approval
	2. Finance Report	Approval
	3. Investment Report	Approval

In complex organizations with rapidly changing legislative, regulatory, or competitive environments, this general approach to issue scheduling will not always be possible. In fact, on occasion, special meetings of the board may be required to address unexpected, emerging issues. If crises requiring immediate board action become a standard agenda item, the planning process is failing. More importantly, requiring the board to deal regularly with matters on a crisis basis reflects poorly on the competence of management.

A Script

In some sense the agenda can be thought of as a script and the meeting as a performance. The goal is to make the performance interesting, efficient, and productive. Complicating the achievement of this goal is the unavoidable fact that for legal and/or administrative reasons a board must deal with a number of items that are repetitive, routine, and less than exciting. Additionally, a board must receive a number of essentially standard reports.

With regard to the routine noncontroversial nonpolicy items, the objective should be to minimize the amount of time spent on them. This can be accomplished by the use of a parliamentary device known as a "consent calendar." (See Exhibit 8-3.)

Exhibit 8-3

SAMPLE CONSENT CALENDAR

Agenda
Enterprise, Inc. Board of Directors
September XX, 20XX

I. Introduction and Opening Remarks

A. Call to order, establishment of quorum and member attendance, and opening comments. (Mr. Samuel Austin)

B. An overview will be provided of the political, economic, and competitive environment facing the corporation and the strategic and operating implications/consequences, as well as a summary of key agenda issues. (Ms. Rebecca Moore and Ms. Claire Preston)

II. Consent Calendar

Unless objections are raised, the following matters are proposed for adoption or approval by consent. These minutes and recommendations address issues, which have either been discussed by the board in the past or are routine operational matters which do not involve new policy decisions. The consent calendar is presented for adoption as a single agenda item. Specific matters can be removed, by request of any board member, for discussion as part of the regular agenda. The remaining items should then be adopted as a single agenda item.

Board approval of the consent calendar is required. Mr. Samuel Austin

A. Minutes of the July 21, 20XX Enterprise, Inc. Board of Directors Meeting. (Tab II.A.)

B. Minutes of the July 21, 20XX Audit and Finance Committee Meeting. (Tab II. B.)

C. Minutes of the July 21, 20XX Operations and Administration Committee Meeting. (Tab II. C.)

D. Minutes of the July 21, 20XX meeting of the Executive Committee/Committee on Directors. (Tab II. D.)

Item A is presented for the board's approval. Board approval is requested.

Items B through D are presented for the board's information and acceptance.

The consent calendar is a way of grouping nonpolicy ministerial matters into a single agenda item and then acting upon all of them, without discussion, as if they were one item. Any consent calendar item that a board member questions, or would like to discuss, is automatically and without debate removed from the calendar, and addressed in what would be its normal place in the agenda. The remaining items are then acted upon as a single item, saving the board's time.

Making standard reports interesting is a more difficult problem. Here the challenge is to keep them from becoming soliloquies that drone boringly on. One way to accomplish this is to sidestep the problem. Simply, to the extent possible, eliminate oral reports. The report item would be included in the agenda, along with written support materials. However, no oral report would be given. Management instead would be available to answer questions or provide any supplemental information that board members might request.

This approach both saves agenda time and reduces the risk of meeting tedium. In its place, however, it creates the possibility, if board members do not pursue their questions and concerns, of issues not being fully explored. Therefore, it should be used conservatively, limited to routine items, and uncontroversial matters.

Another approach, particularly for committee reports, is to ask the board member who chairs the committee to give the report. The benefits of this alternative are several. It more actively engages board members in their work and responsibilities as committee chairs. It is also an automatic way of actively involving members in the dialogue of the board meeting, while simultaneously adding a degree of presentational variety. Finally, it avoids the appearance, as well as the reality, of the meeting consisting of a passive board just listening to management presenting one report after another.

Annotated Agenda

The agenda also should note whether an oral report is to be given, along with who the presenter will be. An annotated agenda is the mechanism for doing this. As illustrated in Appendix 8, Exhibit A-8-1, an annotated agenda summarizes the substance of each item. It also indicates
• if there will be an oral presentation;

• if supporting materials are included or will be provided at the meeting—or, in the case of proprietary or confidential information, not provided at all;

• the recommended action that the board is hoped to take.

An annotated agenda has a number of benefits, both for management and the board. For management, it adds definition and specificity to the planning and meeting preparation processes. It requires decisions as to what will be presented, how it will be presented, who will present it, and what actions or next steps are needed. For the board it provides members with a guide to (and quick summary of) the topic to be addressed and the board action that is needed.

Annotations should be brief. Their purpose is not to provide an in-depth explanation of an issue. Rather it is to "prime the pump" for discussion of the issue at the actual meeting.

A second element in priming the discussion pump is the written support material, which should generally accompany each agenda item. These materials provide the background and fact base for the questioning and discussion that is expected to take place at the meeting.

Agenda support materials always should be accompanied by a transmittal memorandum (see Appendix 8, Exhibit A-8-2) that establishes the background and expectation for the item. The transmittal memorandum should describe the origin or source of the document as well as the issues, concerns, or opportunities that are raised by the subject. It should also include a recommendation as to next steps or how the matter should be handled.

The transmittal memorandum enables board members to develop a general understanding of the topic to be discussed and to decide if they wish to pursue the issue in greater depth, either through the support material or questions at the meeting. It also improves the efficiency of the meeting process by making it clear what type of board action is expected.

The transmittal memorandum is, in effect, a linking pin, connecting the agenda annotation and the support material. It holds the agenda together as it builds on itself from meeting to meeting and in layers of detail.

The most detail is in the support material, the least in the annotation. As the amount of detail expands, management's editorial discipline must correspondingly increase. Written support material should not overwhelm the board. Rather, it should be designed and edited so that it increases the likelihood of a knowledgeable and productive board discussion. To do this, it must have focus, making the issues and the choices as clear as possible.

While most agenda items benefit from advance support material, some exceptions occur. Passing out material at the meeting or even eliminating it completely is often necessary when addressing confidential matters where the availability of written material could create a competitive or proprietary issue. The obvious disadvantage is that this approach does not allow time for board members to consider the topic before they need to discuss it. To compensate for this, the agenda should allow more time for these matters, so that sufficient opportunity exists for the board to deliberate the issues fully without feeling uninformed or rushed.

This approach clearly has a legitimate place and role. It also has risks. The board should not allow the absence of advance agenda support material to become a strategy for masking complicated issues. Similarly, management must not allow itself to fall into the trap of substituting stand-alone oral reports for adequate preparation. Oral reports, without support or background material, should not be the agenda solution to management's inability to adequately prepare.

Agenda Design

In addition to routine operating matters, committee reports, legal requirements, and ministerial matters, a board meeting agenda can also include three other categories of topics.

Strategic and core policy issues must always be brought to the board. These types of issues may not be on every agenda. However, they should be frequent for they are part of the board's fundamental work and responsibility. Importantly, they should be early in the agenda so that time will be available for full discussion.

Second, to the extent that time allows, the agenda should include topics (or a topic) intended to engage the board in extended discussion. This aspect of agenda design provides the opportunity to bring spirit and excitement to the meeting. Its focus should be on topics that might later shape strategy or management actions but that are currently in the formative stage.

Accomplishing this is challenging. It requires both preparation and meeting management skills. The preparation can be thought of as involving several pieces. First is the inclusion, with the agenda, of written material that sets out the background data and issues for discussion. The second part is management's presentation, which must build on the background data, highlighting its specific relevance—both threat and opportunity—to the organization. The final component is actually the conclusion of management's presentation and the beginning of the board's discussion. It is the formulation and posing of a set of provocative questions that try to direct the board's discussion to the strategic and operating questions that should be addressed.

The third common feature of agenda design is the executive session. An executive session is a parliamentary device for setting aside time for the board to meet in private, without management or staff (unless they are invited to stay).

An executive session should be included as a standard item on each board meeting agenda. It should be included to assure that at each meeting the board members have the opportunity, if they wish to exercise it, to talk amongst themselves about issues of concern, as well as confidential or proprietary subjects and fiduciary matters. By including an executive session as a standard item, board members know that, simply by asking the chair, they will have the opportunity to raise any matter they wish, without having to ask for special consideration.

Management should develop the agenda but should include the chair in the agenda review process, along with those senior staff making presentations or having responsibility for particular agenda items. The chair should review the agenda not from an operational perspective, but instead to assure that the board is carrying out its responsibilities and making decisions on appropriate matters.

This simple action is not intended to reduce management autonomy, responsibility, or flexibility. Rather it reflects the facts that the chair manages the board and that the chief executive works for the board. More pragmatically, it is also the first step in the chair's preparation for managing the meeting and the anticipated discussion.

The final piece in agenda design is to time the agenda—that is, to establish how much time is planned to be spent on each agenda topic. If the agenda is the road map, the timing of it is the schedule. Certainly, a timed agenda is only a planning vehicle. If the board is engaged in productive discussion, it should not be rigidly held to a fixed schedule. Nevertheless, by adding an explicit time element to the agenda, the chair has a better tool for guiding the board's discussion and managing the flow of the meeting.

The Event

Managing the event (that is, the meeting, the periodic formal gathering of the board's members) is the most obvious and public part of the chair's job. The meeting can be thought of as a series of presentations, discussions, and decisions. Given this flow the goal is to efficiently get to, and then effectively make, good decisions.

The most efficient strategy for presentations is to not make them. Instead support materials should be sent out prior to the meeting—either as part of a formal agenda package (agenda book) or as they are ready, for pre-meeting reading. At the meeting no formal oral report would be made on these items. Management, however, would be available and ready to answer questions. This approach is most useful for routine matters and uncontroversial nonpolicy management reports. It is also appropriate for routine board committee reports.

Some matters, however, will require presentations either as a supplement to the written support material or on a stand-alone basis. When presentations are necessary, they should be designed to be as brief as possible. They should reference but not repeat what was available for board members to read. Presentations should serve as a catalyst for the board's deliberations, creating a context and highlighting the key facets and subtleties of the issues. They should be explanatory, not defensive, providing a foundation and direction for discussion.

Finally, presentations should conclude by clarifying:
- the question(s) or issue(s) to be discussed and/or the matter(s) on which guidance is being sought;

- the actions(s) or decision(s) needed.

All of this is preparatory to the heart of the meeting, the discussion of various agenda items and issues. This is the most active part of the meeting and also the part that largely determines for members both how much they have contributed to the governance process and the quality of their board experience. Therefore, it is a place where the chair's public leadership is needed.

The goal of the meeting's discussion is to achieve a broad and productive dialogue that yields a clear expression of the group's collective wisdom. How this is accomplished will vary with the character and traditions of the board, the comfort of individual members in speaking out, the size of the board, and the issue.

To generate broad discussion, particularly with a large group, the chair might want to do one or more of the following:
- plan with the chief executive to have the management presentation "set up" or ask key questions;

- ask particular board members, on either a prearranged or spontaneous basis, to comment on the matter after management's presentation has been made;

- ask the board open-ended questions and then call on specific members to respond;
- ask the presenter to clarify or elaborate on a point, as the preface to asking the board for questions or comments.

While other approaches may be used, the common goal of all of these techniques and processes is to draw people into a discussion so that they become engaged in the deliberations. Once this is successfully done, the chair is confronted with a second challenge: managing the flow of discussion. If participation is the first objective, here the goal is productivity.

Board members share the responsibility for keeping the conversation on task. Individual members should wait until one line of inquiry is completed before moving the discussion in a different direction. To facilitate this, the chair should make it clear that waiting to raise a point will not result in the point or the opportunity to comment being lost.

Individual members should also recognize their obligation not to dominate the conversation. Members have the right to comment; they do not have the right to monopolize the discussion or repeat a point over and over. The guideline simply should be that members can say anything they wish, but they can only say it once.

If discussion is the heart of the meeting, the board's decisions are the product. The character of the action to be taken should be clearly understood, from both the presentation and annotated agenda. Based on the discussion and the suggested action, the chair should call for a decision.

From a parliamentary-procedure perspective, discussion should follow the offering and seconding of a specific motion for some action or decision. More often than not, discussion of the matter follows the presentation—before a formal motion is offered—in order to clarify the issue and needed decisions. Regardless of the specifics, when the discussion is exhausted the chair must move the board to closure, providing management with guidance and decision.

At this point the board has done its job. It is ready to move on to the next agenda item and repeat the process or, if finished with the agenda, adjourn.

Follow-Up

The last major component of the meeting process is the follow-up activity, which must be done after the meeting adjourns. Follow-up activity can be either formal or informal. Common to both, however, is a sense of urgency, an understanding that management must respond or act as quickly as practical.

Informal activities are responses to questions or requests that individual board members have made. It is unreasonable to expect, regardless of how well prepared, that management will always have the answers or data for all the questions that will be asked. When management does not have the information, they should not speculate. They should admit that they do not have the data or answer available and commit to getting what is needed and forwarding it. Depending on the discussion, the question and the level of interest, the answer either should be shared with just the board member who asked the question or with the full board.

Requests for additional information or background material should be handled in the same way. A general exception is if the request is made privately. In these instances, the response should be given just to the board member who made the request.

Formal activities are management actions that must be taken as the result of decisions made at the meeting and the preparation of the meeting's minutes. The "management actions" element requires little elaboration. It is simply the understanding that management works for, and is accountable to, the board and is obligated to carry out the board's instructions and decisions.

Minutes are a more complicated matter. They are the formal, legal record of the meeting. Therefore, they must be accurate with respect to their conclusions.

However, they also must be more than that. Meeting minutes must clarify the intent of the discussion and decision as well as document that the board had clear and thoughtful deliberations. Preparing minutes requires a mix of legal skills and technical writing skill. The legal requirement is that minutes document what happened, why it happened, and that the conclusion was carefully reached, meeting the standards of loyalty and care. The skill comes in crafting the minutes in a manner that accomplishes the foregoing without betraying confidences, inappropriately divulging proprietary information, or embarrassing any of the participants. To help assure that this balance is struck, minutes should be broadly reviewed (also by counsel, if practical) before they are distributed.

Minutes also should be distributed as soon after the meeting as possible and included with the agenda materials for the next meeting. Rapid publication is suggested to provide board members the opportunity to review the minutes while their recollection of the meeting is still fresh.

Meeting follow-up activities should also include some form of feedback. Depending on the tradition and character of the board and the preference of the chair, the feedback process can be either formal or informal. Some boards may traditionally conduct an end-of-meeting executive session, which the chair uses for a review of the meeting and the solicitation of suggestions for future meetings. Others may prefer a more structured approach using questionnaires and the rating of each agenda item in terms of such factors as the appropriateness of the matter for board attention, the usefulness of the agenda support material, the quality of management's presentation, and the quality of the discussion.

CONTINUOUS IMPROVEMENT

The final element of leadership is the commitment to continuous organizational governance and operational improvement and the related need to plan for the future.

Continuous improvement is an ongoing process of:
- assessing performance
- assessing the process/processes underlying performance shortfalls
- adjusting/enhancing the process/processes based on that assessment, and
- reassessing performance.

Performance assessment involves measuring actual performance against established goals or standards. Goals should evolve from year to year, reflecting past performance and experience, benchmark and best practice data, emerging priorities, and rising expectations. Importantly, goals should always trend upward, as actual performance should continuously improve.

Performance adjustment and enhancement is the process of operational management. Its objective is to increase sales, quality, productivity, financial condition, etc. It is the result of experience, analysis, imagination, and innovation, all driven by education and training. Performance enhancement is a process with no end, as performance is expected to improve continuously.

For governance, continuous improvement begins with board member education. This is the starting point because it is the support on either end of the assessment process.

CONTINUING EDUCATION

In addition to new member orientation (see Appendix 9), the enterprise should also have an explicit continuing education program for all board members. Oversight of this effort should typically be the responsibility of the board's governance committee.

For first-year board members, regardless of organizational size, one or more sessions should be held to examine and discuss the enterprise's business—both its regulatory and competitive environment and its operations and operational issues. The purpose of these presentations is to establish a baseline level of information that will help new members to knowledgeably and confidently participate in board and committee meetings.

Second-year and all other board members also should be offered ongoing educational opportunities. These can be provided directly by the organization, sponsored by the organization, be a covered or subsidized board member expense, be an expectation of membership, or some combination of any or all of the alternatives. Regardless of the approach, the initiative has a dual focus. One part should be aimed at emerging legal, regulatory, competitive, and business issues, the other at emerging issues in governance.

The second set of issues is perhaps a new concept, reflecting the chronic shortfalls of governance performance in corporate America and the resulting need to:
- pursue continuous governance performance improvement and

- reinforce, for directors, the importance of effective governance.

While continuing education cannot guarantee either of these outcomes, focusing on them provides a forum for keeping them in the forefront of the attention of the board and its individual members.

Educational opportunities also should be provided, on a planned basis, to individual board members. This should be done as part of the process of grooming members for future board leadership positions. As a consequence, these events should not be random. They must be explicit steps in an overall plan that includes committee and board assignments of increasing breadth and responsibility, supported by educational opportunities.

ASSESSMENT

Assessment dovetails with continuing education, both measuring the results of what has happened and providing guidance for what should come next. In addition to identifying gaps and direction, the assessment process provides a means for helping the board keep fresh. Just as term, tenure, and retirement provisions provide a mechanism for refreshing the board's human capital, assessment is the means for refreshing the board's structural and intellectual capital.

Intuitively, the reasonableness of assessing performance may seem obvious. The reality is that board assessment is not the common practice.[7] Assessment is, at its core, a management-of-change process. It must be paced to the organization's ability to change, not to an arbitrary timetable or calendar. Moreover, it is an initiative that requires flexibility, eschewing blind obedience to detailed mechanics. Even so, some general observations can be set out as guides. (See Appendix 10 for sample assessment surveys.)[8]

In terms of a conceptual framework, there are three broad types of governance assessments: self-assessments, peer assessments, and whole board (governance process) assessments. Self-assessments and peer assessments are focused on improving individual director effectiveness. Board assessments are aimed at enhancing the performance of the governance process as a whole.

DIRECTOR EFFECTIVENESS

Self-assessments are exactly what their name suggests. They are an evaluation by the board member of his or her own performance. An assessment questionnaire typically should be provided to help the board member navigate a course of self-discovery aimed at identifying areas requiring increased personal attention. The results can be kept by the board member as part of a personal inventory, and plan for his or her future board activity; and/or shared with the governance committee as part of a peer-assessment program; and/or serve as part of a continuous improvement program wherein individual board members commit to certain activities for the next year or so.

Peer assessments are reviews of a board member's effectiveness by the member's colleagues. They are usually done by the governance committee, as opposed to the full board, as part of its responsibilities for evaluating incumbent board members for re-election.

Peer assessment is a delicate matter. To be beneficial to both the member and the organization, it must be handled with organizational and personal maturity, integrity, and prudence. Because of its sensitivity, it often emphasizes objective data, such as board and committee meeting attendance and preparedness, as opposed to subjective judgments of the members' contributions to discussions and decisions.

> ### ASSESSMENT & CONSULTANTS
>
> Assessment should be a core governance activity and competency. For some boards, an effective assessment process may require the use of a third-party—not just to manage the process, but more importantly to assure candor.
>
> Without candor, the assessment has no validity. In some instances, to achieve candor, a consultant is needed to interview each board member and filter, collate, and synthesize the findings into useful information.
>
> This can be an expensive undertaking. Therefore, if done at all, it should only be done periodically (i.e., once every several years).
>
> Is it worth the cost? The answer depends on the circumstances. If the board is clearly dysfunctional and not capable of facing its own issues, then it is a justifiable expense. If the consultant can only provide marginal benefit, the answer is no.

Because of its potential for adverse personal reactions, peer assessments should be the last phase of a board member-assessment program. The first phase should be confidential self-assessments. At some point, board member comfort levels will evolve to a willingness to share self-assessments with the governance committee. When this happens, the committee should use this input and its own judgment to guide general board education programming, as well as individualized member coaching and counseling. The importance of this last step should not be lost. The goal of member assessment, whether self or peer, is to improve effectiveness—not to embarrass anyone.

BOARD ASSESSMENT

Board assessment has a different perspective. It is aimed at measuring the performance of the board as a whole. Its purpose is to evaluate the effectiveness of the board in fulfilling its governance accountabilities to:

- assure the enterprise's pursuit of its purpose

- approve policy and strategy

- monitor performance processes and results

- add value to the enterprise, and

- assure continuous improvement in the performance of management and the board.

Accomplishing this kind of evaluation involves more than just examining outcomes. While it is easy to argue that effort should not be confused with results, and that results are the litmus test of performance, such an argument is shortsighted. It is unrealistic to think that consistently good results can be produced without a base of sound administrative processes and organizational structures. Governance assessment should therefore examine processes and structures as well as outcomes.

This does not require three separate assessment initiatives. It is simply the recognition that the enterprise's governance assessment program should include all three aspects.

Process assessments look at what the board does and how it works. Examples include questions about board practices such as the existence of a formal governance-assessment process, a new member recruitment program, a continuing education series, and so forth. Process questions also can be open-ended, asking about board member satisfaction with, and suggestions for improving, operational matters such as agenda background/discussion materials, meeting management, and committee roles. This should include any concerns about committees overstepping their bounds and usurping prerogatives that the board should retain for itself.

Structure factors consider "things," as opposed to activities. It asks if the board has, for example:
- a forward agenda for the upcoming year

- a conflict of interest policy and program

- a code of conduct

- adequate meeting facilities

- regular executive sessions, and

- regular chief executive communications.

The list can be quite extensive and should expand as the board's level of governance competence and comfort grows.

Taken together, process and structure provide the tools for, and the pathway to, achieving good results. The ultimate measures, however, are outcomes. Here, the metrics are a mix of objective and subjective considerations. Objective factors focus on whether a process was implemented or not. For example, did the board or a designated committee:
- review and approve the enterprise's strategy and operating plan

- monitor actual performance against operating plan objectives

- conduct an annual chief executive performance assessment
- review and approve conflict of interest declarations
- meet with the independent auditors, and
- review and approve the code of conduct?[9]

There are also subjective measures, focusing on how well a process was done. They ask about the quality of the board's work—were questions penetrating, were discussions robust and thorough, did decisions reflect the board's cumulative wisdom and judgment? The totality of the assessment process provides a checklist for determining whether the board is working in an efficient and effective way.

OUTCOMES

Outcomes are arguably the litmus test of performance.

In the for-profit setting, outcome metrics are relatively easy to come by, as they concentrate on financial results. Such is not the case in the community sector, nonprofit world.

As discussed in the next section, the planning process provides the basis for firms that are not judging performance simply by "bottom line" results to establish objective outcome measures.

Assessing governance includes this, by looking at the board's role and actions in reviewing and

approving the enterprise's operating plan and budget—and then monitoring actual performance against the approved quantified objectives. But it also goes beyond in the sense that it must also examine the elements of good governance that in turn provide the foundation for good operational results.

Good operational results do not necessarily evidence good governance. In the same vein, good governance by itself cannot guarantee good operational results in any particular year. However, over the long run poor governance will deliver poor operational performance.

BRINGING IT TOGETHER

The data from the board assessment questionnaires should be tabulated, organized into a report, and presented to the board, along with any comments or remarks that respondents have offered.

Comments should be edited to protect the identity of the authors. Also, to the extent possible, ratings and comments should be grouped, or otherwise noted, to reflect board experience and activity. This is useful as a safeguard to understand the responses. New or relatively inactive board members may have different conclusions from those of experienced or active members. These data should neither be discounted nor ignored. Rather they should be kept in perspective.

The assessment report should be the central agenda item of an annual assessment review meeting or an extended board meeting. Regardless of the logistics, the goal is to provide the board with a specific opportunity to focus on its performance results and to decide on any follow-up actions that it wishes to pursue. This will not happen if board performance assessment is "sandwiched in" within the regular flow of meetings and agenda items.

In addition to reviewing the results of the current assessment, the board's discussion should include at least two other matters. One should be the review of the "forward agenda." This is necessary to give board members an opportunity to shape the year's agenda and assure that the board is addressing items and issues that it feels are necessary and important (i.e., the year-long meeting roadmap that identifies the major recurring issues, events and actions—as well as their timing—that the board must address). (See Appendix 8.)

The second topic should be a report on the status of the actions taken as part of the discussion of the previous year's review. This step is completing the "feedback loop" in a normal management control process. Its value lies in the discipline it brings. It prevents the process from just running in place—reaching the same conclusions year after year without substantively acting upon them. Just as executive management requires that operational management act on decisions that have been made, the board must expect the same of itself.

While the overall governance-assessment process comes together at a dedicated board discussion, individual member assessment comes together at the governance committee, as it addresses incumbent member re-election. While the process at the committee may be less formal, because of its political and psychological sensitivity, its goal is the same—to improve the enterprise's governance.

Because assessing individual member effectiveness is so personal and board members can be such proud people, any of the committee's suggestions for change must be pursued diplomatically. Moreover, they must be handled by either the chair of the board or the chair of the committee. The chief executive, even though he or she might be a member of the board, is an employee and servant of the board. To ask the chief executive to provide unsolicited advice to one of his or her bosses is an inappropriate request, fraught with both personal risk and the potential for creating dysfunctional board and operating relationships. Peers must deal with peers. If they are not willing to do so, then it is better that no action—as contrasted with the wrong action—be taken.

MAKING A JUDGMENT

While there are no absolute standards, two things to consider in making a judgment regarding board effectiveness and performance are:

Difficulty in Recruiting

- If the board is finding it difficult to recruit new members, then:
  - the board may be too large;
  - the recruiting process may not be efficient/effective; and/or
  - the organization may not be necessary —or lacks general interest.

Difficulty in Maintaining Members

- If the board is finding that members are stepping down as soon as their term ends or

even leaving earlier, then:

- the recruitment process may not be efficient/effective—particularly in identifying people who believe in the enterprise's mission and can, and are willing to, make time available to achieve that mission; and/or
- board members may not feel that they are able to make a difference—because (1) the meetings and discussions are not meaningful, in terms of debating issues, shaping policies or making decisions, and/ or (2) they are not involved in, and are not able to participate in, shaping the board's agenda and therefore its work and contribution to the success of the enterprise.

CAUTION

As noted earlier, formal board and board member assessment is not the common practice. The publicly stated reasons for this vary. They range from concerns about undermining the collegiality of the boardroom to suggesting that informal systems—director to director coaching and counseling—are enough.[10] The real reason is that assessment is a threatening process, demanding increased board accountability and holding some psychological risk to board members' egos. Understanding this, it is not surprising that governance assessment is an emerging process.

Nevertheless, assessment should be pursued, albeit cautiously and at a pace that minimizes any perception of threat. Pragmatically this means that the starting point should be the evaluation of overall board performance, with peer assessments coming last—if at all. It also means that the assessment initiative must have a champion, a respected board member who advocates for it and assures that it evolves at a safe rate. Generally, the board chair, along with his or her predecessors, should be the assessment process champions.

In the same cautionary vein, assessment should not become a cottage industry, taking on a life of its own. (See Exhibit 8-4.)

Exhibit 8-4

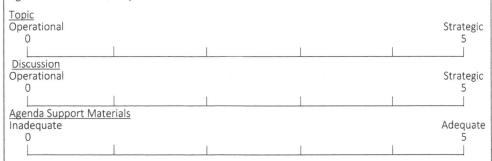

MEETING ASSESSMENT

Relatively little is gained from fanatically assessing each presentation at each meeting. Nevertheless, some form of meeting assessment can be an important component of continually improving the governance process. It can also help to assure that board members feel good about attending meetings, having spent their time well.

A variety of approaches are available for assessing meetings, both agenda topics and pre-meeting briefing materials, as well as the meeting discussion. At one extreme, a formal questionnaire process can be used to focus on selected agenda items and asking about their relevance for board attention; e.g.,

Meeting Assessment
Agenda Item III. A.: Quality Assurance Initiative

Topic
Operational   Strategic
   0   5

Discussion
Operational   Strategic
   0   5

Agenda Support Materials
Inadequate   Adequate
   0   5

At the other extreme may be informal conversations, initiated by the chair, either in person, via telephone or email, asking individual board members about the meeting and how meetings can be enhanced.

Some boards also use routine executive sessions as a means of eliciting meeting assessment feedback. The risk of this approach is that disconnected, ad hoc suggestions will be made that will have to be dealt with, respectfully and diplomatically, regardless of their intrinsic merit. Therefore, at least on an ongoing basis, a more manageable assessment approach should be employed.

LOOKING TO THE FUTURE

The last task that each board chair must complete to fulfill his or her leadership responsibilities is to assure a competent successor. Certainly, ordinary people become board chairs. The weight of evidence shows that for the most part, they step up to the challenges and perform well. The selection of a board chair cannot, however, be a random event. The job is too important and the costs of under-performance too great.

Board chairs are, first and foremost, board members. Therefore, unless the bylaws provide an explicit exemption, the enterprise's policies with respect to board membership tenure and turnover apply to them. Also, many organizations have explicit bylaw limits on the length of the chair's term and how many successive terms can be served.

This can be both good and bad. On the positive side, it allows the board and its leadership to periodically be refreshed. It also protects against the chair creating an independent fiefdom or insulated leadership cadre. The downside is that a skilled and knowledgeable asset is lost—or at least sidelined for a short period. Often, the bylaws permit past members, after the appropriate break in service, to be re-elected. On balance, this is a fair trade-off.

Even so, it creates an issue. Chair succession must be managed just as board member succession is managed. Potential chair candidates must be identified early in their board tenure and then developed through education, appointment, or election to positions of increasing board responsibility, and mentoring by both the current and past chair and by the chief executive. Often this process is specific and formal through the movement of potential candidates through various committee chairs and the ultimate designation of a chair-elect. It can just as easily be informal. Regardless of form, in substance it must be explicit and systematic.[11]

As part of the process of candidate identification, explicit consideration must be given to the type of leader that the organization requires or will require. Trying to do this—to in effect look over the horizon—is a difficult task. Often, it is so frustrating that boards give up. This is a mistake. The very challenge of trying to anticipate the kind of leadership that will be needed is beneficial, clarifying the board's thinking and with each attempt bringing it closer to an answer.

A SENSE OF CONSCIENCE

Successful governance requires active and committed leadership. The key to leadership is caring—not in the sense of unfettered passion, but rather in terms of the responsibility of ownership, regardless of the economic or legal reality, and the consequent obligation to do the right thing, the right way, the first time.

The challenge for any nonprofit enterprise is to establish this sense of operational ownership and responsibility without the driving force of economic ownership.

The goal is to create a sense of conscience to guide the legal creation of the corporation. The mechanism for doing this is the governance process and the accountability to the community that the board provides through the leadership of its chair and the support of its chief executive. (See Appendix 11 for a listing of suggested best practices for the governance of nonprofit enterprises and a governance practice checklist. Also included, for general information, is a copy of the IRS Governance Check Sheet.)

WHEN YOU MIGHT BE GETTING INTO TROUBLE

For board leadership, as well as for individual board members, the question always lurking in the background is, "Are we ok?" It is difficult to provide a fixed template for answering this question. However, there are some warning signs. The enterprise might be moving toward trouble if:

- Revenues (both operating and donations) are down

- Revenues are growing but the margin is not

- Administrative costs (either absolutely or relatively) are increasing

- Creditors are not willing to advance credit

- Board member absenteeism increases

- There are significant negative variances between planned and actual performance, over a several year period.

CHAPTER 8

Takeaways and Questions for Consideration and Discussion:

TAKEAWAYS

1. Boards have chief executives. Chief executives do not have boards. Chief executives report to the board chair but are accountable to the board as a whole. Only the action of the board can hire or fire the chief executive.

2. Just as an organization is expected to strive toward continuous operational improvement, so should the organization's board and its governance function. This requires: assessment, corrective action, and education.

3. You cannot have an effective governance function without leadership by both the chair and the chief executive. The chair has the final responsibility for the behavior and performance of the enterprise—but no direct operational responsibility or control.

4. The chief executive is simultaneously the servant of the board and because he or she is the principal staff to the board and the enterprise's subject matter expert, the substantive leader of the board.

5. The board chair and the chief executive are two different positions playing two different roles. Therefore, for reasons of checks and balances as well as stakeholder credibility, they should be separated—two different positions occupied by two different people.

QUESTIONS

1. How should the chief executive support the chair in the chair's management of the board?

2. How does the chair support the chief executive, without getting involved in operational management?

3. What are the risks involved in peer assessment of fellow board member performance? Do the benefits exceed the risks?

4. How do the chair and the chief executive create a sense of conscience within the board? How do they create a sense of operational ownership of the enterprise?

PART III

MANAGEMENT: PLANNING AND IMPLEMENTATION

Man plans—and God laughs

Regardless of enterprise size or board and management experience and sophistication, the only thing that boards and managers can be assured of is that what is planned will not happen as planned. Even so, if the enterprise does not plan, how does it:

- know what it wants to achieve;

- move from where it is to what it wishes to achieve;

- know when it has accomplished what it wishes to achieve?

Planning, while not guaranteeing success, provides focus. More importantly, it gives the enterprise a basis for making judgments, allocating resources, assessing accomplishments, making adjustments—and determining what not to do.

Plans provide the enterprise with a rudder for guiding its progress, the board with a means of fulfilling its accountabilities, and managers with the protection of a mandate as to how to proceed.

Large enterprises may have extensive planning books overflowing with data and complexity. Small organizations will generally have less formal and less voluminous planning documents—sometimes only a page or two and simply listing goals, quantified objectives, and summarizing a budget.

Both approaches have merit. However, the value of business planning lies in the process of creating and recreating the plan, not in the style or length of its documentation. In fact, care must be taken to ensure that the document does not become a managerial end point, once completed either forgotten or little used.

The planning process is the key because it provides a systematic way for the board and management to:

- thread their way through the enterprise's shifting environment—with the best chance of both avoiding trouble and capitalizing on opportunity and

- assess what has been accomplished and what adjustments should be made or actions taken to be successful.

Recognizing that it is the dynamic "process" which is important, there is some risk in trying to codify it. However, from the point of view of establishing an implementation structure and flow, there is value in dissecting the process into a series of sequential steps and interactive actions and adjustments.

The following chapters provide a road map through the business planning journey. Though presented as a mechanical, step-by-step activity, it must be remembered that planning is a governance and managerial process—characterized by both hard facts and human nature and defined by data and imagination. It is a process that is simultaneously sloppy and elegant, linear and circular, and intuitive and data-driven—not a static recipe.

Chapter 9:
PLANNING AND STRATEGY

Because of its corporate form, an organization has extraordinary potential. The governance function provides the mechanism for harnessing that potential, so that the enterprise can make a difference.

How, though, do you convert potential into results? How do you steer an enterprise to actually make a difference to its community? How do you achieve mission?

The building blocks for achieving results are:

- knowing where you are;

- knowing where you want to go; and

- having the leadership to:
  - envision the route to that destination, and
  - guide the enterprise to that end.

For leadership to be effective, leaders must have a clear idea of where they want to go and a plan for how they want to get there.[1]

COMPLEMENTARY BUT DIFFERENT

Management and the board both have roles to play in creating and implementing the organization's plan. The roles, while complementary, are different.

Management creates the plan. The board reviews, tests, perhaps modifies, and ultimately approves it. Along the way, the board acts as both a partner to management in creating a vision of what the enterprise can aspire to be and do, and as the "devil's advocate," providing a sounding board, and giving advice and guidance.

Depending on the maturity and size of the organization, the board's specific involvement will vary from being very active, in those organizations that are just starting or have limited professional management capacity, to consultative—providing ongoing oversight, counsel, and commentary, prior to the formal review and approval of the business plan.

Regardless of where along the spectrum a particular enterprise falls, three points should be noted. First, boards have a fiduciary responsibility (as a consequence of their stewardship and agency obligations and duties of obedience and care) to be engaged in the planning process. Second, boards want to be engaged in the process, albeit in a meaningful way—sensitive to their obligations, skills, and role. Third, the heavy lifting with respect to the work of planning has to be done by management.

This last point reflects the reality that management will have to implement the plan and no one wants to have to implement a plan imposed on them or created by others and just passed on to them. Quite simply, if management is to take real ownership of the plan, it must be management's work product.*

Similarly, the board must be involved, for just as management cannot accept something that is imposed on it, neither can the board. However, management must take the lead in the planning process—both creating the review drafts of the plan and constructively involving the board.

*This does not mean that consultants and other outside resources cannot be used. In fact, they can be quite helpful, assisting in developing the planning system, cycle and calendar, preparing support materials, documenting discussions and decisions, facilitating discussions, helping in consensus building, etc.

ANY ROAD

If you don't know where you want to go, then any destination is fine, and any road will get you there.

From a governance perspective, an "any road" approach fails to fulfill either a board's stewardship or agency accountabilities. An "any road" approach is both a failure on the board's part to meet its community, and legal obligations, and a recipe for operational disaster.

In a similar vein, no one wants to follow someone who does not know where he or she is going and has no idea/plan for getting there. For management to be effective, it must either plan or be very lucky. Since luck is fickle, prudent managers and boards plan. The simple reality is that planning, while not providing a guarantee, increases the probability of organizational progress—if not success. It does this because it provides the means for the organization to:

- align all its efforts;

- establish clear accountabilities (i.e., identify what is to be accomplished, at what cost, by when, and by whom);[2] and

- protect its future.

Planning cannot remove the uncertainties of the future. It can, however, increase the enterprise's ability for handling, and even capitalizing on, those uncertainties. The pivotal question, therefore, is how does management create its plan, and then how does it implement it, to use the plan to guide the enterprise toward achieving specific performance results?

COMPLEXITY

The first step in creating an enterprise's plan is understanding that business planning is a complex, though not necessarily complicated, process.[3] It is complex because it is an amalgam of facts, analysis, imagination, insight, and skill.[4] It is also complex because it involves simultaneously thinking in two different time perspectives. One is focused on establishing the enterprise's destination and direction. The other concentrates on the mechanics of assuring a successful journey. The first can be thought of as strategic management; the second as operational management. The primary distinction between the two is timeframe and detail.

Strategic management takes a longer view, trying to establish a certainty of destination and stability of direction. Operational management's reach is more immediate. It concentrates on what must be done now to achieve the planned results.

The first provides the macro level, overarching plan. The second provides the detailed project and work planning necessary to achieve the anticipated results. The starting point for both, however, is the same.

Finally, planning is complex because it is not a neat linear process or a single event. It is non-linear in the sense that the individual steps in the process do not always flow either neatly or sequentially from one to the other. Often what is found or determined in a later step forces the review of the conclusions or decisions of a previous step. Also, some steps, though falling into a sequential order, can start at the same time. The result is a process that is both linear and iterative.

Business planning is also an ongoing process, not a single event. The goal should be for planning to be a continuous management process. To be real and meaningful, planning must become part of the fabric of the organization's culture and management's character. Just as it should not be a single event, it also must not be a stand-alone activity, pursued outside of the flow of operational management and performance. Planning is not a parallel activity to operational management. Rather, it is the core of management, providing the insights, directions, and discipline for success. As a consequence, it is an activity that must be personally carried out by all levels of management, not delegated to "staff" or a separate planning department. Planning must be what all managers, at all levels of the enterprise, do all the time. It must be how managers think, solve problems, and accomplish results.

REALITY

For many enterprises the reality is different. Business planning is only done on a periodic basis, often once every three years, and is highlighted as a special event. In this instance, time is set aside to:
- review the mission of the enterprise and the operational progress that has been made since the last major planning event;
- examine the operating, financial, competitive, and political environment facing the enterprise;
- establish the direction to be taken over the next multi-year period.

Generally, external resources are utilized both to bring apparent expertise to the effort and to facilitate the discussions and overall process. In particular, a facilitator can be useful in assuring that the board is actively involved in examining and subsequently understanding the strategic and operating implications of the enterprise's environment and in confirming the goals to be pursued.

These kinds of strategic planning events introduce the organization to planning, while simultaneously providing the foundation, as the organization evolves, for more fully integrating planning into the enterprise's day-to-day management fabric. They also provide an opportunity to discuss the enterprise's purpose and aspirations as well as to teach the board about the enterprise's business. Importantly, they provide a means of building the social capital (e.g. cooperative spirit, willingness to compromise, and trust one another's ability to collaborate, etc.), necessary for the board members to be able to engage both one another and management, in the kind of robust discussions necessary for value-added decisions.

Often these strategic planning events are organized as board retreats. This approach provides the opportunity both to distinguish them from the regular/ongoing work of the board and to dedicate more time to the matters to be discussed and decided. Between these "strategic planning events," management develops and implements, within the context of the strategic decisions that have been made, ongoing financial and operating plans—reporting results back to the board. Also, if events require it, either management or the board can call for an "off-cycle" planning review.

Periodic planning events are positive organization initiatives. However, the reality of a continually-changing environment makes clear the weakness inherent in a once every "X" years approach to business planning. Simply, because the enterprise's operating world is always changing, to be successful, it must recognize the changes, understand their implications, and if not able to anticipate them, at least react/respond to them. To do this, planning must be an ongoing part of both the board's and management's work.

Other organizations may take an annual approach to strategic planning but use the opportunity more for board capacity building than setting business directions. In these instances, the enterprise is generally in a board development process, and a business planning discussion provides a safe venue for board education and member-to-member board relationship building. Here strategic planning serves both as a vehicle for creating board capacity and capability, and sets the precedent for later, more rigorous and involved strategic and operational planning.

The result of this kind of effort is a stronger board, which understands the purpose of the enterprise, and an agreement on the strategic directions that are going to be pursued. Again, this kind of planning program is a positive initiative. Its weakness is not its frequency, but rather its breadth of analysis and depth of direction. As a capacity building effort, it focuses more on creating general business understandings than on translating those understandings into the elements of strategy.

Business planning can also be a useful tool in times of transition, either because the enterprise is facing a crisis and/or it will be going through a leadership change (i.e., the chief executive will be leaving). In these instances, strategic planning gives the board (and/or new management) an opportunity and mechanism to bring focus to the enterprise in terms of both direction and priority. It also serves as a device for calling particular attention to the fact that the enterprise is facing a unique event, requiring special attention and thought.

As suggested, none of these uses of strategic planning is bad. Each adds something positive to the management and governance of the enterprise. The real goal, however, is to integrate planning into the governance and management of the enterprise. It is this approach that, while perhaps the most difficult, yields the greatest benefits.

TRANSLATION

Stripped of all its mechanics and jargon, planning is a translation activity.[5] It provides a vehicle for managers to translate a mixture of facts, insights, intuition, and dreams into a coherent, focused organizational direction, with specific prioritizing decisions and resulting investments and work actions. (See Exhibit 9-1.)

As a translation process, planning involves communication—vertically, both upward and downward, as well as horizontally. It also requires an interactive dialogue throughout the organization, where ideas, conclusions, and decisions are tested and refined. The result is an understanding of the priorities to be molded into actions and achieved.

Exhibit 9-1

PLANNING	
No Plan	**Plan**
Dreams ⇱ ⇲ Ideas Actions ⇦ Insights ⇨ Facts ⇱ Actions Ideas ⇨ Intuition ⇲	⇨ Dreams ⇨ Intuition ⇨ Facts ⇨ Insights ⇨ Ideas ⇨ Decisions ⇨ Actions ⇨ Strategic Plan ⇨ Operating Plan/Budget ⇨ Program/Project Plan ⇨ Implementation

Planning forces management to express its intangible and subconscious thoughts, as well as subjective and objective (quantitative) data, in logical terms that can then be debated and, if found wanting, modified. Planning provides, and most importantly, provokes the opportunity for management to explain its view as to what the enterprise must do, and why it must do it. At this level, the purpose of planning is to create a common understanding throughout the organization of what must be accomplished and how it is to be achieved.

An understanding of what is to be done is not the same as an agreement on what is needed. Planning cannot assure that there will be universal agreement as to how the enterprise should invest its time and capital. It can, however, achieve a universal understanding of the path that is going to be taken.

Hopefully, both understanding and agreement can be achieved. Management, however, is not a democracy. Everyone's agreement is not mandatory. Failure to achieve a consensus should be taken as a warning sign that the plan may need further debate and work. Lack of consensus, however, is neither a veto of decisions nor an excuse for inaction.

The planning process also involves the translation of management's philosophy and values, and accompanying rhetoric and admonitions, into specific resource allocation decisions. This requires that management and the board declare itself so that priorities can be set, investments made, and resources deployed. The vehicles for doing this are the operating and capital budgets. These budgets are fundamentally another translation process. In this instance, a conversion of the enterprise's plan into measurable financial terms.

How do you translate the statement of mission into achievement of mission? In simple terms, plan, execute, assess, correct; plan, execute, assess, correct; plan, execute...etc.

The planning process is the mechanism for creating and communicating the enterprise's intended actions. The plan is basically a map to be followed in pursuit of the enterprise's mission. It is the organization's guidebook, becoming increasingly specific and detailed both as the enterprise's planning skills, experience, and needs grow and as the process moves deeper into the structure of the organization—from the macro level of mission to the micro detail of functional work units, budgets, and natural expense accounts (e.g., wages and salaries, supplies, travel, etc.).

In spite of its increasing detail, it is a living document that must be continually reviewed and adjusted, as needed. Planning must be an ongoing process. Static plans, regardless of how many contingency scenarios are developed, can never have the relevance of a dynamic planning process that is constantly being tested against actual performance targets and results and continuously refined. It is also why and how planning increases the enterprise's opportunity for success.

LANGUAGE

As both a communication and management process, planning is both a mechanical and intellectual activity. As noted earlier, it involves a series of discrete yet interactive steps leading to decisions and actions. Like many similar processes, it also has its own vocabulary.

While eagerness and curiosity favor immediately pursuing a discussion of mechanics, experience suggests that a better starting point is understanding the language of planning. Just as it is difficult to learn how to sail a boat if you do not understand what a halyard is, and how it differs from a shroud, or the difference between a winch and a block, it is difficult to understand planning without first knowing what business planning, mission, vision, strategic planning, operational planning, goals, objectives, budgets, etc., are, and how these concepts and work products build upon one another, as well as fit together to create the enterprise's strategy.

Admittedly, management terminology can be used differently in different settings (see endnote 9). Recognizing this, the purpose here is to provide an understandable definition of business planning terms and to use them consistently in the following discussion.

Some might take issue with how these terms are used. This misses the point. The focus is not to debate alternative definitions. Rather, it is to enable the reader to understand how a particular term is used and how ideas and actions flow together.

The nature of this problem can be seen just by considering the idea of "strategy."

STRATEGY

Any discussion of strategy begins with an inherent semantic difficulty.[6,7,8] This is because the word is used to convey multiple ideas. It is often used interchangeably with strategic plan and strategic planning, as well as tactics and schemes.[9]

Strategy, strategic plan, and strategic planning, though all part of business planning and sound similar, are not synonymous. Business planning is the comprehensive process whose product is the enterprise's strategy. (See Exhibit 9-2.)

Exhibit 9-2

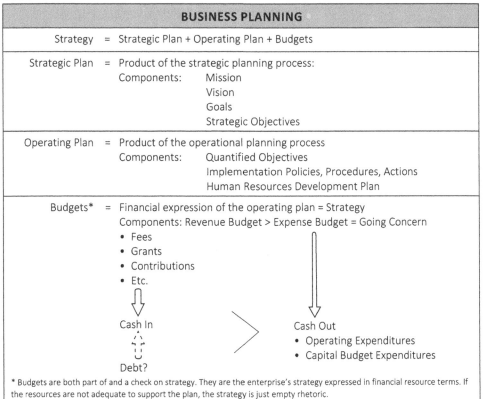

BUSINESS PLANNING		
Strategy	=	Strategic Plan + Operating Plan + Budgets
Strategic Plan	=	Product of the strategic planning process:
		Components: Mission
		Vision
		Goals
		Strategic Objectives
Operating Plan	=	Product of the operational planning process
		Components: Quantified Objectives
		Implementation Policies, Procedures, Actions
		Human Resources Development Plan
Budgets*	=	Financial expression of the operating plan = Strategy
		Components: Revenue Budget > Expense Budget = Going Concern
		• Fees
		• Grants
		• Contributions
		• Etc.

Cash In

Debt?

Cash Out
• Operating Expenditures
• Capital Budget Expenditures

* Budgets are both part of and a check on strategy. They are the enterprise's strategy expressed in financial resource terms. If the resources are not adequate to support the plan, the strategy is just empty rhetoric.

Strategy is the board's and management's answer to the questions of "what" and "how"—what the enterprise intends to do to achieve its mission, and how it intends to do it. Functionally, strategy is the sum of the enterprise's strategic plan (mission, vision, goals, and strategic objectives) and the operational plans and budgets for achieving that strategic plan. The enterprise's basic strategy is management's comprehensive statement of how it is going to achieve the mission of the enterprise, i.e.:

- What is going to be accomplished?

- How it is going to be accomplished?

- How are resources going to be deployed and utilized to get it done?

- At what cost?

WHAT/HOW CASCADE

One way to visualize the flow of the organization's strategy (strategic and operating plans) is to think of strategy as a cascade with one element or component flowing organizationally downhill into the next—asking and answering the questions of "what" and "how."

At the starting point, the enterprise level, the strategic plan defines the "what" that is to be accomplished. The operating plan explains "how" it is to be done. At each successive level of the organization (think in terms of hierarchy of the organizational chart) the tier above describes the "what" and the current tier explains the "how."

As planning cascades down through the organization, the operating plan of one level becomes the strategic direction for the level below. (See Exhibit 9-3.)

The following describes the process that can be utilized to craft this statement, regardless of the organization's size or maturity.

Strategy reaches throughout the organization, from top to bottom, cascading from one level to the next. The operating plan at the corporate or enterprise level provides the strategic guidance for the operating plan for the organizational tier below it, whose operating plan in turn provides the direction for the next level of the organization's operating plan. The process continues, cascading down the organization until it reaches the functional work unit level. At this point it, in effect, reverses itself, with budgets being built at the functional work unit level and rolling back up through the organization, summing into the enterprise's operating budget, which in theory should match the rhetoric and quantification of the strategic and operating plans. (See Exhibit 9-3.)

Exhibit 9-3

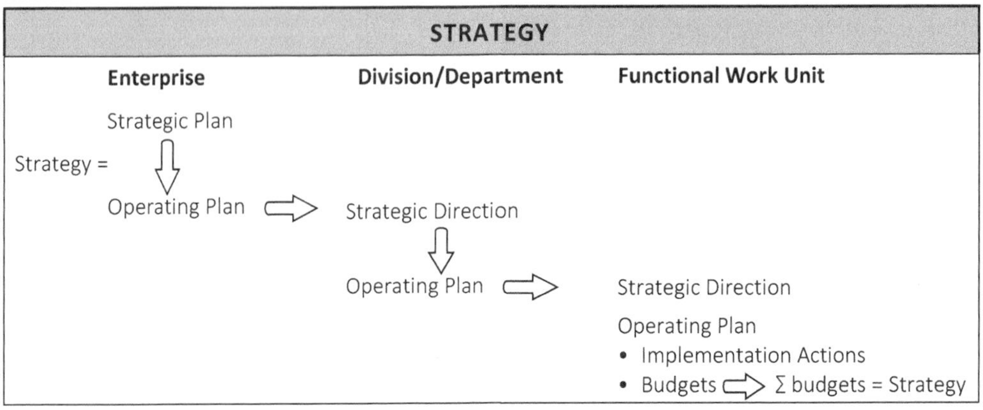

The budget is both a part of and apart from the strategy, providing a check on management's and the board's plans. The budget can be thought of as the strategy expressed in financial terms. Therefore, if management and the board are committed to the strategic and operating plan, the resources necessary to carry it out should be available. The budget provides this reality check. If the budget is inadequate for the needs of the plan, then the plan must be adjusted to fit fiscal reality.

Strategic planning is a process. It is the mechanism for carrying out the strategic management of the enterprise.[10] Its product is the enterprise's strategic plan. The strategic plan is a component of the strategy, setting out in a timeless, overarching, and memorable way the organization's direction (i.e., the direction the enterprise is going to take and the priorities within that direction). Its components are the enterprise's mission, goals, and strategic objectives.

It is timeless in the sense that it has a degree of certainty of destination and stability of direction. In contrast, the enterprise's operating plan will continually change to reflect shifting environmental conditions and actual operating results. In fact, operating plans and budgets are typically reviewed and approved annually, but are modified on an ongoing basis, in effect providing dynamic contingency planning.[11]

The enterprise's strategic plan may also be reviewed annually, but should be less subject to change—providing, as a consequence, stability to the overall strategy. If the enterprise's entire strategy is changing from year to year, then resources are continually being redeployed and motion is being substituted for progress.

The strategic plan should also be overarching, providing a "big enough tent" to include all that the enterprise must do, but at the same time establishing limits so that the enterprise does not try to do all things. Finally, it should be understandable and memorable.

As a communication process, one of the purposes of planning is to try to have the entire organization understand the direction that is being pursued. If the board and staff of the enterprise do not understand and/or cannot remember its strategy, then a basic step in the overall communication process not only falls short, but also erodes the foundation that all of the other elements in the strategic planning process rest upon.

MISSION

The first step in actually building the enterprise's strategy is understanding its mission.[12,13] Mission is the fundamental reason why the enterprise exists. It is the expression of the essence of the organization, setting the direction and providing the impetus that drives the enterprise toward the future. Mission sets out in a brief declarative statement what the organization was created by its founders to do. By omission it also makes clear what the enterprise will not spend its time and resources on.

Mission is an independent variable in the planning process. It is known and not subject to easy change (i.e., approval of the state is needed to change an enterprise's mission).[14] Everything that the enterprise does must be bent to the will of pursuing its stated mission—the condition in society/the community that the enterprise was created to address. Mission is the organization's guide star. (See Exhibit 9-4 for examples of mission statements.)

Exhibit 9-4

MISSION STATEMENT: Examples[15]	
Rehabilitation Hospital	To be a national leader in providing comprehensive rehabilitation services for people with disabilities.
Health Plan	To assure affordable access to effective, needed health services to as many people as possible.
Housing	To end homelessness and preserve affordable housing in the City.
Health System	To deliver health and healing to all people through trusting relationships.
Hospital	To measurably improve health and well-being of all people in Franklin County and neighboring towns, using a coordinated approach of education, health promotion, and outreach.
Nursing Home	To compassionately and affordably care for our community's elderly.
Social Service Agency	• To assist people who are blind or visually impaired to achieve their highest level of independence in all aspects of their lives. • To help women at a crisis or turning point move beyond the challenge of poverty, hunger, unemployment, homelessness, drug and alcohol dependency, and teenage motherhood.
Collective Fundraiser	As an organization of donors, our mission is to motivate and organize people to work for a better life for all by meeting our community's most important human care needs.
American Red Cross	To provide relief to victims of disasters and help people prevent, prepare for, and respond to emergencies.
YWCA	Eliminating racism, empowering women, and promoting peace, justice, freedom, and dignity for all.
Aging Services Agency	To provide services that help older adults take on both the challenges and opportunities of longer life.
Settlement House	To provide a foundation for growth, empowerment, and stability for those in our community.
Food Pantry	To provide hunger relief, eliminate the root causes of hunger, improve health, and promote economic development.
Nonprofit Agency Association	To be a membership organization that informs, inspires, and supports the nonprofit executive who strives to lead with excellence.

VISION

The enterprise's vision flows from its mission. It is built upon mission but shaped by the imagination of the board as filtered through the realities of the enterprise's operating environment.

Mission reflects the purpose of the enterprise, as seen by its founders. Current boards are often far removed from the enterprise's founders and the needs and emotions that guided their framing of the organization's mission. Similarly, the original mission statement, over time, inevitably risks becoming dated. Periodically crafting an enterprise level vision statement provides a mechanism for addressing these issues. It enables the current board to shape the enterprise's direction and to become invested in that decision. By, elaborating on the mission statement, it enables the purpose for which the enterprise was originally established to remain relevant, contemporary, and emotionally attractive.

> **WHAT COMES FIRST— MISSION OR VISION?**
>
> Arguably when an enterprise is first being conceived, the emotional vision of what is needed, what might be possible, and the hopes to be pursued, precede any formal statement of mission. However, once legally established, the enterprise's stated mission becomes a fixed, independent factor, only changeable through court proceedings.
>
> Vision thus precedes mission and then logically flows from it.
>
> Functionally, enterprise vision can be portrayed as either coming before or after mission. It makes little difference because the two—mission and vision—have to be aligned and linked.
>
> Vision is presented here as following mission simply to make clearer the logic of the business planning sequential flow.

The enterprise's strategic vision statement has two major elements, an enterprise level vision created primarily by the board and reflecting its dreams and hopes, and a managerial vision statement.

Managerial vision can also be thought of as consisting of two components: strategic vision and tactical vision. Strategic vision, in turn, can be thought of as consisting of two intertwined elements. One is management's theory of change. The other is what management envisions the enterprise becoming and doing.

The two pieces in practice fuse into a single concept. For the sake of discussion, theory of change is management's idea of how to move from the current condition or status, to achievement of mission or at least progress toward achievement of mission.

For example, the management of an enterprise whose mission is to improve the performance of nonprofit organizations might have as its theory of change—improving board performance. Its strategic vision then would be to be a leader in governance education and support. The two ideas become one, in the form of management's strategic vision (i.e., the focus on governance education builds on the concept of improved board performance as the catalyst for improved enterprise performance).

> **STABILITY VS. CHANGE**
>
> How often the board should review and revise the enterprise vision statement depends on the traditions of the enterprise, changes in the operating environment, and the needs of the current board versus the value of organizational operational stability. The needs of the current board may be the most powerful of all the factors. The enterprise vision statement is the current board's expression of its aspirations for what it hopes can be done and achieved. Therefore, while consistency is a strong force, it pales when confronted by the emotion of dreams.

Another example can be seen in the strategic vision of a hospital. (See Exhibit 9-5.) The hospital's mission is "to measurably improve health and well-being of people in Franklin County." Management's theory of change would be: "Improved health status requires a combination of social, human, and clinical services." For an Aging Services Agency, the mission might be "to provide services that help older adults to take on both the challenges and opportunities of longer life." Management's theory of change could be a "recognition that retirement is morphing from a sedate and recreational phase of life to an active Third Phase—between adulthood (Phase Two) and old age (Phase Four)."

In counterpoint to strategic vision, tactical vision is management's perspective on how it is going to do things; how it is going to organize and deploy resources to achieve what the enterprise wants to accomplish. Enterprise vision is the board's statement of its aspirations for the enterprise. It is a statement that is borne of the board and owned by it. In contrast, management creates and owns its vision for the organization, both strategic and tactical. The two are linked in that management supports the board in creating the enterprise's vision. The board, in turn, provides oversight and ultimately approval of management's vision. This check and balance assures that the two efforts are not just simply consistent, but mutually supportive.

Exhibit 9-5 provides additional examples of enterprise and managerial strategic vision statements. In reviewing the exhibit, it is important to realize that there is no one right answer to what board or management vision should be. Moreover, the process is fluid and complementary and that in some instances the same answer can serve dual purposes. Finally, in crafting a vision statement the board must take care to assure that its efforts do not result in mission drift (i.e., the enterprise slipping away from the fundamental reason for which it was created). To this end, management and the board must always remember that the vision flows from mission and must therefore always fit within the larger sphere of activities as defined by the enterprise's founding purpose. Understanding this, the key is less the actual rhetoric of the statements than the process of asking the questions and testing the answers. One step must flow into the next with each subsequent step supporting the previous one—and all grounded in the bedrock of mission.

Starting with mission, the enterprise's strategy is the product of two processes that flow seamlessly from one into the other.

The first of these is the "Strategic Process." Its product is the enterprise's strategic plan (i.e., the overarching statement of the organization's mission, vision, goals, and strategic objectives). The second is the "Tactical Process." Its work product is the operating plan (i.e., the statement of the organization's quantified objectives and planned actions for achieving those objectives, including its capital and operating (revenue and expense) budgets).

The strategic plan identifies where the enterprise has determined it needs to have impact in order to achieve its mission. The operating plan refines these directional judgments, specifying what is going to be done to accomplish the desired impact. Finally, strategy and plans are turned into reality, as a third process, implementation, details how the desired impact is going to be realized.

The strategic process reflects the art of management. The tactical process reflects the science. The step beyond planning, the implementation process, goes from preparation (planning) to execution (implementation), also reflecting the science of management.

Exhibit 9-5

STRATEGIC VISION: EXAMPLES	
HOSPITAL	
Mission	To measurably improve health and well-being of all people in Franklin County and neighboring towns, using a coordinated approach of education, health promotion, and outreach.
Enterprise Vision	To cure hopelessness.
Managerial Strategic Vision	To combine public health and clinical services in a mix that increases community health status.
NURSING HOME	
Mission	To compassionately and affordably care for our community's elderly.
Enterprise Vision	To enable people to remain in the most independent living environment for as long as safely possible.
Managerial Strategic Vision	Alternative 1: Same as enterprise vision. Alternative 2: To bring services to where people live, relocating clients as a last resort.
HOUSING	
Mission	To end homelessness and preserve affordable housing in the City.
Enterprise Vision	To become the largest manager/owner of low-income housing in the City.
Managerial Strategic Vision	To use architectural and technological innovation to create aesthetically attractive, affordable rental housing.
AGING SERVICE	
Mission	To provide services that help older adults take on both the challenges and opportunities of longer life.
Enterprise Vision	To capture the growing human resource of the healthy elderly to improve the community's quality of life.
Managerial Strategic Vision	To build virtual markets that will enable the supply of healthy elderly to be matched with paid and unpaid opportunities.
HEALTH PLAN	
Mission	To assure affordable access to effective, needed health services to as many people as possible.
Enterprise Vision	To become a national model, demonstrating how a health plan can build a healthier community.
Managerial Strategic Vision	To combine health care finance with a wholly-owned ambulatory care delivery system to serve as an incubator for testing and demonstrating new approaches to effective, needed care.

Exhibit 9-5 continued on next page.

Exhibit 9-5 continued

HEALTH SYSTEM	
Mission	To deliver health and healing to all people through trusting relationships.
Enterprise Vision	Build healthy communities.
Managerial Strategic Vision	Use revenue from clinical services to build community-based preventative services.
FOOD PANTRY	
Mission	To provide hunger relief, eliminate the root cause of hunger, improve health, and promote economic development.
Enterprise Vision	Empower individuals through nutritional and agricultural programs.
Managerial Strategic Vision	Pursue a dual task of: • Creating food distribution networks and • Building sustainable urban agricultural programs.
NONPROFIT AGENCY ASSOCIATION	
Mission	To be a membership organization that informs, inspires, and supports the nonprofit executive who strives to lead with excellence.
Enterprise Vision	Create a more vibrant and caring community through nonprofit management excellence.
Managerial Strategic Vision	Train senior leaders, build networks, develop supporting infrastructure.

GOALS

If mission and vision are the starting points, the next step in translating mission into results is the identification of the enterprise's goals.

Mission identifies the purpose of the enterprise, and the enterprise's vision statement gives emotional life and contemporary bearing to that purpose. Establishing goals begins the process of specifying how mission is to be achieved. Goals are high-level, non-quantified statements, (i.e., neither detailed nor prescriptive), that set out general areas where effort is to be focused. Because they begin to bring focus, they should be limited to a manageable number (e.g., three to five). It is important to limit the number of goals. Human nature is such that only a limited number of choices can be productively managed. If too many areas are identified as goals, both the reason for planning (i.e., to make choices as to how the enterprise is going to move forward), is defeated and motion is substituted for progress.

Goals are the component elements of mission. Therefore, they are priority areas where results must be produced if mission is to be achieved. (See Exhibit 9–6 for examples of the flow from mission to goals.)

Exhibit 9-6

STRATEGIC VISION: EXAMPLES	
HOSPITAL	
Mission	To be a national leader in providing comprehensive rehabilitation services for people with disabilities.
Goals	Be a preferred technology site for post-graduate medical education. Advance the potential for people with disabilities to live independently.
HOUSING	
Mission	To end homelessness and preserve affordable housing in the City.
Goals	Increase the stock of affordable, low income housing.
	Establish social and financial safety nets to prevent the loss of residence.
HEALTH PLAN	
Mission	To assure affordable access to effective, needed health service to as many people as possible.
Goals	Increase both market share and absolute numbers of members, both individuals and groups.
	Assure financial stability.
	Make a difference to the people and quality of life in the community.
SOCIAL SERVICE	
Mission	To assist people who are blind or visually impaired to achieve their highest level of independence in all aspects of their lives.
Goals	Enhance education opportunities for all visually impaired people.
	Maximize the use of technology for both independent living and career opportunities. Increase the employment rate among people who are blind or visually impaired.
COLLECTIVE FUNDER	
Mission	As an organization of donors, our mission is to motivate and organize people to create a better life for all by meeting our community's most important human care needs.
Goals	Increase the financial support provided by the community.
	Increase the volunteer support provided by the community.
SETTLEMENT HOUSE	
Mission	To provide a foundation for growth, empowerment, and stability for those in our community.
Goals	Offer employment skill development resources for single parents.
	Provide after-school and weekend academic resources/programs.

STRATEGIC OBJECTIVES

As the enterprise's declaration of focus, goals identify broad areas for work without providing quantitative measures or time frames. Even so, they are vital in that they both:

- set direction, translating mission into major areas where results must be accomplished, and

- set the stage for the next step in the planning process—setting of objectives.

STRATEGIC OBJECTIVES AND ORGANIZATIONAL TENSION

Strategic objectives identify key areas where results must be obtained if progress is to be made toward achieving the enterprise's mission. Strategic objectives, however, must also provide the organization with operational energy. They do this by creating a degree of organizational tension, requiring that objectives be balanced against one another with tradeoffs being made to harmonize performance and maximize overall results.

If, for example, a health plan's only strategic objective is focused on growth, it could achieve its objective by simply reducing price—to a level below costs. The ultimate consequence of such an approach would be economic failure. Alternatively, if the focus is on both growth and making money, then a balance has to be achieved between two intrinsically competing objectives. Striking this balance brings energy to the organization in that competing interests must find a form of compromise that enables the enterprise to maximize its progress toward its mission.

Objectives are subsets of goals. They are specific areas of concentration within each goal area where results must be achieved to ultimately accomplish the goal. Objectives, in turn, can be thought of as falling into two categories: strategic and quantitative.

Strategic objectives, not surprisingly, are part of the enterprise's strategic plan. Quantified objectives are the foundation of the enterprise's operating plan. The two differ in terms of specificity and quantification. Strategic objectives are non-quantified statements of focus. They identify an operational area where results are to be achieved, without quantifying the exact result. In contrast, quantified objectives specify both the area of focus and the exact result sought/expected to be achieved.

Consider the examples of Exhibit 9-6. For a health plan, one of the example goals is to "increase both market share and the absolute number of members." The strategic objective flowing from this goal could be to improve the retention of current customers—both individuals and groups.

A quantified objective could then be to increase the retention of customers, in the individual market segment, year over year, by 2%.

Similarly, for a collective fundraising enterprise with a goal of "increasing the volunteer support provided by the community," the strategic objective could be "create more awareness among local college students of the importance of a volunteer service experience to their overall education." The quantified objective flowing from this strategic objective might then be: implement at least two community-engaged learning programs in the next 12 months; increase local college student volunteer service hours by 1% over the next 12 months. (This might be a better quantified objective because it addresses a measurable output—not just a process activity.)

More will be said later about quantified objectives. For the moment, the emphasis is on strategic objectives and recognizing the character of the flow from mission to goal, to strategic objectives.[16] That is, the translation process that takes place in moving from the motivating and embracing statements of mission and vision to the specific focus of strategic objectives.

To assure that focus is maintained, strategic objectives, like goals, should also be limited in number. If goals are limited to three to five and each goal in turn has three or four strategic objectives, the enterprise is now focused on nine to 20 priorities. Adding two or three quantified objectives to each strategic objective increases the number of initiatives to 18 to 60. The reality is simply that the number of focused projects must be tempered to match the enterprise's resources—both skills and size, and quantity and quality. Failure to do this dooms the business plan process to being an exercise in wishfulness, more a work of fiction than a doable statement of what is to be accomplished.

ENVIRONMENTAL ASSESSMENT

In considering the strategic planning process, two other factors must be added to the discussion—if the resulting plan is to be more than just a philosophical statement or an elegy on hope.

First, it must be recognized that the formulation of goals and strategic objectives is not simply an excursion in logic. Rather, it is the application of logic to the dispassionate analysis of the enterprise's environment—as modified by the aspirations of the board and the imagination of management.

Analysis of the environment is generally known as an environmental assessment. Managerial imagination can be thought of, in this context, as "strategic vision."

Environmental assessment and vision are related activities. Mission sets the overall direction of the enterprise. However, the analysis of the environment, the board's vision of what the enterprise can accomplish (enterprise vision), and management's vision of what the enterprise can become or do (strategic vision), shape the actual goals and objectives that will be pursued.

The overall strategic planning process is summarized in the illustrations of Exhibit 9-7.

In Part 1, mission and the environmental assessment are presented as independent variables. Mission is an independent variable because it is established as part of the enterprise's creation and cannot be significantly changed without the approval of the state.

Environmental assessment is similarly an independent variable because it is the objective cataloging and measuring of the facts and conditions that exist at a point in time and which must be recognized if the enterprise is to be able to succeed. The environment is continually changing. Therefore, environmental assessment should be a continuous process—with the enterprise's plans changing as needed. However, at any given moment, mission and environment are fixed—not subject to being changed by the immediate actions of the board and or management.

Part 2 of the Exhibit illustrates the same process. It differs from Part 1 in that, while showing the same major components, it emphasizes context and analytical imagination.

In Part 2, "Definitions" are added as an independent variable to make clear the importance of common understandings to productive communications. Frankly, without a foundation of common understanding, the business planning process while not doomed to failure, is going to be frustrating to the participants and unnecessarily inefficient.

Guidelines are also included as an independent variable to make explicit the usefulness establishing standards and values to promote or limit actions (e.g., prohibition against making commercial product endorsements or understanding that as client neighborhoods shift, services must follow them.

Catalytic variables are amplified to show that the board and management must apply:
- analytical skill to translate the environmental assessment's data into operating assumptions and

- the imagination to distill from the total (of vision, threats, and opportunities) the strategic and operating implications upon which the common agreements necessary for decisions and actions can be reached.

Goals and strategic objectives are dependent variables, shaped by the decisions of the board and management. Strategic vision, like leadership, is a catalytic variable, the lens that mission and the assessment of the environment pass through to bring goals and strategic objectives into focus (i.e., to identify the areas where things need to be done).

Exhibit 9-7 part 1

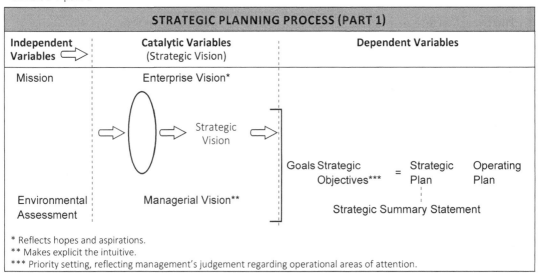

* Reflects hopes and aspirations.
** Makes explicit the intuitive.
*** Priority setting, reflecting management's judgement regarding operational areas of attention.

Exhibit 9-7 part 2

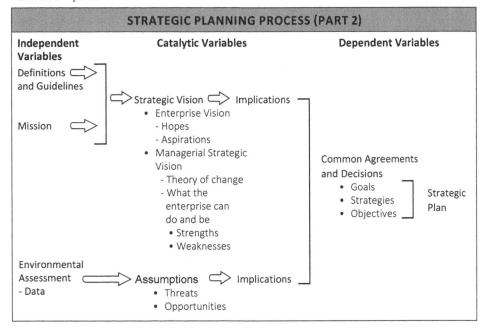

Environmental assessment is fundamentally an analysis of reality. Traditionally, it is viewed as being a review and evaluation of the enterprise's strengths, weaknesses, opportunities, and threats (SWOT analysis).

SWOT analysis is a workable process, having the potential to provide a realistic picture of the organization within the context of its regulatory and competitive environment. Its strength lies in its directness. Its weakness is in its lack of a systematic structure and the resulting possibility for analytical gaps.

An alternative approach to assessing the organization's environment is depicted in Exhibit 9-8. Here, environmental variables are organized as a three by two (3x2) matrix, focusing on external and internal forces, and independent, dependent, and wild card factors.

The principal benefit of the matrix approach is that it provides a systematic structure for drawing conclusions about the enterprise's environment. Either approach can work, producing the managerial dialog needed to distill conclusions about the potential impact of the enterprise's environment on its operations, performance, and priorities. Either approach also holds some similar risks of data overflow and less than rigorous analysis. To guard against the paralysis of too much data, specifically identified environmental factors must be tested against the dual questions of "does it really matter"—and, if so, "what is its real importance (priority)?" An item may be interesting, but not on the organization's critical path. Items fully in this category can be noted but must ultimately be discarded. Items falling on the critical path must then be tested in terms of their priority. The simple reality is, not everything can be of the highest priority. Similarly, the organization can accommodate only a finite number of priorities. This requires that some difficult decisions be made so that the enterprise's attention and resources are not diluted to the point of being ineffective.

Exhibit 9-8

ENVIRONMENTAL ASSESSMENT MATRIX		
	External*	Internal**
Independent (Fixed)	Demographics Technology Legislative/Regulatory	Products/Services
Dependent (Influenceable)	Legislation Regulation Labor Market Funding • Grants • Contracts • Market-Based Resources	Capital • Human • Financial • Physical Products/Services Internal Policies • Pricing • Credit and Collection • Investments Brand Equity Board
Wild Card	Emergency/Disaster, i.e. Pandemic Competition • Action/Reaction	Relationships • Partners • Community Awareness
*External—opportunities and threats **Internal—strengths and weaknesses		

Regardless of the approach, the environmental assessment is a productive place for board education as well as board involvement in strategy formulation. It provides the board, not only with the opportunity to better "learn the business and fulfill its stewardship and agency obligations," but also provides management with a structured approach for gaining the board's insights into the organization's strategic direction. The board's involvement also helps to establish their ownership in the process and its resulting decisions. Most importantly, the board's input enhances management's ability to make sound, even if difficult, decisions.

The net result is an understanding of the threats and opportunities confronting the enterprise and the internal capacities and capabilities available to meet those threats or capitalize on the potential opportunities. All of this is valuable data. However, until it passes through the lens of managerial vision, the areas where action should and can be undertaken are still unclear.

MANAGERIAL VISION

If environmental assessment is the dispassionate, fact-based, analytical component of the strategic planning process, management's strategic vision, as discussed earlier, is the intangible, seemingly "intuitive" element.

Management's vision, both strategic and tactical, is perhaps the most powerful piece in the overall planning process. Its power comes from the fact that it is the point where management brings its unique perspective, insights, and hopes for what the enterprise can become and achieve, to the shaping of its operational direction. By reaching high, it is the factor that begins the chain of events that separates successful enterprises from the "also-rans."

> **STRATEGIC AND TACTICAL VISION**
>
> Managerial vision can be thought of as being of two types: strategic and tactical. Strategic vision brings focus to the strategic plan. Tactical vision brings focus to the operating plan (see next chapter). They differ in that strategic vision sees opportunities that the environment presents. Tactical vision sees the ways for the enterprise to capture those opportunities.
>
> The two are similar in that they both spring from insight and imagination. They are also similar in that they both require the seemingly intuitive to be made explicit.

Articulating "strategic vision" can be a difficult task. It requires, within the vision for the enterprise, that management makes explicit its intangible, subjective understandings of what the organization is capable of, what it can do, and what it must do strategically to get there. It also requires that management engage the board in addressing these same questions so that a common strategic understanding is crafted.

Typically, board members both seek and appreciate being involved in establishing the enterprise's vision and participating in developing the organization's strategic vision. As noted earlier, visualizing what the enterprise should aspire to be resonates with individual board members' basic emotional commitment to the organization and their reason for becoming a board member. It is also a comfortable topic of discussion, centered more on imagination and insight than detailed, technical, subject matter knowledge. Therefore, it is an ideal discussion subject for board retreats—and for building social capital between and among board members.

At the same time, it should also be recognized that while boards and individual board members want to, and should be involved in crafting the enterprise's vision, it must be an exercise in guided discovery by the enterprise's leadership. This requires that management be open and non-defensive. Ideas must be offered, explained, and then hardened in the crucible of debate.

The same discussions that take place at the board level must also happen at the management/staff level. The timing of these discussions is delicate. They must precede the board's conversations, as preparation for that debate, and then follow it as preparation for implementation of the decisions. Again, a degree of managerial openness and courage is required. While the enterprise is not a one-person, one-vote democracy, successful executives understand that success is maximized through an open process with meaningful stakeholder recognition and merit—not hierarchical position-driven decisions.

Management's strategic vision brings focus to the strategic plan. It is the transformational catalyst that moves the hopes and aspirations underlying mission into the reality of the strategic plan.

While reflecting the art of management, vision does not involve a magical eye. Rather, it is the result of managers absorbing the realities of their stakeholder's current needs and future preferences, combining that understanding with a recognition of the enterprise's capabilities, capacities, and possibilities, and then translating it all into a statement of what can be achieved if everyone committed themselves to that end. (See Exhibit 9-9.)

Vision, in all of its manifestations and at all levels, is the spark in the planning process that brings clarity, passion, and excitement to the work of the enterprise.

Exhibit 9-9

ENVIRONMENTAL ASSESSMENT AND STRATEGIC PLAN

Environmental Assessment*	Results in a Statement of Priority ⇨	Establishes areas of concentration, within each goal where results should be achieved	Strategic Plan (What results are needed to accomplish mission)
Identifies: • Opportunities • Threats ⇨ • Strengths* • Weaknesses*	Operational Needs (Goals)	(Strategic Objectives)	=

⇧

Management's Strategic Vision

* Strengths and weaknesses shape quantified objectives—see Chapter 10.

END PRODUCT

The end product of this effort is the enterprise's strategic plan—the statement of its mission and vision, and the sum of its goals and strategic objectives. Obviously, this can be a substantial document, difficult for a person to hold in their "walking around memory." Therefore, as noted earlier, if the planning process is to work best as an organization-wide communication initiative, the strategic plan must also be converted into a summary statement that can be easily remembered as the common answer to the question of: "What is the strategy?" This means that the strategic plan must be translated into a sound bite.

For lack of a better label, this sound bite can be thought of as the organization's strategic summary. It is a short and memorable statement that captures the essence of the plan. It is both broad enough to encompass all

---

WAS IT WORTH IT?

How do you test if the planning effort has been worthwhile? This is a difficult question to answer either quantitatively or definitively. The best that you can do is try to answer two questions:

1. Has the effort added value?

2. Will the resulting plan keep the organization from doing the wrong thing?

If these questions can be answered yes, while there are no guarantees, the enterprise is likely on the right path.

of the enterprise's goals and objectives, yet specific enough to suggest where the focus of work will be directed.

Drawing on Exhibit 9–5, an example of the strategic summary for the health plan could be:

- "Grow, make money, and make a difference." or

- "The right services, in the right place, at the right time."

For a collective fundraiser the strategic summary could be:

- "Through the gifts of time and money, create better lives."

The strategic summary for the rehabilitation hospital could be:

- "Be the nation's rehabilitation hospital of choice for: research, education, and patient care."

Similarly, the strategic summary for the settlement house might be:

- "Enhancing the quality of life, one person, one family at a time."

The above are simply examples. They illustrate the point, however, that the strategic plan can be encapsulated in a compelling way, setting direction while simultaneously evoking emotion.

The next step is to add the next level of detail, to set operational performance specifics (i.e., what is to be done and when it is to be done by). This requires the creation of the operating plan—the second major component of the enterprise's strategy. (See Exhibit 10-1.)

Exhibit 9-10

STRATEGIC THINKING: A SIMPLE EXERCISE

How do you think strategically? It is a simple question that has a difficult answer. To get a feel for strategic thinking consider the following:

We have all played tic-tac-toe, the game where the goal is to connect three "Xs" or "Os" in a row.

Players alternate moves, considering what their opponent has done, what he or she might do, and then deciding their own move.

Now, change the goal. How would the game be different if the goal was to not lose? A tie is as good as a win. How does this change your thinking? The new thought process is an example of strategic thinking.

Now, change the goal again. How would the game be different if the goal was to force your opponent into having to get three in a row? In this instance, you lose if you are forced to link three in a row or if the game ends in a tie. How does this change your thinking?

Strategic thinking is an exercise in looking ahead and, based on your appraisal of the environment (what your competitor has done and might do in the future), identifying a set of actions (and possible alternatives) to achieve a predetermined goal.

CHAPTER 9

Takeaways and Questions for Consideration and Discussion:

TAKEAWAYS

1. Enterprise strategy is the sum of the strategic plan (tells what is hoped to be done) plus the operating plan (tells how it is hoped to be done) and the budget (adds reality to the hopes and wishes).

2. Strategic planning should be done periodically, operational planning should be done annually. (Strategy should be stable. Tactics and operating plans should be dynamic.)

3. It is the planning process, not the planning document that adds value. The process provides a vehicle for a combination of disciplined analysis and creative imagination, to establish direction and metrics to measure how well the enterprise is moving in that direction. However, planning does not guarantee operational success.

QUESTIONS

1. Can the enterprise succeed without having a plan?

2. Why is business planning complex? How can it be simplified? How can it be made manageable for the small enterprise?

3. How do enterprise vision and managerial vision complement one another?

4. How does the environmental assessment bring clarity to the strategic plan?

Chapter 10:
OPERATIONAL PLANNING

The enterprise's strategic plan sets the foundation for its operating plan. Together, the strategic and operating plans describe the enterprise's strategy. Separately, the strategic plan provides the organization with a certainty of destination, a stability of direction, and a sense of priorities. The operating plan provides the specificity of what will be done, and how and when it will be accomplished. It is the keystone both for the board's oversight of the enterprise and management's direction of operations.

> **STRATEGIC PLAN ⇨ OPERATING PLAN**
>
> Another way to think about the flow of activity is to view the strategic plan as identifying areas of priority (i.e., goals), and then more precisely, strategic objectives.
>
> The operating plan gives further definition to the areas by specifying outcomes; exact measures of what will be accomplished and how it will be realized.

How does management move the organization to the operating plan's level of specificity? The answer centers on continuing the translation process that guided the development of the strategic plan. The flow, however, starts not with mission, but rather with strategic objectives and continues to the preparation of the operating and capital budgets.

Before considering the details of this process it is useful to recognize that if strategic planning is thought of as involving the "art" of management, operational planning's focus is on the "science" of management. Operational planning is tactical management. That is, it is the process of identifying the specific results to be achieved, and the methods and procedures for how the enterprise will organize and deploy its resources to accomplish those results. The enterprise's operating plan builds on its strategic plan, providing the specificity necessary to guide actual work, measure results, and take corrective actions.

STARTING

Exhibit 10-1 depicts the major elements in the operational planning process. It starts where strategic planning ends. The principal dependent variable of the strategic planning process, the enterprise's strategic objectives, becomes, along with the environmental assessment, the independent variables of the operational planning process. The dependent variable, the work product, is the planned operational results (i.e., outcomes: accomplishments, costs, and due dates). The sum of all the components is the enterprise's operating plan and budgets.

The previous discussion has explored how an organization identifies its strategic objectives, the specific areas of concentration within each goal area where results must be achieved to reach the goal. The operational planning challenge is to translate strategic objectives into quantified objectives. To accomplish this, management must bring two other factors into the equation. First, the previously discussed environmental assessment; second, its tactical vision of what the enterprise needs to do and can do to realize that end.

Exhibit 10-1

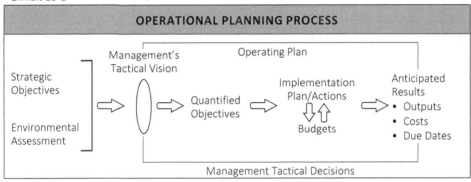

With respect to the environmental assessment, the components of most importance at this point are the evaluation of the organization's internal capacity and capability (i.e., strengths and weaknesses) along with an understanding of the challenges (threats) facing the enterprise and their timing, seriousness, and likelihood. These components must be brought forward into operational planning, because pragmatic decisions must be made about what specific results are going to be sought. These decisions must be grounded in reality—not wishfulness.

The environmental assessment provides data; it does not make decisions. Decisions are made by people, and in this context, while ultimately reviewed and approved by the board, they are made by management. To do this, management must bring its tactical vision of what the enterprise needs to do, and can do, into the decision-making process so that it can identify the specific results to be pursued. Here again, pragmatism must be a guiding force. However, it must be mixed with the imagination and confidence to push the organization beyond its operational comfort zone—anything else irresponsibly limits what the enterprise is able to accomplish for its stakeholders.

QUANTIFIED OBJECTIVES

Quantified objectives are the result of the interplay of these three factors: strategic objectives, environmental assessment, and management's tactical vision. Quantified objectives give reliable, measurable specificity to strategic objectives. They make clear "what," within the strategic objective, is to be accomplished, and by when. They, in effect, give priority to the multiple facets of a strategic objective, singling out the exact result(s) to be achieved.

HUMAN RESOURCES DEVELOPMENT PLAN*

As depicted in Exhibit 9-2, a component of the operating plan is the enterprise's human resources development plan (i.e., the statement of quantified objectives for human capital).

Often when executives are asked, "What is your organization's most valuable asset?" the answer is "Our people." While everyone working in the enterprise likes this answer, if it is to be more than rhetoric it must be supported by actions and results.

A vehicle for accomplishing this is the enterprise's human resources development plan. The enterprise level plan is the amalgam of each employee's individual development plan (IDP). IDPs can be generalized for some levels of the organization (e.g., all entry-level positions take a basic organization and enterprise orientation course) or specific (e.g., the chief financial officer should join an industry leadership group).

The purpose of the plan is simply to identify and agree upon the actions that will enhance individual skills and performance as well as enterprise performance. For the plan to be real, like other operating plan components, its objectives, actions, and results must be:

- supported by budget allocations and
- monitored as part of the operating plan oversight process.

* See Chapter 14, Succession Management, for further discussion and details of human resources development planning.

Most importantly, quantified objectives provide the core of what boards need to fulfill their oversight accountability and what managers need to guide operations. Without them, an enterprise is both aimless and rudderless.

Exhibit 10-2 provides several examples of the translation of strategic objectives to quantified objectives. (These examples flow from the earlier exhibits in Chapter 9.) They also highlight the importance of assuring that quantified objectives focus on outputs—measurable, mission related, results—not process or product inputs.[1] For example, a quantified objective for a charter school might be graduation rates (or better yet, college matriculation rates), not attendance levels. Similarly, for a museum, a quantified objective could be attendance growth, not the increase in the number of exhibits opened during the year.

This focus on outputs is important from two perspectives. First, quantified objectives push the organization in terms of efficiency and performance balance. By setting quantified objectives at a level that forces the organization to try to reach beyond its historical grasp, they provide the impetus for continuous performance improvement. Similarly, by creating organizational tension, by establishing mutually modifying/conflicting results (i.e., grow and increase capital), they force an operational harmony that yields an overall balance of results.

Second, as discussed in more depth in the next chapter, quantified objectives set the foundation, not only for assessing the enterprise in terms of operational performance (Did it do what it said it was going to do,

---

OUTCOMES AND OUTPUTS*

In setting quantified objectives, the difference between outputs and outcomes is key. Outcomes are the desired end results that are being sought. Strategic objectives reflect outcomes (i.e., increased awareness of the importance of volunteer service, improved customer retention, provide subsidized housing, etc.). Quantified objectives identify outputs, the intermediate component deliverables that need to be successfully stitched together to achieve the desired outcome.

* William B. Werther, Jr., and Evan M. Berman, Third Sector Management, (Washington, D.C.: Georgetown University Press, 2000), Chapter 7.

and did it do it in an efficient manner?), but also in terms of stakeholder impact (Did its actions make a significant difference?). Actions produce outputs. Outputs produce outcomes. Outcomes, through research–based evaluative processes, can be expressed in terms of impact (i.e., are the actions being taken and the resulting outputs making a statistically significant, measurable difference in terms of the achievement of the enterprise's mission?[2])

Unfortunately, evaluating impact, in spite of its quantitative precision, may yield confusing, if not, deceptive judgments and counterproductive consequences; chilling innovation as opposed to increasing effectiveness.[3] Recognizing this, as well as the community sector's reality that clear measures of performance cannot be found in the comfort of financial or other quantitative metrics, proxies and judgment must be used as alternatives. The most powerful of these performance proxies are the agreed upon quantified objectives. These objectives reflect management's judgment of what is both important and can be done. However, as noted above, they also must reflect results that can make a significant difference.

Returning to the museum example, opening new exhibits may be important to increasing attendance. However, it is an input that helps lead to the result of increased attendance—that in turn helps make the museum relevant to its community.

Exhibit 10-2

EXAMPLE QUANTIFIED OBJECTIVES	
Health Plan	• Strategic Objective: Improve the retention of current customers—both individual and groups.
	• Quantified Objective: Increase the retention of current customers, in the individual market segment, year over year, by 2%.
Collective Fundraiser	• Strategic Objective: Create more awareness among local college students of the importance of a volunteer service experience to their overall education.
	• Quantified Objective: Increase community-engaged learning program participation by at least 100 students within the next 12 months.
Social Service Agency	• Strategic Objective: Provide adaptive technology to the blind and visually impaired community.
	• Quantified Objective: Within the next year provide Braille computer keyboards to all K-12 blind and visually impaired students in the community.
Housing	• Strategic Objective: Provide subsidized housing for single parents.
	• Quantified Objective: ▪ Increase the number of single-parent, affordable housing units, in the catchment area, by 50 units within the next 12 months. ▪ Achieve an occupancy rate of 93+% in the total supply, including the new units—as they become available—of single-parent units.
Settlement House	• Strategic Objective: Provide academic math support to middle school students in the resource program.
	• Quantified Objective: Increase average score on the 8th grade math test by 5% over last year.

Quantified objectives, in addition to defining what is to be done, provide the platform for the next steps in the planning process—creating the implementation plan (i.e., determining actions and then testing and refining those actions for effectiveness and efficiency). (See Exhibit 10-3.)

ACTIONS

Determining the actions to be pursued to achieve the quantified objectives is an application of tactical decision making. It focuses on determining how, in what quantity resources should be organized, and when they should be deployed. Making successful choices on these questions requires both resource management skills and analytical skills.

> **VISION TO TACTICS**
> **STRATEGIC PLAN TO OPERATING PLAN**
>
> The flow from the strategic plan to the operating plan also explicitly involves a shift in the required management skills. The enterprise strategic plan is driven by management's strategic vision, communication skills, and ability to inspire. In contrast, the operating plan is guided by management's tactical skills. That is, the ability to determine what to do and then how to do it.

In reality, actually determining what to do to realize the intended quantified objectives is often a more difficult task than might initially be assumed. Part of the problem lies in the ambiguous relationship between outputs and outcomes. As noted, actions or sets of actions produce outputs. Outputs, in turn, result in outcomes. The contribution of each output to the ultimate outcome, however, is difficult to assess.

Part of the problem is due to the inherent issues in validly and reliably quantifying the benefits produced by an action or set of actions and the resulting outcomes. The limits of the metrics for quantifying benefits, let alone benefits versus costs, makes quantitative analysis a speculative task—one that should only be pursued with care, understanding that an answer to the "second decimal point" may be no more, and even less, accurate than seasoned judgment.[4]

Part of the problem also lies in the fact that all proposed actions arguably hold positive benefits to one or more stakeholder groups—otherwise they would not be viewed as possible actions. Therefore, both absolute and relative analysis is required.

The lack of good metrics makes absolute analysis difficult. Different benefits for different stakeholders make relative analysis speculative. Together, they compound the decision-making difficulty.

As a consequence, it is a challenge to determine the best resource allocation. Nevertheless, choices must be made. Making those decisions requires knowledge of the work of the enterprise and its operating environment as well as the imagination to stitch together the initiatives required (i.e., programs, projects, and processes that need to be continued or implemented), to effectively and efficiently achieve the planned quantified objectives.

Lacking comprehensive, objective analytical tools, management must rely instead on a mix of metrics and subjective evaluation. As available, metrics can be used to quantify costs and some measure of results (i.e., the number of people impacted, the magnitude of the impact, changes in some measure of outcome, change in some measure of input, etc.). Quantitative analysis, however, falls short both in terms of the scope of the metrics available—they typically are proxies for benefits, not the quantification of the actual benefit—and in terms of assessing the relationship of the potential action to mission. Here, subjective evaluation as well as management and board judgment must be relied upon.

Like all judgment processes, a systematic approach generally yields better results. Exhibit 10-3 provides an example of one systematic approach to making "action" decisions. As the matrix indicates, potential actions are organized by their contribution to mission/benefits and their cost/profitability. While this kind of analytical device does not completely specify what should be done, it does clarify the extremes—both of which should be eliminated (high cost/low benefit). The remaining actions must still be determined based on best business judgment and affordability.[5]

Exhibit 10-3

ACTION ANALYSIS MATRIX—PART 1			
Mission/Benefit			
		Low	High
Financial Impact	Substantial Loss		
	Marginal Impact		
	Modest Profit		
	High Profit		
ACTION ANALYSIS MATRIX—PART 2			
Mission/Benefit			
		Low	High
Financial Impact	Substantial Loss	Eliminate*	Increase Efficiency or Eliminate
	Marginal Impact	Reduce or Eliminate Costs	Increase Efficiency/ Continue
	Modest Profit	Reduce Costs/Continue	Continue
	High Profit	Continue**	Continue/Expand

*   Programs that one enterprise might consider eliminating may be a better fit with another. Therefore, before terminating a program consideration should be given to transferring it to another organization.

**   High profit/low benefit programs represent opportunities for outsourcing or spin-offs so that profits can be captured without the costs and distractions of operating the program.

CONTINUOUS IMPROVEMENT

One of the keys to affordability lies in continuously increasing operational efficiency. The other lies in growing revenues.

If the first part of determining courses of action to focus on is identifying the right things to do (effectiveness), then the second part addresses how to do the right things, the right way, the first time (efficiency). (See Exhibit 10-4.) The emphasis of this second step is on the continuous improvement of the enterprise's operating processes so that resources are allocated in a manner that achieves the greatest impact for the least cost. Simply, the more efficient the enterprise can be, the more it can do, for the same level of revenues.

The need for continuously improving efficiency is beyond argument. In a world of increasing service demands and limited resources, nonprofit enterprises must pursue continuous process improvement. The question is, how to do it? The management literature is rich with sound technical answers to this question, and good managers routinely integrate these process and quality improvement tools into their organization's planning and operations.[6] Exploration of the mechanics of these tools is beyond the scope of this discussion. However, two points should be noted.

Exhibit 10-4

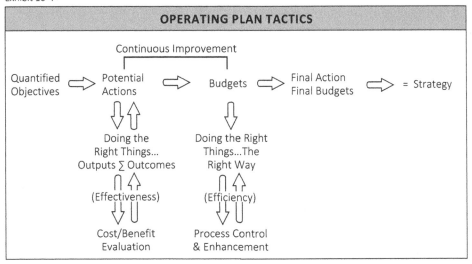

First, achieving continuous process improvement and increased operational efficiency is the result of the mixture of both management science and art. In an ideal setting everything would be quantifiable and comparable. Unfortunately, such is not the case on "the ground," in the reality of nonprofit operations. It would be nice to be able to calculate how many units of mission value/dollar a particular action or set of actions yields, compare that to not only a range of other results within that objective, but as other objectives as well, and select the combination that is always on the margin, yielding the highest mission value return per total expenditures.

While it would be nice, within the limits of current analytical tools and data availability, it is not practical. Therefore, the best that can be done is to bring these kinds of considerations into the action/budget decision process and to try to achieve a directional balance. That is, while it might not be practical to quantify the relative benefit of particular expenditure, it is realistic for management and the board to understand the areas where expenditures should be made and the need to balance (i.e., diversify those expenditures over multiple initiatives, so that spending does not go beyond the margin, yielding diminishing return).

Second, while efficiency must always be sought, it is both a race that has no "finish line" and an effort that by itself cannot achieve long-run enterprise success. No enterprise can save its way to success. Thus, while efficiency in and of itself may not yield direct mission success, success can neither be achieved nor maintained without the continuous process improvement that efficiency demands.

REVENUE GROWTH

In the same vein, for many nonprofit enterprises a seemingly easier, and at first blush less painful, path to providing adequate operational resources is assumed to run through the revenue side of operations. That is, resources for operations can simply be increased by generating more revenue both from current operations and/or from entering into profitable new ventures. These ventures can either be in collaboration with for-profit partners through endorsements and licenses, and/or new product and service offerings—either pursued independently or also in collaboration with either for-profit or nonprofit partners.

Certainly, in a world of scarce resources, nonprofit enterprises must unashamedly do everything they can do to maximize revenues. This not only means that money cannot be left on the table, due to overly conservative pricing, investment, billing, or collection policies, but also that successful, existing products and services that have market-based revenue potential should carry a market rate fee—at least, for those who can afford to pay. It also means that the enterprise must look ahead and determine if, and how, it might be able to wring out new product and service revenue opportunities.

For most nonprofit enterprises, the opportunities for revenue growth are always challenging. Increasing revenues through raising prices generally has limited potential. Yet, even in an economy of modest inflation, revenue growth, at some point, will be needed. In the face of this reality, it is understandable that enterprises will consider the possibility of entering new for-profit ventures as the easiest way to grow the revenues.

The for-profit initiatives pursued by nonprofit enterprises are loosely labeled as "social entrepreneurship." They always bear some arguable relationship to mission and/or perceived existing organizational capacity and capability.

While the logic of such initiatives may seem compelling, the reality is that more often than not, they fail to achieve their purpose. There are dramatic exceptions to this (i.e., Girl Scout cookie sales, Minnesota Public Radio, the gift shop and online stores of many museums, etc.). From these successes springs the hope of all nonprofit organizations that are considering this approach. These exceptions, however, do not change the fact that most social entrepreneurship investments fail. In the main, they fail because the skills and culture necessary for a successful nonprofit venture do not easily transfer to the operating discipline needed for a successful for-profit initiative.[7]

This does not mean that nonprofit managers are any less entrepreneurial or technically skilled than their for-profit counterparts. In fact, there is a growing body of literature that suggests that for-profit firms can learn a great deal from nonprofit enterprises and their managers. Rather, it highlights that on the margin, the skill sets of nonprofit and for-profit managers differ. This is the expected and unsurprising conclusion.

For the nonprofit enterprise, economic success has generally not been found in the pursuit of for-profit ventures that drain managerial and board time, as well as corporate treasure—without generating commensurate returns. Rather, economic success lies in the continuous process improvement combined with aggressive mission-focused revenue and capital generation.

With regard to the latter, the key is mission focused. The enterprise cannot allow the pursuit of a variety of revenue opportunities to dilute its pursuit of mission. There will always be potential grants, contracts, and legislative subsidies looking for an organizational home. Some of these opportunities will look attractive. However, if they change the organization from being mission-directed to becoming a grant or contract "job shop," then the purpose for which the enterprise was created is lost.

FEES

Before moving on, the question of fees merits a further comment. For many nonprofit enterprises (e.g., universities, hospitals, performing arts organizations, museums, etc.), much of their revenue comes from the fees charged to users. The management problem is determining how much to charge. As suggested above, market rate fees should be charged at least to those who can afford to pay.

High fee schedules may generate increased revenues, but they may also create barriers to service. Low fees make services more affordable but may not be economically sustainable for the enterprise. The dilemma is to balance these two conflicting forces.

Often the tendency is to set fees low. The result is that service utilization may be high. Demand might even exceed capacity resulting in people having to be turned away. A low pricing policy will also result in people who have the means to pay, paying the same as everyone else. This latter reality is simply a variant of the free rider phenomena discussed in Chapter 2.

As an alternative to starting by setting fees low, management should consider beginning with market rates and then, as needed, discounting the price based on financial capacity. Market rates can be defined as either what commercial firms charge for similar or alternative services or the full cost of the service plus some profit to support a subsidy for those who are not able to pay the market rate.

Charging less than cost is an economic model that will only result in failure (i.e., increased volume will not offset pricing at less than cost). To support those who cannot afford the full price, revenues must come from another source. Often enterprises look to grants for this support, using grant money to support an artificially low price. The problem with this approach is that money is still being left on the table because those who can afford to pay more are not being charged more. By setting price at the market rate, those who can afford it will contribute toward subsidizing those who cannot. Any grant revenue or other support will simply enable the enterprise to subsidize more services.

These economic, market, and operational realities force the recognition that revenue growth, while an option that should always be considered and tested:

- has limits;

- is not real if the incremental cost of providing the new service exceeds the incremental revenue;

- must be coupled with continuous improvements in operational performance.

BUDGETS

The unavoidable question of resource limits brings with it the unavoidable management challenge of revenue growth and/or expense reduction. It also brings into the overall planning process the final component of the enterprise's plan—and the litmus test of its strategy—the budget.

> ### PROFIT: HOW MUCH IS ENOUGH?
>
> The question of by how much the revenue budget should exceed the expense budget is one of the unfathomable dilemmas facing all nonprofit enterprises. For the for-profit firm the answer is straightforward—by as much as possible. For the nonprofit enterprise, while profit is necessary and should be sufficient for sustainability, the answer is as much as is acceptable. The quandary lies in determining, "acceptable" to whom.
>
> Varying stakeholders will have different answers to this question. Lacking the clarity of an objective financial metric, the answer is a judgment call and the judgment must be made by the enterprise's board—bringing together its sense of what stakeholders want and the right balance between revenue maximization and service maximization, long-run survival, and short-run needs and resilience.

While almost anything can be translated into and expressed as a budget, pragmatically the enterprise has three primary budgets: expense, revenue, and capital. Moreover, these three budgets must be in a balanced relationship. That is, the revenue budget should exceed the expense budget by some agreed upon amount so that the enterprise can maintain itself and its real level of services. The capital budget should be consistent with the expense budget and be affordable in terms of the cash provided by the revenue budget.

The cash budget in effect provides a third dimension to the enterprise's financial picture, assuring that the first two dimensions—revenue and expense—are in balance. The cash budget is a derivative budget. It flows from the revenue, expense, and capital budgets. However, it is a powerful tool, requiring that plans and decisions and their consequent impact on the primary budgets be adjusted if cash is inadequate (i.e., insufficient at a point in time to meet expense and capital needs).

The budget must also match the enterprise's strategy. In this context, balance means that the strategy and budget equal one another. It is important that both the board and management understand that the budget is simply the enterprise's strategy expressed in financial terms. It is the consequence of the planning effort, not a work product independent of that effort. Quite simply, if the resources are either not made available or not spent, then the agreed-upon strategy is not real.

Implicit in this notion of balance is the reality of the fluidity of the planning process. The budgets and the strategy are, until approved, in a state of flux. Based on resource availability, actions (because of their resulting expenses) are being adjusted—while simultaneously, expenses are being scrutinized to determine how process improvement initiatives can be employed to increase efficiency and make more resources available for actions. This interactive process continues until a workable balance is achieved and approved.

Understanding this, the importance of the budget component of the planning process becomes clear. It is the place where the management "tradeoffs and redos" are done in order to create an internally consistent and achievable business plan. It is also the place where process improvement opportunities assume a realistically high priority, for they provide a means for achieving financial and strategic balance. The budget process provides the means for evaluating these opportunities and incorporating the results into operations.

MERGERS/CONSOLIDATIONS

A major failure of nonprofit enterprises is their belief that they must act independently and individually. A person or group recognizes a need and creates a nonprofit organization to address it. Many of these efforts produce remarkable results and, as demonstrated by universities and hospitals, economically significant organizations. These, however, are the exceptions.

The community sector is characterized by small organizations, having limited management capacity and generally being starved for capital. Often, these organizations simply struggle on, moving from one grant to another, one fundraiser to another. The enterprise's focus shifts from its original mission to just sustaining itself.

In this circumstance, the board must give management permission as well as encourage management to pursue consolidation possibilities. Consolidation does not mean that the enterprise must cease to exist or lose its identity. In the extreme, organizations can merge and one or both may lose their identity. However, consolidation can also only involve sharing back office services, to gain economies of scale and cost savings, outsourcing activities, etc.

Regardless of how far along the consolidation continuum the organization goes, it cannot lose sight of the fact that it validates itself not by its survival, but rather by the value it adds toward achieving its purpose (i.e., mission).

The mechanics of how budgets are constructed, like the mechanics of process improvement, are beyond the scope of this discussion. However, like process improvement, a substantial literature exists to aid managers in designing and implementing budgeting processes for their organizations.[8,9] That said, a bit of pragmatism should be recognized, at least with regard to expense budgeting.

In theory, the range of approaches for constructing an expense budget runs the gamut from "zero-base," where all expenditures are supposedly open for reconsideration and possible elimination, to "incremental," where all expenditures continue "as is" with common increases for all similar expense elements. Between these extremes, budgets can be "frozen" from year to year, with no increase in resources, or a mixed approach can be employed, with some activities being eliminated, some frozen, and some growing by either a fixed or varying amount.

Not surprisingly, pragmatism, as contrasted with theoretical zealotry, is the more workable and realistic approach. Zero-base budgeting, with the opportunity to maintain, increase, or discontinue any program or expenditure, holds analytical and doctrinaire attractiveness. The practical problem is that while attractive in theory, it is not realistic in operation. Some expenditures cannot be eliminated (i.e., heat and light, safety requirements, some forms of insurance, etc.). Other assets, like human resources, are not universally interchangeable. Personnel skill sets, while having some degree of overlap, cannot be seamlessly substituted. Also, commitments to the enterprise's staff cannot be unilaterally altered from year to year without costly consequences. Alternatively, increasing all expenditures by a fixed amount may eliminate some painful decisions, but it does not best serve the needs of the enterprise's various stakeholders. It is not realistic to think that all aspects of the enterprise should grow at the same rate.

It is also not reasonable to believe that freezing everything at current levels, with no increase to any program or expenditure, can yield the best long-term results. It can eliminate organizational bloat, and therefore have some short-term benefit.

However, over the long run, continually freezing the budget at current levels forces the enterprise to "consume itself." If freezing expenditures is the enterprise's long-term solution to achieving budget balance, then management and the board must consider operational and organizational consolidation opportunities.

Given the limits of the other choices, a mixed approach to budgeting is the only practical solution. It provides the enterprise with the opportunity to tailor its activities, growing some while simultaneously reshaping or even eliminating others. A mixed approach, however, does not avoid the difficult resource allocation decisions. In fact, it does just the opposite. It brings these choices into focus, requiring management to determine explicitly how resources should be deployed.

REALITY

In the same vein of practicality, three additional points should be recognized. First, while the foregoing describes an orderly, sequential planning and budgeting process, reality does not support this perspective. Business planning involves a number of simultaneously moving parts and decision-making interactivity. While logic is not a casualty of the process, neatness is. The process is reiterative, with adjustments and changes being made until balance and consistency is achieved and the board approves the results.

Second, the smaller the organization, the more important it is to plan and budget. Small organizations have less cushion for either errors or the unexpected. For example, this was made painfully clear during the COVID-19 pandemic of 2020. Recognizing this, the only safety net available to management is planning. Small organizations, however, are invariably "understaffed." Resources are spread thinly, focused primarily on immediate, day-to-day operating and service needs. Tasks, like planning, that do not demand immediate attention, are often easily put off to another time. This is a mistake.

Third, the planning process can be a complicated and time-consuming effort. Understandably, regardless of the size of the organization, it is often viewed by staff as a burden. This behavioral reality should not be brushed aside.

However, an equally important reality is that an enterprise's planning process and plan does not need to be complicated or lengthy. It can be as succinct as a page or two—if it is born of rigorous strategic thinking and includes the factors needed to manage operations and guide the board's oversight of the enterprise's performance. (See Appendix 12—Organizational Planning—Business Plan Skeleton.)

A one-page plan would identify quantified objectives, budgeted surplus, and budgeted capital expenditures. As the organization's comfort and capacity to plan increases, detail can be added. Each iteration of the planning process will automatically increase the organization's planning comfort and ability. The details will similarly flow naturally, as the board learns more about the enterprise's environment—its threats and opportunities—and management begins to translate the board's growing understanding into goals and strategic objectives. Similarly, as experience is gained, managers and staff will expand the details of the actions to be pursued and the resulting budgets.

A one-page plan requires the same kind and degree of management thinking and analysis. It is simply less detailed. But the detail is important. The perfect planning process should not be allowed to become the enemy of, and prevent, a practical, pragmatic planning effort.

The reality is that a bad plan is better than no plan. Organizations with no plan have no way of judging if they are making progress toward their mission. They may just be substituting motion for progress. Organizations with an incomplete plan can at least make judgments about what they are doing, what they are achieving, and what adjustments and changes they have to make to do better.

Boards of organizations with no plan also have no way to carry out objective oversight of the enterprise. They are little more than chowder and marching societies with no way to systematically fulfill either their stewardship and agency accountabilities or legal duties.

The unambiguous conclusion is that managers cannot effectively and efficiently manage, and boards cannot effectively govern, without a board-approved business plan—even if that plan lacks all the detail that management theory suggests is necessary.

A PLAN: A SIMPLE (ALBEIT FICTITIOUS) EXAMPLE

The time: 1492

The place: Spain

The principals: Isabella, Ferdinand and Columbus

Mission: Achieve glory (wealth and power) for Spain and spread the Catholic religion (God and Gospel) Environmental Assessment: Data show that the earth is round. Sailing vessels can stay at sea for long periods.

Strategy: Sail west to India

Isabella and Ferdinand are, in effect, the board. They approved the strategy, setting the destination and the direction. Columbus, as the CEO, took them on a path of guided discovery to recognize the new opportunity for achieving their mission. He then led the journey, determining logistics, course, etc., in effect determining and executing the operating plan and budget.

The result: A failed plan that did not achieve its goal. The Americas got in the way. It did, however, contribute to achieving Spain's mission.

The lesson: A bad plan can be better than no plan.

CHAPTER 10

Takeaways and Questions for Consideration and Discussion:

TAKEAWAYS

1. The strategic plan defines direction and priorities. The operating plan translates priorities, through its quantified objectives, into expected results.

2. The quantified objectives of the operating plan provide the metrics both for guiding operational management and enabling the board's oversight of management and evaluation of enterprise performance.

3. Planning is a necessary exercise in hope, imagination, and aspirations. Budgeting is reality. What is in the budget is the real strategic and operating plan. The budget is the enterprise's strategy expressed in financial terms.

4. Never balance the budget with hoped-for revenue growth or potential philanthropic gifts.

5. Always assure that the revenue, expense, and capital budgets are in equilibrium—as tested by the cash budget (statement of cash flows).

QUESTIONS

1. How does the environmental assessment bring clarity to the operating plan?

2. What is the value of quantified objectives beyond their role as a component of the operating plan?

3. Why is revenue growth a generally seductive, but often impractical, course of action?

4. Why is the budget the litmus test of strategy?

Chapter 11:

IMPLEMENTATION AND OVERSIGHT

Regardless of either how creative or bold an enterprise's plan is, it is still just a plan. It is more a statement of hopes than accomplishments. A plan, like a coiled spring, holds potential for activity and results—not a guarantee. For that potential to be realized, the plan must be successfully implemented. The management and governance challenge is to turn the aspirations embodied in the plan into realities—for the community.

Assuming that the plan is well-designed, grounded in adequate resources, and has been effectively communicated, research still suggests that a substantial portion (over twenty percent) of the plan's hoped-for performance will not be realized. This loss is a consequence of breakdowns in the execution process.[1] Execution, management's skills in organizing and deploying human and capital resources, improving processes, and motivating people to action, is what drives the implementation of the plan.

Implementation is both the last step in the planning process, and the first step in making a real difference to the enterprise's community. It is the place where management must get things done, within the discipline of schedules and budgets, not just conceptualize what should happen. Ideally, management will do the right things, the right way, the first time. However, regardless of how carefully plans have been crafted, the whims of the marketplace and the glitches of operational reality can combine to make a mockery of the board's and management's best intentions. Performance shortfalls, particularly because the enterprise's operational "reach" should, by intended design, exceed its "grasp," are to be expected.

The question is how are the shortfalls to be managed? Sometimes the shortfall is the result of a plan. Operational reality does not simply bend to accommodate the intellectual elegance or imagination of management's plan. Sometimes shortfalls are the result of bad execution—and sometimes it is the product of both.

As a consequence, if plans are to be turned into real stakeholder benefits, managers must dig below the symptom of the shortfall to identify and understand the underlying cause. To do this, several basic realities should be recognized.

HARD WORK

First, implementation is hard work. Expected results do not just magically happen. They require active, hands-on management engagement, starting with identifying the elements of the process that are going to be implemented and then designing the flow of those elements to assure that the process, whether new or old, is done as efficiently as is practical.[2] This requires knowledge of the business[3] as well as the application of leadership, communication and management skills— all aimed at achieving breakthrough performance by simplifying operations.[4]

Understanding process flows and then being able to cobble together the pieces into an efficient system is an exercise in tactical management skills. It involves the process improvement techniques that were previously referenced. It also demands the recognition that the people who are actually doing the work will often have ideas about how to do their jobs better—more accurately, faster and/ or cheaper. Good managers ask their staffs how to improve operations and listen to their answers. They also support their staffs by exposing them to, and utilizing, the technical management skills that can assist them to achieve continuous performance improvement.

Small and medium size enterprises may consider this focus on process improvement as beyond either their needs or capacity. Neither conclusion is true. These enterprises, in fact, with fewer resources for coping with unexpected events and greater needs for efficiency, have arguably more need for continuous improvement than their larger brethren—with their greater capacity for absorbing the dislocations of the unexpected and the unplanned.

WHY MEASURE PERFORMANCE

Organizations measure performance so that managers can manage and boards can carry out their oversight responsibilities. Performance measurement enables the enterprise to:

- determine/demonstrate that it is doing what it said it was going to do (i.e., implementing its operating plan);

- evaluate/document its performance efficiency (i.e., inputs/outputs), and evaluate/document its impact as well as the effectiveness and efficiency of that impact.

Performance measurement and reporting is necessary so that boards and managers can make judgments about the enterprise—its operating results, financial condition, and the difference it is making to its community. "Is the organization making a difference to the community?" is the most important and most difficult question to answer. Generally, it is answered through independent, research-based evaluations. An alternative might simply be to ask the enterprise's community and stakeholders. While not having the quantitative rigor of a well-designed research study, it does have the virtue of relevance—particularly if those who are answering the question are the key to sustainability.

At the same time, because of their smaller size, the tactical management tools used to achieve operational improvements need not be as complex as some of the applications described in management texts and used by larger organizations. Regardless of size, any enterprise can determine what it must do for itself, its core strategic functions. Then, as a way to increase efficiency and continuously improve

performance, consider which of the remaining functions it might:
- sell to others, to increase revenues;

- contract out, to reduce overhead costs;

- discontinue.

Alternatively, any enterprise can flowchart a process and identify the overlaps, redundancies, and bottlenecks. Similarly, any enterprise can look at its revenue processes, billing policies, collection cycle, etc., and identify opportunities for enhancement. Moreover, with technology continually changing, possibilities for improvement are always waiting to be discovered.

The basic fact is that effective implementation requires active management involvement, both in designing and executing processes and in assuring that the actions being pursued achieve results—and if not, taking corrective measures.

This highlights the second key point. As illustrated in Exhibit 11-1, implementation is an iterative process. Management is continually measuring actual performance results against the standard of the approved quantified objectives, and likely making adjustments to its tactics and actions in order to actually achieve the agreed-upon result targets.

Exhibit 11-1

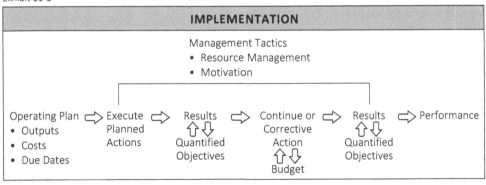

This process of monitoring and then, as needed, making operating adjustments again involves utilizing the skills and experience of front line workers. If they understand what is expected, and of equal importance, know actual performance results, they will be able to offer the insights and make the adjustments needed to improve performance.

The key ingredient in all this is being aware, on a timely basis, of actual results and then comparing them to the appropriate quantified objectives. Without actual results the implementation process is both blind and rudderless.

This operational reality makes clear a third point. Simply, just as management needs actual performance data to guide the organization, the board also needs the same data to carry out its oversight accountabilities. Performance reporting is the catalytic component of the implementation process, providing the ingredient that stimulates the action/results cycle. (See Exhibit 11-2.)

Exhibit 11-2

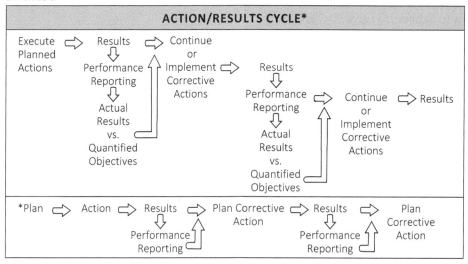

PERFORMANCE RESULTS

Reporting actual performance results, whether financial or operating, is fundamentally an act of score keeping. It can certainly be an involved process, requiring data from a variety of sources and imaginative integration of those data to create actionable information. However, at its core, it is still a mechanical activity.

DATA ≠ INFORMATION

Data does not by itself equal information, let alone actionable information. In fact, large amounts of data can act to obscure information, dooming the recipient of the report to drown in a sea of numbers. Reports therefore, must be spare, providing data in an amount and form that yields a picture of performance that can be used to make decisions and guide actions.

As a mechanical activity, reporting performance results can be done in a number of ways, reflecting the history, current leadership preference, needs of the enterprise, etc. As a consequence, reporting formats and styles will, at some pace, change over time.

Mechanics, however, are secondary to understanding that reports should:
- be neutral, providing quantifiable, verifiable, and reliable data
- contain data in a form and format that changes it from raw data into actionable information.

Reports should provide the information needed for making judgments about both current performance and progress toward mission. They should not make those judgments. To achieve this, managers, in designing reports, must understand the nature of the judgments that must be made and the timing of, as well as the accountability for, those decisions. Implicit in this understanding is the recognition that operational performance reporting is a subset of an overall larger management reporting performance assessment and evaluation function. This overarching reporting requirement involves a hierarchy of performance measures, as well as a mix of operational and financial data, and varying timeframes for being able to assess results.

GLOSSARY

ACTIVITY: an action or set of actions designed to produce an expected output

EFFECTIVENESS: efficient impact (i.e., the measure of change produced, impact, divided by all the costs of the involved activities)

EFFICIENCY: inputs divided by outputs, where inputs are the sum of the resources used to produce the outputs

IMPACT: the ability of an activity or group of activities (outputs → outcomes) to produce changes among stakeholders greater than that which would have occurred if nothing had been done

OUTCOMES: the results achieved as a consequence of the activities pursued and the outputs produced. Outcomes are often the result of two or more outputs and reflect a measure of stakeholder status at a point in time.

OUTPUTS: direct, measurable products of an activity or set of activities

RESILIENCE: the ability to organizationally survive a temporary, reversible, and/or limited financial or operational setback (e.g. loss of major donor or contract, building disaster, etc.)

SUSTAINABILITY: the ability to continue to pursue mission (either independently or in combination with others having a similar mission) in the face of a catastrophic or system financial and/or operating crisis (e.g. the Great Recession, COVID-19 pandemic, etc.).

Arguably, with the exception of special report requests, management reporting focuses on trying to answer six categories of questions:

1. Is the enterprise doing what it said it was going to do? Is it executing its operating plan, producing the anticipated outputs, on time and on budget?

2. Is the enterprise doing what it said it was going to do efficiently? Is cost divided by output at least continually improving—if not, at an absolute best practice?

3. Are the outputs that the enterprise is producing achieving the expected outcomes? Is it achieving the expected results—or benefits for the involved stakeholders?

4. Are the realized outcomes being achieved in an efficient manner? (This is a combination of questions 2 and 3.)

5. Are the outcomes producing a significant impact? Are they producing a result that would not have otherwise been achieved?

6. Is the effort sustainable? Can it be continued or will it fall of its own weight, due to either financial and/or operational imbalance?

These questions are similar to the questions that must be addressed in crafting the operating plan in order to try to allocate resources (i.e., time, talent, and money), to the activities that will produce the greatest, long-run impact. The primary difference is one of time perspective. In developing the operating plan, management is looking ahead, to set out what it intends to accomplish and how it will do it. Here, management is taking a historical perspective—looking at what has actually been accomplished. In both instances, these are difficult questions. However, from a community perspective, in both instances, they are appropriate.

In terms of implementation and oversight, the first question is the most basic— is the enterprise doing what it said it was going to do? However, questions of efficiency/productivity, effectiveness/impact, and sustainability all must be considered at some point in the planning and implementation process. In creating the plan, they are addressed using the best judgment and hopes of management and the board. After the fact, in evaluating the efficiency and effectiveness of performance, they are addressed through historical and comparative data and research based studies of impact.

WHO CARES? *

The question of impact is an important matter for institutional funders (e.g., community foundations, United Way agencies, large foundations, etc.), who want to assure that they are wisely utilizing the assets entrusted to their management. By evaluating the impact of the projects they fund, they can either demonstrate that the money has been well spent or that funding, based on the objective evidence, should be discontinued—because the project is not having an impact or not having the expected impact.

Determination of impact has its own systematic hierarchy, beginning with apparent effectiveness (i.e., documenting results—outputs and outcomes) and assuming that they yield benefits. The second stage is demonstrated effectiveness (i.e., comparing the results of program participants to a similar population that does not receive services). The final stage is proven effectiveness (i.e., research based evaluations), involving one or more control groups and conducted to a scientific evidence based standard.** Often, the research is conducted by an independent third party to assure expertise and objectivity.

In contrast, individual donors are generally not as concerned about impact studies. The individual donor has made a psychological commitment to the mission of the enterprise that they are donating to. They want the enterprise to be honestly run (i.e., no scandal), and to operate in a business-like manner. They are not particularly concerned with impact evaluations because they believe that the enterprise's work produces community benefit and that they want to simply help make the "good work" happen. They are comfortable leaving the operating details about what will be done and how it will be accomplished to the subject matter experts.

*Katie Cunningham, Marc Ricks, "Why Measure," Stanford Social Innovation Review, Summer 2004.

**Jed Emerson, "But Does It Work,?" Stanford Social Innovation Review, Winter 2009.

Efficiency, for example, must be examined when management determines, as part of crafting the operating plan and budgets, the actions that it intends to take to achieve the targeted quantified objectives. (See Chapter 10.)[5] Here, both inputs (cost and activities) and outputs can be quantified. In fact, if the outputs cannot be quantified, this is a signal that the quantified objectives should be redefined.

Effectiveness, as also noted in Chapter 10, presents a more difficult challenge both because of the problems in calculating the value of the benefits produced by the realized outcomes and by the need to measure the impact, both relative and absolute, of those outcomes and the efficiency of their production. Because of these real world difficulties, proxy variables are often relied upon as a substitute measure for what in the for-profit setting would be investment return.

For example, for an after school program intended to increase college matriculation rates, cost per student can be calculated (a measure of efficiency), total number of students served, total number of programs, etc., can all be measured. These can then be compared to matriculation rates, either for the period or over time, to make a judgment as to whether the mission of increased matriculation rates is being achieved. All of these activities can also be compared to the total cost of the effort to make a judgment of both efficiency and effectiveness. Even with all this, the question of impact has still to be answered. To do this, a separate, research oriented evaluation is needed to examine, over time, if the results achieved are significantly better than what would have occurred without any intervention[6]—or with a different intervention.[7]

PRAGMATISM

Again, none of these questions are inappropriate. However, from the perspective of a day-to-day management imperative, several points should be realized. First, all the intended actions and activities that the enterprise pursues are believed to yield positive benefits and contribute to achieving mission. How efficient and effective any particular activity is, at any point in time, is a pertinent question. Similarly, whether the benefits of the activity equal or exceed its costs is a reasonable question—even if seldom asked. Unfortunately, these questions often can only be answered using period-to-period comparisons and special studies.[8]

Second, given that all activities have positive benefit, the first question in the above hierarchy is the most important, is the enterprise doing what it said it would do—on the agreed upon schedule and at the expected cost? That is, is management executing the approved plan? This is the information that the board needs in order to carry out its oversight accountabilities and that management needs to guide operations.

Third, the question of continuity is the litmus test. This may be a harsh arbiter but, it is the ultimate measure. Actions and activities can produce the expected outputs that in turn yield outcomes having great impact. However, if the resources to sustain the activities, even after operations have been re-engineered and streamlined to achieve greater efficiency, are not available, then the initiative will fail. Initiatives must either sustain themselves or only need an affordable level of subsidization. If one or the other of these conditions cannot be met, then the initiative will fall of its own financial weight.

This suggests, as will be discussed later, the importance of profitability and capital generation. For the moment, it is enough to recognize that both the board and management need information regarding the execution of the plan—is it being implemented as intended (i.e., the right outputs on schedule and on budget). How it gets this information moves the discussion to the mechanics of reporting and monitoring.

MECHANICS

In discussing mechanics, two ideas are currently in vogue. One involves the concept of the balanced scorecard and the other, dashboard reporting. The "balanced score card" is simply an understanding that the enterprise must have a range of quantified objectives, and those objectives may at times be in conflict. A simple example of this can be seen in considering the growth and profitability objectives for a health maintenance organization (HMO). Growth can be achieved by under-pricing. Under-pricing, however, will also affect profitability. Alternatively, profitability can be increased by rigorous underwriting. Rigorous underwriting, however, makes growth difficult.

The point is simply that an enterprise cannot be one dimensional in its focus. However, to the extent that it is multi-dimensional, it will at some point unavoidably create tension between objectives. This tension must be balanced to yield the greatest total benefit for the enterprise's stakeholders. The start of this balancing process lies in the strategic plan where strategic objectives, creating the tension, are established. It then moves forward in the operating plan where quantified objectives are set and a balance is created by adjusting the performance levels to be sought for specific objectives in order to meet all of the operating plan objectives. (In effect the relative emphasis placed on the strategic plan's various objectives are adjusted by the results expected for each quantified objective.) Finally, it culminates in reporting where objectives and results are brought together, compared, and judgments made.

Exhibit 11-3 (see this exhibit and others at the end of the chapter) provides an example of the elements that can be included in a balanced scorecard. The example is drawn from a skilled nursing and rehabilitation care provider. It illustrates the tension between operations and satisfaction (employee and patient), as well as the tension between financial and clinical performance and satisfaction. Exhibit 11-4 provides a similar example for a hospital. Again, the tension between the various areas of performance stands out. How and where quantified objectives are set tries to balance this tension, so that, while give and take will still happen, all objectives can be achieved. (Performance regarding specific objectives may be sub-optimized so that overall performance can be pragmatically maximized.)

These exhibits also illustrate dashboard reporting.[9] Dashboard reporting is shorthand for distinguishing between data and information. Dashboard reporting takes its name from the automobile dashboard where all the mechanical/technical information necessary for the driver and driving is available in one easily understandable place and format. For governance oversight, dashboard reports are sensible. For operational management, more detail is required to determine the need for any corrective actions and, if needed, where and what. Exhibit 11-5 provides an example of these more detailed, so called "drill down," reports. (Exhibit 11-5 complements Exhibit 11-3.)

Exhibits 11-3 and 11-4 also illustrate a reporting format known as a spider diagram. The diagram takes it name from the pattern that is created (i.e., it resembles a spider's web). Its value lies in that it provides an easily digestible dashboard report where performance objectives and actual performance are displayed on a single page. The spokes represent objectives, the "bold" line the quantified target, and the diamonds or narrow line, actual performance. Performance relative to the quantified objective can be assessed at a glance by just looking at what is above or below the bold line. Thus, for example, in the case of Exhibit 11-3, shortfalls are occurring relative to three objectives: total occupancy, long-term care resident satisfaction, and rehabilitation care resident satisfaction. The performance results for Exhibit 11-4 are more mixed, but just as easily discernable.

FINANCIAL AND OTHER REPORTS

In addition to operating performance reports, managers and the board also need financial information. Exhibit 11-3 demonstrates how high-level financial information (e.g., operating margin and cash), can be incorporated into dashboard reporting. Most boards and managers, however, will generally want more information. Exhibit 11-6 provides an excerpt from a financial dashboard report that illustrates one approach to providing greater detail.

Depending on the size, history, and capacity of the enterprise, monthly summary reports of expenses and revenues to budget may be all that is necessary. However, in larger organizations or organizations facing financial distress, more detailed reporting will be needed. The financial and management accounting literature addresses the issues and techniques of financial reporting in more depth than can be done here. Readers interested in more information about these topics should refer to these sources.[10]

From a judgment perspective, one note of caution should be recognized. Even if actual performance, whether financial or operational, differs from plan, corrective action may be neither necessary nor appropriate. The budget and plan should be examined prior to taking any action to assure their continued relevance. Circumstances may have changed such that the plan and resulting budget should be adjusted—not actual performance.

In addition to internal reporting needs, every enterprise must give consideration both to the information it wishes to provide voluntarily to its stakeholders, and to the reporting required by various governmental agencies (e.g., IRS, State Charities Bureau, etc.).

It is becoming increasingly common for community sector enterprises to provide an annual public report to their stakeholders. The style and scope of this reporting will vary with the organization. In one sense, these reports are similar to the annual reports that publicly-traded corporations publish. They provide the opportunity to report on the financial condition of the enterprise, as well as share with the community the results of the enterprise's work. In a different sense, they are a public relations and fundraising document that enables the enterprise to humanize its work, telling a compelling story about what it does, how it serves the needs of its community, and what the reader can do to help. Regardless of whether the report is a professionally produced four-color brochure or a photo copied letter, the importance of actively telling the enterprise's story should not be underestimated. It is the first step in fundraising and friend-raising.

Community sector enterprises also must meet certain governmental reporting requirements. City and county governments may require information for purposes of maintaining property tax exemptions. States may also require certain information for tax and business registration matters. Regardless of these reporting obligations almost all medium and larger tax-exempt organizations must annually file Form 990 with the Internal Revenue Service.

Form 990 was substantially revised in 2008. In redesigning the form, the Internal Revenue Service has sought to increase organizational transparency while at the same time promoting tax compliance. Thus, while the Form 990 can still be viewed as an informational form, it requires that a substantial amount of new data about the organization (e.g., governance policies and procedures, where and how it spends its money, executive compensation and benefits, number of volunteers, community benefit information, board member data, etc.), be made available to the public. Appendix 13 provides a copy of Form 990 and excerpts from the Internal Revenue Service's Form 990 general and specific instructions.[11] Even a quick glance makes clear the scope and complexity of the Form. Therefore questions about Form 990, like all tax matters, should be discussed with appropriate tax experts, to assure compliance.

PART IV

Part III has focused on business planning. The discussion, while oriented to community sector enterprise, is equally relevant to all organizations. Part IV shifts the perspective to management and governance issues which are either unique to and/or special changes to community sector enterprises.

Exhibit 11-3

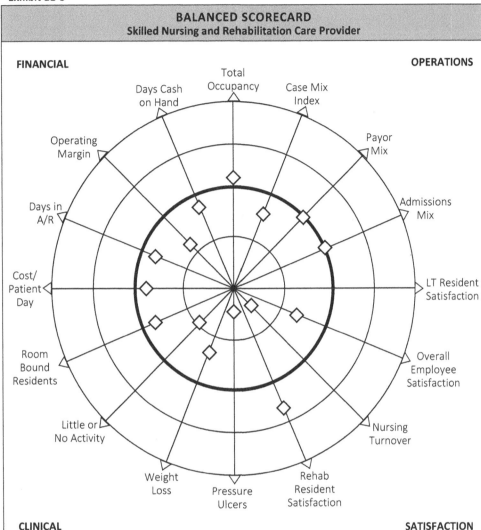

BALANCED SCORECARD
Skilled Nursing and Rehabilitation Care Provider

FINANCIAL

OPERATIONS

Total Occupancy

Days Cash on Hand

Case Mix Index

Operating Margin

Payor Mix

Days in A/R

Admissions Mix

Cost/ Patient Day

LT Resident Satisfaction

Room Bound Residents

Overall Employee Satisfaction

Little or No Activity

Nursing Turnover

Weight Loss

Rehab Resident Satisfaction

Pressure Ulcers

CLINICAL

SATISFACTION

Each spoke represents a separate metric and each metric can be measured differently. Cost per day, for example, will be measured in dollars and may have a target of $425/day. Long-Term (LT) Resident Satisfaction will be measured as a percentage and may have a target of 97% satisfied or very satisfied. Nursing turnover may also be a percentage with a target of 10% or less.

The concentric circles represent performance levels, with the bold circle representing the quantified objective for each metric.

The cost per day circles may be $400/day, $425/day (the bold target circle), $450/day and $500/day. The Long-Term Resident Satisfaction circles would be 98+%, 97%, 95%, less than 95%. Nursing turnover might be 5% or less, 10%, 15%, more than 15%.

In this example, diamonds represent actual performance and the closer to the center, the better the level of performance.

Exhibit 11-4

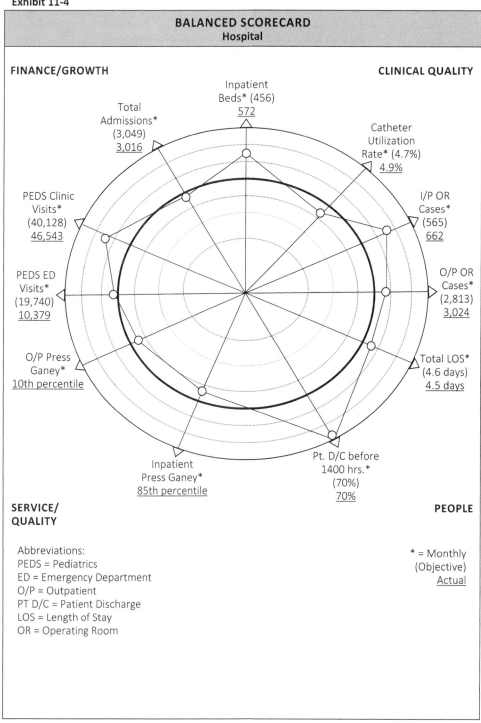

BALANCED SCORECARD
Hospital

FINANCE/GROWTH

CLINICAL QUALITY

Inpatient
Beds* (456)
572

Total
Admissions*
(3,049)
3,016

Catheter
Utilization
Rate* (4.7%)
4.9%

PEDS Clinic
Visits*
(40,128)
46,543

I/P OR
Cases*
(565)
662

PEDS ED
Visits*
(19,740)
10,379

O/P OR
Cases*
(2,813)
3,024

O/P Press
Ganey*
10th percentile

Total LOS*
(4.6 days)
4.5 days

Inpatient
Press Ganey*
85th percentile

Pt. D/C before
1400 hrs.*
(70%)
70%

**SERVICE/
QUALITY**

PEOPLE

Abbreviations:
PEDS = Pediatrics
ED = Emergency Department
O/P = Outpatient
PT D/C = Patient Discharge
LOS = Length of Stay
OR = Operating Room

* = Monthly
(Objective)
Actual

Exhibit 11-5

"DRILL DOWN" REPORTS Satisfaction				
Metric		Actual	Target/ Benchmark	Source
Long Term Resident Satisfaction	Combined percentage of "very good" and "good" responses to overall satisfaction	85.8%	87%	Survey
Overall Employee Satisfaction	Average of all questions on the employee survey (Annually)	80%	77%	Past Performance
Total Nursing Turnover (CNA, LPN, RN)	Annual Percent of Nursing Staff terminated	19.8%	26.8%	Senior Alliance
Rehab Resident Satisfaction	Combined percentage of "very good" and "good" responses to overall rehab satisfaction	86%	88%	Survey

SATISFACTION

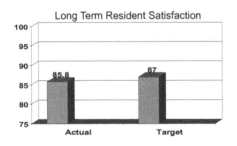

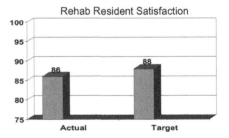

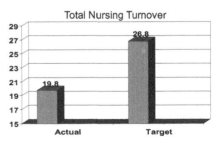

Exhibit 11-5, continued

"DRILL DOWN" REPORTS Financial				
Metric		Actual	Target/ Benchmark	Source
Cost per patient day	Total costs per patient days in dollars	221.68	224.16	Budget
Days in A/R	Total accounts receivable divided by average daily net revenue	50.1	53.7	AHSA (15 nonprofit facilities)
Operating Margin	Ratio of operating income to sales revenue	1.5	-0.46	Budget
Days Cash on Hand	Cash on hand, market securities and investments divided by averaged total operating expenses	23.28	19.6	AHSA (15 nonprofit facilities)

FINANCIAL

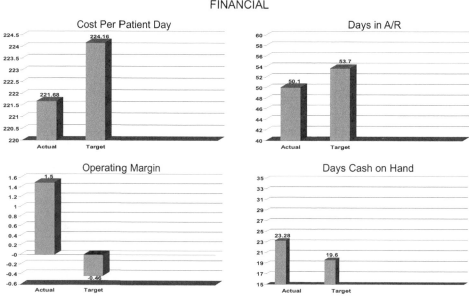

FINANCIAL DASHBOARD

Category	Key Indicator	July-20	Aug-20	Sep-20	Oct-20	Nov-20	Dec-20	Jan-21	Feb-21	Mar-21
Profitability	Excess Margin before investment income ($)	(357,144)	(494,222)	(357,055)	147,804	(315,281)	2,899,140	(929,870)	27,358	97,013
	Excess Margin before investment income (%)	-3.9%	-5.3%	-3.7%	1.4%	-3.2%	22.6%	-10.4%	0.3%	0.9%
	Operating EDIBA ($)	136,929	(12,784)	132,561	636,825	164,744	2,796,332	(482,153)	495,729	540,127
	Operating EDIBA (%)	1.5%	-0.1%	1.4%	5.9%	1.7%	21.8%	-5.4%	5.0%	5.1%
Revenue/ Growth	Patient service revenues	26,948,601	28,706,630	27,232,484	27,596,527	27,654,110	26,710,219	28,643,039	27,508,789	29,988,586
	Admissions	828	832	834	816	753	733	801	777	840
	Non-emergency Outpatient Visits	4,256	4,710	4,181	4,748	4,130	3,740	4,363	4,082	4,278
Expense	Bad Debt	1,221,266	768,262	1,195,597	1,579,524	1,437,120	1,005,982	638,131	936,412	1,368,814
	Uninsured Allowance	515,966	381,240	314,760	441,428	634,039	200,073	386,342	450,667	373,617
	Charity Care	771,575	866,645	730,393	875,865	701,985	857,701	855,256	929,564	879,547
	Salaries, Wages, and Benefits as a % of Net Patient Revenue	57.9%	60.2%	58.8%	51.8%	54.8%	54.9%	67.6%	58.6%	54.0%
	Supply Expenses as a % of Net Patient Revenue	13%	16%	12%	13%	13%	13%	15%	12%	13%
Balance Sheet	Days Total Cash	31	22	39	28	28	20	19	19	16
	Days in Patient Accounts Receivable	52	50	54	46	47	47	48	52	53
	Debt to Capitalization Ratio	60.5%	61.1%	61.5%	61.1%	59.7%	50.4%	51.5%	51.3%	51.1%
Productivity/ Acuity	Paid Hours per CMI adj. Admission	195.33	195.65	186.1	204.03	227.94	220.37	195.43	185.02	208.08
	FTE's per APD	4.6	4.35	4.42	4.57	4.41	4.8	4.35	4.35	4.13
	FTE's per AOB	6.98	6.68	6.65	7.19	6.65	7.16	6.59	6.56	6.21
	Average Length of Stay	4.63	4.58	4.67	4.55	4.9	5.02	4.73	4.47	4.8
	Overall CMI	1.1044	1.0864	1.0786	1.1403	1.2155	1.12968	1.0853	1.0737	1.12198
	Medicare CMI	1.304	1.334	1.308	1.189	1.348	1.512	1.279	1.285	1.445

CHAPTER 11

Takeaways and Questions for Consideration and Discussion:

TAKEAWAYS

1. Plans are aspirational, holding potential for what "could be." Implementation is reality and hard work.

2. Quantified objectives set clear targets, enabling both management and the board to know what is intended to be accomplished. Reporting is score keeping, telling what has been accomplished.

3. Plans are generally never exactly met. They are either exceeded or shortfalls occur. The shortfalls are the issue. They happen. The challenge is establishing a positive culture for managing them. Central to accomplishing this is creating an organizational environment of:
   - Openness (where shortfalls are reported and operationally addressed)
   - Board and management mutual positive support
   - Continuous improvement, and
   - Striving to extend the enterprise's reach beyond its grasp.

4. Implementation is a reiterative process, involving continuous assessment, reporting, and adjustment of either the plan and/or the work process.

QUESTIONS

1. How should performance shortfalls be identified? How should they be managed?

2. Why is performance monitoring important to management? To the board?

3. In assessing results, how do you balance the demands of evidence-based assessment of, and effectiveness against, the economic demands of continuity and pragmatism?

4. How would you design a balanced scorecard report? A dashboard style report? A combination of the two?

PART IV

MANAGEMENT AND GOVERNANCE CHALLENGES

The previous discussion, while highlighting the community sector, has for the most part had broad management and governance relevance. This section takes a more pointed focus, addressing matters that are unique to community sector enterprises (i.e., volunteer management, fundraising, and enhancing the public's trust). It also addresses more general management and governance challenges (i.e., succession and chief executive transition management), from the special perspective of the community sector. It provides a capstone to the management and governance challenges facing community sector enterprises.

Chapter 12:
CAPITAL FORMATION and FINANCIAL SUSTAINABILITY

To survive, all economic entities, over the long run and regardless of whether they are for-profit or nonprofit, must generate total revenues in excess of total expenses. This is an immutable financial equation not just for growth but more importantly for survival.

To the extent that revenues exceed expenses, for-profit firms earn profits and nonprofit enterprises generate surpluses. In the for-profit setting, profits (after taxes) are used to pay a return to investors and/or are reinvested in the firm (increasing owner's equity) so that profitability can be maintained, or hopefully increased, into the future. In the nonprofit world, surpluses are invested in current stakeholder/beneficiary services (similar in financial concept to the dividends paid to stock owners) as well as in the enterprise itself—creating reserves for the unexpected, as well as planned future program needs.

In both instances, profits or surpluses retained in the firm become, in accounting and financial terms, capital and capital is necessary to protect and sustain the enterprise. The fundamental management and governance question then is, how does the enterprise create capital?

CAPITAL IS:

In an operating sense capital is the sum of the firm's physical facilities such as, buildings and equipment, and monetary assets—cash and financial investments—held as reserves. Adding to these physical and monetary assets represents enterprise growth and is the result of revenue exceeding expenses.

In an accounting sense, capital is the bottom right section of the enterprise's balance sheet (statement of position). For nonprofit enterprises it is the unrestricted net assets presented at the bottom of the general fund financial statement.* It is analogous to stockholder's equity on a for-profit firm's balance sheet.

In a financial sense, capital is the owner's (in the nonprofit environment, the community's) residual interest in the enterprise. It is the amount remaining after liabilities are subtracted from assets.

In a management sense, capital is the physical, financial, and human assets available to the enterprise to sustain it and carry out its mission.

Finally, in a practical sense, capital is money.

*Without belaboring the intricacies of fund accounting, a nonprofit enterprise may also have unrestricted capital in its building fund, endowment fund, or other specially created funds. It also may have board restricted funds that at the board's initiative can become available capital.

TWO SOURCES

Capital can only come from two sources: the earnings (profits) of the organization and/or investments by external parties in the organization. Earned capital is profits (surplus) from operations that are reinvested in the enterprise. Invested capital is funds that are derived, in the for-profit setting, from institutions and individuals purchasing an interest in a firm—in the expectation that they will receive a "return" on their capital, from both dividends and increases in the value of their ownership interest, as well as a "return" of their capital when they sell their interest. Invested capital is typically obtained through the sale of stock (equity) in the firm.[1]

In the nonprofit setting, invested capital is contributions/gifts from institutions and individuals. In this instance, the investors are not expecting a personal financial return either of, and/or, on their capital. They are investing private resources for community benefits, expecting a return—not to themselves, but to the community. Invested capital is derived from fundraising or fund development (the contemporary term) efforts.

STOCKHOLDER INVESTMENTS

Equity in the form of stockholder investments in the corporation is generally not associated with nonprofit enterprises. There are, however, exceptions to this general rule. Perhaps, one of the most interesting is the Green Bay Packers.*

The Packers, the NFL (National Football League) franchise in northern Wisconsin, is owned by its fans. Though originally organized as a nonprofit corporation, the Packers are now a for-profit entity.**

Over 100,000 people own 4.75 million shares of Packers stock. The shares include voting rights but, cannot be resold, except back to the corporation at a fraction of their original price, have no dividend and no season ticket purchase privileges. To avoid the risk of a change in control, no shareholder is allowed to own more than 200,000 shares of stock.

The Packers are an example of private resources dedicated to community benefit. In this instance, the community's recognition of the importance of the team to the quality and fabric of life in the community justified the purchase of stock—without an expectation of personal financial return.

Rochester Community Baseball is another example of stockholders making equity investments with the same personal financial expectations as contributors—no personal financial inurement.

Obviously, this source of capital is potentially available to only a limited number of nonprofit enterprises—those that both exist in a commercial, for-profit market segment (i.e., entertainment, sports, publishing, etc.), and add value to the community's quality of life and residential attractiveness.

* See www.packers.com

** The NFL has regulations preventing any other team from adopting a structure like that of the Packers.

Because capital is always scarce and nonprofit enterprises have almost a limitless ability to find good uses for resources, fundraising is a priority matter to most nonprofit enterprises. As a result, organizations place substantial expectations on the person(s) responsible for financial development, expecting he or she to be able, by their own hand and efforts, to lead in finding the capital required to enable the enterprise to meet all its needs and even pursue its dreams. Fundraising is also often a matter of contention and concern between chief executives and boards, with the chief executives typically feeling that the board is not doing enough—either in terms of leadership or personal involvement.[2,3]

While successful fundraising (fund development) may be viewed as the path of choice for generating capital, in reality 70% of nonprofit, social enterprise total revenue comes from fees for goods and services and only 12% comes from private contributions.[4] Therefore, if one believes in the notion of "following the money," the place to start looking for capital is in operating performance results.

EARNED CAPITAL

Profit is the source of earned capital. The more revenues exceed expenses, the greater the surplus and therefore, the greater the amount of money potentially available to retain in the enterprise. To maximize this difference, aggregate revenues must increase (without an equal or greater increase in expenses) or aggregate expenses must decrease (without an equal or greater decrease in revenues)—or even better, both need to happen.

Accomplishing either or both of these results is difficult. The discussion in Part III, regarding the building and implementing of the enterprise's operating plan, spoke to the challenges of growing revenues, particularly in markets that have limited or no resources. Understanding this, perhaps the best that can be said is that:

> **SOCIAL ENTERPRISE?**
>
> What does it mean to be a social enterprise?
>
> Some argue that being a social enterprise means being a profitable nonprofit entity. Examples of this are enterprises like nonprofit hospitals, nursing homes, day care centers, etc. However, profitability may be the consequence of, rather than the defining factor. Operational behavior is the real determinant.
>
> Recognizing this, social enterprises are nonprofit entities that do not put money on the table, by paying more for goods and services than necessary, or leave money on the table, by either underpricing their services or not charging or providing a means for contributions when such opportunities are possible and not inappropriate.

- Thinking that profitable new ventures can be established is an attractive, simple, and wrong conclusion. If the opposite were true, then for-profit firms would be pursuing those very ventures (e.g., if a soup kitchen could be profitable it would be a restaurant, or if a homeless shelter could be profitable it would be a hotel).

- No money should be "left on the table"—either because of underpricing, paying too much for purchased goods and services, or inefficiency. While there may not be many who can pay market rates or even a portion of the market rate, those who can should be charged some amount, with the earned revenue being used to subsidize the program(s) or contributed toward earned capital.[5]

- Similarly, nonprofit purchasing or supply chain managers must negotiate for the best possible prices. Being nonprofit does not mean being economically undisciplined, paying more than market rates to vendors who are donors or suppliers who are "friends" of the enterprise.

- Nonprofit organizations must always have a focus on efficiency. Efficiency is not the exclusive purview of for-profit firms. It is one of the general driving principles of all businesses—and nonprofit enterprises are, at their core, businesses.

From a mechanical perspective, maximizing revenues also means that cash management processes must be examined and, if need be, changed to accelerate the inflow of cash—through continuously improving billing and collection processes—and decelerate the outflow of cash, through supply chain and accounts payable management. The reduced need for cash (working capital), will increase the resources available for long-term capital investment—either in reserves or physical assets.

In a similar vein, maximizing revenue involves maximizing investment income, both by generating earnings on available short-term cash and by prudently investing any available long-term reserves.

With respect to reserves, the enterprise's investment strategy should not be one of chasing high yields, regardless of risk or avoiding all risks. Rather, the enterprise must develop a strategy grounded in prudent risk tolerance.

> **TROUBLE**
>
> Utilizing a board member who is a financial professional to manage the enterprise's investments is unfair to both parties, doing little more than setting the stage for trouble. While conflict cannot be guaranteed, it is likely because it is difficult to satisfy all members of the board, over a multi-year period that performance has been maximized. Someone on the board will always know (urban legend or not) of some situation or circumstance where more was earned and question why the enterprise is not doing as well. At the same time, the financial professional, to avoid criticism for principal loss, will often be more conservative than an external manager without an emotional tie to the enterprise. The net investment results will therefore, almost always, be more modest.
>
> A better role for a board member, who is also a financial services professional, is that of oversight of the hired financial advisor(s). The board member, in effect, acts as a financial advisor and overseer, not the investment manager or the investment consultant. In this role the board member's subject matter expertise can really be used to the enterprise's benefit.

Prudent risk tolerance requires that:
- assets and liabilities are matched;
- investment yields and liquidity be synchronized with cash needs;
- the possibility of principal loss must be balanced with the need for sustainability and not exceed what is either financially or psychologically affordable.

It also requires that management and the board fully discuss the enterprise's risk tolerance and reaches an informed consensus that is both supportable and can be communicated to an investment advisor—as the enterprise's investment policy.

Like other technical areas, investment management is a specialized realm, demanding unique subject matter expertise. Personal investment success neither equates with, nor translates into, institutional investment skills. If the enterprise is fortunate enough to have sufficient resources to make financial investments, it should also be wise enough to utilize the advice of a non-board member, financial professional to inform and guide its actions.[6]

Two general types of outside financial investment professionals are available to work with the enterprise—investment managers and investment consultants. Investment manager services range from simple advisory help to full authority to use their own discretion in determining, within the parameters of the enterprise's investment policy, and implementing investment decisions.

In contrast, investment consultants do not invest funds. Rather, they act as consultants to the enterprise, aiding it in selecting and then monitoring investment managers and investment performance.

DEBT

Health care institutions, universities and colleges, and other nonprofit corporations often have access to tax-exempt debt, that is, debt whose interest payments to lenders are exempt from at least federal income taxation and, often depending on the state and the lender's residence, local and state taxes. Through local economic development programs, for-profit firms may also have access to similar tax-exempt financing.

The value to the borrower of tax-exempt debt is that it requires lower interest payments than taxable debt.[19] This is the result of lenders being concerned about their after tax, not pre-tax, return (i.e., the amount that they can take home). Taxable debt must pay a higher interest rate than its tax-exempt counterpart to produce the same "take-home" return.

Recognizing this, debt, unless it is a perpetual bond with no requirement for redemption, is a source of financing, not a source of capital.[20]

Debt is a way, at a cost (e.g., interest payments and the operating restrictions)—set out in bond covenants or loan agreements—to manage the timing of the availability of capital. While interest payments are an obvious cost of capital, they may be less onerous than bond covenants or loan restrictions. Here, prohibitions against further capital spending, without lender approval or requirements to maintain minimum cash balances, profitability, reserves, etc., can be more problematic and costly than the simple cost of the interest payments.

Debt has a role as a management tool. It enables the enterprise to obtain money on a schedule that meets its needs and that it can control. These are two important advantages. Debt, however, with the above exception, must ultimately be repaid. This can only be done by, at some future date, substituting capital, either earned and/or contributed, for debt.

EXPENSE REDUCTION

Reducing expenses is equally challenging. In the real world of economic scarcity, with demand for services always pressing against supply constraints, continually improving productivity, even if it had no impact on profitability, would still be a business necessity. The point should be well understood by now. Therefore, nothing is to be gained by repeating the discussion of Part III. Even so, it should be emphasized that while the enterprise cannot save its way to success—it cannot achieve ongoing profitability without aggressively managing expenses.

The ability to earn capital rests more on the ability to manage expenses than to grow revenues. Quite simply, without expense management discipline, revenue growth will be consumed by increased expenses. Good managers concentrate on expense management through continually focusing on operational performance improvement.

All other things being equal, the result of this focus on continuous operating performance improvement is earned capital.

CONTRIBUTIONS

The second source of capital is contributions from donors.[7] These gifts are the financial equivalent of equity investments in the enterprise, analogous to stockholder investments in a for-profit firm.

> **TRILLION$***
>
> Over the next several decades, by about 2050, it is projected that over $40 trillion will be transferred from one generation to the next. This is an historic economic event, creating remarkable opportunities for organizations to not only find operating support for specific programs but also to add to their capital base.
>
> * John J. Havens and Paul G. Schervish, Millionaires and the New Millennium: Estimates of the Forthcoming Wealth Transfer and the Prospects for a Golden Age of Philanthropy, Social Welfare Research Institute, Boston MA, 1999.

While a stockholder invests because of a belief in the firm's ability to make money and thereby increase the value of the investment, nonprofit donors invest because of a belief in the work of the enterprise—its mission and its ability to effectively pursue that mission. This means that before they are likely to invest, donors must become aware of the enterprise, its work, its performance, and its needs. Quite simply, awareness and "friend" raising must precede fundraising. It is recognition of this reality that the fundraising function is increasingly being organizationally titled as development, fund development, or institutional advancement, giving weight to the understanding that first, the enterprise must create a constituency that supports its purpose. For it is out of this constituency of supporters, that, in time, donors will emerge.

Fundraising at its core is based on relationships, both organizational and, more importantly, individual. Some of these relationships may be historical, going back to the enterprise's founding and initial growth. Others must be developed on a contemporaneous basis. The former must be maintained, and the latter must be created and nurtured. Effective fundraising recognizes both constituencies, as well as the requirements and needs for cultivating relationships with both groups.

Fundraising is also a complex discipline, part art and part science. The art centers on the cultivation of interpersonal relationships, identifying, developing, and continuously nurturing the interests of people and organizations that can help the enterprise pursue its mission. The science concentrates on data mining, the psychology, technology, and mechanics of communication and solicitation, financial planning and the continuously evolving technology to develop, as well as maintain, relationships with donors and potential donors.

FOUNDATIONS: THREE TRENDS

The number of foundations has increased dramatically from 1999 (50,000+) to 2018 (86,000+). Driving this growth has been the increase in family foundations. One third of family foundations have been established since 2000.

Family foundations are defined by The Foundation Center as independent foundations with material donor or donor family involvement. The growth in these types of foundations reflects the combination of increased wealth and the significant tax advantages available to families of wealth through the creation and use of their own foundation.

A second and related trend has been the growth in donor-advised funds in community foundations, national religious federations, and commercial company-sponsored gift funds like the Fidelity Charitable Gift Fund.

These vehicles legally require that the donor give up ownership and control of the gifted funds. Pragmatically, because they want to continue to grow, donor-advised funds are quite differential to the distribution "suggestions" of donors.

Donor-advised funds provide donors with many of the advantages of a private foundation, but with less overhead cost and work. They also enable donors to take full tax advantage of their gift at the time they contribute to the fund, even though disbursement to charitable organizations might not take place until some point in the future. As a consequence, because money can stay in the donor-advised funds for some time, charitable giving statistics could be somewhat misleading, overstating the amount that actually is given to operating nonprofit organizations in any given year. Conversely in future years, actual gifts to operating entities may increase by more than that year's giving as donor-advised fund reserves are drawn down.

The third trend is an increase in new types of foundations available for nonprofits to seek grants. Two examples are "conversion foundations" set up after acquisitions to benefit the community and "corporate foundations" set up to support a geographic area or genre of nonprofit focus. Researching these foundations on the Internet is usually an easy task.

Like other areas of management (i.e., quality control, operations improvement, finance, etc.), fundraising has developed as its own academic concentration with courses in grant writing and solicitation as well as certificate programs, masters and doctorate degrees in fundraising and/or philanthropy, and professional certification (Certified Fundraising Executive).[8] Given the depth and breadth of this material, a comprehensive examination of fundraising is beyond the scope of this chapter. Nevertheless, the reader should have at least an understanding of certain fundamental fundraising realities. (See Appendix 14.)

First, even for the largest nonprofit enterprises, if for no other reason than the size of their aspirations, fundraising is hard work, made even psychologically harder by the high failure rate—it is estimated that only 25% of requests will be successful in any given year.[9] This is particularly so for small agencies serving poor clients. These enterprises do not have a natural donor base that is continually renewing and often expanding itself like hospitals, colleges, and universities. Recognizing this, the reported data tell an interesting story.[10] (See Exhibit 12-1.)

Private charitable giving in 2018 was estimated to be $427+ billion. This compares with $295 billion in 2006, $310.5 billion in 2007, and $291 billion in 2010. The 2010 giving reflects the lingering effect of the Great Recession and the resulting sensitivity of philanthropy to general economic conditions.

Of the $427+ billion, over 80% of it came from individuals. While larger gifts from foundations draw more attention and visibility, it is individuals who are the nation's major source of philanthropy. Foundations, particularly family foundations, are growing in number and gifting capacity. Similarly, donor-advised funds at brokerage houses, collective fundraisers, and community foundations are having a growing presence.

Exhibit 12-1

THE NUMBERS	
Giving	
$427.71 Billion	Was given to charitable organizations by individuals, foundations, and businesses in 2018.
87%	Of charitable giving by individuals through personal annual gifts, bequests, or family foundations.
59%	Of people give because the cause is important to them. Only 6% give because a person or organization asked them to contribute.
43%	Of giving is from "Baby Boomers" (people born between 1946 and 1964) who represent only 23% of the population.
30.9%	Of all charitable contributions in 2017 went to congregations and religious organizations. 14.3% went to higher education and 12.1% went to human service organizations.
8.7%	Of total charitable revenue comes from donations by individuals. 2.95% comes from foundation gifts and grants; 1.5% comes from bequests; and 0.9% comes from corporations.
Foundations	
86,000+	Grant-making foundations in 2018, making $62.8 billion grants.
42.1%	The increase in foundation giving from 2005 to 2015.
33.2%	The increase in foundation assets from 2005 to 2015.

In 2009, there were an estimated 76,000+ grant-making foundations, an increase over the decade from 1999 by 52%. By 2018, the number of grant-making foundations had grown to more than 86,000. In 2008, foundation gifts were about $45.8 billion. In 2015, gifts had increased to about $62.8 billion.

Given this brief background, it is useful to realize that while important to all 501(c)(3) organizations (entities to which donations can provide a tax benefit to donors), philanthropy:

• Accounts for about 14% of total nonprofit sector revenue. (Over 20% of the sector's revenue if you exclude health care and higher education.)

• Is sensitive to general economic conditions, having, for example, declined by over 11% from 2007 to 2008 and by another 3.3% in 2009. Since then, it has grown to record levels. This growth is in spite of changes to the tax policy that reduced the tax savings (by limiting the percentage of the contribution that could be deducted in determining taxable income from 39.6% to 28%) and later (2017) revisions that changed the standard deduction in such a way that fewer people are expected to itemize deductions, thereby reducing the tax incentives for making contributions. (In 2009, taxpayers using itemized deductions accounted for 77% of total individual contributions.)[11,12]

- In 2020, organizations faced an unprecedented set of challenges due to the COVID-19 pandemic crisis. Fundraising programming had to change as a consequence of the prohibition against large gatherings. At the same time, demand for services increased as people who in the past were contributors became clients needing food and housing assistance.

The conclusions from these data are that:
- Philanthropy is important to all 501(c)(3) organizations—and particularly so for non-health care and non-higher education entities.

- The cultivation of individual donors is vital to fundraising success.

- Organizations that are able to continually generate renewed donor bases— educational and religious institutions—raise the most money.

- While financial angels exist, and from their existence springs the lasting hope that with just a little luck, a fundraising "home run" can be hit, productive fundraising must be built on systematic management processes that identify and engage large numbers of individual donors.

Fundraising, though not the mission of most nonprofit enterprises, is for many vital to the successful pursuit of mission.[13] Given its importance to enterprise success, fundraising must not be treated as an afterthought, but rather as a priority operating objective. That is, it must have strategic and operating objectives, as well as a plan and adequate budget for achieving those objectives. In creating its plan, the enterprise must recognize that fundraising is not a costless activity. (See Exhibit 12-2.)

Exhibit 12-2

FUNDRAISING: COST AND RETURN*	
In establishing fundraising objectives, the budget must be in step with the expectations. Obviously, fundraising has a cost. The return on investment for fundraising expenditures is estimated to be:	
For	**Return: Cost/dollar raised**
Direct Mail Acquisition	$1.00 to $1.25/dollar raised
Direct Mail Renewal	$.20/dollar raised
Benefit Event	$.50/dollar raised
Corporate Support	$.20/dollar raised
Planned Giving	$.25/dollar raised
Major Gifts/Capital Campaign	$.05 to $.10/dollar raised
*Smith, Bucklin and Associates Inc., *Complete Guide to Nonprofit Management*, 2nd ed. and Greenfield, Jim, *Fund Raising Management: Evaluating and Managing the Fund Development Process.*	

In fact, one major factor that erodes trust in an enterprise is inefficient fundraising efforts. Fundraising is an area where financial metrics can be calculated and potential donors can make quantitative judgments. The Better Business Bureau's Wise Giving Alliance Standards for Charity Accountability, for example, recommend that fundraising expenses should be no more than thirty five percent (35%) of total contributions. Fundraising managers must understand the power—in the eyes of donors—of these kinds of performance measures, as well as the reality that efficient and effective fundraising results have to be sensitive to the natural segmentation of the donor market.

ANNUAL GIVING

Annual giving campaigns are different from legacy initiatives. Annual giving is an ongoing effort similar to any other operating program. It is a set of activities, repeated (ideally with enough change to make the program look fresh and imaginative) from year-to-year with the expectation that they will yield income and profit—while simultaneously providing a mechanism for maintaining existing enterprise friends and engaging new people in being aware of the enterprise and hopefully developing an active philanthropic interest in its work.

From this perspective, annual giving activities are the bridge linking earned income capital generation to the longer-term efforts to generate major gifts—in effect, equity capital. On the one hand, annual giving is an operating program intended to produce profits that will support other enterprise costs and activities. or other operating activities. On the other, it is a constituency development and maintenance effort, intended both to maintain and expand the enterprise's circle of friends—and hopefully future financial supporters, particularly major donors.

At a minimum, annual giving initiatives should involve one or more solicitation letters/personal requests asking for support. Recall that though it is a relatively small number, some donors will give simply if they are asked. Therefore, an ask must be made. However, the effort must be more than just a request to "send money." The solicitation, regardless of form, must develop an explanation and justification (i.e. a "case") for donors to provide their support.

The case for support is the gateway for

GOVERNMENT SUPPORT*

While it may seem to be counterintuitive, as government support increases, private giving decreases. The research suggests that a dollar in government spending on nonprofit activities displaces about 50 cents in private giving. Economists refer to this phenomenon as "crowding out." It reflects the reasonable human reaction of perceiving government support and private giving as interchangeable. Therefore, as government contributions increase, private contributions decline. Fortunately, the tradeoff is not one for one. Unfortunately, there is trade off. The financial result is that the net increase in total funding is less than anticipated. Of equal importance is the operational consequence.

For nonprofit enterprises that rely on both public funding and private gifts, government support both lessens the results of fundraising and makes the enterprise more dependent on continued government support. That said, while "crowding out" reduces the overall financial impact of public support, total support is increased, albeit by not as much as the increase in government's contribution.

*Arthur C. Brooks, Who Really Cares, (New York: Basic Books, 2007), pg 58.

MEMBERSHIP

In considering annual giving opportunities, one possibility is promoting organizational membership in the enterprise. In this context, membership is not the formal corporate membership discussed in Chapter 4, with its legal accountabilities. Rather, it is effectively a social membership where individuals and corporations pay an annual fee (dues) to be part of the group supporting the enterprise's work.

Membership offers a relatively low-cost way, both to the enterprise, since membership solicitations and renewals can be done by mail, and to the donor, by providing the donor with options for membership levels, for people and organizations to be part of the enterprise. As importantly, it also builds a database of contacts that can be cultivated to increase both their volunteer and financial support.

engaging donors to become part of the work of the enterprise. As such, it must have an emotional element (i.e. marketing hope and the potential to make a difference) capable of transferring the attraction and vision of the enterprise to the imagination of the donor, and a business component, explaining in a compelling way why support is needed and how the donation will be used.

Donors must understand that what the enterprise is doing, as well as what it hopes to do—and why it needs their help. To do this well, the enterprise must tell a story and telling a story requires a planful approach, that builds throughout the year before it asks for money. Contact between the donor and the enterprise must be about more than the enterprise always having its proverbial hand out. It must try to embrace the donor as a partner in the enterprise's attempt to make a difference.

Beyond direct mail solicitations and annual appeals, other annual giving activities are essentially transactional philanthropy, involving the donor buying or paying for something (e.g. a membership, a golf foursome, event sponsorship, a gala table, etc.). The only limits on what can be done are the creativity of management and the willingness of the board to support and participate in the event.

As noted above, annual giving campaigns provide the vehicles for building the enterprise's base of potential new donors as well as nurturing existing donors. The value of the latter cannot be overestimated. The organization's best prospects are people who have already given—and the more a person gives, the more likely he or she is to give again. At the same time, the importance of the opportunity to create new donors and build the environment for major gift requests should be understood. It is out of annual giving, that major gifts often come.

MAJOR GIFTS

Major gifts are legacy donations, helping to assure the future of the enterprise. Often major gifts are sought as part of capital or endowment campaigns, with naming opportunities for the most significant contributors. These campaigns differ from annual giving efforts both in terms of frequency and the size of their goals (i.e., they occur less often and try to raise significantly more money).[14]

DONOR FATIGUE

In developing its annual giving plans the enterprise should be sensitive to the reality of donor fatigue. Donors are attacked from all directions with requests for gifts. For one appeal to stand out it must be able to get through the clutter of all the other messages. This is why personal solicitation, even if just a handwritten note on a formal letter, is so important and powerful.

Avoidance of donor fatigue also requires that the enterprise periodically update/redesign its annual giving product options, so that donors not only have options but also variety.

Legacy campaigns are major undertakings, often requiring dedicated staff and a multi-year time horizon. Unless they are in reaction to a crisis, major gift campaigns usually begin with a feasibility study (i.e., can the campaign be done and, if so, how much might be raised). If the campaign is judged to be feasible, then strategy must be shaped, the case statement (i.e., what is needed, why it is needed and the difference the donor can make) crafted, naming opportunities identified and priced, and the donor market identified and segmented. All of this has to be done even before the non-public, "quiet part" of the campaign begins.

It is in the "quiet part" of the campaign that potential major donors both become aware of, and comfortable with, the enterprise's aspirations as well as satisfied that the organization is well run and capable of achieving its goals. It is also the time where leadership gifts or commitments (i.e., a pledge to give "X" dollars over "Y" years) are sought from potential major donors so that when the formal, public campaign is announced it can be accompanied by successful supporting news of gifts received and/or commitments made.

In addition to legacy campaigns, from time-to-time, the enterprise might have special projects that require extraordinary financial support. Developing support for these kinds of projects differs from legacy initiatives in that their duration is shorter, the amounts sought are less, and the focus is narrower (i.e., a one-time only or a unique event in the enterprise's business life). A home care agency establishing an inpatient hospice facility or a day care organization needing to replace its heating system are examples of possible special project fundraising opportunities.

These kinds of highly focused special need campaigns also often offer donors a means to be visibly associated with the enterprise, through naming and other recognition programs, at a lower cost than a legacy campaign gift. The only cautionary note is to be aware of the potential for donor fatigue. Regular special project funding requests may not only desensitize donors to the needs of the enterprise but also, raise questions about management's planning and operating abilities.

Planned giving also provides a means for raising major gifts. Planned giving is theoretically considered to be any contribution that requires more thought to execute than a normal donation. More pragmatically, it is a tax efficient way for donors to make substantial gifts to charitable organizations.

Typically, planned giving is a decision, made near the end of life, by a donor to make a deferred gift. In its simplest form, a planned gift can be a bequest set out in a donor's will or designation (by the donor) of the enterprise as the beneficiary of a life insurance policy or a cash gift from the estate. It can also be more complicated (see Exhibit 12-4). Each mechanism offers a means of providing a future gift to the organization, often with current and estate tax nuances (i.e., the tax benefits occurring to the donor before the actual gift is received by the enterprise). Therefore, from the donor's perspective the advice of tax and legal counsel should be sought before planned giving commitments are made.[15]

From the enterprise's perspective, planned giving is a bit of an unknown. To put it into context, the available data suggests that although 40+% of Americans have wills, only about 9% have included charitable bequests in their wills. Surprisingly, once a bequest has been put into a will, it is estimated that only 3% of those bequests are later revoked. Equally surprising is that, until they are received, 70+% of bequests are unknown to the benefiting organizations.

While the logic and opportunity of planned giving seems clear, the process has historically been marked by frustration in terms of securing gift commitments. The specific reasons for this are as varied as the attempts. However, the underlying problems are three: lack of good data systems, lack of good research, and lack of good follow through. The importance of data, research, and follow through apply, not just to planned giving, but to all of the enterprise's fundraising efforts.

MANAGEMENT

If the key to successful fundraising is personal contact, then the key to productive personal contact is good underlying databases, systems, and processes. The need for efficient and effective systems and processes applies as relevantly to fundraising as it does to any other function that must be managed successfully to achieve its objective.

If the first two realities of fundraising are that it is both hard and important work, the third is that its sustainable success, setting luck aside, is determined by its supporting systems, research, and follow through.[16]

From an operational management perspective, the fundraising process starts with building a donor (and potential donor) database. Donor lists can be purchased from commercial sources. Their cost, however, is high, if measured in terms of yield versus acquisition and campaign implementation expenses. A more productive alternative is for the enterprise to build its own donor database. This need not be a daunting task. However, it must be a continuous and ongoing task. The underpinning for any donor database should be the enterprise's own known contacts. This includes current and past board members, vendors, current and retired employees, current and past contributors, volunteers, attendees and guests at enterprise-sponsored events and

> ### ANGELS
>
> Fundraising angels, donors who make a large and even sometimes surprising gift, exist. When an angel emerges, it is both a cause for celebration and a noteworthy event. It is an event, in part, because of its rarity. This rarity also evidences that angels are an example of the triumph of hope over reality. The reality is that fundraising is hard work, requiring the personal commitment of board members and other friends of the enterprise. The hope is that an angel will appear and solve the enterprise's capital problems, making the hard work unnecessary.
>
> Certainly, the hope and quest for angels should always go on. A professional fundraiser—either on staff or as a consultant—can help with the search. A professional fundraiser, however, does not come with a "pocket full of angels." The professional fundraiser can guide the process of developing a database, building and maintaining relationships, helping to determine whom can be asked for what, when to ask, who should make the request, and how the follow up should be handled. The professional fundraiser can also be responsible for assuring that the enterprise's fundraising activities are comprehensive and carried out as planned and budgeted.
>
> The simple fact is that angels come more from systematic, continual fundraising work than from luck.

programs. It also may include some of the enterprise's past clients who have achieved success, beneficiaries or graduates (this is particularly an opportunity for many institutional health care providers and universities/colleges), and additional names that primary contacts suggest as persons who would be interested in the work of the enterprise, etc.

The database should be as extensive as it is productive, and as complete as it is practical. Fundraising costs both time and money and therefore, should be targeted to those with an interest and an ability to support the enterprise. The database is the foundation upon which research, solicitation, and follow up will be built. Therefore, it should have not only basic contact information, but also as much additional data as possible both for relationship building and for making the appropriate gift request (i.e., birth date so that birthday cards can be sent out, relationship to the enterprise (how the person is known either directly or indirectly), past giving history (if any—and its timing and amount, estimate of gift potential—both type and amount, etc.)

Donor database management systems are commercially available, so the enterprise does not have to create software. It will, however, have to build and maintain the database, pruning as necessary (to reflect deaths, relocations, and people with a history of failed support) and simultaneously working to increase the fundraising yield by adding productive names and background information—for both new and existing database entrants.

This last point suggests the importance of research. The database must be "mined" to identify not simply prospects but, prospects for what type of appeal— annual, major gift, planned gift, and/or special project gift. (See Exhibit 12-3.) This is where the science and art of fundraising come together and where the fundraising subject matter expert plays the major role.

Exhibit 12-3

EXAMPLE OF SOLICITATION MARKET SEGMENTATION		
Market Segment	**Priority*** (Likelihood of Contribution)	**Possible Gift**
Current Board Members	1	Annual, Major, Planned, Membership, Special Projects
Senior Management	1	Annual, Planned, Membership
Vendors	1	Event Sponsorship, Special Projects
Major Businesses in the Community	2	Event Sponsorship, Special Projects
Past Donors	2	Annual, Major
Volunteers	2	Annual, Planned, Membership
Former Board Members	2	Annual, Major, Planned, Membership, Special Projects
Retired Employees	3	Annual, Planned, Membership
New Contacts	4	Annual, Membership
Former Clients/ Beneficiaries	5	Annual, Membership
General Public	6	Annual, Membership
*Grants and funding from government agencies, foundations, and corporations represent a parallel fundraising.		

Once the technical data parts of fundraising are in place, the focus must shift to execution and follow through. There are technical elements to this aspect. Crafting a newsletter, annual giving solicitation request, or a proposal is a challenging task, as is grant writing. The database should identify who gets what, and when (i.e., newsletters, letters from the chief executive, membership requests, annual giving solicitations, small group meetings, personal meetings, etc.). Execution also requires planned follow up (i.e., when contact should be made and how it should be done including whom, if the contact is going to be personal).

THE BOARD

It is here where another reality of fundraising comes into play. Successful fundraising requires the personal involvement of the enterprise's board.[17] Involvement, however, can take a variety of forms. Certainly, all board members must make a personal financial commitment (contribution) to the enterprise. (See Chapter 6, The Unspoken Criterion.)

The need for board member financial commitment is straightforward. It is difficult to ask someone who is not as involved with the organization as its own board members to make a contribution—if the board, in its entirety, has not already led the way. That said, all board members do not have to contribute at the same level.

Expectations can be set but, it must also be understood that circumstances differ and, if full board participation is to be achieved, people can only contribute what they can afford. A rule of thumb, however, is that if you are on the board of an organization, that organization should be among your top three places for gifts.

In addition to their financial contributions, board members must also participate in the enterprise's overall fundraising efforts. The degree of this participation, as noted earlier, is often a matter of tension between management and the board. Each expects more of the other than they perceive is being done. Some chief executives believe that the board's principal purpose is to raise money. Some boards believe that they have fulfilled their fundraising responsibilities when they hire a chief executive, expecting the chief executive to raise needed capital. Importantly, because it is a task that has easily recognized performance metrics,

---

WHY DO I HAVE TO FUNDRAISE?

A common question from board members is, "Why do I have to fundraise? Isn't that the job of the CEO, the finance committee, the development director —or anyone else but me?"

The answer is straightforward. As a board member, part of your fiduciary responsibility is to review and ultimately approve the enterprise's business plan. Part of that review and approval process requires that you make a judgment that the realistic level of resources available is consistent with the plan (i.e. you don't have a $3 million plan and a $2 million checkbook).

If you don't believe the resources and the plan are consistent, then you should not approve the plan without either changing the required level of resources or committing to working to get more resources. If you approve the plan with the understanding that more resources are going to be needed, then you are at the same time committing to helping find those resources.

Your approval is your agreement to get personally involved in fundraising.

This does not mean that you personally have to solicit contributions—though it might. Rather, at a minimum, it means that you have to be an active part of the systematic fundraising process.

many boards are quick to question if the chief executive is doing enough or accomplishing enough. Not surprisingly, chief executives look to the enterprise's board for fundraising help. As a consequence, they are equally quick to judge performance, wondering if the board, either in whole or its individual members, are doing all they can (or should) do for the enterprise. Both perspectives are troublesome. The facts are that each must be involved, and both must work together.

WHERE TO START?

In fundraising it is said that the enterprise should:

"Solicit inside-out and top-down," meaning that you should solicit those closest to your organization first (i.e., your board and previous donors), then donors with the highest giving potential, and on down to those with the lowest potential."*

* Smith, Bucklin and Associates, Inc., "Raising Money to Serve Your Cause," *Complete Guide to Nonprofit Management*, 2nd ed., (New York: John Wiley & Sons, 2000), Chapter 5.

Every chief executive must recognize not only his or her personal, central position in fundraising, providing explicit time for fundraising activities and taking a "hands on role" but also, the legitimate reluctance and anxiety of many board members to become involved in fundraising. As a consequence, management must find initial fundraising support roles for these board members to play—and hopefully, grow them over time into more active participation.

The board must similarly recognize both their inherent credibility and that their combined network of contacts exceeds that of management's. They must therefore, at least, if not necessarily asking directly for financial support, make as many people as possible aware of the enterprise's work and provide a pathway to begin to engage them in that work.

Every board member must be an ambassador of the enterprise to the community. Board members must be willing to suggest people to contact, write personal notes on solicitation letters and invitations, write thank you notes to contributors whom they know, introduce management to potential enterprise supporters, host potential supporters as guests at enterprise-sponsored events, etc. All of this is short of actually soliciting a gift—though, in the course of time, some board members may become comfortable enough with their fundraising skills to expand their personal role and become active solicitors.

Many boards and managers believe that all of an enterprise's problems could be solved, or at least made easier, if it only had more money. Obviously, money helps, and capital generation and accumulation is necessary. The mission of the enterprise, however, is not simply to raise money from donors. Therefore, fundraising, while important, must be kept in perspective. It is a means to an end, not an end in itself. When management and the board fail to recognize this, consciously or unconsciously placing fundraising ahead of mission, they doom fundraising efforts to ultimate failure.

THANK YOU

Before moving on, a last point should be noted with respect to fundraising. Quite simply, it is the importance of saying "thank you" and staying "in touch." Certainly, as noted above, board members should thank contributors whom they know. Beyond this, all donors, regardless of the size of their contribution, should get the enterprise's thanks.

Just as a contribution must be solicited, all must also be acknowledged with appreciation if for no other reason than to set the basis for the next request.

How the thank you is accomplished can vary with the size of the donation and the amount of information available as to how to reach out to the donor. Small contributions can be acknowledged with both letters and, if available, email. Larger donations should get more attention ranging all the way to personal contact and follow up invitations to come and see how the contribution is being used and the difference it is making.

This year's thank you is simply the first step in securing next year's donation. Appropriately and publicly recognizing donors is also part of securing the next donation. If the organization publishes an annual listing of donors, care must be taken to assure that no one is by accident left out or mis-listed.[18] Particular care should be taken with donors who wish to be anonymous, both to protect their anonymity and to assure that they understand that their generosity—even if not publicly known—is recognized and appreciated.

> **PRACTICAL GUIDELINES***
>
> Fundraising is about relationships—people support causes to which they feel personally connected.
>
> **Be in touch**
> - Ask for the gift last—answer questions first.
> - Identify top 50 donors or potential donors; visit or have a conversation with at least one donor per week.
>
> Talk to your potential contributors—tell stories about the work you do, not the business you're in.
>
> **Be clear**
> - Focus on mission
> - Share vision, not problems
> - Be relevant
>
> Thank three times—thank more than you ask. Make the thanks personally focused and grateful.
>
> **Be near**
> - A letter is good
> - Telephone is better
> - Face-to-face is best
>
> *Daniel Meyers, Retired President, Al Sigl Community of Agencies, Rochester, NY

Quite simply, donors, even those who say they wish anonymity and no recognition, should never be taken for granted. In fact, the emphasis should be just the opposite. Even if they can no longer offer current financial support, all donors—past and present—must be treated, and feel that they are being treated, as friends of the enterprise.

SUSTAINABILITY

The simple reality is that regardless of whether the enterprise's strategic objective is to remain stable or grow, additional capital (earned or contributed—financial or volunteer) is necessary for organizational survival.

The role of volunteers in nonprofit enterprises and compensation of paid staff are discussed in the following chapter. One of the unique features of community sector enterprises is their ability to use volunteers as substitutes for paid staff and thereby reduce both operating costs and capital needs. Therefore, volunteer recruitment and management is a parallel activity to fundraising and if well managed can become a source of people committed to supporting the enterprise financially, as well as with their time.

Exhibit 12-4

DEFERRED GIVING	
Planned giving programs, sometimes called deferred giving, help donors make philanthropic gifts that are to be delivered at a future date. There are many variations of planned giving. The most common are:	
Bequests	Donors specify in their wills or estate plans a specific amount, percentage of their estate, or the remainder of their estate after all other bequests are paid as a gift to a charitable agency.
Charitable Gift Annuities	Donors give a significant gift, receiving a tax deduction at the time of the gift, and then receive payments from the charitable organization for a specific period or for their lifetime—after the specified period ends or upon the donor's death, the remaining funds become the property of the corporation.*
Charitable Lead Trust**	Donors give assets to an irrevocable trust designed to provide financial support to a charitable organization for a specified period of time. At the end of that period, any remaining assets are returned to specified non-charitable beneficiaries. (Note: a charitable lead trust is the inverse of a charitable remainder trust. However, unlike a remainder trust, it is not tax-exempt.)
Charitable Remainder Trust	Donors give assets to a tax-exempt, irrevocable trust that makes annual payments (either a fixed amount or a fixed percentage) to the donor (or specified beneficiary) for a certain number of years and then donates the remainder to the charitable corporation.*
Pooled Income Funds	Donors contribute to a trust, established by the charitable organization, that pays dividends to the donor during their lifetime, with the remainder then reverting to the organization.*
Planned giving programs, particularly for small enterprises, can be simple bequest programs. However, they can also be complex, requiring expert legal and tax help for both the donor and the organization. They are effectively multi-year initiatives, designed to help assure the financial sustainability of the enterprise. In the short run, however, they also require the commitment of the board and management, as well as an adequate budget to support staff, demographic and donor database research, marketing, donor education, and follow-up.	
Are they worth it? Yes. Historically, planned gifts are more than twice as large as a donor's lifetime charitable giving.***	
* The amounts that can be paid are limited by IRS regulations. ** Charitable trusts are complicated and subject to specific IRS rules. *** Source: www.donorsearch.net	

CHAPTER 12

Takeaways and Questions for Consideration and Discussion:

TAKEAWAYS

1. Survival and growth require nonprofits to generate income in a regular and sustainable way. Earning income and equity through philanthropic gifts does not just happen. It requires a continuous commitment from both the board and management—as evidenced by an adequate budget, research and planning, and personal involvement.

2. Philanthropy is important to almost all nonprofit enterprises, particularly human service agencies. Therefore, investing in fundraising should be viewed as a necessity.

3. Individual donors are the nation's major source of philanthropy, both in annual giving and legacy donations.

4. There are two primary and reliable sources for that income—earned income and contributions. Both sources of income require focused efforts from the board leadership and staff and must be effectively managed.

QUESTIONS

1. Why is it important to pay attention to investment income performance?

2. What factors should the enterprise's earned revenue policies take into account? Particularly, how should revenue for subsidies be obtained, and what role should government funding be allowed to play?

3. Why should annual fundraising be thought of as an ongoing profit center?

4. How does management support the board in fundraising? How does the board support management? How important is it that board members know about fundraising expectations as part of the member recruitment process?

Chapter 13:
HUMAN RESOURCES: VOLUNTEERS AND PAID STAFF

Volunteer time and work can also be thought of as a source of contributed capital. To the extent that volunteers are substitutes for paid staff, they either maintain or extend the enterprise's ability to achieve its mission. From a financial perspective, volunteer work has an effect similar to monetary contributions, dedicated to operations. Both enable the enterprise to maintain or extend its work.[1]

In 2010, total community (nonprofit) sector paid workforce was estimated to be about 13.7 million employees.[2] This, in turn, is estimated to be about 61% of the total nonprofit workforce. Volunteers provide an estimated 8.8 million full-time equivalent workers.[3]

The bulk of volunteer work effort is given to charitable organizations. However, substantial volunteering also takes place in the public sector through the public schools and increasingly in state and local governments through programs to promote community volunteer work.[4] Also, it can be argued that programs that pay modest stipends or salaries, such as VISTA (Volunteers In Service To America), Teach For America, City Year, and the Peace Corp., are really hybrid volunteer efforts.

In 2010, 26.3% of the population age 16 and older (62.8 million people) are estimated to have provided volunteer service during the year.[5,6] Not surprisingly, given the earlier financial contribution data, most volunteering was done in religious organizations—followed by education and youth services. (See Exhibit 13-1.) What volunteers did by activity is summarized in Exhibit 13-2. As indicated, the largest single use of volunteer time was in administrative activities, including fundraising, office work, writing, and editing. The second most popular area of activity was social services and care, which included food preparation, collecting and delivering clothes and other goods, providing direct care, teaching, and mentoring.

Exhibit 13-1

VOLUNTEERS BY ORGANIZATION CLASSIFICATION 2006 & 2010*		
Classification	Percentage of Volunteer Effort (Approx.) 2006	Percentage of Volunteer Effort (Approx.) 2010
Civic and Political	6.1	5.3
Educational and Youth Service	26.4	26.5
Environment or Animal Care	1.6	2.4
Hospital or Other Health	8.1	7.9
Public Safety	1.3	1.3
Religious	35.0	33.8
Social or Community Service	12.7	13.6
Sport, Hobby, Culture, or Arts	3.7	3.3
Other	4.9	5.9
* Data Source: Nonprofit Almanac 2012		

Exhibit 13-2

VOLUNTEERING AS MEASURED BY ACTIVITY 2006 & 2010*		
Classification	Percentage of Volunteer Time (Approx.) 2006	Percentage of Volunteer Time (Approx.) 2010
Administrative and Support	20.6	21.7
Social Service and Care	17.8	24.3
Maintenance, Building, and Cleanup	5.7	6.6
Performing and Cultural Activities	6.9	5.4
Meetings, Conferences, and Training	10.6	10.6
Public Health and Safety	0.9	0.4
Travel	14.2	10.8
Other	23.0	20.0
* Data Source: Nonprofit Almanac 2012		

While the data are interesting, the details are less important than two conclusions. First, it is not surprising that so many Americans volunteer. Reflecting on the discussion in Chapter 2, voluntary action and collective association are keystone elements in American democracy. Without volunteers, America, as we know it, would not exist.

Historically, community service was viewed as a "high calling," the responsibility of all residents. More recently, the courts have used community service as a form of punishment and recompense, imposing "X" number of hours of community service as the penalty for various forms of law breaking. This is unfortunate. Community service is not a form of punishment, an alternative to incarceration. Rather, it is every person's contribution both to enhancing their community (whether defined by geography or interest) and more importantly, to maintaining democracy.

This understanding of the importance of volunteering is recognized in the fact that successive population cohorts from 1926 on (e.g., 1926-1935, 1936-1945 and 1946-1955—first baby boom cohort), have each volunteered more than their predecessors. If this trend continues, the total number of volunteers, due to the large absolute size of the baby boom generation, will continue to increase.[7]

At the same time, the nation's high schools, colleges, and universities, are increasingly recognizing the importance of community service and the need for it to be a learned activity. High schools are often making a specified minimum number of hours of volunteer service a requirement for graduation. Colleges and universities are incorporating service learning into their curriculum as a way of exposing students to the value of community service volunteering while simultaneously enriching the student learning experience—supplementing classroom theory with practical, field experience.

Second is the realization that volunteer workers are an important part of the nonprofit business model. They are a significant source of skill and service, providing, as needed, either short—and/or long-term, human resources to meet the enterprise's personnel needs. Therefore, they must be well managed if the enterprise's stakeholders and beneficiaries are to be well served.

In terms of a management paradigm, the enterprise's approach to volunteers should be conceptually similar to how it determines the need for, as well as the deployment, supervision, and assessment of paid human resources. Exhibit 13-3 provides a macro-level overview of this process.[8]

> **WHO CAN YOU TRUST?**
>
> Most volunteers step forward out of an inner motivation to give back to their community. Volunteering is community service and is a noble calling. Understanding this, it is naïve to not realize that we live in difficult times and vetting of volunteers has become increasingly important for some positions (e.g., working in schools, working directly with young children, youth recreation programs, etc.). In addition to normal human resources employment and reference review, law enforcement background checks of applicants may either be good policy or required. Certainly, such checks may involve an added expense. This cost, however, is deminimus compared to the cost of an avoidable tragedy.

As it applies to volunteers, a board level policy approval process should precede the initial operating step of needs assessment. If an enterprise is going to use volunteers in its work, the board should adopt a policy regarding volunteers. The importance of this step is not only that it is informative to the board in a strategic sense, but also that it starts to make clear that while volunteers are not compensated in the traditional wage and salary sense, they do have a cost. This cost is reflected in both the organizational infrastructure needed to support and the recognition necessary to motivate and retain volunteer workers. Appendix 15-Part 1 provides an example of a board policy on volunteers, including a listing of volunteer rights and responsibilities. Part 2 of the Appendix provides a summary outlining the key factors in Volunteer: Supply, Demand, and Outcomes.

Exhibit 13-3

HUMAN RESOURCES MANAGEMENT FLOW: VOLUNTEERS*		
Need	What is the volunteer needed for? • Ongoing support • Special event	What is the volunteer needed to do? • Technical expertise • Service delivery • Administrative • Other
Recruitment	Sourcing • Broad based—event support • Targeted—ongoing support Matching to the task	
Vetting	• Employment history • Reference check • Background checks	
Orientation and Training	Organizational orientation training • Initial • Corporate policies • Security policies • Ongoing	
Management (Supervision)	• Organized management support and oversight • Flexible work policies—grounded in clear expectations • Psychosocial—not economic—motivation • Individual uniqueness • Meaningful work • Appropriate recognition	
Assessment	Job volunteer	
*Adapted and modified from The Jossey-Bass Handbook of Nonprofit Leadership and Management, Chapter 22.		

NEED

Given a policy foundation supporting the use of volunteers, the first step, like in any hiring decision, is to determine need. The importance of this step is not reduced by the fact that volunteers do not generate a salary/wage budget expense. As is made clear below, volunteers are not free. More importantly for the long run, if volunteers do not have a good experience, they will leave the organization, perhaps not disgruntled, but certainly not as "raving fans." The consequences of this for future "friend" and subsequent fundraising may far exceed the cost that would have been incurred if the job were paid.

The safest way to assure the possibility of a positive volunteer experience is for the enterprise to build its volunteer commitments on a foundation of need. That is, the enterprise must begin by knowing what it needs volunteers for, and then, within that framework, what specifically it needs its volunteers to do. For example, is the enterprise looking for a few people for ongoing volunteer work or a large number for a special event? Even if it is looking for both, it should make clear what its expectations are to the volunteers so that there is no misunderstanding that might later lead to ill will. In the same vein, if the enterprise is looking for continuous or long-term volunteers as either an alternative or complement to paid workers, is it seeking administrative support, technical expertise, service delivery, or some other need? Simply, if the volunteer experience is going to be good for all concerned, it must start with the organization knowing what it needs.

Identifying what a volunteer is going to be expected to do is similar to creating a job description for a paid employee. A volunteer's job description must make clear the tasks and assignments the person will be expected to do, what support they will receive, as well as expected to give, what supervision and reporting relationships will be in place, what ongoing training will be provided and, if appropriate, testing (including medical testing) that will be required, etc. The volunteer's job description should also address the questions of attendance and time. In this latter regard, a note of caution is required, for in dealing with volunteers flexibility will often be necessary.

Recognizing the importance of flexibility, it should also be understood that the details of the job description should be open for some tailoring to better fit the needs of the organization to the needs of the volunteer. Volunteers are volunteers because they have given up the structure of their paid full or part-time job or they are fitting their volunteer work around their paid work. In either instance, while expectations must be set, they also must be tempered to the reality of volunteering, including how anticipated seasonal, as well as unanticipated, absences are to be handled. This need for flexibility is simply a reality and a challenge of volunteer management—and one of the costs of volunteers.

Knowing what it needs volunteers for, and then more specifically what it needs them to do, is vital for both recruiting and making a proper placement match. It is also a key to assuring value both for the volunteer and the enterprise. While volunteers will, for the most part, tolerate poor work conditions and underutilization for an event, on a long-term basis a bad match will only create ill will for the organization—as volunteers become critical of the enterprise and its management and then leave, reducing the enterprise's ability to accomplish its work and create future "friends."

RECRUITMENT

If the task that volunteers are needed for is an event, then the goal of the recruitment process is to gather a relatively large number of people who require minimal training and are willing to work for a short period.[9] The focus is more on numbers than organizational knowledge or skills. The recruitment effort must concentrate on disseminating information, as widely as possible, about the need for volunteers. The information distribution challenge is for the enterprise to get its unique message to stand out from all the other messages in the market. To do this, like any advertising problem, it must focus on the right demographic, in this case individuals or groups likely to volunteer, and achieve the highest message frequency possible. Accomplishing the latter is only limited by the organization's budget and imagination. Of the two, imagination is the more limiting constraint, because, as the data demonstrates, people are willing to volunteer.

To distribute information on the need for volunteers to staff an event, the enterprise should consider:

1. contacting the local media—through press releases and also personal calls;

2. making announcements at local community service centers (i.e., recreation centers, churches and synagogues), as well as reaching out to scout groups, college community/ civic engagement centers, business/employees volunteer program, professional and service organizations, the local volunteer recruitment organization (i.e., United Way's volunteer center), and, if it exists, the city's or town's office on volunteers.

3. asking staff and board members (both past and present) to volunteer along with others in the enterprise's "friends" database.

Recruiting long-term volunteers presents a different challenge. Here, the enterprise must balance its recruiting efforts with its needs so that it does not incur ill will as a result of not being able to utilize a willing, committed, and competent volunteer, or worse, under-utilizing that volunteer. For event-based volunteers and some service-providing volunteer jobs, the task generally has a degree of elasticity that will allow a greater or lesser number of workers to be accommodated. Tasks that lack such elasticity require a more paced recruitment effort and process. That is, a process that seeks out volunteers in the same way that paid, permanent workers are recruited and hired. To accomplish this, the enterprise needs a job description (see above) that it can share with organizations (i.e., retired executive agencies, human resources departments of large corporations, union retiree offices, United Way, Volunteer Connection, senior citizen organizations, etc.), that try to match interested volunteers to jobs. The enterprise can also use its current volunteers as a recruiting base.

MANAGEMENT

Regardless of the nature of the volunteer work, volunteers must be well managed. (See Exhibit 13-4 and box "Volunteer Management.")

The volunteer management process begins with recruitment and continues through orientation and training. Just as paid staff requires orientation to the enterprise and initial, as well as in some instances ongoing skills training, so do volunteers.

Ongoing training for both staff and volunteers is key to an organization's stability and creative growth. Without this training, both staff and volunteers lose focus on the mission and purpose of the organization and the members it serves. Several key areas of training are important to focus on, including:

• Skills training for all staff and volunteers on what their responsibilities are and how best to perform them.

- Board training on the responsibilities of governance.

- Training for all on the culture of the organization, which is defined in the Mission and Vision Statements and interpreted jointly by the board and staff leadership.

- Training on the key issues facing the community that the organization serves. These issues may be the local "environment" and dealing with local government, increasing local needs, etc. or they could be broader issues such as racial equality and justice facing all communities and organizations.

In fact, such efforts may be even more important for volunteers because they provide a tangible demonstration of the meaningfulness of the work that the volunteer is doing and the importance that the organization places on volunteers. It also sheds positive light on the quality of the enterprise's management.

Of greater importance to volunteer satisfaction, however, is supervision and appropriate recognition.

Exhibit 13-4

MANAGEMENT PRACTICES: VOLUNTEERS* More than one-third (1/3) of those who volunteer in one year do not do so in the next year.	
Good Practice	**Percentage of Organizations Regularly Using****
Screen Volunteers**	88%
Conduct background checks on volunteers***	60+%
Matching volunteer skills with appropriate assignments	45%
Recognizing the contributions of volunteers	35%
Providing volunteers with training and professional development	25%
Training paid staff to work with volunteers	19%

*   The New Volunteer Workforce, Stanford Social Innovation Review, Vol. 7, No. 1, Winter 2009, pg 34, and Nonprofit World, Vol. 26, No. 9, September/October 2008, pg 6.
**   Volunteer Management Capacity in America's Charities and Congregations, 2004.
*** National Center for Victims of Crime, 2008.

Volunteers come to their work with a variety of motivations, linked in a complex amalgam of goals that are both altruistic (i.e., help others, improve the community, etc.), and non-altruistic (i.e., companionship, fill time, feel useful, self-fulfillment, etc.). Supervisors must understand that:

- what motivates each volunteer is unique to that volunteer, and

- what that motivation is must be discovered and built upon for each volunteer.

These two steps are necessary so that a psychological, as contrasted with simply an economic (wage/salary), relationship can be structured, maintained, and, over time, enhanced.[10]

A key element for achieving this non-economic bond is providing each volunteer with meaningful work. Creating a value-added match between the volunteer and the enterprise, however, is an increasingly difficult task as the demographics of the volunteers begin to shift to energetic retirees who are leaving their career jobs with a desire not only to continue to be active but, more importantly, to make a meaningful contribution to their community.[11]

To satisfy this new generation of volunteers, organizations must structure work opportunities that capitalize on their technical skills and personal experiences, challenging them professionally as well as emotionally.[12] Certainly, not all volunteers are seeking a professional challenge.

However, for the increasing number who want to do more, traditional volunteer tasks, that emphasize the rote and the repetitive, will only generate frustration and dissatisfaction, potentially sacrificing the opportunity to create an organizational "friend" and possibly a financial contributor.

In addition to meaningful work, volunteers also need appropriate recognition. An element of this is a well-managed work environment which recognizes that volunteers are part of the enterprise's staff and demonstrates that the organization values them by having efficient and effective support and supervisory systems in place.

Recognition also involves more personal and sometimes even tangible expressions of appreciation. How the enterprise acts to accomplish this recognition will vary with its circumstances and traditions. Regardless of the specifics, the gesture, even if it is only a "thank you" must be made.[13]

The final step in the process is assessment. The need here is twofold. First, basedon actual experience, is the job really necessary to the organization? The fact that the position is not compensated is not an adequate reason to continue it—if it is not really contributing to enabling the enterprise to better serve its mission. Second, if the position is needed, is the volunteer doing a good job?

These two questions can obviously become intertwined in that the position could be needed if it were performed better, or the volunteer could be working hard and doing a good job on an unnecessary task. Regardless, the questions must be sorted out and answered. Of the two, the latter is the more delicate and must be sensitively handled.

Continuous supervisory feedback and ongoing coaching and counseling are likely a more appropriate approach to volunteer assessment than an annual, explicit performance evaluation. An ongoing

---

VIRTUAL VOLUNTEERING

At the time of this publication, one of the things that organizations are finding challenging is the restrictions imposed by the COVID19 pandemic on volunteers actually coming into their location and volunteering. While the 2020 pandemic will not last forever, the idea of working from home is likely to stick and impact how people want to volunteer. Organizations need to be prepared for this change and build that into the definition of their needs—and how those needs can be met by volunteers working remotely.

VOLUNTEER MANAGEMENT*

If an enterprise is going to involve a large number of volunteers in its work, it would be well served to have both a subject matter expert manage its volunteer program and to invest in training its own paid staff on how to work with and relate to volunteers. The need for a professional skilled in: recruiting, matching, and training volunteers as well as in overseeing the enterprise's overall volunteer program should come as no surprise. Managing volunteers, if it is to be done well, requires special knowledge and skills—just as other areas of the enterprise require particular expertise.

Similarly, the paid staff should receive training regarding how to work with and relate to volunteers. Because, at least in the traditional sense volunteers "do not need the job," they must be managed in a manner that recognizes that their different motivations are aimed toward a different set of goals. It is unreasonable to expect that this kind of understanding is intuitive. Therefore, it must be taught and this requires an investment in training.

* Rick Cohen, "Volunteering by the Numbers," *The Nonprofit Quarterly*, Fall 2008, 40.

COST OF VOLUNTEERS

Volunteers, though unpaid, are not free. They have a cost; this cost involves both tangible and intangible expenses.

The tangible expenses are the costs of the enterprise's volunteer infrastructure (i.e., supervision, recruitment, training, etc.), and the expenses associated with maintaining volunteers (i.e., coffee, snacks and perhaps meals, parking and the costs of recognizing their work).

In some instances as noted, there may also be other costs such as background checks.

The intangible expenses, while having no accounting dollar value, may have a greater actual cost for they involve the impact of the volunteer on the organization.

This impact includes both the reaction of and ongoing relationship with paid employees and the shift in managerial control over the total workforce.

The latter is particularly important to understand for it requires managers not only to develop flexibility, but also to utilize different supervision and motivation techniques—substituting a psychosocial relationship for the traditional economic/compensation contract.

In addition to these costs, a failed volunteer experience (that results in a disgruntled volunteer) may also have costs in terms of the enterprise's reputation, credibility, and future fundraising opportunities.

FIRING A VOLUNTEER: CAUTION!

How do you fire someone you do not pay?
From time to time, in spite of rigorous candidate screening and training, a volunteer is simply just not a good fit with the organization. The results of such a mismatch are both organizational and interpersonal, producing tension and poor client service.

The volunteer in question may well have a wonderful community reputation. He or she also likely has friends who are active in and/or supporters of the enterprise. Importantly, they may not understand what the problem is, what has happened, or why it has happened.

There is no simple answer to this kind of problem. Obviously, the preferred circumstance is to avoid the problem through front-end

screening, training, and careful matching of people to the volunteer position. Failing this, the best that can be done is to rely on systematic management processes. Active volunteers should have annual evaluations and ongoing skills training. This process at least offers a pathway for identifying and talking about problems, exploring alternative placements, or agreeing on a workable exit strategy.

It should be remembered that volunteers volunteer to fulfill a personal need and to provide some good to the enterprise and the community. They do not want to do a bad job. If the volunteer opportunity is not working out, the volunteer, as much as the enterprise, wants a way to make a non-embarrassing change.

approach allows issues to be addressed when they are small, and problems to be defined and solved, before they take on a life of their own. Ongoing feedback also provides the opportunity for interpersonal relationships to be nurtured.

All this said, while the cost of a failed volunteer experience may be high, it is not as high as the cost of a resulting failed beneficiary experience. While volunteers are important, they are not as vital as the enterprise's beneficiaries.

STAFF COMPENSATION

The second major human resources issue confronting nonprofit enterprises is at the other end of the economic spectrum.[14] It centers on determining paid compensation and, particularly, the compensation of the enterprise's highest paying positions.[15]

The importance of this issue can be seen in the facts that:
- the compensation committee is generally recognized as one of the three core committees that all corporations should have (see Chapter 7);

- Congress added a section (4958) to the Internal Revenue Code, establishing intermediate sanctions, in the form of excise taxes, which can be imposed on individuals who receive excessive compensation from a tax-exempt organization (see Appendix 16),[16] and

- the IRS Form 990 places compensation data more clearly in the "public eye," increasing scrutiny and inviting questions about the amounts (regardless of what they are) being paid. (See Appendix 13.)

The reasons for focusing the discussion of compensation on the highest paying positions are twofold. First, the highest paying positions will draw the most attention and face the most scrutiny. Therefore, it is important that the compensation for these positions be properly determined so that organizational criticism and embarrassment can be avoided.

Second, the compensation paid to the highest paying positions represents the base from which all other wage and salary payments flow. If it is too low, then it sets a non-market-based ceiling for all other compensation, making it difficult for the enterprise to hire qualified people. If it is too high, then the rest of the organization will expect the same level of compensation premium. Regardless of the direction of the error, if the process is flawed, the rest of the enterprise's pay levels will be viewed as being unfair, with resulting employee and stakeholder dissatisfaction—as well as the risk of IRS penalties and public credibility issues.

Before addressing the management and mechanical issues involved in establishing and maintaining equitable and defensible compensation, it is useful to consider several general, albeit practical/experiential, observations about compensation.

PRACTICAL LESSONS

Compensation is usually thought of as a strong motivating factor. If people are asked, "Why do you work?" the answer is usually, "for money." Since people say that they work for money, it is natural to view compensation as a primary motivating force. In actuality, unless they are volunteers, people work because they need money to support themselves and their families and to do the things they want to do. Compensation is the output they seek, so that they can do other things, not the primary motivation. This simple answer masks a more complicated relationship. Certainly, compensation has the power to bring focus and attention to the pursuit and achievement of specific objectives (see Variable Compensation); its greater potential, however, lies in its risk of becoming a dissatisfier (i.e., a demotivator).

While people often find professional and/or personal satisfaction in their jobs and, as a consequence, view work as a positive activity, they are working for money to support other needs and desires. It is these factors that are the motivators—not money.

Recognizing this perhaps non-intuitive reality, it should then be understood that usually paying more will generally not result in people working harder or better. People generally feel that they work hard and do a good job.

> ### MENIAL TO ESSENTIAL
>
> Once volunteering was thought of as centering on stuffing envelopes and licking stamps.
>
> In the age of email, fewer envelopes and stamps are needed. Similarly, volunteers are bringing more skills and interest in utilizing those skills to their organizations. From teaching college courses to serving as interim CEOs, volunteers are increasingly looking to help with essential tasks. The lesson for the enterprise using volunteers is that if volunteers are to be satisfied, they should be used to their highest, not least, capability.

> ### AN EXCEPTION: COMMISSIONS
>
> An exception to the general observation about compensation's limits as a direct motivating factor is commission-based salary arrangements and the returns that independent contractors and owners receive for their efforts. Here, the more the worker accomplishes the more he or she is paid. Because payment and work are directly tied together, arguably compensation itself becomes a motivating factor.

Therefore, if they were paid more, they might work longer hours, but not harder or better. Paying more will only produce better results if the increment is used to acquire staff with better skills.

The relationship between compensation and performance is complex and, therefore, often misunderstood. As noted above, increasing pay does not by extension lead to better performance. As discussed earlier, performance must be measured against the expectations established in the enterprise's business plan. As a result, performance should be directly linked to retention—not compensation.

Compensation, as discussed below, must be linked to labor market requirements as well as the enterprise's own financial condition. To make this distinction clear, some human resource executives suggest that performance assessments (reviews) be separated in both time and process from compensation adjustments.

It should also be understood that the power of compensation is intertwined with human nature. The result of this mixture is that regardless of how large a pay increase a person gets—a year later, they will have convinced themselves that they have both earned it and that they now merit another pay increase. The net result is that while compensation can temporarily make people feel good, its power quickly decays. More importantly, it can become a dissatisfier if people begin to perceive that they are not being fairly paid. Herein lies one of the real risks of getting compensation wrong.

While employees may not work harder if they are paid more, the risk is very real that they will be less diligent if they perceive that the organization is taking advantage of them by underpaying. There are two issues here. One relates to reality and the other to perception. Reality must be addressed through structure, policy, and facts. These three factors apply not only to the highest compensated positions, but also throughout the enterprise.

The organization must have a human resources pay structure that establishes a salary range (with a minimum and maximum), based on verifiable and reliable data by position, for all positions in the enterprise. It must also have compensation policies that prevent people from being paid below the position's minimum or above its maximum. In addition, it should have a payment policy that establishes the pay raise that accompanies a promotion (i.e., pay at the minimum, or grant a fixed percentage increase, whichever is more).

Finally, compensation must reflect the facts. That is, salary and benefit surveys must be done periodically, to assure that pay ranges and benefits are consistent with both the relevant market for each position (i.e., the market from which replacement recruitment will take place), and with the enterprise's overall compensation policies.

As importantly, to deal with the perceptions, the findings of these reviews should be shared with employees—at least, in terms of the overall trends and results. Between surveys, community-based estimates of wage and salary trends should be used. These data should also be shared with the organization so that everyone is confident that, at least from a market perspective, compensation is equitable.

In the same vein of assuring positive perceptions, the enterprise's compensation policies should also be available to all employees. These policies should make clear how compensation is determined (i.e., salary and wage structure, use of market survey data), and how it is administered (i.e., review schedule, use of actual performance data in determining pay increases, promotion increase guidelines, approval process, exception and appeal process, etc.).

COMPENSATION AND GOVERNANCE

The enterprise must also pay attention to compensation in a governance context. The clear reality of contemporary corporate life is that if the enterprise and its board are to avoid regulatory and public relations problems, compensation must be a focus of governance attention. The first step in doing this is that the board, if it is not functioning as a committee of the whole, assigns responsibility for compensation oversight to a specific committee. Ideally, it should be a separate committee charged with focusing on compensation and succession management. (See Chapters 7 and 14, and Appendix 6.)

Some organizations elect not to establish a separate compensation committee. Due to circumstance and tradition, compensation governance responsibility is added to the work of another committee, most often the executive committee for chief executive and senior management compensation and a personnel or human resources committee for the remainder of the organization, including oversight and approval of general compensation (salary, wage, and benefit) policy and procedures. Regardless of the location or division of responsibility, specific committee accountability, particularly for chief executive compensation determination and review, is necessary. Moreover, the committee(s) must:

- have in its charter the explicit accountability for compensation policy and for the oversight of at least the chief executive's compensation;[17]

- meet periodically, preferably two or three times per year to review current market and actual enterprise salary data, review actual performance against the operating plan's quantified objectives, and make compensation decisions—either for recommendation to the full board or for implementation;

- be composed entirely of independent board members;

- utilize external data and, if needed, independent consulting advice to guide its work;

- take a comprehensive view of compensation and operational performance, recognizing the value of benefits in the total compensation equation and the need for total compensation to reflect actual performance against expected results;

- document its actual work processes, discussions, and decisions;

- meet in executive session both for decision-making and periodically for reviewing its own processes and performance;

- coordinate its work regarding general compensation adjustments and compensation policy with the work of the finance or budget committee, and

- report its decisions to the full board for either (depending on the committee's charter) their information or action.

These steps are necessary to protect the enterprises from the internal costs of flawed decisions. They are also necessary to establish the "rebuttable presumption of reasonableness" needed to protect the enterprise and any of the involved parties from penalties.

The Internal Revenue Service (IRS) guidelines that enable an enterprise to justify its compensation levels by, among other things, simply comparing them to similar organizations (i.e., "the rebuttable presumption of reasonableness"), is an interesting concept. Basically, it is a justification, which says that an enterprise's actions are justified, simply because everyone else is doing the same thing. Such a justification would not be tolerated for a looter, a traffic speeder, a child's behavior, etc. Just as importantly, it flies in the face of common sense, creating a disconnect between what is permissible under the law and what is perceived as fair by the public.[18] Both boards and chief executives should bear in mind that compensation must both be fair in fact as well as in perception.

POLICIES

Once the committee assignment has been made and the membership appointed, the committee's first task should be to review the enterprise's compensation practices and policies. As a matter of good governance practice, policy reviews should be done on a regular basis to assure that the enterprise's operating rules are both relevant and being observed. In addition to the matters listed above, the enterprise's compensation policy should also set out its position regarding:

- the organizations it compares itself to—at least in terms of establishing compensation market equity;

- the frequency of salary and benefit surveys and the data sources to be considered between surveys;

- the size of the salary range around the mean (e.g., salary range equals the mean ±10% or mean ±15%, etc.);

- the compensation guidelines regarding paying less than the minimum of the range or more than the maximum (e.g., never paying less than minimum or more than maximum);

- the criteria for hiring and/or paying beyond the position's midpoint;

- the compensation target (i.e., pay at 100% of the mean, or to be considered as a sought-after employer—pay at 105% of the mean, or because of the richness of the benefit package—pay at 95% of the mean, etc.);

MAXIMUM & MOTIVATION

While it may not be a strong motivator, a person at the maximum of his or her salary range, and not receiving any salary adjustment, faces a real demotivating circumstance. People in this position are often long-term and/or highly skilled employees whose performance is important to the enterprise. Paying above the maximum is a policy that will only create equity and economic problems.

A better tactic is to consider non-cash recognition alternatives, like professional development opportunities, additional vacation time, representing the enterprise in appropriate forums, etc. These kinds of alternatives maintain the integrity of the personnel and compensation policies, while still providing means and opportunities to demonstrate appreciation and recognition of value.

- employee benefits, both current and retirement, and including professional development and education/training;

- the process for approving exceptions to its policies.

The committee's compensation policies should also address any other matters which it feels important to the management and oversight of the enterprise's overall compensation program.

DATA

Building on this policy base, the next step is to determine the market data for each position's compensation (i.e., the market rate of pay and benefits). This is an empirical question that can be answered through survey data developed by the organization and/or the data and advice provided by a compensation consultant.

Whether the enterprise is going to develop its own data, by having its human resources staff reach out to their counterparts in other organizations, or rely on the help of a consultant, there are two key variables

> **WHY SHARE?**
>
> Why would one enterprise share its compensation data with another? One would think that compensation data would be viewed as proprietary information. This is correct. But at the same time each firm has the same need for comparative compensation data. Therefore, to get what they need, they are typically willing to contribute their data, under the conditions that the data are not identified by organization and that they get a copy of the results. Neither of these conditions should be problematic.
>
> In addition, compensation consultants do their own surveys so that they have data that they can share with their clients. This is part of the value add that the consultant brings to the assignment.

common to all survey efforts that must be considered. The first is the matter of validity. That is, are the relevant peer group organizations being surveyed? If data are obtained from the wrong places, then the results will be wrong in both fact and perception. As a rule of thumb, to assure validity, data should be gathered from firms in the regions that the enterprise would likely reach out to, to recruit a replacement for the position in question—or who might recruit the enterprise's staff, if they were seeking a new person to hire. In the same vein, in order to assure the perception of validity, other selected firms should be added to the survey database to satisfy any concerns/questions about the comparative data.

The second issue involves the reliability. As suggested above, total compensation consists of several distinct components. For the survey data to be reliable, it must produce the same result if it were replicated in the same time frame. The key to insuring this is to include all the relevant components of compensation in the survey. This is important for both assuring confidence in the data and establishing and defending compensation equity. A technique for accomplishing this is to develop a tally sheet for each of the positions being surveyed.

TALLY SHEETS

A tally sheet is simply a listing and totaling of all of the components of compensation, current and deferred, cash and non-cash. Exhibit 13-5 provides an example of the elements of a tally sheet. Most of what is shown in the tally sheet is straightforward. Several items, however, merit comment.

Perquisites are benefits provided by the enterprise that are only available to certain employees. Examples of perquisites are club memberships, automobiles, and entertainment allowances. For the most part, perquisites are not a concern for nonprofit enterprises because, for either economic and/or organizational philosophy or public perception reasons, they are generally not provided to any employees. However, for some health care, education, cultural, and entertainment organizations, perquisites have traditionally been part of compensation.

Regardless of the precedent of tradition, with the increased scrutiny that can be expected to be focused on compensation, if for no other reason than as a consequence of the IRS Form 990, boards would be well advised to reconsider their position regarding providing perquisites as a separate element of compensation. If, on reflection, all or some of the perquisite items are needed for business reasons (i.e., club memberships for donor contact and entertainment, automobiles to travel between various enterprise operating locations, etc.), consideration should be given to providing them through increases in current cash compensation (salary)—and eliminating them as stand alone, conspicuous items.[19] This approach will enable the enterprise to meet its business needs, without leaving it vulnerable to questions and concerns about excessive or inequitable compensation.

Exhibit 13-5

EXAMPLE ELEMENTS: TALLY SHEET		

Current Compensation	**Cash Compensation**
	• Base Salary
	• Variable Payments
	  ▪ Short Term—Annual
	  ▪ Long Term—Multi-Year
		Benefits
		• Perquisites and Allowances
		• 401(K) Match
		• Education and Training Support

Deferred Compensation	• Pension Plan (Defined Benefit and/or Defined Contribution 401(k), 403(b), 457(b), 457(f)) • Supplemental Retirement Benefit Plan • Other	
Other Items of Compensation	• Retention Payments • Supplemental Life Insurance • Separation Pay Arrangements	

Supplemental retirement benefits are another potential element of compensation that can be subject to abuse, or at least questions. These benefits are, in theory, a means of creating pension plan equity for employees whose salaries exceed the ceiling of the organization's qualified, defined benefit pension plan.[20]

Pensions are a complicated matter, well beyond the scope of this discussion. Fortunately, supplemental retirement plans are not an issue for most nonprofit enterprises. This is due to several factors, not the least of which is that nonprofit enterprise salary levels are typically within the ceiling limits. Also, many nonprofit organizations do not operate their own pension plan, relying instead on making contributions to the pension programs of their trade or professional associations, local shared administrative service organizations, or national entities like TIAA-CREF.[21]

For those where it is an issue, again most likely the large health care and entertainment organizations, a supplemental retirement benefit plan that continues the benefits design of the qualified benefit plan beyond the salary ceiling is an equitable solution. It eliminates the inherent penalty imposed on highly-compensated employees, by providing them with the same benefits as all other employees.[22] In this circumstance, supplemental retirement benefits are understandable and defensible, and should not be a compensation issue. However, where supplemental retirement benefits are provided only to specific employees, for example as part of salary negotiation, they are more like a perquisite than a standardized benefit and leave the enterprise vulnerable to the same issues and criticisms as apply to all other perquisites.

VARIABLE COMPENSATION

Variable compensation is also sometimes called incentive or at-risk compensation because it is not assured.[23] It differs from base salary in that in any particular period it may or may not be earned or paid. The determinant of whether it is paid or not, and if paid, how much is paid, is actual performance—as measured against certain agreed-upon results. Ideally, whether it is paid or not should depend on actual performance as compared to the quantified objectives of the operating plan.

Variable compensation is similar to being graded on a curve or being paid on a sliding scale. Based on actual performance, an individual may earn all of the potential variable pay amount, part of it, or none. In contrast, base compensation is more like "pass/fail" grading. That is, if the individual's performance is acceptable, employment is continued, and payment is made (pass).

Acceptable performance need not be a subjective judgment. It can be related to the operating plan's quantified objectives. For example, acceptable performance for a chief executive may require meeting the operating plan's financial objective. Actual performance results should be clear cut. The objective is either met (or exceeded) or not. While a person may be given more than one year and more than one opportunity to achieve the planned, agreed-upon objectives—if after time, coaching,

> **BONUSES**
> **How can a tax-exempt organization pay bonuses? Aren't they a form of inurement?**
>
> While some people think of variable compensation as a bonus, if structured as discussed, it is part of competitive compensation. There is nothing, per se, illegal about variable compensation.
>
> While not illegal, for many community sector enterprises, it may be impractical. The impracticality may lie in variable compensation not being a common business practice for the involved agency, resource limits and/or public relations and fundraising concerns.
>
> The key points, however, are simply that variable compensation is neither illegal nor inurement. It is allowable and may even be necessary if variable compensation is the competitive practice of the involved organizations. However, for most community sector organizations, significant variable compensation element of total pay is not needed.

counseling, and training, performance is still substandard, then employment, at least in that position, should not be continued.[24] This may sound harsh, but if performance, over time, is not acceptable, how can the enterprise justify the failure to take action to correct and improve the situation? Clearly, it cannot.

While compensation may have limited power as a motivator, variable compensation has substantial power to bring focus to performance. By linking variable compensation to the achievement of the operating plan's quantified objectives, attention and reward are focused on the specific results that are important to the enterprise.

By tying variable compensation to the accomplishment of the operating plan's measurable objectives, not only is the focus intensified, but more importantly, theory and practice, planning and results, and pay and performance are melded into a closed, cause and effect systematic relationship. Quite simply, variable compensation is the catalyst that takes performance beyond just the "acceptable" judgment associated with base salary to higher levels. It turns the dreams and the strategic and operating plans into reality.

AFFORDABILITY?

How can the enterprise afford to pay more than just base salary? In a real world of shrinking resources and increasing demands for services, how can the enterprise add to its costs by including variable compensation, in addition to base compensation—in effect paying a bonus?

A glib answer is that the enterprise cannot afford not to have a variable compensation program because variable compensation is the element needed to bring the attention and focus necessary to go beyond acceptable performance and achieve the enterprise's plan. This may be true, but it does not answer the financial question of affordability.

If the comparative markets tally sheet shows that variable compensation is a standard practice, then affordability should not be an issue. In this instance, total compensation has just been split into two elements and while it could all be viewed as base compensation, this perspective would lose the motivating force of variable compensation.

Alternatively, if the tally sheet shows that variable compensation is not a common element of total compensation, then the enterprise must

make a decision. If, because of the focus it brings to the achievement of the operating plan's quantified objectives, the enterprise wants to include variable compensation in at least the compensation packages of its senior leadership, it must reduce (split) base compensation by some amount to be able to finance the expected cost of the variable compensation program. In doing this, the variable compensation program should be designed to enable anticipated or expected performance to result in the sum of base plus variable compensation to equal what would have been paid under just a base salary program—and for exceptional performance to earn compensation greater than what would have been received from just base salary program alone. This increase in compensation should be able to be financed by the higher than expected/planned performance results.

Recognizing that mechanical solutions are available, imagination and will—not affordability—are the prohibiting factors to the use of a variable compensation program.

Variable compensation, in turn, can have an annual and/or a multi-year performance-measurement time horizon. The link between the annual operating plan and annual variable compensation payments is obvious. The addition of long-term variable compensation is historically more common in the for-profit world, where boards wanted to protect against short-run decision making, driven by annual incentives which, while improving current performance, would have a negative long-run impact.

Whether the same dangers exist for most nonprofit enterprises is arguable. Moreover, without the financial metrics of the for-profit environment, it is unclear that reasonable long-term performance measures, beyond the sum of a series of annual objectives, could either be formulated or be meaningful. As a practical matter, before trying to structure long-term variable compensation systems, nonprofit enterprises should focus on enhancing their annual compensation programs, particularly gaining experience in using compensation to support more aggressive annual operating planning—and variable compensation as a means of harmonizing conflicting quantified objectives.

DECISIONS

At this point, the pieces for decision making are in place. The policy foundation is set and the external data needed for making judgments is available. The next step is to determine if any adjustments have to be made to the salary ranges of the positions being reviewed. Based on comparing the current salary ranges to the survey data and the enterprise's pay policy (i.e., where the enterprise's salary range mid-points should be relative to the market), judgments can be made regarding the need, and if needed, the magnitude of any adjustments. (See Exhibit 13-6.)

Exhibit 13-6

SALARY RANGE ADJUSTMENT
Based on the market survey data, the average salary for a position can be determined. This average can then be compared to the enterprise's salary range mid-point for that position to determine if an adjustment has to be made. The salary range is typically the mid-point ± a fixed percentage.

For example:
- Current Salary Range: Director of Client Service = $98,000± 10%

- Salary Range:
  Minimum: $88,200
  Mid-Point: $98,000
  Maximum: $107,800

- Comparative Salary Data = $101,000

- New Salary Range:
  Minimum: $90,900
  Mid-Point: $101,000
  Maximum: $111,100

This assumes that the enterprise wants to pay at 100% of market. If it wanted to pay at 95% of market, then the new range would be:
  Minimum: $86,355
  Mid-Point: $95,950
  Maximum: $105,545

The same process should be used with the other elements of compensation to assure that they are consistent with both the market and the enterprise's compensation philosophy and policies. Finally, the committee should conduct a pay equity audit to assure that the salary administration policies are being consistently applied throughout the entire organization. For example, if the enterprise's policy is to have a 30% spread between positions and the market salary rate for position "B" increases, does the salary rate for the position above it, position "A," have to increase to maintain the 30% spread? The committee must decide, following its established policies and processes for adjustments or for making exceptions, and then document its deliberations and actions.

The fact that a salary range is changed does not mean that an incumbent's salary is automatically also changed. What happens to individual compensation is a separate matter, guided by the unique circumstance (i.e., the individual's salary position within the salary range and personal performance), as well as the enterprise's overall economic condition and decisions regarding compensation, increases.

The details of salary administration management are another of those technical subject matter areas that are beyond the scope of an introductory, general management discussion. However, in terms of basic guidance, boards and managers should heed the following principles:

- **EQUITY**: Employees must be paid fairly, expected to neither explicitly nor implicitly subsidize the enterprise by being underpaid.

- **PERFORMANCE**: Employees must be paid in a manner that directly reflects performance. To accomplish this, the enterprise should utilize a variable compensation program tied directly to the quantified objectives of the operating plan.

- **VALUE**: Employees are the enterprise's most important resource; good employees yield benefits greater than the expense saving associated with lower cost/under-qualified, or underpaid, and consequently underperforming staff.

Paying the right people, the right amount, in the right manner will enable the enterprise to yield the greatest return to its community. Underpaying people is simply a false economy that will ultimately cost more in terms of not just the waste and remedial expenses of increased turnover, but also in lost opportunities.

Done consistently, market base pay practices, equitably administered will, over time, enable management and the board to create the foundation needed to build a good—and possibly even a great—organization. However, to accomplish the latter, more than just enlightened compensation policies are needed. The organization must continually plan for its future through active succession and periodic transition planning. As discussed in the next chapter, this may well be the key ingredient for going from a good to a great enterprise—and for creating a positive legacy.

CHAPTER 13

Takeaways and Questions for Consideration and Discussion:

TAKEAWAYS

1. Americans volunteer in a large variety of different fields for a huge number of organizations. The number of volunteers is increasing with each generation, fueled at least in part by an increasing emphasis on the importance of "giving back" at the high school and college levels.

2. Nonprofit human resources consist of two distinct yet mutually supportive groups, volunteers and paid staff. Volunteers are a valuable resource to an organization offering services that would otherwise have to be provided by paid staff. As a valuable resource, they must be recruited carefully, matched to their volunteer responsibilities effectively, and well managed.

3. Volunteers must be given the tools to be successful through a management approach that includes orientation, ongoing training and support, proper supervision, meaningful recognition, and regular assessment.

4. Board leadership and ultimately the entire board of directors have the responsibility for setting compensation levels in the organization. First, develop and adopt the policy guidelines that will govern compensation. Second, use that policy to set the compensation of the senior executive leader(s).

5. Paid staff are the enterprise's most important investment and valuable asset. To protect that investment, paid staff must be compensated at, at least, current labor market rates. Compensating people at less than market rates is a false economy, increasing future expenses and jeopardizing current performance.

QUESTIONS

1. How does the environmental assessment process support the volunteer management process?

2. What are some of the organizational costs, both tangible and intangible, of using volunteers? Does the enterprise assure that these costs do not exceed the benefits of having volunteers as part of its work force?

Continued on next page.

3. Is paying employees as little as possible a cost savings or cost increasing policy? Does compensation have more potential as a motivating force or a demotivating factor?

4. Is the disclosure of the compensation of highly-paid employees good governance policy? If transparency is thought to be beneficial, how can the public relations risks associated with disclosure be mitigated?

Chapter 14:
SUCCESSION MANAGEMENT

As experience demonstrates, achieving organizational success in even a single year is no easy task. However, an even more difficult challenge that faces every chief executive and every board is how to build an enterprise that is capable of achieving sustained success over an extended period.[1] How do boards and chief executives create and/or enhance a tradition of significant progress regarding mission? How do you first build a good—and then a great—organization?

The answer to these questions, like the solution to most management problems, lies in processes and people. In terms of process, the enterprise must exercise the managerial discipline to replicate the previously discussed annual planning and implementation actions in a manner that continuously increases their rigor—stretching their reach out to grasp more opportunities and achieve more results.

CONTEXT

To put the following discussion in context, by this point there should be a sense of:
- why there are community sector organizations,
- why they take a corporate form,
- how governance can provide organizational conscience, values, discipline, and business judgment to an enterprise's corporate form.

The following should also be clear:
- need for a strategic plan to guide the pursuit of mission;
- fit and flow of the operating plan from strategic direction to the specifics of quantified objectives;

- mechanics of implementation, including the role and importance of capital generation, volunteers, and equitable compensation.

To paraphrase Jim Collins (author of Good To Great), the bus has been built, the direction has been set, everyone has the same map and the journey is underway—with good progress being made.* The remaining operational question is, "How do we assure continued and even accelerated progress?"

* James C. Collins, Good To Great, (New York: Harper Business, 2001).

PERSONNEL DEVELOPMENT

The more powerful part of the answer, however, lies in continually developing the enterprise's human resource capabilities, enabling people to enhance their knowledge, skills, and subsequent performance. People create and execute processes and plans. As a product of their greater experience, growing knowledge, and increasing skills they are both able and motivated to enhance process as well as personal and organizational performance.

Whether for altruistic reasons of helping people or, as noted earlier, the more pragmatic standard of business need, organizations must invest in developing

---

SACRED COWS

In difficult times, organizations have to make hard decisions regarding expense reductions. Typically, two places that are often looked to are maintenance and employee training. These are tempting areas for savings because they do not involve program expenditures, are generally entirely within management's control, and have seemingly little short run negative consequences. In reality, these areas of expenditure should be the organization's "sacred cows." While cutting expenditures for a year or two may seem harmless, it becomes addictive and the resulting catch up becomes so large that the organization is never able to recover from the shortfall. Eliminating maintenance and employee training and development is the organizational equivalent of burning seed corn.

---

employee skills. How this is done will vary from enterprise to enterprise, reflecting tradition, size, resources, etc. That it be done, irrespective of enterprise size, is not a matter for argument. Investing in personnel is as important as investments in programs or facilities. In fact, it may be more so, for without competent staff these other investments will never produce a return. This is so, regardless of the enterprise's size. However, it is perhaps even more vital for the small organization, whose staffs often have multiple functional responsibilities, than it is for the large.[2]

Regardless of the specifics, to be successful, the process must be systematic and comprehensive. Just as other management activities require systematic processes (i.e., actions and schedules), personnel development has the same need. A mechanism for accomplishing this is the human resources development (HRD) plan. As discussed in Chapters 9 and 10, the enterprise's HRD plan should be part of its overall business plan.

The enterprise level HRD plan is the sum of the individual development plans (IDP) created for each of the enterprise's employees. An example of both a blank and completed IDP is shown in Exhibit 14-1. As is so with all mechanical processes and forms, the enterprise can and should modify both the process and form to better fit its unique circumstances.

The IDP is, from one perspective, nothing more than a multi-year plan. It describes the support that the enterprise will provide an employee to address the development/improvement needs identified as part of his or her annual performance assessment.[3]

From this point of view the IDP need not be as complex as the model in Exhibit 14-1. It can be as simple as an email or a memorandum setting out the commitment of the enterprise to provide tuition support or pay for a professional development seminar, etc. Alternatively, as the exhibit demonstrates, it can be a complex document. It can specify the training objective to be achieved, the expected timing and, if appropriate, the commitment of the employee to remain with the enterprise for a specified period of time or to prepay the enterprise for the payments made on his or her behalf. While mechanics are important, they are less so than the underlying commitment of the enterprise to support employee development.

Exhibit 14-1, Part I

PART I	INDIVIDUAL DEVELOPMENT PLAN: BLANK			
	Name	Title	Division	Manager
Development Needs	Development Actions			
	Job Based Assignments–70%	Relationships – 20%		Formal Training – 10%

Exhibit 14-1, Part II

PART II	INDIVIDUAL DEVELOPMENT PLAN: COMPLETED			
	Name	**Title**	**Division**	**Manager**
	Jane Smith	Director	Services	C.L. Killingsworth
Development Needs	**Development Actions**			
	Job Based Assignments – 70%	**Relationships – 20%**		**Formal Training – 10%**
Further develop management and leadership skills	• Assignment with formal management responsibilities of cross functional project. Act as project lead for XYZ Project working effectively with IT and Operations staff. Complete project objectives by 20XX. • Increased size and scope of existing management platform. Complete team restructuring considering people, process, and structure by Q3 20XX.	• Seek opportunity for nonprofit board membership—by end of Q3 20XX. • Engage internal coach to support transition of expanded management responsibilities, relationship in place by Q2 20XX.		• Participate in Leadership Excellence development program (internal capstone leadership development program in partnership with Syracuse University) by November 20XX. • Participate in Enhanced Business Knowledge (EBK) by September 20XX. • Complete Executive Presentation Skills course by May 20XX.
Increase working knowledge of strategic planning	• Complete 3-year strategic plan for restructured department by end of Q3. • Align all team members' goals with corporate objectives, design tracking, and communication process. Goals by Q1, rest ongoing. • Working with HR establish recruitment, retention, and development strategy to maximize team performance by Q4 20XX.	• Seek mentor with expertise in strategic planning. Establish relationship by end of Q2 20XX. • Create learning opportunity for entire division on the integration of corporate and division strategy by end of Q3 20XX.		• Investigate local MBA programs by year end for consideration in 20XX. • Attend an executive level development program sponsored by established business school by end of Q3.
Notes/Accomplishments: Registered for Executive Presentation Skills – May 20XX Engaged mentor to support development of strategic planning skills – April 20XX Completed first draft of 3 year strategic plan – July 20XX				

Importantly, employee development is the foundation for successful succession management.

While it is unreasonable to expect, or even set as an objective, that all promotional hiring come from internal candidates, it is important for workforce morale and organizational success that employees feel they have opportunities to advance. Internal succession is also valuable because it enables the enterprise to maximize its return on its employee training and education investment.

COMMITMENT AND OPPORTUNITY

At its core, succession management (i.e., the succession plan and the subsequent actions to implement it), is both a matter of organizational commitment and an opportunity for making tactical organizational decisions for enhancing performance.

In terms of commitment, succession management requires a decision to provide advancement opportunities to current employees (a "grow your own" personnel strategy), and the necessary training and education support (both time and money) to make those opportunities realistically possible. It also includes a management and governance commitment to actively oversee the individual development plan and succession management processes (i.e., are the IDPs being implemented, and when vacancies are occurring, are they being filled in accordance with the intention of the succession management plan?)[4]

Succession planning also provides management the opportunity and vehicle for making tactical organizational structure and individual personnel decisions. Having to plan for how vacancies will be handled provides both the opportunity to review, within the context of the organization's future performance requirements, individual development needs and form explicit plans for how to address those needs. As importantly, it also provides the chance to review the overall organizational structure to assess whether continuing it as is best serves the enterprise's emerging demands.

Over time, the environment that the enterprise must work within changes. More often than not, the change is evolutionary—not revolutionary—and therefore, perhaps, not dramatically obvious. Nevertheless, experienced managers should from time to time ask themselves, "If I was just starting in this position, would I structure the work unit or even the entire organization the way it is, or would I make changes?"

COMPREHENSIVE, SYSTEMATIC PROCESS

The succession management process consists of the succession plan and the implementation of that plan. The succession plan is the specific identification of backups (successors) for each key position.

Implementation of the plan involves both the identification of the skills and competencies that individuals need to develop and/or enhance in order to be able to be ready to succeed the identified incumbent, and the pursuit of those competencies.

The litmus test of the plan and its implementation is—are people moving from secondary to primary successor and are primary successors being selected to actually fill vacancies per the actions outlined in the plan? If this is happening, the plan is being implemented and succession management is working.

The answer is probably less important than the question, because there is no one right way to organize. Asking the question, however, enables managers to think through the issues and make thoughtful decisions. The succession management process provides the forum and the opportunity to do this.

How the organization actually handles succession management will depend on its traditions, size, available resources, and the history and training of its leadership. In its simplest form succession planning can be a single sheet of paper, created by the chief executive and shared with the board chair. The piece of paper need not contain anything more than the current organizational chart, restructured if necessary, to better meet the needs of the future, and listing the enterprise's key positions. Beside each key position should be the incumbent's name and the name of his or her primary and secondary successor—if either or both can be identified.

A key position is any job that is pivotal to producing enterprise success. Holders of key positions can be either managers or individual performers. The defining criterion is whether or not the effectiveness of other positions is dependent on the performance of the key position. At a minimum, positions that report to the chief executive, as well as the chief executive position itself, should be viewed as key positions and be part of the formal succession plan.

The difference between a primary and a secondary successor is a matter of the readiness of the person to move into the position, should it become vacant. A primary successor should be ready to step immediately into the vacancy. A secondary successor needs several more years of preparation and grooming to be able to assume the responsibilities of the new position. How this preparation and grooming is to be accomplished should be set out in that person's individual development plan. Exhibit 14-2 provides an example of a succession management plan as well as a narrative explaining how vacancies that occurred during the last year were handled.[5]

The exhibit reflects what might happen at a large enterprise. For smaller organizations the same principals apply; the detail and formality are just less. It should also be noted that for a number of positions, no primary successor is listed. This reflects the reality that in environments of limited resources, it is difficult to build significant bench strength.

The difficulty involved in creating the succession plan is not in constructing the form or filling in the blanks. These tasks are reasonably straightforward. Rather it is in understanding that personnel are continually changing and that vacancies are a condition of organizational life. Some vacancies will be anticipated (e.g., retirements, terminations, etc.). Others will be complete surprises, leaving the organization in a difficult circumstance. Some will be good and some bad. Regardless of the cause or timing, they will happen, and they represent either a threat, if unmanaged or the result of systemic organizational problems; or, if managed, an opportunity.

Exhibit 14-2, Part I

PART I	SUCCESSION PLANNING: 20XY SCHEDULE		
		Potential Successor	
Position	**Incumbent**	**Primary**	**Secondary**
1. CEO	ME	UNO	DUE

LEVEL I		**Potential Successor**	
Position	**Incumbent**	**Primary**	**Secondary**
2. EVP/CFO	DUE	---	PED WIS
3. EVP/COO	UNO	ILK	NAP

LEVEL II		**Potential Successor**	
Position	**Incumbent**	**Primary**	**Secondary**
4. Div. Pres: A	HAM	---	WIS NAP
5. Div. Pres: B	IIK	---	WIS NAP
6. Div. Pres: C	HAM	---	WIS NAP
7. Pres.: D	MULE	---	DREWS
8. Gp. VP, Svcs.	NAP	---	

LEVEL III		**Potential Successor**	
Position	**Incumbent**	**Primary**	**Secondary**
9. Chief Medical Officer	LANK	---	EBB FLOW
10. Sr. VP, Opns.	LANGE	---	SAM
11. CIO	---	SKY	---
12. Sr. VP, Corp. Relations	SACK	PAIGE	---
13. Sr. VP, Legal	ORE	---	LOCK WALL
14. EVP, Benefit Mgt.	EAR	---	---
15. Sr. VP, Human Resources	KID	SACK	---

Exhibit 14-2, Part II

PART II		
	SUCCESSION PLANNING: 20XY	
	NARRATIVE	

Since the last report:
- EAR was appointed as the division manager of the newly created Management division, reporting to UNO.
- EBB, M.D. was hired as the Medical Director, reporting to LANK, M.D.
- SKY was appointed as the Chief Technology Officer, reporting to DUE.
- KID was hired as the Senior Vice President for Human Resources, succeeding DJ and reporting to UNO.
- ORE was hired as the Senior Vice President for Legal and Regulatory Affairs, reporting to ME.
- DREWS was hired as the Medical Director reporting to LANK, M.D. and PAT.

Two senior managers, Jacqueline Bickhaus and Carlie Normyle left during the year.

As evidenced by the above, change continued in 20XX, as implementation of the local front office, consolidated (decentralized) back office model continued.

At the moment, no senior level retirements are anticipated for the next year.

20XX Succession Plan

1. CEO Position:
UNO can be a leader, CEO. I believe, when the need arises, that he will be ready to succeed me. To help assure this, with the board's knowledge, an explicit developmental program was initiated in September. Developmental progress continues on—or perhaps, slightly ahead of—schedule.

Currently, UNO is not being actively recruited by another organization. However, from time to time, he still receives inquiries.

2. Executive Vice President: CFO (DUE)
WIS and PED are both potential successors. Neither is presently ready to succeed DUE. Of the two, while PED has more seniority, WIS has begun to demonstrate more leadership and business acumen.

An accelerated individual development plan is being pursued for WIS.

3. Executive Vice President: COO (UNO)
IIK is demonstrating strong growth and is expected to be ready to succeed UNO when needed.

4. 5. 6. Division President: (HAM, IIK)
No internal replacements are immediately available.

The changes of the past year have consumed the "bench strength" which was previously available. WIS is a high potential, possible successor for any of these positions. As noted above, an accelerated developmental plan is being pursued for WIS.

NAP could possibly step into either of these positions. However, this would obviously create a problem in term care. Over the long-term Brooke Bickhaus (VP) has the potential to develop into a possible candidate.

7. Group Vice President: Services (MULE)
No immediate internal successor. At this point, if an immediate replacement were needed, it would require recruitment from outside of the organization. However, in the short run, the position is likely to be left vacant until the opportunities and needs of the merger are sorted out.

8. President: Term Care (NAP)
No immediate internal successor. At this point, if a replacement were needed, it would require recruitment from outside of the organization.

Continued on next page.

Exhibit 14-2, part II

PART II, continued
SUCCESSION PLANNING: 20XY **NARRATIVE**

9.   Senior Vice President/Chief Medical Officer: (LANK)
No internal replacement is immediately available.

EBB was promoted last year to fill LANK's former position. EBB is doing well and has the potential to develop into the chief medical officer position. Over the longer term, Madeline Schiffman may be a candidate.

Similarly, FLOW, M.D. has the potential to develop into a senior executive.

10.   Senior Vice President: Operations (LANGE)
No internal replacement is immediately available. However, Sam Millstone is being groomed as a potential successor.

11.   Senior Vice President: Information Technology (Jacqueline Bickhaus)
Jacqueline Bickhaus resigned this year. Information Technology was combined with Operations under LANGE. Future senior leadership for this area will have to be recruited from outside the organization.

12.   Senior Vice President: Corporate Relations (Flynn Leo)
Paige Millstone would be promoted to fill a vacancy in this position.

To understand if turnover and vacancies are a systemic issue, exit interviews should be conducted to sort out why people are leaving as well as why they are leaving at this particular time. For the exit interviews to elicit useful information, they may have to be conducted by a neutral third party. Certainly, this may involve some expense but, this cost pales in comparison to the cost of unplanned and undesired turnover.

Regardless of how good the enterprise is and what it does to be an attractive employer, turnover will happen. Managers should not be afraid of it. Each vacancy presents an opportunity either to reorganize, to become more efficient and effective, and/or to promote or hire a person who better meets the organization's current and emerging needs. Succession management enables managers and the organization to sort through the maze of opportunities (and dangers) in a thoughtful manner.[6]

That said, succession management is a special challenge for small and/or developing enterprises. Because of their size, these organizations generally have limited, if any, internal human resource bench strength. Additionally, their resources are often stretched, as they try to grow and therefore, they have limited slack capacity. As a result, vacancies create real operational problems.

With less capacity for dealing with vacancies, small organizations must be more aggressive in their succession planning. To do this, the chief executive must create a virtual human resources pool. This can be done, for example, by:

• Continually surveying the market and identifying people that could be approached as the need arises;

• Developing relationships with colleagues who may have someone in their organization who is ready for a larger position, but who have no internal opportunity available for them;

- Staying in touch with past employees who have gained new skills and experiences.

Regardless of the approach, chief executives should have at least an informal list of people they would approach if a vacancy occurred and no internal successor is available.

CHIEF EXECUTIVE SUCCESSION

While succession management is of obvious general importance to any organization, it takes on particular significance, as discussed in Chapter 15, when the position to be replaced is that of the chief executive.[7] Chief executive succession, typically labeled as transition management or leadership continuity planning, can be viewed as simply a subset of overall succession management. While this perspective is valid, it risks missing the strategic character of chief executive transition. Changing the chief executive, whether it is the result of voluntary planned actions or involuntary circumstances, presents the enterprise with an opportunity to reflect, to reinvent itself, and to do things that were previously thought not to be either practical or possible. It is a strategic opportunity for organizational transition and transformation.

The lack of succession management, and particularly a chief executive transition plan, is at a minimum a failure by the board to manage risk.[8] Organizations that do not capture the opportunity of succession management, as Exhibit 14-3 illustrates, face a performance future of little gain. They also face an immediate operational threat. Momentum is lost as a result of a delay in finding a new chief executive. Alternatively, if a hurried and/or flawed search process is pursued, the enterprise faces the risks of not only a bad hire and resulting declining performance, but also the unnecessary expenses, both tangible and intangible (staff morale and enterprise reputation), of a repeated search.

Exhibit 14-3

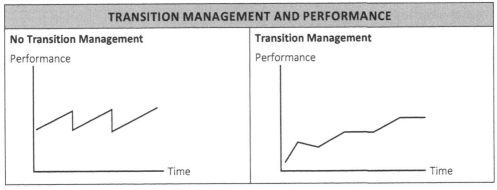

In contrast, those that are able to manage transition well are also able to at least maintain performance, if not continue to improve. This is the result, in part, of the performance of a series of competent chief executives, well vetted and chosen.

Even though the value of chief executive succession/transition management is clear, it is estimated that less than 25% of community sector enterprise boards have systematically addressed transition management and taken formal action. The obvious question is why? What is holding boards back from acting—and what has to be done, once moved to act, to capture the opportunity?

OBSTACLES

The obstacles to addressing transition management are less technical than a reflection of the realities of human nature. Since the chief executive is hired by the board, transition planning must be a board activity. Within the reality of already full board schedules, transition planning is another demand on time that, while recognized as being important, can be put off to another day. Surely the chief executive will leave at some point, but that point is generally not imminent and therefore addressing it can be postponed in favor of more pressing matters.

Board chairs also generally have limited experience in transition planning and management. For the most part, chairs come and go, but the chief executive remains, providing organizational stability and continuity. The chair that draws the "short straw" and has to begin the transition management process is entering the equivalent of a governance wilderness. Therefore, the chair understandably feels insecure, fearful of getting it wrong and anxious to pass on the task to his or her successor—who, it can be rationalized, if for no other reason than having more time to anticipate the problem, will be better able to deal with it.

It is also an issue, at both the personal and organizational level, of some sensitivity. If the board (through either the board or a committee chair) takes the initiative, raising the question of succession and transition planning, will the chief executive view it as a vote of no confidence? Will the organization perceive it as the board wanting to push the chief executive out? These reactions, while perhaps ungrounded and irrational, are real and not uncommon. To avoid them, and the counter-productive consequences they can produce, two actions are necessary.

First, the enterprise must act to make succession management an ongoing and regular part of its annual operating and governance activities. Making succession management part of an annual human resources budgeting process converts the unavoidable guesses about organizational changes from speculation to just one more routine item on the board's annual agenda of oversight activities. This step will not eliminate rumors, for organizational prognostication is as much driven by its entertainment value as the inextricable human need to be in the know. Nevertheless, it provides a systematic mechanism for both dealing with questions about timing and process and, more importantly, enables each individual to know where he or she stands in terms of personal growth and career development (i.e., what is expected of them and what opportunities are potentially available to them).

With respect to governance oversight, boards should demand that the enterprise have at least a simple succession management process:

- a plan covering the chief executive and his or her direct reports,

- an annual review of how the IDPs are being implemented, and

- a yearly review of how the succession plan is being followed in actual practice.

Management should encourage the board's review, for it enables the board to carry out its responsibilities without overstepping into either operational decisions or feeling the need to re-examine individual senior management personnel decisions.

> **PREPARATION***
>
> Serving on the board of another corporation, either for-profit or nonprofit, can be a useful experience for helping potential chief executives prepare for becoming chief executives. Board service enables a potential chief executive to understand the structure and mechanics of governance as well as the difference between oversight and operations. These are all lessons that most senior executives are not exposed to until they either become a chief executive or serve on a board.
>
> To enable chief executive candidates to have this kind of preparation and governance experience, not only must it be part of their IDP but also incumbent chief executives and board leaders must use their networks to identify opportunities and make connections.
>
> * Beverly Behan, "The Boardroom," Business Week, August 24, 2009. (Interview with Bill Mitchell, Arrow Electronics, Chairman.)

The second necessary action centers directly on the chief executive. He or she must take the initiative to make themselves and their position part of the succession management process. By taking the initiative, the chief executive's action signals not only personal support, but also that there is no hidden organizational agenda. The former sets the foundation for others to support the process. The latter makes clear that the initiative is intended to improve enterprise performance—not threaten careers.

By both supporting and participating in the process, the chief executive also provides a vehicle, given the changing skill demands of their position, for enhancing their own competencies. Also, as discussed in Chapter 15, participation enables the chief executive to initiate the timing of when succession management changes to transition management (i.e., the preparation for the succession of a new person to the chief executive's position).

EMERGENCY SUCCESSION

Before turning to transition management, the process and mechanics of chief executive succession (see Chapter 15), a bit of a detour is needed. Transition management is a subset of overall succession management. Emergency succession, in turn, is a subset of transition management.

Emergency succession involves the need to unexpectedly replace the incumbent chief executive. This need can arise for a variety of reasons, both controllable and uncontrolled, and can demand immediate action or allow for some time. Regardless of the circumstance, the requirement is the same. The board must know what it is going to do to replace the out-going chief executive. In the most extreme and at the same time the easiest to understand example, presume the incumbent chief executive is hit by the proverbial bus. What does the board chair do? Glibly, the answer is look for the "name in the envelope."

The name in the envelope is shorthand for the conversation that each board chair and chief executive must have as to how the enterprise is to be cared for if the chief executive is suddenly unavailable to lead it. What should the board chair do in that circumstance? What action would the chief executive recommend that the chair take? To know what that is, the chair and the chief executive must have a conversation. This conversation is not only a non-threatening way to introduce the importance of succession management to the organization and enlist the chief executive's support for a systematic program, but also to answer the question of what should be done if an emergency occurs.

The answer to this question is the so-called name in the envelope, implying that the envelope will only be opened in the case of an emergency. Who that person is need not necessarily be the person who can assume the long-term leadership of the enterprise. In fact, the criterion for the candidate is someone who can step in immediately and provide short-term leadership and stability, without causing long-term operational or succession issues.

Depending on the enterprise's size and personnel bench strength, it may be a senior executive who had no interest in being the next chief executive or who can step down without difficulty if/when the incumbent chief executive is able to return. Alternatively, it could be the board chair, a past board member, or even a past chief executive or senior executive. In the extreme, it could be someone from outside of the enterprise's family, an interim chief executive from another agency or from a firm that provides temporary executives. The answer depends on the enterprise's circumstance. The importance is to know what to do if the need arises.

If there is no name in the envelope, then the problem falls to the chair. In this instance, the chair should seek the advice of both current and past board leadership to reach a consensus on the best course of action. Again, the same options as outlined above are available.

When a non-chief executive, senior management position becomes unexpectedly vacant the organization has more flexibility than when it is the chief executive position. The chief executive can, on an interim basis, assume the responsibilities of the position. In fact, there may be some benefit to this in that it enables the chief executive to better understand the current operational details of the position and decide if:

- the position should be replaced—with no changes;

- assignments should be redistributed, and the position reorganized or eliminated;

- the position should be maintained, but a different set of skills are needed.

If it is determined that the position should be replaced, then the chief executive should look to the succession plan for the action to be taken—promote from within or look to an outside candidate who may or may not have already been identified by the chief executive.

IMPORTANCE

Central to all of the above is an understanding that human resources are the enterprise's key asset. While a board's stewardship responsibilities and the duty of care make obvious the need to manage financial assets, managing human resources generally does not attract the same attention.[9] This is a dangerous failing, particularly for management who must rely on the enterprise's staff to accomplish its goals and objectives.

To protect against this risk, management must take the leadership initiative to manage human resources with the same vigor that it applies to financial resources and financial performance. Management must nurture the incumbent staff, continually enhancing their professional capabilities. Simultaneously, it must also build a human resources safety net, so that the changes in personnel that will inevitably occur—fail safe.

CHAPTER 14

Takeaways and Questions for Consideration and Discussion:

TAKEAWAYS

1. Sustained organizational success depends on products (services), processes, and people. Of the three, the most powerful factor is people—human capital.

2. Human capital (human resources) is potentially the enterprise's most valuable asset. For this value to be realized, human resources must be continually nurtured and improved.

3. Human capital value maximization requires:
   - At the enterprise level, a succession plan that identifies individuals for advancement and the skills and competencies needed for their next step.

   - At the individual level, a development plan that accommodates both needed current competencies and the necessary advancement skills identified in the succession plan.

4. Every enterprise needs a "name in the envelope" identifying the chief executive's emergency/unanticipated replacement.

QUESTIONS

1. How does succession management differ from transition management?

2. How can small organizations afford the time and money for succession planning? Does succession planning have to be either costly or time-consuming?

3. How can emergency succession be handled for the chief executive position? For other key positions?

4. How does the individual development planning process support the succession planning management? How is time an ally in the succession planning?

Chapter 15:
TRANSITION MANAGEMENT

Fortunately, true emergency chief executive succession events are the exception. Unplanned transitions, however, are more common, particularly for enterprises having young chief executives who in the course of their careers can be expected to look for increasingly challenging opportunities. If for no other reason than this pragmatic reality, the chief executive position should be part of the annual succession management process. In these instances, only limited time is available to begin to manage the transition process. Therefore, it is not unusual for the board to appoint an interim chief executive, possibly relying on the name in the envelope, to manage the enterprise as it pursues the planned transition actions discussed below.[1]

For most enterprises, chief executive transition will be both a rare event and an event that can be plainly anticipated. This means that the opportunity will exist for chief executive transition to be managed. Due to its infrequency, it also means that the board's skills around this event will be rusty at best. But boards need to capture the opportunities presented by a chief executive's leaving.

Moreover, if boards and chief executives procrastinate, what could be a managed transition process turns into a rushed search or worse, an emergency succession problem. To avoid these pitfalls, time must be used as an ally. This requires that as the possibility of the chief executive's leaving moves into the time frame of the board's planning horizon (i.e., the time when meaningful action can begin to be taken), the board must find the internal commitment and time to act.

> **FOUNDER'S DILEMMA**
>
> An interim chief executive can also be useful, regardless of the adequacy of the time that is available, when the outgoing chief executive is the founder of the enterprise.
>
> To be the immediate successor to a living founding chief executive is often a position doomed to failure because the new chief executive is compared to the mythic (and embellished) standards and accomplishments of the person who created the enterprise.
>
> An interim chief executive provides a circuit breaker, enabling the enterprise to pursue a two-stage transition, using an interim chief executive for 12-18 months and then recruiting a long-term successor who does not have to stand in the full shadow of the founder.

Not surprisingly, like any complex process, managed transition involves a number of decisions and resulting actions. Each of these steps builds on the previous one, creating a flow of activity leading to a new chief executive. For ease of discussion and understanding, it is helpful to group these individual actions into five phases of activity. (See Exhibit 15-1 on next page.)

PRELUDE

The first phase—The Prelude—starts well ahead of any explicit board action or personnel decisions. However, because of its early start and the opportunity it holds for repeated conversations with the incumbent chief executive, it is the foundation of the entire transition process, providing the opportunity for establishing common understandings and expectations.

By anticipating the other steps in the process, the prelude provides both time for the stage to be set for an effective chief executive transition and the mechanism for bringing everyone to the same starting point—at the same time. It also turns time into an ally, giving the enterprise the flexibility and space to work its way through the complexity of the transition process. This is particularly critical for small and/or developing enterprises where getting transition right is the key not just to survival—but future growth.

Exhibit 15-1

MANAGED TRANSITION	
I. **The Prelude**	• Conversation • Economics • Starting Point ▪ Announcement
II. **Board Transition Organization and Management**	• Leadership and Committee Assignment • Decision Regarding Stakeholder Involvement • Timetable and Process • Communication Plan • Spokesperson
III. **Strategic Considerations**	• Consolidation/Shared Services • Skill Sets/Competencies
IV. **Search, Interview, and Selection**	• Candidate Identification • Interviews • Selection
V. **Transition**	• Announcement • Notice and Relocation • Overlap/Succession/Transformation • Farewell Recognition • Welcome

The prelude ends when the incumbent chief executive informs the board that he or she will be leaving and the expected date. How much advance notice should be given is an important question. The answer will vary with the circumstances of the enterprise and the capacity and capability of the board.

The goal of managed transition is to provide a smooth movement from one chief executive to the next. This means that enough time has to be provided for board deliberations and decisions, possible successor relocation, and incumbent/successor overlap.

However, if the process starts too early, it can become dysfunctional, concentrating the enterprise on questions of succession instead of performance. It also risks, in larger enterprises where there are alternative internal candidates, creating unproductive organizational tension as possible successors compete with one another as well as have an extended period to wonder about their future and whether they should begin to look elsewhere. Similarly, if there is too much time for overlap between incumbent and successor chief executives, the enterprise may begin to lose momentum, because staff may not be able to determine the enterprise's leader, or decisions are delayed while the incumbent and successor try to be respectful of each other's prerogatives.

In counterpoint, experience has shown that the Strategic Consideration and Search and Selection phases of the process will usually take longer than expected—as the board organizes itself, deliberates, and adds candidate interviews to already busy schedules. Recognizing this ambiguity, the following can be used as guidelines. It must be understood that they are just a starting point. The enterprise must tailor the process to its own unique needs and traditions.

First, the chief executive should begin to talk to the board several years before any formal announcement. Ideally, these conversations should be initiated by the chief executive and should take place during one of the board's executive sessions. The chief executive should take the lead so that there is no misunderstanding about either intention or timing. The conversation should be in executive session so that speculation and rumors can be kept to a minimum.

If the chief executive does not take the lead, then the board chair or the chair of the appropriate board committee should raise the matter. This can be done as part of the chief executive's annual review or the annual discussion of his or her individual development plan. If the discussion is board-initiated, the timing and matter may be sensitive. However, as the chief executive approaches a point in his or her career when change can be expected, the subject is an appropriate matter for the board's concern and discussion with its direct employee—the chief executive, just as it would be for the chief executive's discussion with any of his or her key employees.

By initiating the discussion, the board is simply carrying out its governance and oversight responsibilities. Regardless of the initiating party, transition planning should become an annual agenda item for board discussion. Because of the time required for transition preparation and implementation, these conversations should begin as simply an annual agenda discussion item and start well ahead of any formal announcement. These discussions should be used for at least four purposes:

1. managing expectations;

2. preparing the organization for transition;

3. providing adequate time for a seamless change in leadership;

4. eliminating personal economic barriers to a timely transition.

The first and third objectives are self-explanatory. The other two purposes of these discussions merit further examination.

Depending on its current status, preparing the organization for transition may be a multi-year task. Just as employee-focused individual development plans are part of the process of preparing people for growth and change, the enterprise as an operational entity also needs to prepare itself for leadership change. Exhibit 15-2 presents an example of the factors that should be considered in developing the enterprise as an organizational entity for chief executive transition. Many of the matters that are important for preparing the organization for a planned change in leadership are the same management and governance practices that have already been discussed.

Exhibit 15-2

ORGANIZATION DEVELOPMENT PLAN EXAMPLE CHECKLIST*
When the following conditions are in place, an enterprise can expect a relatively smooth transition to new leadership whenever it might occur. An enterprise might determine which elements below are lacking in its current operations and then create a "capacity building plan" that prescribes activities and timelines for filling the gaps. The organization is then ready for leadership transitions, foreseen or unforeseen.

1. A strategic and operating plan is in place with goals and objectives, including objectives for leadership talent development.
2. The board evaluates the chief executive annually.
3. The board evaluates itself annually.
4. The chief senior executives receive annual performance reviews with continuously updated individual development plans.
5. Another staff person or board member shares important external relationships (major donors, funders, community leaders) maintained by the chief executive.
6. A financial reserve is in place with a board established minimum amount of operating capital.
7. Financial systems meet industry standards.
8. A succession management process is in place, utilized and monitored by the board.

* Adapted from Tim Wolfred, The Annie E. Casey Foundation, "A Succession Readiness Checklist," Building Leaderful Organizations, 2008.

The goal of the organizational development plan is straightforward. It is simply to assure that the new chief executive is able to assume leadership of a strong, stable entity, instead of having to begin his or her tenure with the need to turn things around. The importance of this is clear for both recruiting a new leader and for enabling the enterprise to prosper.

The last objective, eliminating personal economic barriers to a timely transition, is also a key element in enabling the enterprise to make a productive transition.

No one can be expected to "fall on their own economic sword" for the sake of the enterprise having a seamless transition. Chief executives will overstay their value and welcome, if leaving presents them with a personal economic penalty. To get the personal and personnel side of transition right, the enterprise must first get the personal economic side right. This takes time. Time is needed for conversation, deliberation, and decision—and then, as importantly, for prudently accumulating the resources needed for putting an economic structure in place that neither forces the chief executive out, nor forces him or her to stay—in order to protect their personal economic future.

Some board members will feel that getting the proper economic incentives in place is an unwarranted expense. The facts are that the costs of a chief executive staying too long, simply to avoid some loss of retirement benefits, are enormous in terms of lost opportunities, reduced morale, and organizational stagnation. The problem is that these costs are not only intangible but also lie in the future. In contrast, the costs of getting the incentives right are tangible and current. Nevertheless, these future costs, because they impair the enterprise's ability to achieve its potential for success, far exceed the defined and manageable expenses of enabling chief executive transition to proceed in an operationally necessary and timely manner.

Second, time should be allowed for both considering and acting on strategic options and, if needed, for conducting a search for an external successor. As suggested, this will likely take longer than expected. This is particularly so for a smaller enterprise, as the strategic options may have profound implications and therefore require careful and unhurried analysis and decision. Also, the search process may be less formal and as a result take longer.

Third, time should be built into the process for a period of actual transition overlap between the incumbent and successor, providing an opportunity for the new chief executive to get a sense of the flow of the enterprise's activities and to be introduced to key stakeholders. This period should be no more than a year, or less than a month. Also, time may need to be allowed for the new chief executive to provide his or her current employer (if an employed, external candidate) with fair notice. If a geographic and/or family relocation is involved, even more time will be required.

With regard to fair notice, the executive leaving his or her position often believes that a great deal of time is necessary. Realistically, once the announcement is made, he or she immediately becomes a lame duck—whose authority deteriorates at an accelerating rate. Therefore, unless required by contract or some special event that must be completed, the length of notice should typically be one to three (1–3) months.

In a planned transition, the incumbent who is leaving suffers the same loss of authority. However, the starting point for the loss of influence is not the announcement of the incumbent's intent to leave, but rather the announcement of the successor.

Recognizing all of the foregoing, the prelude, in the form of transition-focused conversations between the board and the chief executive, should begin several years before any formal announcement. Ideally the chief executive's formal announcement to the board, not the enterprise's various stakeholders, should provide six to eighteen (6–18) months of lead time. This is based on the board needing:

- one month to organize itself for transition management;

- two to six (2–6) months for strategic considerations and decisions;

- two to six (2–6) months for search, interviews, and selection (and perhaps longer if an extensive external search is needed);

- zero to three (0–3) months for notice and relocation (zero time is needed if the successor is an internal selection);

- one to three (1–3) months for transition overlap (to provide an understanding of the flow of activity, as well as introductions to key stakeholders).

ORGANIZATION

The prelude ends with the chief executive's announcement to the board of his or her plans to leave the enterprise. The internal announcement to the board is also the first step in the next phase of the process—Organization and Management. In practice there must be a bit of an overlap between these first two phases, in order for the public announcement to be handled in a planned manner. Therefore, the board must organize itself prior to any public announcement—so that the public announcement is presented as the enterprise would like it to be. This means that decisions must be made with respect to at least the following matters:

- Who will chair the transition process?

- What board committee will be used for conducting the "search" process—or will an ad hoc committee be used, and if so, who will serve on it?

- How, if at all, will former board leaders and others in the community be involved?

- What external support and resources will be required (i.e., internal staff support, consultants, etc.)?

- What is the target timetable?

- Who will speak for the enterprise and what is the communication plan?

Regarding the last point, the importance of a communications plan and an ongoing flow of information to key constituencies for both maintaining confidence in the enterprise and starting to build a positive climate for the new chief executive cannot be overstated. (See Exhibit 15-3.) In this vein, the announcement to the board must precede the public announcement. The public announcement in turn should not only share the news that the incumbent chief executive will be leaving, but also begin the process of thanking, and recognizing the accomplishments of, the incumbent. It should also, at least, outline how the enterprise will be proceeding to select a successor.

Exhibit 15-3

COMMUNICATION PLAN OUTLINE	
1. Internal Announcement	**Chief Executive Leaving**
2. Identify single person to communicate for the enterprise	
3. Establish Communications Guidelines	• Only one voice • All inquiries channeled to the spokesperson • No individual board member or staff comments • Confidentiality of information

4. External Announcement: Chief Executive Leaving	• Informal—Key stakeholders, should precede the public announcement
	• Public—Share the news as well as begin:
	  ▪ Thank you and recognition of incumbent
	  ▪ Managing expectations

5. Status Reports	• Internal—To manage rumors and false information
	• External:
	  ▪ Key stakeholders—To manage expectations and maintain relationships
	  ▪ Public—Optional, depending on role and place of the enterprise in the general community

6. Selection Announcement	• Board—Should be informed first • Staff—Ideally should be both personal introduction to senior staff as well as formal notification • Key stakeholders—Should be informed prior to the general public; process should be tailored to stakeholder circumstance and begin the introduction of the new chief executive • Public—Share the news and celebrate the legacy of the incumbent and the qualifications of the successor

How the enterprise organizes itself to manage the transition process will be shaped by its circumstances, traditions, and resources, as well as the preferences of the board's leadership. There is no fixed formula. However, the process must be credible and result in a selection that is accepted positively by the enterprise's stakeholders. To achieve credibility, the process must have legitimacy and transparency.

To accomplish legitimacy, it must be headed by the board chair, the chair of the governance or compensation committee, or another current or past board member whose personal credibility will give community legitimacy to the process. To have transparency, the process must involve two-way communications. The enterprise must not be reluctant to share with its stakeholders its plans and timetable. It also should not be fearful about involving them in the process, either through informal conversations or in a more formal advisory committee role or even participation in the search process itself.

STRATEGIC CONSIDERATIONS

The next set of steps involves the entire board and concentrates on considering the strategic opportunities that become available when a chief executive is leaving. The precursor to this is the board's review of the enterprise's current strategic plan to assure itself that it is directionally correct, with the appropriate priorities—or if not, how it should be modified. (See Exhibit 15-4.) This review should not be thought of as being a comprehensive business planning effort. Rather, it should be an examination of the enterprise's strategy in terms of the board's comfort level with the direction that is being pursued and its sustainability.

Exhibit 15-4

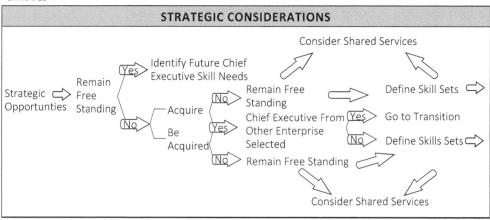

STRATEGIC CONSIDERATIONS

Leadership transition provides a special opportunity to consider both mission and enterprise sustainability. As discussed below, transition opens organizational strategic opportunities that are typically only reluctantly considered. By looking at these possibilities through the position of enterprise sustainability, a neutral, yet compelling, perspective for decision making is available. Sustainability, however, is not simply a binary—"Yes" or "No"—conclusion. For the most part, it's the identification of vulnerabilities and what must be acted on to address them in order to protect sustainability.

As a byproduct of this effort, a summary of the strategy should also be developed that can be shared with potential successor candidates. This is a useful document both for introducing the enterprise to the candidate and for the candidate assessing his or her comfort with the direction that the board has decided to pursue.

In considering strategic opportunities, the most obvious is the possibility of some form of consolidation with another enterprise. Not surprisingly, determining what will happen to one or both of the incumbent chief executives is a major barrier to organizational consolidation. If one of the incumbents is leaving, this problem becomes soluble.[2]

Enterprise consolidation can take a variety of forms. For the sake of clarity, Exhibit 15-4 illustrates the extremes—acquire or be acquired. It also shows that the foundation for the possibility of shared services should be considered when defining future chief executive skill needs.

Typically, consolidation, in whatever form, is first thought of as a way to reduce enterprise costs. Certainly, savings can be obtained if consolidation is combined with aggressive operational management. However, the smaller the organization, the more difficult it is to generate significant savings. This is due to the simple fact that in small enterprises people play multiple roles, carrying out multiple jobs. Therefore, there are not two financial officers or two human resources directors who can be consolidated into one. Nevertheless, occupancy costs as well as some back office, legal, and auditing costs can be saved. Also, governance administrative burden (i.e., number of directors that must be recruited and oriented, number of board meetings, etc.), can be reduced.

While reducing costs is important, it is not a sufficient reason to consolidate. For any form of consolidation to be successful, it must result in the enterprise being better able to pursue and achieve its mission.[3] If this is the case, and if it is broadly recognized by the enterprise's stakeholders, then the strategic opportunity for, and benefits of, consolidation can be grasped. If it is not, then pursuit of consolidation, in whatever the form, is an empty task that will only drain resources, divert attention from more productive alternatives, and frustrate board members.

Consolidation may be of interest for another reason. As referenced in End Note 2, consolidation (merger/acquisition) can be the enterprise's strategy for obtaining the human resources it needs to be able to survive and succeed, to continue to lead the enterprise, or to take it to the next level of performance and achievement.

Implicit in thinking about consolidation as a human resources strategy is a related strategic requirement. The board must determine the skill sets and competencies that it is looking for in its next chief executive. This determination is difficult, but it is also necessary. Without explicit decisions about the skills that the next chief executive should bring to the enterprise, the enterprise will not be able to grow.

The next chief executive should not be a clone of the incumbent. The skills that the incumbent brought to the job are the drivers that have taken the enterprise to its current place. The next chief executive must be able to take it from where it is and continue to move it forward. This means that different competencies, either in depth and/or breadth, may be needed. The search committee needs to understand what these are so that it knows what it is looking for. Similarly, the entire board has to know what it is seeking in its next chief executive to be able to make a strategic decision regarding consolidation, or a personnel selection choice.

Consolidation as a human resources strategy is reasonable as long as the resulting chief executive has the requisite skill. If not, then consolidation will be a failed initiative, wasting the opportunity that chief executive transition offers to the enterprise.

An external consultant can be helpful in accomplishing the strategic assessment— both from a time perspective, being able to accelerate the process, and from an altitude perspective (i.e., keeping the review at the right level of board member involvement and detail). Also, depending on the results and conclusions, he or she can be useful in assisting the enterprise in pursuing the next step—either exploring consolidation opportunities or initiating the search for the new chief executive.

TACTICAL CONSIDERATION

Before moving on to the actual search process, it is useful in some situations to pause in the process and consider if the enterprise is facing what could be considered a special circumstance.

Generally, chief executives can be viewed as coming and going, each serving for perhaps 8 to 12 years. In these circumstances, transition, while still disruptive, is a normal and understood part of enterprise life.

The exception to this non-routine yet normal flow of organizational life is the replacement of a long-tenured (20 to 30 years), well-loved chief executive. In this instance, the board must ask itself a tactical question. Is it searching for an immediate, permanent successor or would it be better to first find an interim chief executive? An interim chief executive can be a "circuit breaker" between the beloved and admired retiring chief executive and a new, sometimes completely unknown, successor.

The long-tenured chief executive is, as evidenced by length of service, viewed as having had a particularly meaningful career. Regardless of the facts, he or she will be considered as holding a special place in the enterprise's history. Moreover, some people, both inside as well as outside the enterprise, may view the retiring incumbent as being irreplaceable in terms of skills (business and social), industry knowledge, and or sensitivity.

In this circumstance, a successor chief executive is confronted with a daunting challenge: how to replace an icon. Simply as a consequence of the circumstances, a good candidate, who by all rights if given a chance would be successful, leaves or is asked to leave after a relatively short period. While the reasons for his or her departure may be expressed in politically correct terms, the root cause of such failures is almost always the fact that the board and the organization were not really ready for change.

When this happens, the enterprise's reputation is diminished, and the competency of the board is called into question. The result at a minimum is increased cost, as a second recruitment effort has to be undertaken and perhaps even a hiring premium has to be paid to lure another good candidate. Even more costly is the disruption to the organization as it is left rudderless. These costs and self-inflicted wounds should be avoided.

One approach for doing this is to first hire an interim person to serve as the chief executive for a fixed, short-term period—and with the understanding that he or she will not be a candidate for the permanent position.

An interim chief executive provides an opportunity to break from the past, implement business practice and operational changes that might be needed and even, if necessary, restructure the organization all without incurring the costs of a failed transition.

The interim chief executive in effect;

• prepares the organization for a new, permanent chief executive, and

• provides the opportunity for that person to have a fair chance to be successful.

Whether an interim chief executive is needed will depend on the particular circumstances of the organization and the personalities of the involved individuals. It is a decision that only the board can make and is not simply a function of the incumbent's length of service. In fact, it is likely more dependent on how the board and the incumbent have prepared the enterprise for change and particularly chief executive succession than anything else.

If the decision is made to pursue an interim executive, the pool of likely candidates is generally recently retired executives, from the same or related fields or recently retired members of the enterprise's own board. These people are either already known to the board or can be identified through professional associations or local resources like the United Way. Also, if a consultant has been engaged to help with the transition, he or she can be useful both in weighing the decision and in sourcing potential interim candidates.

How long an interim executive should serve is also a judgment question for the board. As a guideline, it should be short-term (a year or less)—yet long enough to make a break with the past, while short enough not to be misunderstood as being a permanent hire.[4]

SEARCH

Now knowing what is being looked for, the next major set of activities in the transition management process is the search, interview, and selection component. As illustrated in Exhibit 15-5, it is a straightforward series of steps. The primary leadership and work is done by, regardless of its formal name, the enterprise's search committee.

Exhibit 15-5

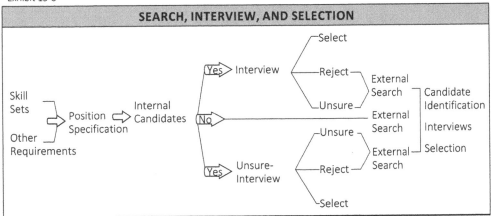

In pursuing search and selection, the search committee must make several decisions before it interviews its first candidate. The skill sets and competencies being sought have already been discussed and specified. To this, the committee should determine if there are any other requirements they would like to add to the search criteria (i.e., educational background, knowledge of the business, licensure needs, etc.). As the surrogate for the board, the committee should also consider what it is that the board worries about, what the board's governance priorities are, and how much change the organization needs or can tolerate. The committee must define what it is looking for—so that it will know when it has found it.

In the same vein, the committee must also determine if there are any internal candidates to consider. If there is an internal candidate, the committee must make a difficult decision. Should it interview the candidate, and if the candidate meets the enterprise's needs, select that person and forego an external search, or should the committee do a comprehensive search and include the internal candidate in this larger and lengthier process?

The justification for the latter comprehensive, external search approach is fiduciary based with the board or committee feeling that it must examine a universe of candidates, then selecting the best available choice to fulfill its stewardship and agency responsibilities. The logic of this approach is attractive. Moreover, it is a solid defense against any criticism of the process or the committee. Its flaw lays in that it:

- Adds time to the process,

- Adds cost to the process,

- Possibly risks losing the best candidate, if the internal candidate feels unappreciated and offended by the process,

- Is inherently unfair.

The first two points are obvious. The third reflects the realities of both human nature and internal organizational politics. It may be irrational. However, its consequences can be powerful, undermining morale and driving away good candidates.

The fourth point relates to the third, but goes beyond it. Mixing external and internal candidates in the same review scheme puts the internal candidate at a disadvantage.

While he or she knows the organization, they are also known by the organization. The board has seen the internal candidate at his or her best and worst. The board has seen frailties as well as strengths.

In contrast, external candidates are comparatively unknown. They come with good references and recommendations, if for no other reason than that they have selected the sources. They meet with the search committee and perhaps others for a relatively short time, under controlled circumstances and while on their best corporate behavior. The result is that external candidates are in a position to look good.

A more pragmatic approach is to determine if there are any qualified internal candidates and if so, make a judgment about them before undertaking the time and cost of an external search or even a combined internal/external search. The committee's judgment should reflect both strategic and personal considerations. At the strategic level, if the board is comfortable with the enterprise's strategy and the way it is being implemented, then it should evaluate internal candidates. If it is not, then the search should recognize that an external candidate is necessary and look beyond the organization.

If the strategic hurdle is successfully passed, the committee should look at the personal skill sets, competencies, and other qualifications of the internal candidates. If an internal candidate meets these criteria, then the internal candidate, or the best of the internal candidates should be selected and the committee's job is completed.[5] If they do not, or if the committee is unsure, the process should proceed to an external search.

As noted, an external search adds time and cost to the process. It also adds a substantial degree of logistical complication. Therefore, if it is affordable, the enterprise should engage a search consultant to help navigate the external search process. (See Appendix 17—Selecting and Retaining a Consultant.)

A consultant can be useful not only because the firm will have information regarding potential candidates, but also because the consultant can help to guide the entire process from strategic considerations, forcing the board to define its and the organization's real needs, strengths, and weaknesses, through candidate management and referencing. The consultant can also provide a buffer between the candidate and the board, protecting the board from unwarranted direct contact.

If a consultant is not affordable, then the search committee, and particularly the chair of the committee, must play the consultant role. The incumbent chief executive must also provide increased support, particularly with respect to candidate identification.[6] In doing this, time can be made into an ally, allowing potential candidates to meet with the board by being invited to make presentations and using national associations and local agencies, such as the community foundation and the United Way, to help identify candidates.

RETENTION INCENTIVES

If there is no internal candidate or if there is a choice of internal candidates, leaving one or more not selected, the board may want to consider providing retention incentives to stabilize the organization. An incentive can be offered to keep people in place until both they and the new chief executive can make a judgment about the future. The incentive can either be financial or non-financial. A financial incentive might involve a retention bonus (i.e., a lump sum payment if the person stays for six (6) or twelve (12) months after the change in leadership). A non-financial incentive might be a change in control severance agreement. While the financial incentive guarantees a payment if the person stays, the change in control severance agreement only involves an expense if, within a specified time frame, the person leaves.

SELECTION

Regardless of whether the candidate is internal or external, the committee must develop a position description or job specification that outlines, in some detail, the responsibilities and expectations of the position, the qualifications and skills the enterprise is seeking and expected compensation and benefits. (See Appendix 18—Chief Executive Officer Position Descriptions: Examples.) In regard to compensation and benefits, the committee may in effect wish to prepare a prospective tally sheet (see Chapter 13) outlining the range of salary and benefits the enterprise is willing to consider.

If the committee has engaged a consultant, he or she can be helpful in drafting these materials. If not, the committee will have to do it itself—hopefully with the aid of the incumbent chief executive or the assigned human resources development staff to the committee. This document is important for it both markets the position and sets the base for the later negotiation to close the deal. It must reflect an understanding of the economics of market conditions as well as the board's expectations both with regard to the authority that it is expecting to give to the new chief executive and the support that it will provide for the chief executive to be successful.

Also, regardless of whether the candidate is internal or external, the committee must decide on a candidate selection and interview process. Typically, the committee should act as a filter. The chair (or the chair and the search consultant) should identify candidates who merit an interview, either through a paper review of their qualifications or an informal personal conversation. Depending on the personal preference and the board's guidelines, the chair can either do this unilaterally or with the concurrence of the committee.

Once selected for an interview, candidates should meet with as many members of the committee as possible, enabling the committee to determine who should go on to a second set of interviews with non-search committee board members. Here, as many board members as possible should have an opportunity to talk with the candidates.[7] This is important both for the board and the candidates.

From the candidate's perspective, it enables a better assessment about board/ chief executive chemistry and the board's commitment to the enterprise. From the board's vantage point it gives members involvement in the process and ownership of the decision. Both are important in setting the base for the new chief executive's selection and assumption of responsibility.

Beyond the search committee and the board, the interview process obviously has a bit of a public relations opportunity to it. The board may want the candidate to meet with key stakeholders and other community leaders so that they feel that they are part of the process. In all these interviews, board and community, the chair should seek feedback. The feedback, however, should focus on matters such as: can you work with the candidate and would you veto the candidate for the position—not should the particular candidate be offered the position or how he or she ranks relative to the other choices. Once the interview process is complete, the committee must make a selection and then close the deal.

These steps have no magic formula. They do, however, involve a lot of moving pieces because the deal has to be closed both with the candidate and the board. The first step is making the selection. Here the committee should, if it has multiple candidates, rank the order of their choices. The first choice, depending on the committee's charge and authority, should then be reviewed with at least the board's leadership to assure comfort level. Assuming success at this point, the candidate can then be approached and, hopefully, agreement reached.

Prior to this point, the candidate will already have information, provided in the job specification or the job description, about the position, its compensation and benefits. It can be assumed that if these terms were not felt by the candidate to be reasonable, that he or she would not have continued to pursue the position. Even so, from the candidate's perspective this is a time for salary and benefit negotiations.[8]

Negotiations with a potential new chief executive are no different than any other negotiations. It is a mistake to think that because it involves a job and, that the candidate is interested in the job, that it is a fundamentally different kind of conversation.

The search consultant can again be useful at this point, guiding the process through difficulties, without burning future relationship bridges. The importance of this last point should not be underestimated.

The new chief executive does not want to begin with ill will due to contention generated in closing the deal. Recognizing this, if agreement does not come quickly and relatively easily, perhaps with both sides compromising to show good faith and optimism about the future, the committee should discontinue the negotiation and move on to its next choice—or start over. Either decision will be less costly in the long run to the enterprise.

Depending on the committee's authority, it can either approve the agreement and sign the hiring letter/contract or bring the matter to the full board for approval. Setting aside the specifics, closure will be achieved, an offer will be made and accepted, and a new chief executive will be ready to go to work. The new chief executive's acceptance of the position begins the last phase of the process, the actual transition.

TRANSITION

Exhibit 15-6 outlines the major components of the transition phase of the process.

Exhibit 15-6

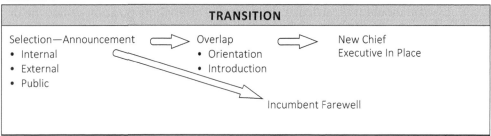

As discussed earlier, there should be an announcement of the board's selection decision, timed appropriately, for the internal/external stakeholder and public audiences, and some period of overlap between the incoming and outgoing chief executive. The period of overlap should be used to introduce the new chief executive to the organization and to key stakeholders. With one exception, this is the incumbent chief executive's final significant task.

The exception is the incumbent's participation in his or her own farewell recognition. To some chief executives this is a grand event, the final moment in the corporate spotlight. To others it is an awkward time. For most it is somewhere in between, and for all it is something that must be done. The breadth, scope, and grandeur of the event can be adjusted to accommodate the incumbent's comfort level. The organization, however, needs to say "goodbye" and "thank you." The organization must in effect have the opportunity to reach closure with the change of leadership.

After this, the former chief executive must assume a new, non-management role. He or she must eschew any explicit formal leadership position in the enterprise, becoming instead the chief leader for the new chief executive.[9] If the former chief executive hangs around as either part of the enterprise's operational leadership and/or as a board member, the new chief executive, at least initially, is in an awkward position. Over time, as the former chief executive's day-to-day knowledge of the organization and emerging business and regulatory event decays, the former chief executive's influence will diminish. At the outset, however, he or she will know more than their successor and if sitting at the executive management or board table, it is only human nature for people to look in their direction for confirmation of what is being decided. This kind of second guessing, even if unintended and benign, is not helpful to the transition process. The best way to protect against this is for the former chief executive to remove him/herself from any involvement in the governance and/or management of the enterprise.

SENSITIVITY

While it is important for the outgoing chief executive to be as supportive as possible of his or her successor, the new chief executive must also be sensitive to the feelings and ego needs of the former chief executive. The new chief executive should always speak positively about his or her predecessor, the leadership that was provided and the legacy left for the future. How the new chief executive treats his or her predecessor will set the precedent for how, when the time comes and the new chief executive is leaving, he or she will be treated. Therefore, the new chief executive has a vested interest in being respectful and gracious.

SUCCESS

Transitioning to a new chief executive, regardless of how well the process is constructed and managed, is always organizationally traumatic. The board must recognize this and their resulting obligation also to introduce the new chief executive to the organization, the community, and the enterprise's stakeholders. Just as the former chief executive must be a cheerleader for the enterprise and his or her successor, the board must also be the new chief executive's ambassador.

Effectively managed chief executive transitions can provide a competitive advantage and a platform for enabling the enterprise to become a better organization. For this to be accomplished, the board must recognize that the responsibility for leadership transition lies directly with it. While internal, and if needed and affordable, external resources can provide support; the selection decision must be made by the board—and uncategorical support to the new chief executive must be given by the board. If the board gets chief executive transition right, then it has taken, perhaps, the most critical step to getting governance right and guaranteeing the success of the enterprise.

CHAPTER 15

Takeaways and Questions for Consideration and Discussion:

TAKEAWAYS

1. Successful enterprises require a series of competent chief executives. Selecting a competent chief executive is the board's most important task and a matter of careful process design and implementation—not luck.

2. Chief executive transition provides the enterprise with the opportunity (and arguably the excuse) to objectively consider strategic questions such as the appropriateness of its current strategy, enterprise's sustainability, and the value of consolidation with other organizations.

3. If the board is satisfied with both the enterprise's strategy and its operating performance, then internal candidates should not be put at either an implicit or explicit disadvantage. The strengths and weaknesses of internal candidates are better known than those of external candidates. (Remember external candidates pick their references and only have to be well behaved for the relatively short time of the interview and vetting process.) A board's fiduciary obligation requires a careful transition management process not necessarily an external search.

4. The outgoing chief executive must be his or her successor's chief cheerleader, just as the board must be the new chief executive's leading ambassador to the community, providing unconditional support.

QUESTIONS

1. How can time be an ally in transition management?

2. Does the board have a fiduciary responsibility to always consider external candidates before it makes its decision? Is there a risk in looking for external candidates to compare to internal candidates?

3. How does successful transition management contribute to long run organizational success?

4. What has to be done to prevent the incumbent chief executive from being an impediment to transition management? Is it more than a question of just economics?

Chapter 16:
THE PUBLIC'S TRUST

The previous chapters have focused on fundamental governance and management problems. These matters are important for enterprise success. However, for an enterprise that requires the support of more than just its nuclear corporate family, sustainable success involves performance beyond just sound business mechanics.[1] Success requires that the enterprise continually maintain, and ideally enhance, the public's trust in it. Donors give to, volunteers get involved with, and government creates a special place for community sector enterprises because they are trusted to focus singularly on and carry out their missions, to be good stewards of their resources, and to act as responsible agents of their stakeholders, demonstrating the highest ethical standards.[2] Community sector enterprises validate themselves not by their financial metrics, but rather by how they act and how they serve their community—by the value they add to their community, both those they serve and those with whom they live and work.

As discussed in Chapter 10, quantifying benefits and therefore, being able to assess added value is a difficult task, laced with subjective valuations and speculative estimates. Therefore, the public, except in blatant instances of misbehavior (e.g., hospitals "dumping" mentally unstable, uninsured patients who cannot pay for care; inefficiency; excessive fundraising costs; more money being spent on overhead costs than client services; secret dealings; private enrichment by management and/or the board, etc.), turns instead to proxies for making its judgments.[3] Not surprisingly these proxies are characterized more by their general understandability than their validity for drawing conclusions about either enterprise performance or trustworthiness. This may change with the enriched database that will be provided by the new Form 990.[4,5] For the present, however, the public will rely on indicators that it can relate to and place in a personally understandable context.

Paralleling this substitution of metrics is a shift in focus from the specifics of what the enterprise does to how it does it. While the public, for example, cannot judge how efficient a food pantry is in acquiring supplies and providing food to the needy, it can judge how people are treated when they come for help and how well the agency reaches out to those in need. Similarly, while most people cannot accurately assess the quality of clinical care, they can judge the sensitivity of the nursing staff, the speed with which call buttons are answered, etc. As a result, public trust is assessed on the basis of such things as how open the enterprise is in its management and operating style, how sensitively and respectfully it treats its clients and employees, how it organizes itself (i.e., if it is structured for the convenience of its clients or its professional staff, its closeness to its community and stakeholders, how it collaborates with others, how it raises money, and how it spends it, etc.).

Public trust also has a corollary public policy issue, involving the criteria for tax exemption. Here the question centers on both what the enterprise does in order to achieve its tax-exempt status, and then how it performs on an ongoing basis in order to maintain that status. Does the enterprise both act responsibly and do enough for its community to justify its being a 501(c)(3) corporation, with both the accompanying exemption from income taxation and donor ability to deduct contributions to the enterprise from taxable income? The larger question of public trust and the more narrow matter of tax exemption become intertwined around the specifics of community benefits, executive compensation, profitability, and regulatory equity.

Qualification for tax exemption is obviously a major proxy for public trust. However, public trust involves more and runs deeper than just the criteria for tax exemption. It is dependent on the enterprise's commitment to the public good, its openness and honesty, and its management and board commitment beyond self.

GOOD WORKS

One does not have to suspend reality to accept that all legitimate community sector enterprises strive to do good—to provide benefits to and for their stakeholders. Whether the outcomes produced yield real results/benefits and whether the actual value of the benefits equals or exceeds the cost of providing them is almost a secondary consideration, honored more in rhetoric than analytics and overshadowed by the enterprise's striving to do good works.[6] Therefore, public trust must consider more than what the enterprise's mission is and the services that it provides. Public trust is dependent on how it goes about doing its work.

Certainly, as noted, the public can make some judgments based on quantitative data such as administrative costs as a percentage of total revenues or fundraising costs as a percentage of fundraising yield. Its ability, however, to assess the intricacies of resource stewardship and agency responsibility and the quality of managerial decision making and internal operational performance is limited. As a result, the public reaches its conclusion about trust based on other information. It relies on stories that circulate in the community, limited events that may have been personally experienced, the negotiations of board members (see Chapter 6), and other tangible and intangible factors that create perceptions that can then be put into a personal judgmental context. Unfortunately for the enterprise, these factors are subjective—not necessarily based on facts and difficult to change.

While it may be unfair, the public's trust is the product of its cumulative subjective impressions as to how the enterprise acts with regard to its clients and beneficiaries and how it performs as a citizen of the community. If it is arrogant in its relationships with its peers, bureaucratic in its operations, secretive in its decision making, slow in its responses to requests, fixed and inflexible in its ways, does not keep commitments, etc., its level of public trust will decline. In contrast, if it is collaborative, visible in the community and in community affairs, sensitive to its clients and benefactors, innovative, close to its community, etc., its level of public trust will increase.

In addition, how it operates, not directly in terms of bottom line financial performance, but with respect to how it manages its money, both earning it and spending it, affects public trust. In fact, how much profit the enterprise earns and how much it pays its senior managers are key factors in shaping the public's judgment. This is due to the facts that these factors can be both quantified and compared and that they are metrics that people can relate to in terms of their own situations and experiences.

FOLLOW THE MONEY

In the public's eye, profitability and executive compensation are perhaps the community sector's principal public trust vulnerabilities. Clearly, for the vast majority of organizations, these matters are not issues. Most community sector enterprises generate modest, if any profits requiring, as discussed in Chapter 12, fundraising for meeting capital needs, as well as in many cases ongoing operating expenses. Similarly, many community sector executives knowingly subsidize their organizations by accepting below-market rates of compensation.[7] However, for the large enterprises (i.e., health care providers, health care plans, national organizations and associations, universities, etc.), these are matters that draw newspaper headlines and consequent public attention. Moreover, the public's reaction to the behavior of these large, highly visible, and well-known organizations spills over into its views and judgments about the entire sector.

How much is enough with regard to either compensation or profits, is the management equivalent of a metaphysical question. While there are formulas, profit cannot be determined simply by a formula (see Chapter 10 and Exhibit 16-1). Similarly, while there are processes (see Appendix 16), the results of either the formulas or processes will not guarantee that there will be no criticism.

As discussed previously, compensation must at least start with reflecting the requirements of the market. Profits are also needed over the long run for survival. Therefore, the question for boards and managers is more an issue of how much, not if.

The simple answers are:

1. Compensation must be enough, but no more than is necessary, to attract and retain the management capacity and capability needed for the enterprise to be successful.

2. Profits must be enough, but no more than are necessary, for the enterprise to continue its progress toward achieving its mission—at a minimum, contributing to building reserves to assure short-run resilience and long-run sustainability.

Boards, with the advice and guidance of management, must make these decisions, recognizing that:

- Though objective quantified data may be part of the decision mix, these decisions are subjective judgments.

- They must live with the consequences—either organizational stress and perhaps failure and/or public criticism.

Of the choices, facing public criticism is preferable to the alternative of an under-managed and under-financed failed enterprise. A failed enterprise accomplishes nothing, denying the community the services and benefits that it needs. The enterprise, if it is behaving ethically and following sound management and governance practices, can survive public criticism, particularly since the reality is that it is impossible, or at least highly unlikely, that the entire public can always be satisfied on these issues. Some voice, some place, legitimate or not, will always write a letter to the editor, a regulator or a legislator arguing that someone is being paid too much or that the organization is making too much, and as a result denying benefits to those in need. If the board were to reduce compensation and/or shrink profits to the point of enterprise failure, these same voices would still be critical. The only difference would be that the criticism would be focused on the lack of governance and management competency that allowed the enterprise to fail.

Recognizing these proclivities of human nature, management and the board must be sensitive to the importance of compensation and profitability levels in shaping public confidence and rely on independent, objective, and transparent processes and the best available data to guide their decisions. Of the two, compensation is the more important for it is both entirely within management's and the board's control and for the average person more comparable to something they know and understand. Therefore, it is vital that the determination of compensation be an independent, data-supported process, with the processes and results known to the entire board. While this will not eliminate the potential for criticism, it will provide a mitigating defense.

Exhibit 16-1

SURPLUS

While no general formula can determine the surplus objective for any specific enterprise for any given point in time as a guideline each year the overall financial objective should be to generate a surplus. A surplus is needed so that the enterprise can build a reserve to assure both its resilience and sustainability, as well as to fund any future growth.

Resilience: Three Months of Reserves
Resilience is the financial ability of the enterprise to weather short-term setbacks such as:
- a significant operating error/problem (e.g., unexpected failure of a major customer and a resulting bad debt write off or loss of revenue—or an unexpected change in the priorities or the financial performance (e.g., 2008 Great Recession) of a supporting foundation) or
- an unexpected economic/political event (e.g., 9/11, pandemic, etc).

A general guideline for assuring resilience is that the enterprise should have a liquid reserve equal to three months of operating expenses.

Sustainability: Inflation, Growth, Catastrophe
Sustainability is the financial ability of the enterprise to continue to provide, in real terms, services at the same level as it currently is over the long term.

Financially, this means that it must generate surplus (from all sources—both operations and fundraising/development) at least equal to the estimated inflation rates for its operating assets—both working capital and fixed assets. In addition, if growth is planned, additional surplus must be generated.

In terms of a formula:

$$\text{Surplus} = \left(\begin{array}{l}\text{working}\\\text{capital}\end{array}\right) \times \left(\begin{array}{l}\text{short-run}\\\text{inflation}\end{array}\right) + \left(\begin{array}{l}\text{fixed assets, net}\\\text{of depreciation}\end{array}\right) \times \left(\begin{array}{l}\text{long-run}\\\text{inflation}\end{array}\right)$$

The novel coronavirus pandemic of 2020/2021 made clear that sustainability can require more than just accounting for the challenges of inflation and growth. Every enterprise's board and senior management must try to imagine the unthinkable and then consider how it can be managed. The hurricane devastation of Puerto Rico and Louisiana, the tsunami in Fukushima, Japan, and the coronavirus pandemic and other events have made clear the reality of the unimaginable.

While fixed plans are unrealistic, consideration should be given to: financial (credit facilities, asset mortgages or sales, cash conversation measure, etc.), operational (alternate work sites, operational consolidation, virtual meeting capability and capacity, etc.), and strategic (sharing facilities with others, back office sharing, affiliation and/or consolidation with other organizations having compatible missions, etc.) actions that can be taken.

Notes:
1. Surplus can be expressed as a percentage by dividing the surplus target by the operating expense budget.
2. If growth is needed, the capital costs of growth must be added to the surplus objective.
3. If operations are not capable of generating sufficient surplus, the enterprise must turn to fundraising. If this is not a realistic option, business plans either have to change and/or strategic decisions must be made regarding the future of the enterprise (e.g., possibility of acquiring or being acquired, changing scope of operations, etc.).

At the same time, the reality that it is not possible to avoid criticism emphasizes the importance of getting the other aspects right of how the enterprise does its work. Key to this is clear and demonstrated:

1. bond with its community,

2. respect for the worth and dignity of individuals,

3. commitment to racial equity and justice,

4. honorable and humane operations,

5. ethical and legal business behavior, complying with both the letter and the spirit of the law and regulations.

To know whether it is meeting these standards, the enterprise must systematically ask, "How are we doing?" and "How can we do better?" (See Exhibit E-1, Epilogue.) How it gets this input (i.e., focus groups, client questionnaires, informal conversations, open community meetings, etc.), will vary with the traditions and circumstances of the organization. The mechanics, while important, are less critical than the enterprise's willingness to seek out feedback and its explicit commitment to act on the information obtained in a clear and explicit manner.

TAX EXEMPTION

The corollary question of tax exemption must still be addressed. (See Chapter 2, "Sector Equity" and Exhibit 2-7.) An enterprise's involuntary loss of its tax-exempt status will obviously undermine the public's trust in it. Tax exemption, however, has a cost attached to it. Moreover, it is likely, with the data provided by the Form 990, that this cost will grow as the government, facing increasing economic pressures, will demand more community benefits in exchange for tax exemption. The management issue is, at what point does the cost of tax exemption exceed its value?

In general terms, for 501(c)(3) organizations the benefits of tax exemption are five:
1. Exemption from paying federal income tax on profits resulting from mission-related activities.[8]
2. Exemption from state and local income tax on business-related profits.
3. Exemption from state and local property taxes.
4. Eligibility for low-cost debt financing.
5. Donor deductibility of contributions to the enterprise from taxable income.

The first three benefits apply to almost all nonprofit organizations, the major exception being nonprofit Blue Cross and Blue Shield plans who since the late 1980s have been subject to federal (though for the most part not state) income taxation. The latter two apply to only 501(c)(3) entities, though tax exempt financing is also available in many communities to for-profit organizations through a variety of economic development schemes.

For most community sector enterprises, the benefits of tax exemption will always exceed the costs of earning and maintaining it. The issue is relevant for large enterprises, which are in markets that have significant nonprofit and for-profit competitors (i.e. health care, health insurance, entertainment, and/or who have profits, executive compensation and/or endowments, that attract public attention and consequent public questioning of their performance. In these instances, public officials are pushed to question if the community benefit (e.g., the free or subsidized care provided by a hospital, the low-income, safety net coverage provided by a health plan, the community education and free tickets provided by a museum or orchestra, etc.), received from such enterprises at least equals the tax revenues that are foregone. Putting the question in this context changes the underlying reason for tax exemption from a policy decision intended to encourage certain activities to an economic, quid pro quo, exchange.

Certainly, this change in perspective and purpose is well within government's prerogative. However, like any managerial or economic action, it will produce a reaction having both intended and unintended consequences. This can be particularly expected from those community sector enterprises that are not dependent on philanthropy for survival.

The experience of the nation's Blue Cross and Blue Shield plans (though not 501(c)(3) corporations) has shown that the loss of tax exemption does not automatically result in abandonment of the business decision to operate as a nonprofit enterprise. When the Blue Cross and Blue Shield plans lost their federal income tax exemption, the majority of plans, at that time and still to this day, elected to remain nonprofit. For 501(c)(3) entities, because of the importance of:
- contributions to organizational sustainability, and

- tax deductibility of charitable contributions to the donors, it is likely that few would change to being for-profit.

Therefore, if the price of tax exemption becomes too much, some enterprises may just give it up, while still continuing to operate as nonprofit organizations. In fact, an argument could be made that this kind of action would be beneficial public policy, encouraging nonprofit enterprises to spend more on beneficiary services and/or lower their prices to minimize their tax liability.

RESPONSIBILITY

Exemption from property tax presents a different kind of issue. Property taxes are not dependent on performance results. Moreover, while they can be managed through the assessment process, with accompanying lobbying, appeals, and litigation, they are not subject to day-to-day operating control. Property taxes simply add to the cost of doing business, increasing overhead expense. In terms of reducing the costs of services, avoidance of property taxes is obviously beneficial.

That said, community sector enterprises have an obligation to their communities to support public services. While as a matter of both principal and economics they can be expected to fight the loss of their property tax exemption, they also must recognize, particularly as their property holdings increase, a responsibility for contributing to sustaining the community in which they are located. Whether this is accomplished through payments in lieu of taxes, payment of an annually negotiated amount for unspecified services, voluntary support for specified programs, or some other approach, the mechanism is less important than the recognition that tax exemption cannot be used as a reason to abrogate an organization's community responsibility.

Property tax exemption is an example of differential regulation favoring the community sector enterprises. Other regulation and oversight (i.e. prior approval of rates, scrutiny of compensation, barriers to existing services, etc.), have the opposite impact. Economically unjustified differential regulation, regardless of direction, generates inter-sector tension and public confusion. Public confusion reduces public trust.

Community sector enterprises must recognize both their responsibility beyond mission and that regulatory advantage must be economically justified and continuously earned.

Private sector (for-profit business) firms must also recognize that their self-interest lies in a strong community sector. They must support it both with resources and by realizing that a purely level playing field, while perhaps providing short-run satisfaction, is also short sighted.

Finally, the public sector must not penalize community sector enterprises for electing to be community sector enterprises. If pressure on compensation increases to the point where qualified managers can no longer be attracted to the community sector or the profit levels necessary to meet continuing capital needs cannot, because of political pressures, be achieved, then some of the largest and most important community sector organizations will give up their tax exemption and their nonprofit charter—to be able to better pursue mission.

CONCLUSION

Public trust is the key element in establishing and maintaining the legitimacy of an individual enterprise as well as that of the entire community sector.[9] While perhaps unfair, the misdeeds of a single, visible organization blemish the entire sector, opening it to criticism and jeopardizing the sector's special tax treatment.[10] Certainly, tax treatment does not define the sector. However, for many enterprises it is of critical importance. Large enterprises, even those that do not fully benefit from tax exemption or that in the future might forego it, must take the leadership role in protecting and enhancing the public's trust in their own operations and in the entire sector. While public trust may not be quantified in the math of determining either current or future tax exemption—without it not only will the sector lose its tax benefits, but more importantly its special place in society, leaving empty the gap it was created to fill.

The argument by this point has come full circle. Public trust is dependent upon the enterprise performing with a responsibility to more than just itself. Performance beyond self,

---

PUBLIC TRUST

Earning and maintaining public trust is difficult work. However, like many hard tasks, at its core it is also straightforward and simple. For an enterprise to have the trust of the public it must always:

- do what it should do, even if that is the harder road, and then
- do what it says it will do, even if it finds that keeping that commitment may no longer be necessary or in its best interests.

however, requires enlightened and sound governance. Good governance provides the environment and energy for enterprise success. As illustrated in Exhibit 16-2, governance yields sustainability.

Exhibit 16-2

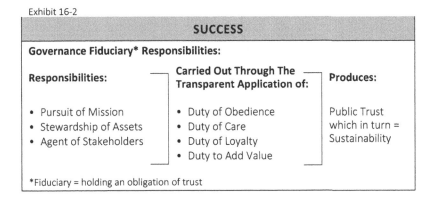

Just as organizations, like fish, rot from the head down, they also achieve great things from the head down. Management and governance matter. They make a difference.

CHAPTER 16

Takeaways and Questions for Consideration and Discussion:

TAKEAWAYS

1. Ongoing success requires that the enterprise continually maintain the public's trust.

2. In the public's eye, profitability and compensation are the community sector's principal public trust vulnerabilities. Profitability must be enough to enable pursuit of the mission, as well as to assure resilience and sustainability. Compensation, as can be demonstrated by objective, unbiased analysis, must be enough to attract and retain the managerial skills needed for the enterprise to be successful.

3. To maintain the public's trust and to be a successful, integral part of the community, an enterprise must do more than just serve itself. It must do what it should do, even if that is the more difficult path.

QUESTIONS

1. How can an organization develop a management and governance culture that enables it to think and act beyond itself?

2. Does the enterprise validate itself by its bottom line or by the value it adds to its community? If it can increase the value it adds to the community by collaborating with other enterprises, does it have an obligation to do so?

3. Even if exempt from property taxes, does an enterprise have a responsibility to contribute to the support of its community's governmental services?

4. What steps must an enterprise take to maintain the public's trust? To enhance it? Can the enterprise survive without the public's trust?

EPILOGUE

Society gives to the community sector its most difficult and thankless human services problems to solve and its most cherished values to protect, as well as to pass on from one generation to the next. Our democratic society looks to the voluntary, collective association aspect of the community sector as a means of protecting the rights and interests of both the majority and the minority. The community sector provides the means of giving voice to the voiceless and standing to those who might not otherwise be able to rise for themselves.

Communities, either defined by geography or common interest, look to nonprofit enterprises to provide the programs and services that either the private sector will not do, or that society does not want the public sector to do. (See Chapters 2 and 3.) Without the community sector, America as we know it would not be possible, and America as we dream it could not be realized.

Does the community sector make a difference? Of course it does! Or at least it does if the enterprises that compose it succeed in accomplishing what they were created to do. To achieve this, to be successful, these enterprises must be well governed (see Chapters 5, 6, and 7) and well managed. (See Exhibit E-1.)

The previous discussion has tried to provide the foundation for such success. Many topics (i.e., grant writing, fundraising processes and techniques, project management, endowment investment management, compliance, design of board presentations, etc.), were not addressed or not addressed in depth. These omissions are not a measure of their importance. Rather, they reflect the fact that these and similar topics are either too mechanical or too technically advanced to fit within the borders of this kind of introductory text. These and many of the other matters mentioned in the previous pages are all possible subjects for either specialized or more advanced works. The purpose of this text is simply to give the reader a basic perspective and the fundamental tools to start down the road of making a difference.

Community sector enterprises are complicated, difficult to manage, and often disadvantaged. Overcoming these obstacles takes special people, doing special jobs. When managed well, they can accomplish the seemingly impossible. Welcome to contemporary management's greatest challenge and most fruitful area for personal satisfaction. Nothing is more worthy of our best efforts and uncategorical commitment.

Exhibit E-1

RISK SELF-ASSESSMENT
It is not unreasonable for chief executives, board chairs, or even the full board to ask, "Is the organization well managed?" A full answer to this straightforward question requires a great deal of thought and work. It involves a careful review of the annual financial audit, management letter, corporate compliance and risk analysis, as well as an environmental assessment and a review of programs in terms of their contribution to mission versus financial performance. (See Chapters 9 and 10.) A less detailed approach is to do a snapshot risk-assessment. The snapshot is not designed to tell if the enterprise is either healthy or well managed. Rather, it is intended to look at several key variables to determine if the enterprise is at short-term risk. If the conclusion is that it is, then more analysis and work must be done to evaluate and then improve performance as well as perhaps plot a new strategy.
Snapshot Different enterprises will have unique factors that they might want to examine to judge their degree of short-term risk. In general, the following elements should be part of any snapshot self-assessment.
Leadership Is a succession plan in place for both board leadership and key management positions? (See Chapters 8, 14, and 15.) If no plan is in place the enterprise is at some risk. If an attempt has been made to identify successors and the effort has failed, the enterprise needs to examine the underlying reasons and assess its long-term ability to continue as a freestanding entity.
Capital Are needed repairs to physical facilities being put off for lack of capital? If so, this is a leading indicator of trouble ahead. Is the donor base diversified or dependent on a small number of "angels"? (See Chapter 12.) The greater the diversity, the stronger the base. Is the donor base, regardless of its degree of diversity, increasing in average age? The older the base, the greater the risk. Have recent capital campaigns, either annual or legacy, been successful?
Operations Has recent performance met planned expectations? (See Chapter 11.) Performance shortfalls can indicate poor planning and/or poor management execution. Either way chronic performance shortfalls represent a risk. Has operational performance, including annual fundraising proceeds, been profitable? The unavoidable reality is that no margin yields no mission. (See Chapter 3.) Sustained losses present a major going-concern risk. Are revenue sources diversified? Most nonprofit enterprise revenue comes from fees for services and contracts; the more concentrated the sources of revenue, the greater the risk, particularly if government contracts are a major source of operating revenue.
Cash How many weeks or months of cash are on hand? The fewer the number of days of cash in reserve, the greater the risk. With enough cash any problem can be resolved. Too little cash places the entire enterprise in jeopardy.
Other Obvious Risks Are there any bond covenants or loan agreement restrictions that are being violated or at risk of being violated? Has the last independent audit been "qualified"? Has the auditor raised going-concern questions? Are required tax payments being made on time? Clearly some of the above questions carry more weight than others (e.g., operating losses, cash availability, qualified audit, etc.). However, even if these factors do not represent immediate risks, the enterprise can still be in jeopardy if the trend of the other factors is negative. In this instance, management and the board must confront the issues, and recognizing that time is of the essence, simultaneously pursue both operational improvement and business planning processes.

AFTERWORD

Where does this leave us?

First, it is clear that the tools, techniques, and processes exist to create well-governed and managed nonprofit enterprises.

Second, it is clear that since the tools exist, the challenge is to effectively implement and utilize them.

Third, the key variables for effective implementation and utilization is competent management and engaged, disciplined governance.

Competency and discipline, not greatness, are the requirements. Given the costs of failure and the benefits of success, these are not high hurdles to achieve.

APPENDIX 1

Excerpts:
Internal Revenue Code*

In 2015, more than 1.5 million organizations registered with the Internal Revenue Service (IRS). This means that they had applied for and received an exemption from having to pay federal income tax on business-related income. However, this does not mean that they do not have to file a tax return, avoid prohibited activities, pay standard taxes on unrelated business income, or make available their annual 990 filing.

Nonprofit groups that generate more than $50,000 in gross receipts are required to file a 990 tax return with the IRS. This return has to be signed by officers of the corporation, approved by the board, and be publicly available.

Under the Internal Revenue Code, more than 30 types of entities are classified as 501(c) organizations and are exempt from corporate income tax. Though all are exempt, not all are charitable. Charitable tax-exempt organizations are classified as 501(c)(3) and must meet and sustain certain requirements.

Section 501. Exemption from tax on corporations, certain trusts, etc.

COMMENTARY: TAXATION AND COMPETITION

The Internal Revenue Code imposes the standard income tax on the (material) unrelated business income of an otherwise tax-exempt organization. Taxation, however, is not the pivotal matter—mission is. More precisely, it is a question of the appropriate use of resources, both human and financial, in the pursuit of mission.

Managers of social enterprises argue that even if a particular activity is only indirectly related to mission (e.g., a museum's offsite retail gift store), if that effort generates a surplus that can be used to support mission, then it is an appropriate use of resources. Others take a more orthodox view, contending that profitability does not justify the diversion of

time, attention, and financial assets. The question of unfair competition may also be raised by private sector managers, who contend that income tax-exemptions as well as property tax exemptions, the use of contributed capital and tax exempt financing provide an inappropriate cost advantage to what is essentially a business competitor.

There is no simple answer to this dilemma. It is also a problem that is not going to naturally disappear. In fact, unless an external policy innovation is introduced, because of increasingly limited resources, it can be expected to grow, accelerating inter-sector tension and raising continuing questions about the role of the community sector.

An organization described in subsection (c) or (d) shall be exempt from taxation under this subtitle.

* Excerpted from the Internal Revenue Code and related sources.

Subsection (c) Partial list of exempt organizations:

Any corporation organized under Act of Congress, which is an instrumentality of the United States, but only if such corporation is exempt from federal income taxes. 501(c)(1)

Corporations organized for the exclusive purpose of holding title to property, collecting income there from, and turning over the entire amount thereof, less expenses, to an organization which itself is exempt under this section. 502(c)(2)

Religious, Charitable, etc. Organizations 501(c)(3)

Corporations, and any community chest, fund, or foundation, organized and operated exclusively for religious, charitable, scientific, testing for public safety, literary or educational purposes, or to foster national or international amateur sports competition (but only if no part of its activities involve the provision of athletic facilities or equipment), or for the prevention of cruelty to children or animals, no part of the net earning of which inures to the benefit of any private shareholder or individual, no substantial part of the activities of which is carrying on propaganda, or otherwise attempting to influence legislation and which does not participate in, or intervene in (including the publishing or distributing of statements), any political campaign on behalf of (or in opposition to) any candidate for public office.

Social Welfare Organizations (501)(c)(4)

Civic leagues or organizations not organized for profit but operated exclusively for the promotion of social welfare, or local associations of employees, the membership of which is limited to the employees of a designated person or persons in a particular municipality, and the net earnings of which are devoted exclusively to charitable, educational, or recreational purposes.

Select Others

Labor, agricultural, or horticultural organizations. 501(c)(5)

Business leagues, chambers of commerce, real-estate boards, boards of trade, or professional football leagues (whether or not administering a pension fund for football players) not organized for profit and no part of the net earnings of which inures to the benefit of any private shareholder or individual. 501(c)(6)

Clubs organized for pleasure, recreation, and other nonprofitable purposes, substantially all of the activities of which are for such purposes and no part of the net earnings of which inures to the benefit of any private shareholders. 501(c)(7)

Exempt organization when operating under the lodge system or for the exclusive benefit of the members of a fraternity itself, and providing for the payment of life, sick, accident, or other benefits to the members of such society, order, or association or their dependents. 501(c)(8)

Voluntary employees' beneficiary associations providing for the payment of life, sick, accident, or other benefits to the members of such association or their dependents or designated beneficiaries, if no part of the net earnings of such association inures (other than through such payments) to the benefit of any private shareholder or individual. 501(c)(9)

Benevolent life insurance associations of a purely local character, mutual ditch or irrigation companies, mutual or cooperative telephone companies, or like organizations; but only if 85 percent or more of the income consists of amounts collected from members for the sole purpose of meeting losses and expenses. 501(c)(12)

Cemetery companies owned and operated exclusively for the benefit of their members or which are not operated for profit; and any corporation chartered solely for the purpose of the disposal of bodies by burial or cremation which is not permitted by its charter to engage in any business not necessarily incident to that purpose and no part of the net earnings of which inures to the benefit of any private shareholder or individual. 501(c)(13)

Subsection (h)

(h) Expenditures by public charities to influence legislation

In the case of an organization to which this subsection applies, exemption from taxation shall be denied because a substantial part of the activities of such organization consists of carrying on propaganda, or otherwise attempting, to influence legislation, but only if such organization normally:

Makes lobbying expenditures in excess of the lobbying ceiling amount for such organization for each taxable year, or makes grass roots expenditures in excess of the grass roots ceiling amount for such organization for each taxable year.

Subsection (i)

(i) Prohibition of discrimination by certain social clubs

An organization which is described in subsection (c)(7) shall not be exempt from taxation under subsection (a) for any taxable year if, at any time during such taxable year, the charter, bylaws, or other governing instrument, of such organization or any written policy statement of such organization contains a provision which provides for discrimination against any person on the basis of race, color, or religion.

The preceding sentence to the extent it relates to discrimination on the basis of religion shall not apply to an auxiliary of a fraternal beneficiary society if such society limits its membership to the members of a particular religion, or to a club which in good faith limits its membership to the members of a particular religion in order to further the teachings or principles of that religion, and not to exclude individuals of a particular race or color.

Unrelated Business Income

Two additional general points should be noted regarding tax-exempt organizations. First, they must pay tax, at standard rates, on any significant unrelated business income and second, they must file annual tax information returns.

If a tax-exempt organization regularly carries on a business activity, for example, selling advertising in a regularly published journal, that is unrelated to its exempt charitable purpose and that activity produces significant income, then that income is taxable. The significance of this provision is that an exempt organization does not lose its exemption simply due to the fact that it is generating some income from an unrelated activity.

Rather, it simply must pay tax on that income.

Annual Returns

Though exempt from paying income taxes, tax exempt organizations, as noted earlier, are not exempt from filing tax returns. Exempt corporations must file an annual information return with the Internal Revenue Service. These returns require an extensive itemization of transactions and therefore can be quite involved and lengthy. (See Appendix 13: Form 990.) Forms are available through the Internal Revenue Service.

IRS Forms and Publications

For more information on how the tax code applies to nonprofit organizations, consult IRS Publication 557. Among other things, the publication outlines the application and approval process and also indicates where to get relevant forms.

To be exempt under section 501(c)(3), a corporation

- must be organized and operated exclusively for charitable, religious, educational, literary, or scientific purposes
- must not have any of its net earnings inured to the benefit of private shareholders or individuals

(See following section 503 for an excerpt of the Internal Revenue Code with respect to requirements for exemption.)

To maintain its exemption, a corporation

- must not carry on substantial activities to influence legislation
- must not participate, in any way, in any political campaign
- must not give up its charitable purpose or allow any of its net income to benefit, either directly or indirectly, private individuals and must file an annual information return with the Internal Revenue Service

Section 503: Requirements for Exemption

Organizations engaged in prohibited transactions shall be denied exemption from taxation.

For purposes of this section, the term "prohibited transaction" means any transaction in which an organization subject to the provisions of the section:

1. lends any part of its income or corpus, without the receipt of adequate security and a reasonable rate of interest, to;

2. any compensation, in excess of a reasonable allowance for salaries or other compensation for personal services actually rendered, to;

3. makes any part of its services available on a preferential basis to;

4. makes any substantial purchase of securities or any other property, for more than adequate consideration in money or money's worth, from;

5. sells any substantial part of its securities or other property, for less than an adequate consideration in money or money's worth, to; or

6. engages in any other transaction which results in a substantial diversion of its income or corpus to;

the creator of such organization (if a trust); a person who has made a substantial contribution to such organization; a member of the family of an individual who is the creator of such trust or who has made a substantial contribution to such organization; or a corporation controlled by such creator or person.

OTHER MATTERS

In addition to the above, two other matters are of note because they involve some of the largest nonprofit organizations—hospitals and BlueCross BlueShield (BCBS) Plans. With regard to the hospitals, Congress established additional requirements that must be met to qualify for 501(c)(3) tax treatment. These hospitals must meet the

- community health needs assessment requirements
- financial assistance policy requirements
- requirements regarding charges, and
- bill and collection requirements set out in the Code.

The underlying purpose of these provisions is to help assure that hospitals are providing "community benefits" as a quid pro quo for their tax exemption.

BCBS Plans face a different tax treatment.

While some BCBS Plans were established as mutual insurers, most were organized under federal law as 501(c)(4) "social welfare" organizations—engaged in promoting the common good and general welfare of the people in the community. For a variety of reasons, both competitive and tax revenue potential, in 1987 the federal government removed the full tax-exempt status of BCBS Plans and created a special hybrid tax class for them, which imposed, after certain tax preferences and deductions, a federal income tax on profits. This change only affected federal tax treatment. At the state level, Plans retained their full income tax-exempt status.

Other nonprofit organizations, e.g. private foundations, also pay taxes. These taxes are modest and are not income-based.

Tax law is complicated. The foregoing is just a high-level summary of key factors. The best advice is that when dealing with tax issues, amateurs should always seek professional guidance.

APPENDIX 2
Conflict of Interest and Disclosure Statement

Statements should be filed, at least annually, by all board members and key employees; that is, employees who can make purchasing or resource allocation decisions. They should also be updated whenever there is a material change in circumstance, which has the potential to create a conflict. Statements should be submitted to the board's chair or the designated compliance officer.

EXAMPLE CONFLICT OF INTEREST POLICY*

1. Purpose
All directors, officers, and employees of the corporation owe a duty of loyalty to it, and must act in good faith, pursuing the best interests of the corporation. The purpose of this policy statement is to outline the mechanism for eliminating potential and/or managing existing conflicts of interest.

2. Who is covered?
This policy applies to anyone who is a director of the corporation (or an affiliate), an officer of the corporation (or an affiliate), any other key employee, volunteer, contractor, or material donor to the corporation (or an affiliate).

3. Conflicts of Interest
A conflict of interest exists or arises whenever the interest of "X" might come into conflict with the personal interests of a covered person and can be reasonably viewed as having the potential to affect his or her corporate decision-making objectivity.

4. Conflict of Interest Disclosure
All covered persons are required to annually disclose in writing (use attached) all material facts related to existing or potential conflicts of interest. Disclosures must be made in advance of any action by the corporation that has the potential to create or realize a conflict. Conflict of interest disclosure statements (including those of nominees to the board or board committees) must be submitted at least annually to the chair of the board or the designated compliance officer.

* This example of a conflict of interest policy is not intended to be a definitive statement. It is excerpted and modified from an example provided in "Guide to Nonprofit Governance 2019" by Well, Gotshal, and Mange's LLP. Each organization must develop its own statement reflective of its history, circumstances, and operating and legal environment.

5. Review

The board chair or other designated person must initially review all conflict of interest disclosure statements and discuss any matter of concern with appropriate persons, including the involved person and, if necessary, counsel. Matters of concern should also be addressed with the full board, prior to the board's approval of annual disclosure statements.

6. Compliance

If the board has reasonable cause to believe that a covered person has not complied with this policy, it can, after proper investigation, as appropriate, terminate that person from employment with or by the corporation, or in the case of a board member, remove him or her from the board.

WIDGET, INC. **Conflict of Interest Questionnaire Employee**	Form created: _____ By: _____
Name:	Division

I wish to report that no situation in which I am involved could be construed as placing me in a position of having a conflict of interest with Widget, Inc. and its subsidiaries or affiliates (corporation), except possibly the following: (Please use and attach additional sheets of paper, if necessary.)

1. A. Are you or any members of your family a supplier of goods or services to the Corporation? YES ☐   NO ☐

    B. Do you or any members of your family have a connection with any supplier of goods or services to the Corporation? YES ☐   NO ☐

Name of Supplier	Person Connected	Relationship to You	Describe Connection

2. Do you or any members of your family have a connection with any competitor of the Corporation? YES ☐   NO ☐

Name of Competitor	Person Connected	Relationship to You	Describe Connection

3. Are you or any members of your family an owner of more than 10% of the stock of a corporation whose aggregate sales to the Corporation exceed 5% of its total sales? YES ☐ NO ☐

Person	Relationship to You	Describe Connection

4. Do you or any members of your family have an affiliation with a related entity owned or controlled by the Corporation (such as corporation, company, partnership, joint venture, association, trust, foundation, fund, institution, society, union, club or other group organized for any purpose, whether incorporated or not, wherever located and of whatever citizenship)? YES ☐ NO ☐

Name of Entity	Nature of Corporation's Relationship to Entity	Nature of Entity's Business	Interested Person's Relationship to You	Describe Connection

5. Are you a director or officer of any organizations? YES ☐ NO ☐

Name of Organization	Position Held

6. Are you involved in any other situation which could be construed as placing you in a position of having a conflict of interest with the Corporation? YES ☐ NO ☐

If yes, please explain: _____

_____

_____

If any situation involving a conflict, potential conflict, or seeming conflict of interest should arise before the next annual conflict of interest procedure, I will report it promptly to the Compliance Officer.

CONFIDENTIALITY AGREEMENT

In view of my duty of loyalty to the Corporation, I understand that I must preserve for the sole benefit of the Corporation Confidential Information (as described below). Therefore, during the term of my service as an Employee of the Corporation and at all times thereafter: (i) I will hold in confidence and not disclose any Confidential Information I may have about the Corporation, its officers, directors and employees, and (ii) I will not use any of the Confidential Information for any purpose, except for the sole benefit of the Corporation.

For purposes of this Agreement, Confidential Information includes all information about the Corporation and its officers, directors, employees, suppliers and customers of which I have knowledge. This includes not only information communicated to me in writing, but also all information I obtain through oral communications.

I hereby affirm that, to the best of my knowledge, the information given above is complete and accurate.

Signature   Date

APPENDIX 3

Example: Code of Business Conduct and Compliance Program

Code of Business Conduct and Compliance Program

FOR
Company, Inc.

Approved _____

Revised and Approved _____

Dear Fellow Employee,

I am pleased to share with you the Company Code of Business Conduct and Compliance Program. This program focuses on business conduct and ethics— in other words, the way we do business. It is a tool we can all use to apply and maintain the highest standards of ethical conduct in our business practices.

Company, Inc. is committed to applying the values of honesty, integrity, and fairness in all business operations, and the implementation of this program is proof of our commitment. The program is designed to educate all of us on the legal and ethical rules of accepted business practices, raise our awareness of questionable conduct, and provide us with ways to report suspected ethics violations. Through this program, you will gain the knowledge you need to make informed, fair business decisions entrusted to you by Company, Inc.

All our employees have the responsibility to uphold our core values of honesty, integrity, and fairness, and to apply them to their everyday work activities and responsibilities. When you are uncertain about the ethics of a business decision, use the information in this program to guide you through the decision-making process.

Our obligation to comply with the Code of Business Conduct doesn't end with our individual business activities. We have an equal responsibility to report any activities we believe to be unethical or counter to our stated values. Without diligent application of our business values, we could find the company or ourselves at risk for legal consequences.

We have established several resources to help you raise concerns or report possible violations of the Company Code of Business Conduct and Compliance Program. You may speak to your immediate supervisor, your division compliance officer, or the company compliance officer. In addition, members of senior management, human resources, fraud and abuse, and corporate audit are also available to assist you. A special telephone compliance hotline has also been created for employees to report violations.

Please review, as I have, this policy. If you have any questions about the program, please speak with your supervisor or contact the resources listed in this policy.

Thank you for supporting Company's Code of Business Conduct and Compliance Program. Our company's continued success depends on your commitment and diligence.

Sincerely yours,

Chief Executive Officer

Mission

The mission of the Corporation is to improve the health of its members and communities served by:

- Providing access to affordable, effective health care services, including long-term care services;
- Being responsible stewards of our communities' health care premiums and health care resources;
- Seeking ways to continually improve the health and health care of the residents of the communities we serve.

Vision

Our vision is that we will be:

- The preeminent financier of health care services in the area.
- An innovative direct provider of efficient and effective care.
- A nationally recognized and sought-after provider of long-term care insurance.

Principles

In a dramatically changing environment, there are three principles we embrace as timeless guides for both strategic and operating decisions.

- First, we exist to assure, in the communities we serve, that as many people as possible have affordable, dignified access to needed, effective health care services, including long-term care services.
- Second, we recognize the need, and our responsibility, to reach out to all segments of the communities we serve, particularly the poor and the aged and others who are underserved, to enhance quality of life, including health status.
- Third, we are committed to be a not-for-profit health insurer.

Goals

To accomplish its mission, the enterprise must:

- Contribute to, and be recognized as, improving the quality of life in the communities that it serves, including improving access to care and clinical outcomes;
- Achieve and maintain profitable growth in order to ensure the long-term financial stability of the organization and to enhance our ability to care for our communities.

Values

In pursuit of our vision and mission, we are guided by the following values:

Commitment and Passion: We should share and be passionate about our shared vision, including our strategy and how we are organized to execute the strategy.

Communication: We should be open in our communication and be good listeners. Our employees are our best ambassadors.

Integrity, Quality, and Reliability: Our word is our bond. Our service levels and quality of work should be the industry standard.

Efficiency, Decision Making, and Control: Reducing unnecessary, wasteful expense is essential. We should seek suggestions from all levels of staff, especially frontline workers, on improvements to enhance effectiveness.

Change, Innovation, and Risk Assumption: We should be perceived as an innovative leader who is not afraid of risk. We should be open to consideration of alternative approaches.

Respect for the Individual: We should deal with each other courteously, respectfully, and compassionately. Improvement ideas should be sought from all levels of our employees.

Authority and Empowerment: Relying on clear policies, we should trust and empower all employees to resolve internal and external customer requirement.

Feedback to Management: Our culture should encourage all employees to candidly and directly share improvement ideas with management. Management should create an environment of trust and accessibility to foster such feedback.

Teamwork, Collaboration, and Accountability: We succeed only if the team succeeds. Success should be celebrated by all.

Security and Opportunity: We need to take care of our own employees first. For equally qualified candidates, promotion from within should be the norm.

Localism: Our health plan businesses and health care services are local. Our managers and executives need to be involved with their communities.

Diversity: Our workforce should reflect our customers and providers. We should recognize and celebrate differences, creating an environment where discrimination in any form is simply not tolerated.

Work Ethic and Work/Family Issues: Hard, steady, focused work is expected from all. Our company is healthiest when a balance is struck between work and family and/or other interests.

Leadership and Modeling Behavior: Managers at all levels of the organization—from team leaders to senior executives—need to model these behaviors.

Table of Contents

Code of Business Conduct

CODE OF BUSINESS CONDUCT

I. Introduction to the Code of Business Conduct

The Code of Business Conduct (the "Code") is for Company, Inc. and its wholly-owned subsidiaries (collectively the "Corporation"). The Code was prepared with the advice and assistance of legal counsel and has been approved by the board of directors. It is to provide officers, directors, and employees, as well as those with whom we do business and the general public, with a formal statement of the Corporation's commitment to the standards and rules of ethical business conduct as spelled out in this Code.

In addition to being committed to upholding the rules set forth in this Code, the Corporation is also committed to conducting all activities in accordance with applicable laws and regulations. All employees are bound by these laws as well as the policies set forth in this Code.

It is imperative that all individuals associated with the Corporation comply with the standards contained in this Code, immediately report any alleged violations and assist compliance personnel in investigating allegations of wrongdoing. It is the policy of the Corporation to prevent the occurrence of unethical or unlawful behavior, to halt such behavior as soon as reasonably possible after its discovery, and to discipline personnel and representatives who violate the standards contained in the Code, including individuals who neglect to report such violation.

No code of conduct can cover all circumstances or anticipate every situation. Consequently, individuals encountering situations not addressed specifically by this Code should apply the overall philosophy and concepts of the Code to the situation, along with the highest ethical standards observed by honorable people everywhere. If a question still exists in your mind after so doing, the particular circumstances should be reviewed with your immediate supervisor or the compliance officer. In addition, members of senior management, human resources, fraud and abuse, and corporate audit are also available to assist you.

II. Ethics

It is the long-standing policy of the Corporation to observe all laws applicable to its business. Even where the law is permissive, the Corporation chooses the course of highest integrity. While local customs, traditions, and mores differ from place to place, honesty is valued in every culture.

All employees of the Corporation must understand that how results are obtained, not just that they are obtained, is important. You are expected to keep management generally informed of what you are doing; to record all transactions accurately; and to be honest and forthcoming with the Corporation, regulatory agencies, and internal and external auditors.

Q: What does "ethical business conduct" mean?

A: It means you must be open and honest in all business activities.

All employees must comply with the Corporation's policies, accounting rules and controls. All employees must also demonstrate the highest standards of ethical conduct. The intent of this Code is that the entire Corporation function with honesty in internal operations and in dealing with members/insureds, accounts, providers, suppliers, and all others with whom the Corporation does business.

III. Conflict of Interest

You must not allow any outside financial interest or competing personal interest to influence your decisions or actions taken on behalf of the Corporation. You must avoid any situation where a conflict of interest exists or might appear to exist between your personal interests and those of the Corporation. The appearance of a conflict of interest may be as serious as an actual conflict of interest.

- *I am planning a corporate dinner, and my daughter owns a restaurant in town. May I use her restaurant, if the prices are comparable to other restaurants?*

  No. This may seem unfair, but our corporate policy on avoiding conflicts of interest means that you must avoid even the appearance of a conflict of interest. No matter how comparable the prices at your daughter's restaurant, others might see your selection of your daughter's restaurant for a corporate dinner as favoritism, and this clearly violates our policy.

- *My coworker's son has just been hired for a job in our department. Does this represent a conflict of interest?*

  A conflict of interest may exist, if your coworker is directly supervising his or her son.

- *I am a claims examiner, and I need some extra income. I have the opportunity to work part-time for a physician's office, doing medical billing. Is it all right for me to pursue this type of employment?*

  No. This type of employment may put you in a position to pay claims that you submitted from the physician's office where you are employed part-time.

- *Prior to joining this organization, I worked as a health insurance consultant for many years. Although I don't have many clients and none of them are customers of this organization, I would like to continue my consulting business outside of my regular business hours. Can I continue to work as a consultant in the insurance industry as long as it doesn't interfere with my work schedule here?*

  As an employee, you cannot do consulting work with the health insurance industry because it is a conflict of interest with our company. You will need to choose between working for our company or continuing your consulting business.

It is a conflict of interest for you to personally take for yourself opportunities that are discovered through the use of corporate property, information or position; to use corporate property or information for personal gain; or to compete with the Corporation. An example of an actual or potential conflict of interest is a personal or family enterprise that conducts business with the Corporation or competes with it. This does not include a minimal holding of stock or other securities in publicly traded companies that may incidentally do business with the Corporation.

There are many types of situations where potential conflicts may arise. You must promptly disclose actual or potential conflicts of interest to an immediate supervisor or directly to the Corporate Compliance Officer. Senior management and the Special Investigations Unit are also available for assistance in determining whether a situation poses a conflict of interest.

A. Outside Activities and Employment

You may not conduct outside activities during work time. Such activities interfere with your regular duties and adversely impact the quality of your work.

You are an ambassador of the Corporation in your everyday life. Even in outside activities, your conduct should reflect the principles and values outlined in this Code.

You owe a duty to the Corporation to advance its legitimate interests when the opportunity to do so arises.

B. Use of Company Funds and Assets

The Corporation's assets are to be used solely for the benefit of the Corporation. You are responsible for assuring that corporate assets are used only for valid corporate purposes. Corporate assets include not only equipment, inventory, corporate funds, and office supplies, but also concepts, business strategies and plans, financial data, member/insured and provider information, intellectual property rights, and other proprietary information about the corporation's business. You may not use corporate assets for personal gain or give them to any other persons or entities, except in the ordinary course of business as part of an approved transaction. On occasion, the corporation may sell assets that are no longer needed to employees. Such sales must be supported by properly approved documentation signed by an authorized employee.

- *My daughter is celebrating her 10th birthday, and I am having a special birthday party for her. I don't have the cash to buy her invitations. Is it all right for me to copy an invitation that I made on my home computer on the color copier in my office?*

  No. The Corporation's assets—such as equipment and supplies—are to be used solely for the Corporation's benefit and not for your personal use.

- *I'm having a large get-together in my back yard and need tables and chairs. I am a good friend of the maintenance guy at work, and he's going to let me use tables and chairs from the cafeteria. Is it all right to borrow them and return them after the party?*

  No. The Corporation will not sell, give, or lend any corporate equipment, furniture, supplies, or materials to employees for their personal use.

C. Business Dealings between the Corporation and Employees

The Corporation will not be inappropriately influenced to purchase goods or services from any business in which you or your close relatives have a substantial interest. Similarly, the Corporation will not sell, give, or lend any company equipment, furniture, supplies, or materials to you for your personal use. Occasional exceptions may be made when it is in the best interest of the Corporation, but only when senior management and the Corporate Compliance Officer document and approve it.

IV. Maintenance of Books and Records

You must record and report all member/insured, provider, customer, and financial information fully, accurately, and honestly. Records include, but are not limited to, accounting books or records, financial reports, business and time records, expense reports, vouchers, bills, payroll, membership/insured records, correspondence and other records of communication, and claims payment records. You must not omit or conceal any relevant information. You may not create any secret or unrecorded funds or assets.

A. Falsification of Records

You must not make false entries in any of the Corporation's books or records or in any public record for any reason. You may not alter any permanent entries in the Corporation's records. You may only approve payments or receipts on behalf of the Corporation that are described in the documents supporting the transaction. "Slush funds" or similar off-book accounts, where there is no accounting for receipts or expenditures on the corporate books, are strictly prohibited. You may not create or participate in the creation of any records that are intended to mislead or to conceal anything that is improper.

- *My boss asked me to shred some information that I know must be retained. I reminded him that the Corporation has document retention policies, but he said this was an extenuating circumstance and insisted that I shred them. I don't want to be charged with insubordination. Should I shred the documents or not?*

  You should not shred the documents. Retention of corporate records is not optional, and no one is permitted to make an exception to the corporate policies. There are avenues for you to report this type of conduct, and staff who can help you handle these kinds of situations. You should bring this information to the attention of your supervisor's manager, or the Compliance Officer.

- *My department was asked to provide data for a report that is going to the state. To make sure that our performance fell within the recommended parameters, my supervisor changed the numbers that I provided. Should I tell someone, or is this common practice?*

  If, by making the changes, your supervisor falsified a report, that is never allowed and should be reported immediately. You should bring this information to the attention of your supervisor's manager, or the Compliance Officer.

B. Expense Records

You must always charge expenses accurately and to the appropriate cost center or account, regardless of the financial status of the program, project, or contract, or the budget status of a particular account or line item.

C. Retention of Records

The retention, disposal, or destruction of records of, or pertaining to, the Corporation must always comply with legal and regulatory requirements and corporate policy. You may not destroy records pertaining to litigation or a government investigation or audit without express approval from the Corporate Compliance Officer.

V. Protection of Confidential Information

You may not release confidential information without proper authorization. Confidential information includes medical and claims information about members/ insureds, as well as non-public information that might be of use to competitors, or harmful to the Corporation or its customers, if disclosed.

Protected health information, financial data, sales figures, planned new products/ projects or planned advertising programs, areas where the Corporation intends to expand, lists of suppliers, lists of accounts, lists of prospects, lists of member/ insureds, provider data, wage and salary data, capital investment plans, projected earnings, changes in management or policies of the Corporation, testing data, suppliers' prices to us, and any plans the Corporation may have for any of its products are also confidential information.

You must abide by all confidentiality agreements and policies of the Corporation and avoid even inadvertent disclosures of confidential information.

- *I am thinking of taking a job with another insurance company. I have been working on some new and innovative products for roll-out next year. I would like to put this information in my portfolio. Would I be breaching corporate policy if I included only my own ideas in the portfolio?*

  Yes. The work that you perform as an employee of the Corporation belongs to the Corporation. You may not take originals or copies of any materials, even if you created them yourself.

- *I'm leaving for vacation and have some critical work that needs to be completed. May I give my password to my coworker so he can finish my project and make the deadline?*

  No. You may not share your system username or password with anyone else.

A. Termination of Employment

If you terminate employment with the Corporation, you may not use any confidential information gained from employment with the Corporation for your or another company's benefit. The work that you perform as an employee belongs to the Corporation. You may not take originals or copies of any reports, manuals, proposals, or any other property belonging to the Corporation.

B. Information Security

You are responsible for properly using information stored and produced by all of the Corporation's systems. You may not share system usernames and passwords with other employees. Using any username or password other than your own without the express permission of an appropriate official of the Corporation is considered theft of service and a violation of corporate policy.

Microcomputers, personal computers, Internet access, email, or other office communications systems are intended for business-related purposes only and not for use that may be considered disruptive, offensive, harassing, or harmful to others.

All employees are required to comply with the corporation's Electronic Communications Policy, policies for Internet Services, and all other policies contained in the Employee Handbook. If you have any questions concerning information security, contact your immediate supervisor or the Corporate Security Officer.

VI. Fair Dealing

Conducting business with providers, contractors, producers, accounts, members/insured, and competitors may pose ethical problems. You should endeavor to deal fairly with the Corporation's providers, contractors, producers, accounts, members/insureds, and competitors.

This Code is intended to help you make appropriate, responsible, and correct decisions. You are expected to exercise good judgment and discretion in these and all matters.

A. Kickbacks and Rebates

Kickbacks and rebates in cash, credit, or any other form are prohibited. They are not only unethical, but in many cases, illegal.

- *One of our vendors would like to treat my whole department to lunch. We do not have an ongoing contract with this vendor, and I know that the vendor would like to get more of our business. Is it all right for the vendor to pay for lunch?*

  No. As there is no contract in place with this vendor, accepting an invitation to lunch could be perceived as allowing the vendor to gain favor and/or to influence your decision whether to establish a business relationship with the vendor.

B. Gifts or Gratuities

You may not accept or encourage gifts of money under any circumstances. You may not solicit non-monetary gifts, gratuities, or any other personal benefits or favors of any kind from providers, contractors, producers, accounts, or members/insureds.

You or your family may accept an unsolicited, non-monetary gift from a business firm or individual doing or seeking to do business with the Corporation, if the gift is primarily of an advertising or promotional nature. You may also accept a gift of nominal value that a business firm or individual provides to a wide spectrum of existing and potential customers.

In addition, if protocol, courtesy, or other special circumstance requires it, you may accept a gift of more than nominal value. However, you must report any gift of more than nominal value to the Corporate Compliance Officer, who will use the company's Business Courtesies Policy as a guide to determine whether you may keep the gift.

C. Entertainment

You may offer or accept entertainment, if it:

- is not excessive;
- does not involve lavish expenditures;
- is compliant with corporate policy and any applicable laws and regulations.

You must not offer or accept entertainment that is not a reasonable addition to a business relationship but is primarily intended to gain favor or to influence a business decision.

D. Agreements with Contractors and Producers

Agreements with contractors and producers must clearly and accurately describe the services to be performed or items purchased, performance standards, and applicable compensation, if any. Compensation must be reasonable in amount. For example, payment may not be excessive in terms of industry practice and must equal or match the value of the services rendered. The Corporation's legal counsel will help you develop these agreements.

- *After negotiating a new subcontract with us, a subcontractor sent me a clock as a gift. Does this violate the gift ban?*

   Generally, as long as the clock can reasonably be valued at $100 or less, you may accept it for personal use. If the contract involves a government customer, however, you cannot accept the gift because it may violate the anti-kickback laws. If you receive a gift of any kind, it's always a good idea to inform your supervisor or check with your Compliance Officer before accepting it.

- *At a conference I attended, my name was entered in a drawing, and I won a weekend trip to New York City. The value definitely will exceed $100. May I accept the prize?*

   Yes, you may accept a prize with a value greater than $100 if it is awarded randomly, as in a lottery or drawing, or if you win it as part of a competition. If you are a prize recipient or winner of a competition, and you are unsure whether you are permitted to keep the prize, it is a good idea to talk with your supervisor or check with your Compliance Officer.

   When entering into an agreement with a contractor or producer, you must provide the applicable chapter of the Code to that contractor or producer. The contractor or producer will be required to acknowledge receipt of the Code and to adhere strictly to its provisions.

E. Improper Use of Funds or Assets

Use of the Corporation's funds or assets for any improper purpose is prohibited. Examples of improper use of funds or assets include:

- Payments for any unlawful or unethical purposes;
- Payments outside the scope of agreements entered into by or on behalf of the Corporation;
- Personal loans (including the extension or maintenance of credit, the arrangement of an extension of credit or the renewal of an extension of credit) to any employee of the Corporation using the Corporation's funds or assets;
- Use of the Corporation's funds or assets in violation of corporate policy or any applicable laws or regulations.

If you know or have reason to know about an improper use of the Corporation's funds or assets, you must report it to your immediate supervisor or the Corporate Compliance Officer. Senior management and the Special Investigations Unit are also available for assistance.

VII. Federal and State Contracts; Federal Procurement

A. Gifts to Government and Public Officials

Federal and state statutory provisions prohibit public officials, including employees, from accepting anything of value, subject to reasonable exceptions such as modest items of food and refreshments. You may not either offer or make a gift to a federal or state public official.

It is also illegal to give a gift or to offer or promise anything of value to a public official for, or because of, any official act performed or to be performed by such official. Additionally, it is a crime to make a payment to a public employee as compensation for public duties performed.

B. Federal Procurement

The Corporation is subject to the Federal Procurement Integrity Act when bidding on a federal contract, such as a Medicare Advantage contract. This law restricts certain business conduct for a company seeking to obtain work from the federal government. During the bidding process, you may not:

- offer or discuss employment or business opportunities at the Corporation with any agency procurement official;
- offer or give gratuities or anything of value to any agency procurement official; or
- seek to obtain any confidential information about the selection criteria before the government awards the contract. This includes information submitted by another company in a bid or proposal and marked "Proprietary," as well as the selection criteria and the evaluation of bids and proposals.

VIII. Federal and State Programs

The Corporation is committed to abiding by the laws and regulations that govern the state and federal programs it administers.

- *Do all government agencies have the same regulations concerning the acceptance of meals and entertainment?*

  No. Regulations applicable to federal, state, local, and foreign government agencies differ. Before offering any gifts, meals, or entertainment, make sure you know the applicable regulations. Check with the Legal Department or the Compliance Officer for details.

IX. Governmental Investigations

From time to time, the Corporation may be asked to cooperate with a governmental examination or investigation, or respond to a request for information. A request may be formally addressed to the Corporation or directed informally to an individual within the Corporation by a regulator or enforcement agency. All employees are required to report requests for information or cooperation to the Corporate Compliance Department's ad hoc routing coordinator.

X. Political Activities and Contributions

Federal law prohibits and state law restricts the use of corporate funds in connection with elections. Accordingly, pursuant to the corporate policy on political contributions, you may not include, directly or indirectly, any political contribution on an expense account or otherwise seek reimbursement from the Corporation for that contribution.

- *I am working on an election campaign for a local legislator and want to use some Volunteer Time Off (VTO). Does this activity fall within the corporate VTO policy?*

  No. Although the Corporation encourages you to be involved in the community, it is against corporate policy for you to use VTO time for any political activity.

- *I am working on a re-election campaign for a state senator and would like to hang posters on my cubicle and hand out buttons at the office. May I do this?*

  No. It is also against corporate policy for you to use corporate assets (including facilities and supplies) or your work time for any political activity.

XI. Employment Environment

Each employee is entitled to work in a safe and professional setting. To that end, the Corporation is committed to complying with all applicable laws and regulations affecting safety, health, and the environment. The Corporation's commitment to the quality of the workplace includes maintaining a drug and alcohol-free environment.

- *A colleague is upset because a coworker is constantly telling off-color jokes. She is afraid to speak up. What should she do?*

  Sexually-oriented, suggestive or obscene comments, whether written or spoken, may be considered sexual harassment. Your colleague should tell her coworker that these jokes are offensive to her and ask the coworker to stop. If she is afraid to speak to the coworker directly or if the unwanted behavior continues, she should report this offensive behavior to her supervisor, Human Resources, or the Compliance Officer.

- *A coworker in my department often makes "jokes" about certain ethnic groups. I find these "jokes" insulting and demeaning, but I am afraid to confront him. What should I do?*

  Jokes or slurs directed against certain groups of people because of such things as the color of their skin, their country of birth, or even their accents are not acceptable in our workplace. These remarks may also be interpreted as discriminatory or harassing conduct and expose the Corporation and the employees involved to costly litigation and penalties. Tell your coworker that you find his/her jokes offensive. If the jokes don't stop, you should report the incident to your supervisor, Human Resources, or your Compliance Officer.

In addition, the Corporation is committed to providing a work environment that is free of harassment and discrimination in all aspects of the employment relationship, including recruitment and employment, work assignment, promotion, transfer, salary administration, selection for training, corrective action, and termination. Equal employment opportunity will be extended to all individuals who are qualified to perform the job requirements regardless of race, color, creed, gender, religion, national origin, age, marital status, sexual preference, public assistance, disability, military, or veteran status or any other status, protected by law, except as permitted or required by law.

All employees are required to support the Corporation's commitment to a safe and professional work environment and to demonstrate appropriate behavior in the workplace. The Employee Handbook is available to all employees, and any questions concerning it may be directed to an immediate supervisor or a member of Human Resources.

XII. Employment of Government Personnel

There are very strict laws and regulations to prevent a conflict of interest by federal government personnel. Some restrict when and how a federal government employee or appointee may be employed by, or go to work for an entity that the government regulates or with which the employee or appointee has interacted in the course of the federal job. Federal laws also restrict non-governmental organizations in interviewing, recruiting, and hiring current and former federal government personnel, including both military and civil service employees. These rules apply to personnel hired as employees and to those retained as consultants. Violation could result in sanctions against the former government employee and criminal and civil charges against the Corporation.

XIII. Manipulation of Auditors

You may not take any action to fraudulently influence, coerce, manipulate, or mislead any representative of Corporate Audit, Corporate Compliance, or Finance who is conducting an internal audit on behalf of the Corporation; or any independent public or certified accountant engaged in the performance of an audit of the financial statements of the Corporation, for the purpose of rendering such financial statements materially misleading.

XIV. Seeking Guidance and Reporting Violations

You must report to your immediate supervisor or the Corporate Compliance Officer any actual or suspected violation of this Code, any applicable law or regulation, or any corporate policy or procedure. Senior management and the Special Investigations Unit are also available for assistance. Employees may also make reports to the Ethics and Compliance Hotline (1-800-XXX-XXXX).

The person to whom an incident is reported must refer the matter to the Corporate Compliance Officer. Steps will be taken to protect anonymity and confidentiality, where warranted and appropriate. The Corporation will not tolerate any form of retaliation against a person who makes a good-faith report in accordance with this Code.

All employees must cooperate openly and honestly in any corporate investigation into a reported violation of this Code; any applicable law or regulation; corporate policy, practice, or procedure.

- *The person in the cubicle next to me has been making copies of personal fliers for her home business and has occasionally taken office supplies. I really don't want to get involved. Do I have an obligation to tell someone?*

   Yes. If you witness someone violating the Code of conduct and you fail to report the incident, then you violate the Code by not reporting the offense. You should bring this information to your supervisor or your Compliance Officer. Steps will be taken to protect your anonymity and confidentiality where warranted and appropriate.

XV. Corrective Action and/or Discipline

Any employee who violates or knowingly fails to report any violation of this Code, any applicable law or regulation or any corporate policy, practice, or procedure is subject to disciplinary action. Any director or officer who is not an employee of the Corporation and who violates or knowingly fails to report any violation of this Code, any applicable law or regulation or any corporate policy, practice, or procedure may be removed from service as a director or officer for "cause" as provided in the bylaws of the Corporation.

"Disciplinary action," as used in this Code, may range from a warning to suspension or discharge, depending on the nature of the incident and the relevant surrounding circumstances. Discipline will not necessarily be progressive. Additionally, although the Code sets forth the Corporation's goal for complying with all applicable laws and regulations, the Corporation may impose discipline in situations where an employee exercises bad judgment, engages in inappropriate conduct, or otherwise compromises the Corporation's commitment to ethical business conduct, even if there is no actual legal violation. Violations may also result in criminal referral and reports to law enforcement and government agencies.

- *What happens if I report an incident and then my coworkers and supervisor stop talking to me or verbally harass me?*

  Any individual who harasses or threatens you for reporting violations will be subject to disciplinary action. The corporation will not tolerate any form of retaliation against you for reporting an issue in accordance with this Code. You should bring this information to the attention of your supervisor, your supervisor's manager, or your Compliance Officer.

Any employee who harasses or threatens another employee for reporting in good faith a real or perceived violation will be subject to disciplinary action, up to and including discharge; or, in the case of a director or officer who is not an employee, removed from service for "cause" as provided in the bylaws of the Corporation. The Corporation will not tolerate such retaliation.

XVI. Board of Directors and Officers—Special Provisions

In their fiduciary relationship with the Corporation, directors and officers are required to act in good faith and to exercise their powers solely in the interests of the Corporation and never in their own self-interest.

By accepting their positions, directors and officers agree to comply with all requirements of the Corporation for service as a director or officer, to pay diligent attention to the business of the Corporation, and to be faithful and honest in fulfilling their duties to the Corporation. Because of this special relationship, it is particularly important that directors and officers adhere to the standards set forth in this document.

COMPLIANCE PROGRAM

I. Overview

The Corporation always has been, and continues to be, committed to conducting its business with integrity and in accordance with all federal, state, and local laws to which its business activities are subject. It is the long-standing policy of the Corporation to prevent the occurrence of unethical or unlawful behavior, to halt such behavior as soon as reasonably possible after its discovery, to discipline personnel who violate corporate policies, including individuals responsible for the failure to detect a violation, and to implement any changes in policy and procedure necessary to prevent recurrences of a violation. The Corporation has instituted the Code and other related policies to reflect these commitments.

The Compliance Program provides a mechanism to enforce the Corporation's Code and sets an ethical tone for conducting business while creating a corporate culture that enhances the reputation of the institution. A compliance program is simply a mechanism to educate employees, sensitize them to ethical and criminal misconduct, monitor for compliance with such expectations, audit for and investigate wrongdoing, and sanction violators.

The hallmark of an effective compliance program is due diligence—the persistence exercised by a company to uphold its policies. This Compliance Program is designed to promote due diligence in everything from the hiring of employees to the auditing of records in an effort to prevent and detect misconduct and criminal activity.

The compliance officer has the ultimate responsibility for overseeing compliance with all applicable laws, the Code, and all related company policies and procedures. Specifically, the compliance officer will be responsible for coordinating and updating the Code and related policies, the annual review, reporting on the implementation and enforcement of the Compliance Program to the board of directors, and all duties that ensure the overall effectiveness of the program. The role of the compliance officer in no way diminishes the responsibility of employees to comply with all policies and procedures of the Corporation.

The division compliance officer is the chair of the division compliance committee, which consists of human resources, fraud and abuse, corporate audit, and legal counsel.

A critical aspect of the Compliance Program is the effective communication of the Code and Compliance Program and related policies to all employees. This is accomplished by supplying all employees with a copy of these documents and requiring them to sign an acknowledgement that they have read and understand the policies and agree to abide by them. There will also be training for all employees which will serve as a refresher course and an update on timely compliance issues.

The Compliance Program envisions education, training, investigation, detection, and reporting. The Compliance Program also requires that individuals acting for or on behalf of the Corporation comply with the Corporation's Compliance Program.

The Corporation intends to utilize a variety of tools to implement the Compliance Program, such as training and education, employee performance evaluations, a whistle blower reporting system, and internal audits. It is the Corporation's intention to monitor this program to verify compliance with the Corporation's published standards.

The Corporation encourages all personnel to report internally all potential noncompliance with the Code or Compliance Program. The program details a variety of means to report such noncompliance, protecting confidentiality where appropriate. No individual's position or influence is considered to be more important than the goal of institutional integrity. Those who honestly report wrongdoing will be protected from any form of retaliation.

II. Frequently Asked Questions

The following are answers to frequently asked questions in regard to the Compliance Program and are included to help clarify the goals of the program.

- *Why do we need this Code of Business Conduct and Compliance Program?*

  Today's business environment is complicated. We need a specific program to provide a mechanism and a process not only for making sure we comply with the specific statutes and regulations that govern our business but also to ensure that each of us lives up to and helps the Corporation maintain basic ethical standards.

- *What does the program really mean?*

  It means that each of us is expected to be aware of good business and ethical standards and accept responsibility for upholding them. It also means adhering to applicable laws and regulations that affect our business. In addition, we must all behave ethically toward other employees and to external customers.

- *What does the Compliance Program involve?*

  This program monitors the Corporation—what we do and how we accomplish our objectives. The goals of the program are to prevent problems initially and to resolve problems internally. Departments need to establish procedures for auditing and monitoring their compliance with the laws and regulations applicable to their particular tasks (e.g., claims processing or federal contracting). Also, employees must learn to report suspected violations of corporate policy, laws, or regulations. To ensure that issues are addressed objectively, matters of concern should be reported to the compliance officer.

- *What type of information is appropriate to report to the compliance officer?*

  Any event, circumstance or business practice that you believe:
  - violates corporate policy;
  - violates the Code of Business Conduct and Compliance Program;
  - violates a law or regulation;
  - is unethical;
  - is not in keeping with the values of the Corporation.

  Some instances are clear-cut violations, while others may be a judgment call on your part.

- *How do I report a concern to the compliance officer?*

  You may report any concern you have to your immediate supervisor or directly to the compliance officer. In addition, members of senior management, human resources, fraud and abuse, and corporate audit are also available to assist you.

  You may also call the compliance hotline. This call can be made anonymously. In addition, there are reporting forms located in human resources and various places throughout the building. Please submit completed forms to the compliance officer.

- *What happens after a situation is reported?*

  The situation is investigated as thoroughly as possible. If further information is needed and the person who reported the situation gives his or her name, there will be follow-up with that person. All reports will be reviewed and investigated and a semi-annual report will be made to the board of directors.

- *What happens if the report concerns a high-level employee?*

  All referrals will be reviewed and investigated, regardless of the department involved or the level of the employee. In some cases, fairness may require a neutral party to conduct the investigation.

- *Will my name remain confidential?*

  You may make reports anonymously, but giving your name may prove helpful in case further information is needed to proceed. Careful efforts will be made to ensure that investigations are handled with the utmost of confidentiality. Files will be identified by number, not by name. Names will not be used in reporting the status of investigations to the board of directors. However, if an outside agency becomes involved, it may be necessary to give your name to that agency for follow-up. Be assured that your name will NOT be given to the person(s) involved in the situation you have reported, and the Corporation will not tolerate any form of retaliation against a person for reporting an issue under the Compliance Program.

- *If the employee reporting a suspected violation gives his or her name, will that person be informed of the outcome of the investigation?*

To some extent, yes. While we can assure the person that the matter has been investigated and that appropriate steps have been taken, we cannot reveal confidential or private information.

- *Why do I need to sign the acknowledgment form?*

Employees are asked to sign a form indicating awareness of the Code, agreement to abide by ethical business practices, and adhere to laws and regulations. Signing this form also provides the necessary documentation for the Corporation to demonstrate that every employee has received a copy of the Code.

If you have further questions about any of the policies or procedures set forth in this Code and Compliance Program, feel free to ask your immediate supervisor or the compliance officer. In addition, members of senior management, human resources, fraud and abuse, and corporate audit are also available to assist you.

EXHIBIT A

FEDERAL SENTENCING GUIDELINES REGARDING COMPLIANCE PROGRAMS

An effective program to prevent and detect violations of law means a program that has been reasonably designed, implemented, and enforced so that it generally will be effective in preventing and detecting criminal conduct. Failure to prevent or detect the instant offense, by itself, does not mean that the program was not effective. The centerpiece of an effective program to prevent and detect violations of law is that the organization exercised due diligence in seeking to prevent and detect criminal conduct by its employees and other agents. Due diligence requires, at a minimum, that the organization must have taken the following types of steps:

- The organization must have established compliance standards and procedures to be followed by its employees and other agents that are reasonably capable of reducing the prospect of criminal conduct.
- Specific individuals within high-level personnel of the organization must have been assigned overall responsibility to oversee compliance with such standards and procedures.
- The organization must have used due care not to delegate substantial discretionary authority to individuals whom the organization knew, or should have known through the exercise of due diligence, had a propensity to engage in illegal activities.
- The organization must have taken steps to communicate effectively its standards and procedures to all employees and other agents; for example, by requiring participation in training programs or by disseminating publications that explain in a practical manner what is required.
- The organization must have taken reasonable steps to achieve compliance with its standards, for example, by utilizing monitoring and auditing systems reasonably designed to detect criminal conduct by its employees and other agents and by having in place and publicizing a reporting system whereby employees and other agents could report criminal conduct by others within the organization without fear of retribution.
- The standards must have been consistently enforced through appropriate disciplinary mechanisms, including as appropriate, discipline of individuals responsible for the failure to detect an offense. Adequate discipline of individuals responsible for an offense is a necessary component of enforcement. However, the form of discipline that will be appropriate will be case specific.
- After an offense has been detected, the organization must have taken all steps to respond appropriately to the offense and prevent further similar offenses, including any necessary modifications to its program to prevent and detect violations of the law.

APPENDIX 4

Bylaws, Part A Outline of Content

I. **Name, Location, and Definitions**
    a. Name of the corporation
    b. Location or principal place of business
    c. Definition of how terms are used within the context of the bylaws

II. **Membership**
    a. Composition of membership (who the members are)
    b. Term of membership
    c. Termination of membership

III. **Meetings of the Members**
    a. Annual meeting location and date
    b. Special meetings (how convened and scheduled)
    c. Meeting notices
    d. Quorum requirements
    e. Organization (who shall preside)
    f. Voting and proxies
    g. Voting without a meeting; unanimous written consent
    h. Super majority voting requirements (if any)
    i. Electronic communication; participation in meetings through telephone or videoconferencing

IV. **Board of Directors**
    a. Size, number
    b. Composition (any formula requirements concerning source of recommendation/nomination or professional background)
    c. Election and term
    d. Forfeiture of board membership
    e. Removal for cause
    f. Resignation (including automatic causes for resignation)
    g. Filling of vacancies

V. **Meetings of the Board**
    a. Schedule of regular and annual meetings
    b. Special meetings (how convened and scheduled)

    c. Meeting notice

    d. Quorum requirements

    e. Organization of the board (who shall preside)

    f. Actions without a meeting; unanimous written consent

    g. Electronic communication; participation in meetings via telephone or videoconferencing.

VI. Officers

    a. Designation of officer positions

    b. Election

    c. Term of office

    d. Filling of vacancies

    e. Compensation

    f. Responsibilities of officers

    g. Bonds (requirement, at the corporation's expense, for the bonding of officers and certain employees)

VII. Committees

    a. Committees (identification of standing committees and their method of appointment and composition)

    b. Special committees (rules for creating and operating special committees)

    c. Committee charge (specification of accountabilities of each standing committee)

VIII. Authority (specification of who is authorized to commit on behalf of the corporation and any limits to such authorization)

IX. Indemnification (protection for officers and directors)

X. Amendments

    a. Precedence for amending bylaws

    b. Voting requirements for amendment

XI. Miscellaneous (in addition, bylaws may have ministerial provisions relating to such matters as governing law, fiscal year, corporate seal, etc.)

APPENDIX 4

Bylaws, Part B
Example Bylaws*

This example of bylaws may be used as a starting point for developing or revising a nonprofit organization's bylaws. It should not be considered as definitive. It is simply an example to help in your own drafting or revision process.

Article I—Members

1.1 <u>Classification of Membership.</u> The corporation shall have one or more classes of membership.**

1.2 <u>Annual Meetings.</u> The annual meeting of members for the election of directors and for the transaction of such other business as may properly come before the meeting shall be held each year at such time and place as the board determines.

1.3 <u>Special Meetings.</u> Special meetings of the members for the transaction of such business as may properly come before the meeting may be called by the board or its chair, and shall be held at such time and place as may be specified by such order.

1.4 <u>Notice of Meetings or Waiver of Notice.</u> Written notice of all meetings of the members, stating the place, date, and hour of the meeting, the means of any remote communications by which members and proxy holders may be deemed to be present in person and vote at such meeting shall be delivered to each member not less than "X" nor more than "Y" days prior to the meeting, unless the prescribed period for notice shall have been waived. Notice of any special meeting shall state in general terms the purpose or purposes for which the meeting is to be held.

1.5 <u>Quorum.</u> Except as otherwise provided, a quorum for the transaction of business at any meeting of members shall consist of a majority of the members entitled to vote at the meeting, present in person, remote communication, or by proxy.

---

* This appendix is a modified form of the Delaware Nonprofit Corporate Bylaws. The original document is excerpted from "Guide to Nonprofit Governance 2019" by Weil, Gotschal, and Munges LLP.

** Typically to protect against unwelcomed interference, nonprofit corporations have a single class of members who are the directors (board) of the corporation.

1.6 <u>Meeting organization and voting.</u> Meetings of members shall be presided over by the chair, or in the chair's absence, by a presiding person to be chosen by the members entitled to vote. At all elections of directors, a plurality of the votes shall elect.

Article II—Board of Directors

2.1 <u>General Powers.</u> The business, property, and affairs of the Corporation shall be managed by, or under the direction of, the board. The board may delegate the management of the day-to-day operations of the corporation to the officers or other persons provided that the business and affairs of the corporation shall be managed by and all corporate powers shall be exercised under the ultimate direction of the board.

2.2. <u>Composition, Qualifications, and Chair of the Board.</u>
- The number of directors constituting the entire board shall be "X", or such other number as may be fixed from time to time by amendment of the bylaws by the action of the members of the board.
- Nominations for persons to serve as directors shall be made by the governance committee. Directors who are elected at an annual meeting of members shall hold office for a term of "X" years and can succeed themselves for up to "Y" terms.
- Directors who are elected in the interim to fill vacancies and newly created directorships, shall hold office until the next annual meeting of members.
- A "X%" majority of the directors shall be independent. Independent directors should not be compensated by the corporation as employees or independent contractors, have their compensation determined by individuals who are compensated by the corporation, receive directly or indirectly material financial benefits from the corporation, or be related to or reside with any individuals who are compensated by the corporation.
- The board may elect a chair of the board and a vice chair (or chair-elect) of the board as officers of the board/corporation. The chair shall preside at all meetings of the board and shall have such other powers and duties as may from time to time be assigned by the board. In the absence or disability of the chair, the vice chair shall exercise the powers and perform the duties of the chair until a replacement chair is elected or the disability of the chair is removed.

2.3 <u>Annual Meeting.</u> Following the annual meeting of members, the newly elected board shall meet for the purpose of the election of officers and the transaction of such other business as may properly come before the meeting. Such meeting may be held without notice immediately after the annual meeting of members at the same place at which such members' meeting is held.

2.4 <u>Regular Meetings.</u> Regular meetings of the board shall be held at least "X" times per year.

2.5 Action by Written Consent. Any action required or permitted to be taken at any meeting of the board may be taken without a meeting if all the directors consent thereto in writing or by electronic transmission, and the writing or writings or electronic transmissions are filed with the minutes of proceedings of the board.

2.6 Meeting by Telephone or Similar Communications Equipment. The members of the board, or any committee thereof, may participate in any meeting through conference calls or other forms of communication that permit participants to hear and be heard by all other participants, and participation in such meeting shall constitute the presence in person by such member at such meeting.

2.7 Resignation and Removal. Any director may resign at any time upon written notice to the corporation and such resignation shall take effect upon receipt thereof by the chair. Any or all of the directors may be removed, with or without cause, by a majority of the members entitled to vote for the election of directors. A director is assumed to have resigned if he or she misses more than "X" meetings in any year of service.

2.8 Vacancies. Vacancies on the board, whether caused by resignation, death, disqualification, removal, an increase in the authorized number of directors or otherwise, may be filled by the affirmative vote of a majority of the remaining directors.

Article III—Committees

3.1 Board Committees. The board may, by a resolution adopted by a majority of the directors then in office, designate board committees each consisting of one or more directors and non-directors, as long as a majority of the committee is directors.

3.2 Advisory Committees. The board may establish one or more advisory committees to the board. Advisory committees may consist of directors or non-directors and may be appointed as the board determines. Advisory committees may not exercise the authority of the board to make decisions on behalf of the corporation but shall be restricted to making recommendations to the board or board committees.

3.3 Term and Termination. In the event any person shall cease to be a director of the corporation, such person shall simultaneously therewith cease to be a member of any board committee.

Article IV—Officers

4.1 Officers. The board shall elect officers of the corporation which shall include a chair, chief executive, vice chair (or chair elect), treasurer, and secretary.

4.2 Election and Term. All officers with the exception of the chief executive, shall be recommended by the governance committee unless otherwise nominated, and shall serve for a term of "X" years. With the exception of the chief executive, officers may succeed themselves for a maximum of "Y" terms.

4.3 <u>Nominations.</u> At the annual meeting for election of officers, any member may nominate an individual to stand for election to serve as an officer. This is in addition to the nominations of the governance committee.

Article V—Books, Records, Reports, and Audits

5.1 <u>Books and Records.</u> The corporation shall keep correct and complete books and records of account and shall keep minutes of the proceedings of its members, its board, and the board committees.

5.2 <u>Reports.</u> The corporation shall comply with all state and federal tax reporting requirements, including filing a Form 990 with the IRS.

5.3 <u>Audits.</u> The accounts of the corporation shall be audited annually in accordance with generally accepted auditing standards, by independent certified public accountants or independent licensed public accountants certified or licensed by a regulatory authority of a state or other political subdivision of the United States.

Article VI—Miscellaneous Provisions

6.1 <u>Approval of Conflict of Interest Transactions.</u> The corporation may enter into a transaction or other arrangement in which there is an actual or potential conflict of interest only if at a duly held meeting of the board a majority of the directors then in office who have no interest in the transaction or arrangement approve the transaction or arrangement after determining, in good faith and after reasonable inquiry that:

- Entering into the transaction or arrangement is in the best interests of the corporation, while considering the corporation's mission and resources, and the possibility of creating an appearance of impropriety that might impair the confidence in, or the reputation of, the corporation (even if there is no actual conflict or wrongdoing)
- The transaction or arrangement in its entirety, and each of its terms, are fair and reasonable to the corporation
- After consideration of available alternatives, the corporation could not have obtained a more advantageous arrangement with reasonable effort under the circumstances
- The transaction or arrangement furthers the corporation's mission and charitable purposes
- The transaction or arrangement is not prohibited under state law and does not result in private inurement, an excess benefit transaction, or impermissible private benefit under laws applicable to tax-exempt organizations

Where it is not reasonably practicable to obtain approval of the board before entering into a conflict of interest transaction, a board committee may approve such transaction in a manner consistent with the foregoing requirements, provided that at its next meeting, the full board determines in good faith that the board committee's approval of the transaction was consistent with such requirements and that it was not reasonably practical to obtain advance approval by the full board, and ratifies the transaction by a majority of the directors then in office without the vote of any interested director.

6.2 <u>Fiscal Year.</u> The fiscal year of the corporation shall be fixed and shall be subject to change by the board.

6.3 <u>Indemnification.</u> The corporation shall indemnify, advance expenses, and hold harmless, to the fullest extent possible any director investigated, indicted, or sued pursuant to his or her service as a director, permitted by applicable law as it presently exists or may hereafter be amended, any person as provided in the corporation's certificate of incorporation.

6.4 <u>Amendments to Bylaws.</u> These bylaws may be amended or repealed, and new bylaws may be adopted by a majority of the board.

APPENDIX 5

Ongoing Board Member Involvement: Staying in Touch

After individuals have completed their terms as members of the corporation's board, nonmember and non-board alternatives can be created for keeping them involved with the organization. For a variety of reasons (fundraising, advice, institutional memory, etc.) it is often advantageous for nonprofit corporations to do this. Examples of mechanisms commonly used to accomplish this are listed below. If an enterprise wishes to pursue these or other alternatives, the details (eligibility, term, role re-election options, limited legal authority, etc.) should be specified in the bylaws.

Alternative Board Membership

- Emeritus Directors—title which can be given to long-serving board members who have completed their eligibility or reached mandatory retirement age.
- Honorary Directors—title which can be given to individuals whom the corporation wishes to recognize. Honorary directors may or may not have been past members of the board.
- Life Directors—title which can be given to individuals to recognize their long service or significant contribution. Depending on the corporation's decisions, as codified in the bylaws, life directors may or may not have the right to vote or have the other privileges and obligations of board members.
- Ex-Officio Directors—an individual who, as a result of office or position, is granted board member recognition. Like life directors, depending on the corporation's decisions, as specified in the bylaws, ex-officio directors may or may not have the privileges and obligations of board members.

Alternative Boards

- Advisory Boards—bodies which have no legal duties or responsibilities but which the enterprise has established to provide management with advice, competitive and community intelligence, communication networks, etc. Advisory boards can include current and former board members, as well as people who have never served on the board.
- Boards of Governors—bodies that are similar in role to advisory boards but whose membership is generally limited to former board members.
- Foundation Boards—legally separate, 501(c)(3) companion organizations typically dedicated to annual fundraising and endowment development. Often

this can be a long-term organizational home for former board leaders and particularly dedicated general board members. Foundation board members should be selected by the criterion of either being able to give or get money. Foundation boards are active entities that, for the good of the organization, must be productive. Therefore, they are not a place for simply trying to maintain contact with former board members or friends of the organization.

In addition, many nonprofit organizations make extensive use of volunteers. These individuals, while agents of the corporation, are not part of the governance process.

APPENDIX 6

Example: Committee Charters

AUDIT COMMITTEE

COMPENSATION COMMITTEE

GOVERNANCE COMMITTEE

Example A, Committee Charter
AUDIT COMMITTEE

Statement of Purpose

The audit committee will assist the board of directors in its oversight of the integrity of the financial statements, the enterprise's compliance with legal and regulatory requirements, the independent auditor's qualifications and independence, and the performance of the enterprise's internal audit function and independent auditors.

Organization and Membership

The audit committee will be organized and conduct itself as follows:

(A) The board of directors will annually appoint the members of the audit committee, consisting of at least three persons, one of whom will be designated as chair. Each member of the committee will be independent and financially literate.

(B) The members of the audit committee may be removed at any time by a majority vote of the board present to vote on such action. The audit committee member who is the subject of such removal vote will be ineligible to vote on the matter. Upon the recommendation of the governance and/or nominating committee, the board will fill any vacancy at its next regularly scheduled meeting after such vacancy occurs.

(C) In order to discharge its responsibilities, the audit committee will meet regularly. The chair of the committee will report to the board after each meeting of the audit committee.

(D) The chair of the audit committee will be responsible for establishing the agendas for meetings of the audit committee. The agenda, together with materials relating to the subject matter of each meeting, will, to the extent practical, be communicated to the members of the audit committee sufficiently in advance of each meeting to permit meaningful review.

(E) A majority of the members of the audit committee will constitute a quorum. A majority of the members present at any meeting at which a quorum is present may act on behalf of the audit committee.

(F) The committee may meet by conference telephone or similar communications equipment allowing all persons participating in the meeting to hear each other at the same time and may take action by unanimous written consent.

Duties and Responsibilities

The audit committee will:

(A) Be directly responsible for the appointment, compensation, oversight, and termination of the work of any independent auditor employed by the enterprise (including resolution of disagreements between management and the independent auditor regarding financial reporting) for the purpose of preparing or issuing an audit report or related work, and each such independent auditor will report directly to the audit committee.

(B) Pre-approve all auditing services and non-audit services to be provided to the enterprise by the independent auditor.

(C) Review and discuss the annual audited financial statements with management and the independent auditor.

(D) Discuss policies with respect to risk assessment and risk management.

(E) From time to time meet separately with management, with internal auditors (or other personnel responsible for the internal audit function), with the independent auditor, and with the general counsel. The audit committee will meet separately with the independent auditor at each audit committee meeting that the independent auditor attends.

(F) Review with the independent auditor any audit problems or difficulties and management's response.

(G) Conduct an annual performance evaluation of the audit committee and report to the board the results of the self-evaluation.

(H) The committee will annually review its charter and recommend any proposed changes to the governance and/or nominating committee.

(I) Review, at least annually, the scope, planning and staffing of the proposed audit for the current year.

(J) Receive and review from time to time such reports or other materials as the audit committee may deem advisable with respect to significant new developments and trends in accounting and auditing policies and procedures and their impact on the enterprise.

The foregoing list of duties is not exhaustive, and the audit committee may, in addition, perform such other functions as may be necessary or appropriate for the performance of its duties.

The audit committee has the authority to engage independent counsel and other advisors, on such terms as it determines appropriate. The organization will provide for funding, as determined by the audit committee, for payment of compensation to any such advisors.

Audit Committee's Role

The audit committee's responsibility is one of oversight. It is the responsibility of the enterprise's management to prepare consolidated financial statements in accordance with applicable law and regulations and of the organization's independent auditor to audit those financial statements. Therefore, each member of the audit committee shall be entitled to rely, to the fullest extent permitted by law, on the integrity of those persons and organizations within and outside the enterprise from whom he or she receives information, and the accuracy of the financial and other information provided to the audit committee by such persons or organizations.

Example B, Committee Charter
AUDIT COMMITTEE

1. The chair of the audit committee shall be a member of the board of directors, in good standing, and all members shall be independent in order to serve on this committee.

   Although not all audit committee members need be members of the board of directors, a majority of the audit committee members should be members of the board of directors.

2. The audit committee should have access to financial expertise, whether in the form of a single individual serving on the committee, or collectively among committee members. If the financial expertise is provided by one individual, it is desirable that he or she be a member of the board of directors. When no single member of the board has the requisite skills, other arrangements should be made to ensure that the audit committee has the financial expertise to carry out its duties.

3. Review the committee's charter annually, reassess the adequacy of this charter, and recommend any proposed changes to the board of directors.

4. The audit committee will meet as needed to address matters on its agenda, but not less frequently than twice each year. The audit committee may ask members of management or others to attend the meetings and provide pertinent information as necessary.

5. Conduct executive sessions with the outside auditors, executive director, and chief financial officer (CFO). If the organization has a chief audit executive (CAE), general counsel, or outside counsel, executive sessions should be conducted with each of these individuals as well. Circumstances may dictate that additional executive sessions are needed with the director of financial reporting, controller, or others as desired by the committee.

6. The audit committee shall be authorized to hire independent auditors, counsel, or other consultants as necessary. (This may take place any time during the year.)

7. Appoint the independent auditors to be engaged by the organization, establish the audit fees of the independent auditors, and pre-approve any non-audit services provided by the independent auditors, including tax services, before the services are rendered. Review with management the significance of bidding out audit services.

8. Inquire of management, the CAE, Auditors (IIAs) Standards for the Professional Practice of Internal Auditing (Standards), if applicable. Internal Audit should meet separately with the independent auditors.

9. Review with the independent auditors, CFO, controller, and CAE the audit

scope and plan of the internal auditors, if applicable, and the independent auditors. Address the coordination of audit efforts to assure the completeness of coverage, reduction of redundant efforts, and the effective use of audit resources.

10. Review with the independent auditors and the CAE:
    - The adequacy of the organization's internal controls, including computerized information system controls and security;
    - Any related significant findings and recommendations of the independent auditors and internal audit services, together with management's responses thereto.

11. Review with management and the independent auditors the effect of any regulatory and accounting initiatives, as well as other unique transactions and financial relationships, if any.

12. Review all material and written communications between the independent auditors and management, such as any management letter or schedule of unadjusted differences.

13. Review with management and the independent auditors:
    - The organization's annual financial statements and related footnotes;
    - The independent auditor's audit of the financial statements and their report thereon;
    - The independent auditor's judgments about the quality, not just the acceptability, of the organization's accounting principles as applied in its financial reporting;
    - Any significant changes required in the independent auditor's audit plan.

14. Periodically review the organization's Code of Conduct/Ethics to ensure that it is adequate and up to date.

15. Review the procedures for the receipt, retention, and treatment of complaints received by the organization regarding accounting, internal accounting controls, or auditing matters that may be submitted by any party internal or external to the organization. Review any complaints that might have been received, current status, and resolution if one has been reached.

16. Review procedures for the confidential, anonymous submission by employees of the organization of concerns regarding questionable accounting or auditing matters. Review any submissions that have been received, the current status, and the resolution, if one has been reached.

17. The audit committee will perform such other functions as assigned by the organization's charter or bylaws, or the board of directors.

18. The audit committee will review its effectiveness.

19. Oversee the preparation of, or prepare, an audit committee annual report.

Example C, Committee Charter
AUDIT COMMITTEE

Purpose

The audit committee's primary purpose is to represent and assist the board of directors in fulfilling its oversight responsibilities relating to: (a) the integrity of the organization's financial statements and the financial information provided to the public; (b) the organization's compliance with legal and regulatory requirements; (c) the organization's internal controls; and (d) the audit process, including the qualifications and independence of the organization's principal external auditors (the "independent auditors") and the performance of the organization's internal audit function and the independent auditors.

Membership and Meetings

The committee shall be comprised of at least three directors, as appointed by the board upon the recommendation of the governance and compensation committee, including one chairperson. Each member of the committee shall meet the independence requirements of the board and shall be financially literate.

Meetings shall be held at least quarterly and additional meetings shall be held as needed. The committee shall report to the board on its activities on a regular basis. The committee shall meet separately with representatives of the independent auditors and the head of Internal Audit at least once a quarter and periodically with members of management as the committee determines appropriate.

Duties and Responsibilities

In furtherance of its duties and responsibilities, the committee shall have the authority to undertake the following:

Financial Reporting

1.   The committee shall review with the independent auditors and internal auditors, the adequacy of the organization's financial reporting processes, both internal and external.

2.   The committee shall review: (a) the planned scope and results of the audit examinations by the independent auditors, including any problems or difficulties the independent auditors encountered in the course of their audit work, any restrictions on the scope of the independent auditors' activities or on access to requested information, and any significant disagreements with management, and in each case management's response to such matter; and (b) the scope and results of the internal audit program.

3.   The committee shall review significant changes in accounting principles, and any significant disagreements between management and the independent

auditors and other significant matters in connection with the preparation of the organization's financial statements.

4. The committee shall meet to review with management and the independent auditors the organization's audited financial statements and the independent auditor's management letter.

Independent Auditors

5. The committee shall be directly responsible, in its capacity as a committee of the board, for the appointment, compensation, retention, and oversight of the work of the independent auditors. In this regard, the committee shall select and retain, evaluate, determine funding for, and where appropriate, replace the independent auditors.

Compliance

6. The committee shall receive reports regarding, and review with the independent auditors, internal auditors and management, the adequacy and effectiveness of: (a) the organization's internal controls, including any significant deficiencies in internal controls and significant changes in internal controls reported to the committee by the independent auditors or management; and (b) the organization's disclosure controls and procedures.

7. The committee shall oversee the organization's compliance program by reviewing: (a) legal and regulatory compliance matters; and (b) the organization's policies and procedures designed to promote compliance with laws, regulations, and internal policies and procedures, including the organization's code of conduct. This will be facilitated through the receipt of reports from management and, as determined appropriate by the committee, legal counsel and third parties.

8. The committee shall establish and oversee procedures for the receipt, retention, and treatment of complaints received by the organization regarding accounting, internal accounting controls and auditing matters, including procedures for confidential, anonymous submission of concerns by employees regarding accounting and auditing matters.

Evaluation of Charter

9. The committee shall evaluate its performance annually and review and reassess the adequacy of this charter annually.

Example A, Committee Charter
COMPENSATION COMMITTEE

Statement of Purpose

The compensation committee is a standing committee of the board of directors. The committee shall have the authority to determine the compensation of the executive officers and such other employees as the board may decide.

Organization

1. *Charter.* At least annually, this charter shall be reviewed and reassessed by the committee and any proposed changes shall be submitted to the board of directors for approval.

2. *Members.* The members of the committee shall be appointed by the board of directors and shall meet the independence requirements of applicable law, and applicable policies of the board of directors. The committee shall be comprised of at least three members. Committee members may be removed by the board of directors. The board of directors shall also designate a committee chairperson.

3. *Meetings.* In order to discharge its responsibilities, the committee shall each year establish a schedule of meetings. Additional meetings may be scheduled as required.

4. *Agenda, Minutes, and Reports.* The chairperson of the committee shall be responsible for establishing the agendas for meetings of the committee. An agenda, together with materials relating to the subject matter of each meeting, shall be sent to members of the committee prior to each meeting. Minutes for all meetings of the committee shall be prepared to document the committee's discharge of its responsibilities and shall be distributed to the full board of directors. The committee shall also make regular reports to the board of directors.

Responsibilities

The following shall be the principal responsibilities of the committee:

1. *Compensation Philosophy and Program.* In consultation with senior management, the committee shall establish the organization's general compensation philosophy and oversee the development and implementation of compensation programs and policies. The committee shall review on a periodic basis the organization's compensation programs and make any modifications that the Committee may deem necessary.

2. *Chief Executive Officer Compensation.* The Committee shall annually review and approve the organization's goals and objectives relevant to the compensation of the chief executive officer and shall evaluate the performance of the chief executive officer in light of those goals and objectives. Based on such evaluation, the committee shall recommend to the full board of directors the compensation (including base salary and incentive compensation) of the chief executive officer.

3. *Officer Compensation.* The committee shall also review and approve the compensation (including base salary and incentive compensation) of officers above the level of vice president of the organization.

4. *Benefit Plans.* The Committee shall review the terms of the organization's incentive compensation plans, retirement plans, deferred compensation plans, and welfare benefit plans. Unless their administration is otherwise delegated, the committee shall administer such plans.

5. *Appointment and Monitoring of Named Fiduciaries.* With respect to any funded employee benefit plan covering employees of the organization subject to the fiduciary responsibility provisions of the Employee Retirement Income Security Act of 1974, the committee shall have the authority to appoint, terminate, and monitor the named fiduciary or named fiduciaries of such plan, unless such fiduciaries are specified in the constituent plan documents.

6. *Annual Compensation Committee Report.* The committee shall produce an annual report for review by the board of directors.

7. *Committee Performance Evaluation.* The committee shall evaluate its own performance on an annual basis and develop criteria for such evaluation.

8. *Access to Consultants.* The committee shall have the resources and authority to discharge its duties and responsibilities as described herein, including the authority to select, retain, and terminate counsel, consultants and other experts. The committee shall have the sole authority to select, retain, and terminate a compensation consultant and approve the consultant's fees and other retention terms.

9. *Other Duties.* The committee shall also carry out such other duties as may be delegated to it by the board of directors from time to time.

Example B, Committee Charter
COMPENSATION COMMITTEE

This compensation committee charter governs the operations of the compensation committee (the "committee") of the board of directors (the "board") of the company. This charter is intended as a component of the flexible governance framework within which the board, assisted by its committees, directs the affairs of the company.

Purpose

The committee shall assist the board of directors in: (a) determining appropriate compensation levels for the company's executive officers; (b) evaluating compensation plans, policies, and programs, and (c) reviewing benefit plans.

In addition to the powers and responsibilities expressly delegated to the committee in this charter, the committee may exercise any other powers and carry out any other responsibilities delegated to it by the board from time to time consistent with the company's bylaws and applicable laws and regulations.

In discharging its role, the committee is empowered to investigate any matter brought to its attention that is within the scope of (or otherwise relevant to) its responsibilities, with all requisite access to all books, records, facilities, and personnel of the company. The committee has the power to retain, subject to concurrence of the chair of the board, outside counsel or other advisors and will receive adequate funding from the company to engage such advisors. Such counsel and/or advisors shall report directly to the committee. The committee shall have the requisite authority to retain, compensate, terminate, and oversee executive compensation consultants.

Committee Membership

The committee shall consist of two or more members of the board, each of whom is determined by the board to be "independent" in accordance with the company's corporate governance guidelines.

The members of the committee shall be appointed by the board and continue to be members until their successors are elected and qualified or until their earlier resignation or removal. Any member of the committee may be removed, with or without cause, by the board at any time.

The board may appoint one member to serve as chair of the committee annually, to convene and chair all regular and special sessions of the committee, set the agendas for committee meetings and determine and communicate to management the information needs of the committee, and to report committee determinations and action on behalf of the committee to the full board.

Committee Meetings

The committee shall have regular meetings. Meetings of the committee may be held telephonically. A majority of the members of the committee shall constitute a quorum sufficient for the taking of any action by the committee. The committee shall meet separately, on at least an annual basis, with the chief executive officer (CEO), the vice president of human resources (or similar position) and any other corporate officers as the board and committee deem appropriate to discuss and review the performance criteria and compensation levels of key executives; provided, however, that the CEO shall not be present at such portion of the meeting during which the compensation of the CEO is discussed.

Key Responsibilities

The following functions and responsibilities are set forth as a guide for fulfilling the committee's purposes, with the understanding that the committee's activities may diverge as appropriate given the circumstances. The committee is authorized to carry out these responsibilities, and other responsibilities assigned to it by the board from time to time, and to take any actions reasonably related to the mandate of this charter.

Compensation Arrangements

1. Establish and review the overall compensation philosophy of the company.

2. Review and approve corporate goals and objectives relevant to the compensation of the CEO and other executive officers, including annual performance objectives.

3. Evaluate the performance of the CEO and other executive officers against those corporate goals and objectives and determine the compensation level for each such person based on this evaluation and consideration of the recent compensation history of each such person.

4. Review on a periodic basis the company's compensation programs to determine whether they are properly coordinated and achieving their intended purpose(s) and recommend any appropriate modifications.

5. Review and recommend to the board for approval any new executive compensation programs.

6. Review and recommend to the board for approval any changes in employee retirement benefit programs and review broadly employee salary levels and ranges and employee fringe benefits.

7. Review and recommend to the board for approval any changes in incentive compensation plans.

Reports

8. Report to the board on committee recommendations or any other matters the committee deems appropriate or the board requests.

9. Maintain minutes or other records of committee meetings and activities.

Annual Self-Evaluation

10. Conduct an annual self-evaluation of the performance of the committee and its members including their effectiveness and compliance with this charter.

11. Review and reassess the adequacy of this charter at least annually.

Example Committee Charter,
CORPORATE GOVERNANCE COMMITTEE

Purpose

The purpose of the corporate governance committee includes: (a) recommending to the board corporate governance guidelines applicable to the company; (b) leading the board in its annual review of the board's performance; and (c) through and based on the recommendations of the nominating subcommittee, identifying individuals qualified to become board members consistent with criteria approved by the board, and recommending to the board director nominees for election.

Members

The corporate governance committee shall consist of at least six (6) members of the board. The board shall designate either its current chair or its immediate past chair as chair of the committee.

Duties and Responsibilities

The functions of the committee, on behalf of the board, shall include having responsibility to:

1. Adopt, regularly monitor, and recommend to the board any modification of the Principles of Corporate Governance which may be necessary.

2. Conclude each committee meeting with an executive session.

3. Form from its ranks a nominating subcommittee consisting of the chair of the corporate governance committee, plus at least three members, selected by the chair of the corporate governance committee, to recommend to the full committee:

   a) Process and criteria for selection of new directors and nominees for vacancies on the board.

   b) Candidates for board memberships and for the positions of chairman and chair of the corporate governance committee.

   c) A decision on the tendered resignation of a director for reason of change of employment.

   d) To evaluate the performance of any director whose term is expiring and whether such director should be invited to stand for re-election.

4. Act on recommendations made by the nominating subcommittee.

5. Establish any special committee which may be necessary to properly govern ethical, legal, or other matters which might arise.

6. Review the corporate governance committee's own performance annually and review this charter annually and recommend any changes to the board for approval.

Meetings

The corporate governance committee and nominating subcommittee shall meet as often as may be deemed necessary or appropriate in their respective judgments, but not less frequently than three times annually, either in person or telephonically, and at such times and places as they shall determine. The committee and subcommittee may request any officer or employee of the company or the company's outside counsel to attend meetings. The corporate governance committee shall report its activities to the board regularly.

Example Committee Charter, NOMINATING AND CORPORATE GOVERNANCE COMMITTEE

Purpose

The nominating and corporate governance committee (the "committee") is created by the board of directors of the company to:

- Identify individuals qualified to become board members, and recommend director nominees for election to the board;
- Recommend directors for appointment to board committees;
- Make recommendations to the board as to determinations of director independence;
- Evaluate board and director performance; and
- Develop and recommend to the board the corporate governance guidelines of the company and oversee compliance with such guidelines.

Membership

The committee shall consist of at least three members, comprised solely of independent directors. In consultation with the chair of the board, the board shall recommend nominees for appointment to the committee annually and as vacancies or newly created positions occur. Committee members shall be appointed by the board and may be removed by the board at any time. The chair of the committee will be designated by the chair of the board.

Responsibilities

In addition to any other responsibilities that may be assigned from time to time by the board, the committee is responsible for the following matters.

Board/Committee Nominees

- The committee shall oversee searches for, and identify qualified individuals for, membership on the company's board.
- The committee shall recommend to the board criteria for board and board committee membership, including as to director independence, and shall recommend individuals for membership on the company's board and its committees.
- In evaluating current directors for re-nomination to the board or re-appointment to any board committees, assess the performance of such directors.
- Periodically review the composition of the board and its committees in light of the current challenges and needs of the board, the company, and each committee, and determine whether it may be appropriate to add or remove individuals after considering issues of judgment, diversity, age, skills, background, and experience.

- Consider rotation of committee members and committee chairs.
- Consider any other factors that are deemed appropriate by the committee or the board.

Evaluating the Board and Its Committees

- At least annually, the committee shall lead the board in a self-evaluation to determine whether it and its committees are functioning effectively. The committee shall oversee the evaluation process and report on such process and the results of the evaluations, including any recommendations for proposed changes, to the board.
- At least annually, the committee shall review the evaluations prepared by each board committee of such committee's performance and consider any recommendations for proposed changes to the board.
- The committee shall periodically review the size and responsibilities of the board and its committees and recommend any proposed changes to the board.

Corporate Governance Matters

- The committee shall develop and recommend to the board the corporate governance guidelines for the company. At least annually, the committee shall review and reassess the adequacy of such corporate governance guidelines and recommend any proposed changes to the board.
- The committee shall oversee compliance with the company's corporate governance guidelines and report on such compliance to the board. The committee shall also review and consider any requests for waivers of the company's corporate governance guidelines for the company's directors, executive officers and other senior financial officers, and shall make a recommendation to the board with respect to such request for a waiver.

Director Orientation and Continuing Education

- The committee shall oversee the company's orientation and continuing education program for directors.

Reporting to the Board

- The committee shall report to the board periodically. This report shall include a review of any recommendations or issues that arise with respect to board or committee nominees or membership, board performance, corporate governance or any other matters that the committee deems appropriate or is requested to be included by the board.

- At least annually, the committee shall evaluate its own performance and report to the board on such evaluation.
- The committee shall periodically review and assess the adequacy of this charter and recommend any proposed changes to the board for approval.

Procedures

The committee shall meet as often as it determines is appropriate to carry out its responsibilities under this charter. The chair of the committee, in consultation with the other committee members, shall determine the frequency and length of the committee meetings and shall set meeting agendas consistent with this charter.

APPENDIX 7

Example: Board Chair Job Description*

Example: 1 (Bylaws Language)

The board chair shall preside at all meetings of the organization, and of the executive committee and board of the organization. The board chair shall exercise general supervision over the affairs of the organization and shall be an ex-officio member of all committees of the board. He or she shall have the power to sign with the chief executive, in the name of the organization, all contracts authorized either generally or specifically by the board. The board chair shall appoint the chairs of all committees and task forces of the board and perform other duties as may be assigned by the board.

In the absence of the board chair, the board chair-elect shall perform the duties of the board chair.

Example: 2 (Bylaws Language)

It shall be the duty of the board chair to preside at all meetings, to guide the board in the enforcement of all policies and regulations relating to XYZ, and to perform all other duties normally incumbent upon such an officer. The board chair shall appoint all members, including the chair of each standing committee and all other committees deemed necessary by the board. The board chair may serve as an ex-officio member of each committee, except the nominating committee, but may not vote.

Example: 3 (Bylaws Language)

This brief sample clarifies the authority of the chair as the leader of the board and the manager of board practices:

The responsibility of the board chair is, primarily, to ensure the integrity of the board's process. The chair is the spokesperson for the board itself, other than in specifically authorized instances when others fill that role. The chair ensures that the board operates within its own rules and those legitimately imposed upon it from outside. Business meetings will focus on policy clearly belonging to the board, not the staff. The chair has no authority to make policy decisions for the board but is expected to help the chief executive interpret board policy.

* Excerpted from *The Nonprofit Policy Sampler, Second Edition* by Barbara Lawrence and Outi Flynn, a publication of BoardSource. For more information about BoardSource, visit www. Boardsource.org. BoardSource ©2006

Example: 4 (Operational Outline of Chair's Role in an Organization Having Limited Staff)

1. Be directly responsible to the board for the administration of the organization.
2. Appoint committee chairs and members as necessary and delegate committee activities, with board approval.
3. Appoint members to fill other positions, such as liaisons, editorial positions, section chairs, and focus group leaders, as appropriate with board approval.
4. Preside at all board meetings.
5. When appropriate, serve as the official representative and spokesperson of XYZ.
6. Approve all contracts into which XYZ enters. Responsibility may be delegated to the chief executive.
7. Serve on the executive, budget and finance, and other committees as appropriate.
8. Provide a report at each board meeting of his or her activities since the previous board meeting.
9. Perform any other duties that are necessary for the successful execution of XYZ's mission.

Example: 5 (Operational Job Description)

Board Chair Job Description

General: Ensures the effective action of the board in governing and supporting the organization and oversees board affairs. Acts as the representative of the board as a whole, rather than as an individual supervisor to staff.

Community: Speaks to the media and the community on behalf of the organization (as does the chief executive); represents the organization in the community.

Meetings: Develops agendas for meetings in concert with the chief executive. Presides at board meetings.

Committees: Recommends to the board which committees are to be established. Works with committee chairs in seeking volunteers for committees and coordinating individual board member assignments. Makes sure each committee has a chair and stays in touch with committee chairs to be sure that their work is carried out. Identifies committee recommendations that should be presented to the full board. Determines whether executive committee meetings are necessary and convenes the committee accordingly.

Chief Executive: Establishes search and selection committee (usually acts as chair) for hiring a chief executive. Convenes board discussions on evaluating the chief executive and negotiating compensation and benefits package; conveys information to the chief executive.

Board Affairs: Ensures that board matters are handled properly, including preparation of pre-meeting materials, committee functioning, and recruitment and orientation of new board members.

Example: 6 (Operational Job Description)

Title: Chair of the Board

Purpose: The chair is the senior volunteer leader of XYZ who presides at all meetings of the board, the executive committee, and other meetings as required. The chair is an ex-officio member of all committees of the organization. The board chair oversees implementation of organizational policies and ensures that appropriate administrative systems are established and maintained.

Key Responsibilities:
- Works with the chief executive, board officers, and committee chairs to develop the agendas for board meetings, and presides at these meetings.
- Appoints volunteers to key leadership positions, including positions as chair of board committees and service committees.
- Supports annual fundraising with his or her own financial contributions. Recognizes his or her responsibility to set the example for other board members.
- Thanks and solicits other board members.
- Works with the board and paid and volunteer leadership, in accordance with XYZ bylaws, to establish and maintain systems for:
  - Planning the organization's human and financial resources and setting priorities for future development
  - Reviewing operational and service effectiveness and setting priorities for future development
  - Controlling fiscal affairs
  - Acquiring, maintaining, and disposing of property
  - Maintaining a public relations program to ensure community involvement
  - Ensuring the ethical standard

Elected By: Board

Length of Term: _____year(s)

Time Commitment: Negotiable to meet the requirements of the organization

Reports To: Board

Support: Chief Executive

Qualifications:
- A commitment to XYZ and its values; an understanding of XYZ's objectives, organization, and services; and the responsibilities and relationship of paid and volunteer staff
- Knowledge of and influence in the community
- Ability to understand concepts and articulate ideas

Budget Support:
Travel and maintenance, workspace, telephone, postage, and computer equipment, as appropriate, and costs of conference and conventions.

APPENDIX 8

Meeting Management

Exhibit A-8-1

ANNOTATED AGENDA

Agenda
Enterprise, Inc. Board of Directors
September XX, 20XX

I.   Introduction and Opening Remarks
Call to order. The key agenda matters and goals of the meeting will be highlighted.
Mr. Samuel Austin and Ms. Rebecca Moore

II. Review and Approval of Minutes
Review and approval of the minutes from the July 21, 20XX meeting. Minutes are attached.

This is an action item. The board should act to approve the minutes as presented, or as modified by the board's discussion. Mr. Seth (Tab II)

III. Committee Reports
A. Compensation Matters
Annual review of the charge of the enterprise's Compensation Committee. In addition, the board will review the operating policies and procedures for establishing and monitoring the Management Compensation and Benefits Program.

This is an action item. The board should act to affirm or modify by the discussion, its charge, policies, and procedures. Mr. Seth (Tab III.A)

B. Advisory Board Task Force
Attached are three documents. Attachment A outlines the evolution of the advisory boards and summarizes their current status. Attachment B is the forward agenda and Attachment C is the advisory board general agenda template.

This is a discussion item. The board should provide management with its advice and counsel. Ms. Lindsay (Tab III. B.1., B.2., and B.3.)

C. Minutes of the July 21, 20XX Operations and Administration Committee Meeting. (Tab II. C.)

D. Minutes of the July 21, 20XX meeting of the Executive Committee/Committee on Directors. (Tab II. D.)

IV. Other Business
Succession Planning: This is in follow-up to the discussion at the March meeting. Management will complete the succession plan, describe the management development progress, and report on the present development activities planned, identified, or implemented for specific individuals.
This is an information item. No committee action is required. Mr. Alex Moore (Tab IV.)

V.   Other Business
Any other business or questions that members of the committee would like to raise.

VI. Executive Session
Adjournment

Exhibit A-8-2

TRANSMITTAL MEMORANDUM

Example 1

MEMORANDUM

Date: September XX, 20XX

To: Board of Directors

From: M.B. Millstone

Subject: Committee Charge: Compensation Matters

Origin of Document

The following has been prepared by management. The original document and the December 20XY revision were approved by the then-sitting Compensation Committee.

Issues

The attached sets out the charge of the Compensation Committee. The language of the charge has been revised to reflect the changes which have taken place, since 20XY, in the enterprise's governance structure.

Recommended Disposition

The board should review the attached and approve it, as modified by its review and discussion.

Example 2

Action Requested by the Committee	Receive the Key Issues Report of the National Employee Benefits Committee from its meeting of January 20XX.
Summary	Investment Programs: Revised investment performance of managers for the 401(K) program.
	401(K) Program: Received an update on the conversion to Trustworthy and the termination of Flybinite.
	Received a report on amendments made to each 401(K) program at the time of transfer to Fidelity to provide administrative efficiencies and enable best practices.
	401(K) Investment Options: Approved the LBIC Family of Funds as a replacement for lifestyle funds.
Other Committee Involvement	N/A
Other Considerations	N/A
Votes Required Contact	Majority of the board present and voting.

Rebecca Moore
Vice President, Finance and Administrative Services

APPENDIX 9

Orientation and Mentoring

Systematic director education starts with the new member orientation program. It is helpful to think of a new member orientation program as having three basic components. The first is an orientation meeting. Here the new member is introduced to the corporation in terms of its: corporate and management profile; operating, competitive, and legal regulatory environments; vision, goals, and strategy; financial performance, and its board meeting system and logistics. Whether the orientation meeting is formal or informal is secondary to the requirement that it must be organized with specific and explicit presentations. (See Exhibit 1 for an agenda example.) It should also be attended by senior management and, if possible, the chair of the board and senior board members.

Exhibit 1

EXAMPLE AGENDA: NEW MEMBER ORIENTATION

X, Inc.
New Board Member Orientation Agenda
December XX, 20XX, 2:00 P.M. to 4:00 P.M.

————

I. **Welcome**
II. **History and Structure**
Review of the factors leading to the formation of X, Inc. As part of this agenda item, management will review the organizational structure from both legal and functional perspectives. Ms. J. Scarbrough (Tab. 1.1)
III. **Regulatory Environment Overview**
Review of the federal, state, and regulatory environments in which X, Inc. operates. Mr. I. Flack (Tab III)
IV. **Board Structure and Operations**
A. A review of the X, Inc. Board Structure and Operations Plan, which outlines the processes and procedures for the ongoing operation of the X, Inc. enterprise governance, structure. In addition, governance operating guidelines and principles will be discussed. Ms. E. Marcus (Tab IV.A.)
B. Code of Business Conduct and Compliance Program. An overview of the corporate Code of Business Conduct and Compliance Program will be provided by Mr. W. Dorr (Tab IV. B.)
V. **Governance Matters**
A. Governance Assessment Process
Management will provide an overview of the governance-assessment process. Mr. I. Flack (Tab V. A.)
B. Board Mentoring and Development Program
Each new board member will be assigned a board mentor. Management will provide an overview to the mentoring and development program. Mr. I. Flack (Tab V. B.)
VI. **Strategic and Operating Plan: 20XX-20XY**
Review of the 20XX-20XY X, Inc. Strategic and Operating Plan. Ms. L. Moore (Tab VI.)
VII. **Questions**
VIII. **Adjournment**

Ideally, all board members should attend an orientation program prior to their first board or committee meeting. If there is more than one new member joining the board, the new members should be oriented as a group—both for reasons of efficiency and for building collegiality. If this is impractical, members should be oriented in individual sessions.

Regardless of the scheduling mechanics, all new members must undergo an orientation process. Orientation provides the foundation upon which much of a director's future board service is built. If the foundation is firm, the likelihood of a positive, productive board experience is increased. If there is no foundation, then a member's ability to remain interested in the corporation and contribute meaningfully, is severely compromised.

To help assure that the orientation presentation is tightly organized, it should be accompanied and supported by an orientation manual (the second component of the program). The orientation manual is the enterprise's basic reference book. It should be designed with the understanding that members can and will refer back to it throughout their board careers. Therefore, it should include documents such as the corporate charter or certificate of incorporation, bylaws, mission and vision statements, strategic and operating plan, board operating policies, and so forth. Moreover, as these documents are changed from time to time, members should receive updated copies. Exhibit 2 presents an example of an orientation manual table of contents. It is provided to give the reader a sense—as opposed to a prescription—of the kinds of materials to be included in an orientation manual.

Exhibit 2

EXAMPLE OF TABLE OF CONTENTS: BOARD ORIENTATION MANUAL	

I. History and Structure
  A. Organizational History
  B. Market Data
  C. Organization Charts
  D. Legal Structure
  E. Overview of Regulatory Environment
 	
II. Role of the Board
  A. Duties and Responsibilities
  B. Personal Liability Protection
 	
III. Governance
  A. Board Structure and Operations Plan
  B. Board Governance Operating Guidelines and Principles
  C. Board Mentoring and Development Program Guidelines
	D. Governance-Assessment Processes
	    i. Governance Assessment
	    ii. Member Evaluation
	    iii. Governance Processes Schedule
	  E. Code of Business Conduct and Compliance Program
	  F. Conflict of Interest Questionnaire
	
	IV. Strategic and Operating Plan
	
	V. Appendices
	  1. Current Board Member Biographies
	  2. Articles of Incorporation
	  3. Bylaws
	  4. Board of Directors' Members and Committees
	  5. Glossary of Common Terms and Acronyms

The third component of the orientation program is the assignment of a mentor to each new board member. Mentors should be experienced board members who can translate the organization's culture, jargon, and board processes to the new member and answer questions that the new member will have.

The mentor program should also be a structured initiative, including its own assessment component. (See Exhibit 3 on next page.) Mentors must clearly understand their obligations to meet with the new member and be available to the new member throughout his or her first year of board service.

Ideally mentors should attend the new member orientation session to meet their assigned new members (protégés). The mentor should also try to meet with his or her protégés prior to the new members' first board or committee meeting. Additionally, mentors should greet their protégés at their first board meeting, introduce them to the other board members, and sit next to them at the meeting. Mentors also should meet individually with their protégés at least once or twice during the first year of board service to answer questions, increase their comfort level, and identify any issues that must be addressed to enhance the new members' contribution to the governance process.

With respect to this last point, members should encourage new members to offer both their perspective on board operations and suggestions as to how to improve governance performance. These ideas, in turn, should be shared with the board chair and discussed with the full board as part of the board's regular performance review.

Assessment of the mentor program should involve both mentors and protégés. Since a small number of people are typically involved each year, the assessment process can be informal with the chair of the board and/or the chair of the governance and/or nominating committee meeting individually with each participant. The purpose of the meeting is to gather feedback regarding both the individual's experience as well as ideas as to how the program can be improved.

If in any particular year a large number of people are participating in the mentor program, individual meetings may not be practical. In this instance a more formal process relying on participant questionnaires can be considered. Regardless of the approach, the results should be included, in at least a general form, as part of either the governance committee's review of the mentor program and/or the full board's discussion of governance performance.

Exhibit 3

EXAMPLE OF BOARD MENTORING PROGRAM GUIDELINES

X, Inc.
Board Mentoring Program Guidelines

Goal

The purpose of the Board Mentoring Program is to provide:

- an efficient and effective mechanism for introducing and integrating new board members into the operations of the board and the responsibilities of being a board member;
- a resource which new board members can call on, both for background information and for answers to current questions;
- a catalyst for introducing new board members into the social fabric of the board.

Mechanics

- Each new board member will be informed by the chair of the board as to whom their mentor is.
- Mentors and new board members will both be invited to the regular new member board orientation.
- Following the new member orientation, mentors will take the initiative to schedule meetings with their assigned new board members.

Mentor Checklist

- At their initial individual meetings, mentors should review board operating logistics with new board members:
  - Meeting schedules
  - Expense reporting
  - Payment
- At follow-up meetings, mentors should seek opportunities to answer questions and explain board operations.

Feedback

- At the end of the year, the board chair will contact both mentors and new board members and seek their feedback as to how the mentor program and the new-member-orientation program can be improved.

APPENDIX 10

Example: Assessment Surveys

Example 1: Individual Board Member Self-Evaluation

Question	Yes	No	Unsure
1. Do I understand the mission of the organization?			
2. Am I knowledgeable about the organization's goals and objectives?			
3. Do I follow trends and important developments related to this organization?			
4. Do I assist with fundraising?			
5. Do I read and understand the organization's financial statements?			
6. Do I prepare for board meetings and committee meetings?			
7. Do I openly share my thoughts at board and committee meetings?			
8. Do I listen to the positions of others, seeking understanding and clarification?			
9. When requested to do so, do I advocate for the organization in the community?			
10. Do I support the mission of the organization?			
11. Do I think the organization's strategy, goals, and objectives make sense?			
12. Do I personally financially contribute to the organization every year?			
13. Do I act as a goodwill ambassador to the organization?			
14. Do I find serving on the board to be a satisfying and rewarding experience?			

Example 2: Individual Board Member Self-Evaluation

1. How satisfied are you with your overall performance as a board member?

   ☐ Very satisfied ☐ Satisfied ☐ Neutral ☐ Dissatisfied ☐ Very dissatisfied

2. How satisfied are you with your overall performance as a committee member?

   ☐ Very satisfied ☐ Satisfied ☐ Neutral ☐ Dissatisfied ☐ Very dissatisfied

3. Do you enjoy your role as a board member and in the organization itself?

   ☐ Yes ☐ No

4. Do you act as an ambassador for the organization?

   ☐ Yes ☐ No

5. What would help you to better fulfill your obligations as a board member? Comments:

   _____

   _____

   _____

   _____

6. What would help to make your service as a board member more satisfying? Comments:

   _____

   _____

   _____

   _____

7. In light of your personal commitment to the mission of the organization, time availability, family/professional obligations, and health status, etc., will you be able to continue to contribute to the board and its committees?

   ☐ Yes ☐ No

   Note: A negative answer to question 7 should trigger the member reconsidering if he or she should continue to serve on the board. This form is to be completed by the member for his or her own use.

Example 3: Individual Board Member Self-Evaluation

<u>Background Data*</u>   Date: _____

Year First Elected: _____

Remaining Years of Eligibility: _____

Remaining Years in Current Term: _____

1. Service Record

During your service, you have chaired or served on the following committees.
(Please review this record of your participation, correct, and update as needed.)

Dates	Committee	Chair/Dates

2. Attendance at Board Meetings

Minutes of board meetings reflect that you have attended _____ of the _____
meetings held since your term began. (Please review and correct this information,
if needed).

3. Attendance at Committee Meetings

Minutes of Committee meetings reflect that you have attended _____ of the
_____ meetings held by the committees which you chaired or on which you
served since your term began. (Please review and correct this information, if
needed.)

*Background data to be provided by the Governance Committee.

4. Self-Assessment

A. In light of time commitments, family/professional obligations, and health status, will you be able to continue to contribute to the board and its committees?

☐ Yes   ☐ No

B. Are you satisfied with your performance as a board member? Why or why not?

Comments:

_____

_____

_____

_____

C. What would help you to better fulfill your obligations as a board member in the future?

Comments:

_____

_____

_____

_____

D. Are there areas of interest or expertise in which you would like to expand your involvement with the board? If yes, please specify.

Comments:

_____

_____

_____

_____

Note: This form is to be completed by the member, for review by the Governance Committee.

Example 4: Board Member Peer Evaluation

Name: _____ Date: _____

Board Service History (To be completed by management)

Year Elected: _____ Current Term to Expire: _____
Years of Eligibility Remaining: _____
List Committee and Officer Appointments: _____

Board/Committee Meetings	Term	Number	Attendance %
Comments:			

Participation*			
Actively participates in discussions: • Asking questions • Offering opinions	Yes	No	
Votes on Issues Abstains	Never	Occasionally	Often
Actively serves as an ambassador for the organization	Always	Occasionally	Seldom
Comments:			

Conflicts of Interest and Independence	Yes	No
Do you have any significant business relationships with the organization?		
Have any potential conflicts of interest developed since you last reported on conflicts?		
Comments:		

Preparedness*	Good	Fair	Poor
Adequately prepared for meetings			
Knows the organization's history and missions			
Understands the organization's long-term strategies			
Understands the role of the organization in the community and the implications of the organization's actions on the community			
Development Opportunities Comments:			

*To be completed by the governance committee.

Example 5: Board Member Self-Evaluation

Questions to be answered by individual board members. For any questions that are answered "no," what steps will you take to improve?

Question	Yes	No
1. Do you understand the difference between governing and managing the organization?		
2. Are you clear on the mission of the organization?		
3. Are you clear on the strategy of the organization?		
4. Are you an effective communicator with your board colleagues?		
5. Have you developed productive peer relationships with your board colleagues?		
6. Are you prepared for meetings?		
7. Do you actively participate in meetings?		
8. Do you avoid real, as well as perceived, conflicts of interest?		
9. Do you avoid real, as well as perceived, threats to your independence?		
10. Do you surprise management with unplanned issues?		

Plan of Action:

_____

_____

_____

_____

_____

_____

_____

_____

_____

_____

_____

_____

_____

_____

Example 6: Board of Directors Governance Assessment

The board chair is requesting that all board members complete this governance assessment form. It is through such a self-examination process that board governance can be improved.

Although the governance assessment process is an annual review, board members are encouraged to contact the chair directly, at any time, to voice comments and questions.

General Information

1. Please indicate number of years of board service: _____

2. Please indicate the number of committees in which you participate and the approximate total number of board and committee meetings you have attended during the last year:

   • Committee Membership: _____
   • Approximate Number of Meetings Attended: _____

Board Meetings	Yes	No	Needs Improvement	Not Applicable
1. Adequate time is given to review board agenda books prior to meetings.				
2. Sufficient information is provided in board books so that an informed decision can be reached.				
3. Sufficient time is allocated at board meetings for each agenda item.				
4. Thoughts, views, and perspectives of members are encouraged.				
5. Management's presentations provide sufficient information on each item so that an informed decision can be reached.				
6. Do you think we have the right number of staff at board and committee meetings? (If no, please elaborate.)				

Additional comments regarding board meetings:

_____

_____

_____

Board Education	Yes	No
1. Did you participate in any of the continuing education programs offered this year?		
If yes, what can we do to improve the programs?		
If no, what can be done to entice you to participate?		

Strategy	Yes	No	Needs Improvement	Not Applicable
1. The organization's strategy is clearly defined.				
2. The board has sufficient participation in reviewing the strategy.				
Additional comments regarding strategy:				

Maintaining Legal and Ethical Practices	Yes	No	Needs Improvement	Not Applicable
1. The board has adequate information and exposure to ensure ethical, legal, and socially responsible action by the organization.				
Additional comments regarding maintaining legal and ethical practices:				

Overall Performance	Needs Improvement	Not Applicable
1. In general, how is the board functioning?		
Regardless of how you answered this question, what can be done to improve board performance? _____ _____		
2. In general, how is the governance process functioning?		
Regardless of how you answered this question, what can be done to improve board performance? _____		

Overall Performance	Yes	No	Needs Improvement	Not Applicable
Board membership requires, among other things, undivided loyalty and active participation of all board members.				
3. Do all board members show undivided loyalty?				
4. Do all board members participate actively?				
Do you have any suggestions for improvement? _____ _____				

Example 7: Board of Directors Governance Assessment

November 20XX

Please assign one of these three ratings to board performance in each of the following categories:

"Acceptable"   The board's performance is satisfactory in this area.

"Discussion"   There is room for improvement or clarification, and the board should schedule time to talk about it.

"Improve"   There is a problem and the board should establish a plan to improve.

Question	Acceptable	Discussion	Improve
1. Board members know how to raise issues and get them on the meeting agenda.			
Comments			
2. Board members read the background materials before meetings and are prepared to discuss and decide the issues.			
Comments			
3. Board members, in general, listen to each other and decide issues only after all relevant information has been discussed.			
Comments			
4. Board members have an equal opportunity to speak.			
Comments			

Questions (continued)	Acceptable	Discussion	Improve
5. Board members have adequate information by the time they vote on action items.			
Comments			
6. Board members limit themselves to making policy, and do not attempt to manage operations.			
Comments			
7. Board members, in general, have diverse opinions, but interact without rancor or ill will.			
Comments			
8. Board members, in general, support conclusions reached by the board, even though they may at times disagree with each other about them.			
Comments			
9. Board meetings begin and end on time.			
Comments			
10. Board members, in general, understand the mission and policies of the organization.			
Comments			

Questions (continued)	Acceptable	Discussion	Improve
11. The meeting room is pleasant and comfortable, with no distractions.			
Comments			

12. GENERAL COMMENTS:

I am:

☐   on the Board of Directors

☐   on the Board of Governors

☐   a past Board Chair

☐   I have been involved with the organization:

    ☐   more than five years

    ☐   fewer than five years

Name (OPTIONAL) (Please Print) _____

Example 8: Board Chair Self-Evaluation

Factors to be considered by the board chair in assessing performance. For any question that is answered "no" or "unsure," what steps will be taken to make the future answer "yes"?

Question	Yes	No	Unsure
1. Do I understand the differences in the roles of the board chair and the chief executive officer?			
2. Do I understand and support proper relationships among board members, including the chair, and the chief executive and other members of executive management?			
3. Am I well prepared for meetings?			
4. Do I insist that management is well prepared for meetings, including presentations and follow-up questions?			
5. Do I manage the agenda effectively, including: • flow of discussion? • time for discussion? • decision making?			
6. Do I ensure that candidates are developed for board and management leadership positions?			

Plan of Action:

_____

_____

_____

_____

_____

Suggested Best Practices for Governance of Nonprofit Enterprises[1]

I. **Board of Directors/Governance**

Best Practices	Suggestions for Achieving Best Practices
A. The board determines the organization's mission, sets policy, and assesses and approves programs and services that are appropriate to that mission.	
Board annually reviews the organization's mission.	The board annually reviews the organization's mission and purpose.
Board sets and monitors policies and attends to emerging policy issues.	The board sets and reviews organizational policies to ensure specific outcomes and organizational safeguards are achieved.
Board reviews reports on programs and services that demonstrate links to organization purpose and tracks progress toward desired outcomes.	The board regularly reviews programs and services to ensure that they are tied to specific outcomes.
B. Board membership is well managed.	
Staff support the board and its committees in order to maintain interest, commitment, and productivity of members.	The board chair and the CEO find ways to sustain maximum board attendance, through development of compelling agendas and presentations, recognition and appreciation of service, and incentives to participation.
	The board chair and the CEO develop a well-defined structure of effective board committees and an appropriate advisory committee that have a clear purpose and task.
	CEO ensures that there is consistent staff support for board committees and other activities.

1 Material excerpted from: Whatcom Council of Nonprofits (Whatcom County, Washington) document on "Best Practices for CEOs and Boards of Nonprofit Organizations." The excerpt has also been amended to reflect the proactive needs of organizations of various sizes. Further information can be found at www.wcnwebsite.org.

Best Practices	Suggestions for Achieving Best Practices
Board members receive orientation regarding member responsibilities, legal requirements, and conflicts of interest.	The board chair and the CEO understand legal requirements and restrictions and communicate those effectively to the whole board. Board leadership develops, and when necessary, implements procedures for removal of non-compliant board members.
Board members receive orientation and continuing education.	The board chair and the CEO ensure that there are regular orientations and ongoing training opportunities for board members.

C. The board ensures that the organization is in compliance with regulations affecting nonprofit organizations and has sound risk-management practices.

The CEO provides the board with information and consultation regarding risk management practices that apply to the organization.	Board leadership defines and applies the various bylaws and regulations (funding, program, health, audit, personnel, and facility) that affect the organization's risks. The CEO identifies appropriate types of liability and other insurance and benefit plans to meet the organization's needs, including facility management, professional services, personnel, health care, Employee Assistance Programs, and Director and Officer coverage.

D.   The board ensures effective fiscal management.

Board reviews financial reports that are accurate, easy to understand, and timely.	The CEO ensures effective staff support to the finance committee, including the provision of reports that meet the committee's needs for financial information. Board leadership defines board roles in fiscal management and oversight and identifies which board members have the skills to provide that oversight.

Best Practices	Suggestions for Achieving Best Practices
The board's financial review and follow up actions focus on assuring that the organization has adequate cash to meet operating needs, and adequate capital to pursue its mission.	The CEO ensures that the board is provided with appropriate cash flow reports. The board leadership and the CEO ensure that board members understand their personal responsibility, if any, for assuring adequate capital.
Employees and volunteers are able to make a confidential report regarding suspected financial impropriety or misuse of organization resources.	Board leadership ensures that there is a procedure for confidential reporting of suspected improprieties.
E. The board represents the organization in the community.	
Board members serve as ambassadors of the organization to the community. Board members actively solicit input from the communities and constituencies they represent.	The CEO and board leadership develop processes for supporting board members in their outreach to the community, including, as appropriate, utilizing board members to represent the organization.
F. The board represents the interests of the community to be served and brings the proper balance of expertise to the organization.	
Board membership provides the skills required by the organization and reflects the interests of the community served.	Board leadership, such as a governance committee, defines the criteria for strategically selecting board members, based on experience, organizational needs, and diversity. Board leadership develops a process and timeline for board recruitment based on the above criteria and needs.

Best Practices	Suggestions for Achieving Best Practices
G. The board ensures that the public has reasonable access to information about mission, activities, board membership, and basic financial data.	
An annual report to inform the public is produced.	The CEO ensures that the organization provides the public with an annual report as well as meeting all public regulatory filing requirements. CEO and staff leadership prepare elements necessary for an annual report. CEO and staff leadership communicate key organization information in writing in a way that is understandable to the public.
Orderly records are accessible to the public.	The CEO organizes all appropriate documents in a file accessible for public review.
H. The board recruits, hires, sets salary, and evaluates the performance of the CEO and oversees succession of that position and other key staff.	
Board conducts annual review of the CEO performance and sets goals for coming year.	The board chair ensures that an effective CEO evaluation process is in place and implemented.
The board, at least annually, reviews succession management plans and programs. A written policy is maintained regarding board oversight of the CEO and succession of key staff.	The CEO develops and has approved by the board a management development program and succession process. Board leadership identifies steps for succession appropriate to organization and writes a policy for board approval.

GOVERNANCE BEST PRACTICE CHECKLIST

DUTIES AND FUNCTIONS

☐ Board officer job descriptions

☐ Board member job descriptions (responsibilities and expectations)

☐ Committee charters

ORGANIZATION AND OPERATIONS

☐ Conflict of Interest Policy

☐ Annual board work plan (forward agenda)

☐ Committee charters and work plans

☐ CEO evaluation process

☐ CEO succession plan

☐ Strategic Plan—review and regular monitoring

DEVELOPMENT AND SUSTAINABILITY

☐ Recruitment/cultivation plan

☐ New member orientation and development process

☐ Board officer succession plan

☐ Board improvement process, including periodic review and feedback

APPENDIX 12

Organizational Planning (Business Plan: Skeleton)*

It can be helpful to think of the enterprise's business plan as a puzzle whose pieces must interlock to create a balanced, workable whole. When done correctly, the pieces set direction, establish priorities, describe expected results, and turn rhetoric into quantitative measures that are in a sustainable equilibrium. When put together, the pieces that comprise the enterprise's business plan are as follows below.

Strategic Plan

Mission: statement of the enterprise's mission—so that everyone is clear as to the purpose of the organization.

Goals: statement of the major goal areas that will be pursued.

Strategic Objectives: within each goal, statement of the objectives that will be pursued to achieve the goal—should be a limited number in order to establish focus/priorities.

Operations Plan

Quantified Objectives: Within each strategic objective, a statement that identifies, in an objective, measurable form the outputs to be achieved and the expected dates of accomplishment—should be a limited number in order to establish focus/priorities.

Budget

Revenue
- Ongoing services and operations
  (Revenues of any form containing fee-for-service operations)

- One time and short-term revenues
  (Revenues from time-limited grants and contracts)

- Development
  - Annual campaigns
  - Income from endowment
  (Revenue from both current fundraising and past fundraising)

Total Revenue

* At a minimum, quantified objectives should be listed so that judgments can be made about achievement.

Expenses**

- Direct Costs: expenses by goal and objective within each goal.

- Indirect Costs: overhead costs and non-cash expenses (e.g. depreciation).

Total Expense

Surplus: Total Revenue—from all sources—minus Total Expense. This should be a predetermined positive amount.

Capital: the current year's cash cost of acquisitions that are large enough to be depreciated (expensed) over a period of years.

Cash Budget (Cash Flow Statement): revenues received (not simply billed), expense and capital spending must be in balance, such that there is always sufficient cash (internally generated, borrowed, and/or donated) available—without impairing funds needed for resilience and sustainability—to meet obligations.

If cash is not in balance, the other pieces of the puzzle must be reworked to create a realistic, balanced picture.

** As an alternative, expenses can be organized by major cash classification (e.g., salaries and wages, supplies, occupancy, depreciation, etc.). Organizing expenses by goal and objectives within each goal provides a check on the relationship between the business plan/strategy and the budget.

APPENDIX 13

Form 990*

Form 990, the Return of Organization Exempt From Income Tax, is the Internal Revenue Service's (IRS) document that provides financial and operational information about nonprofit organizations.

Form 990 is not a new document. It was first used for the tax year ending in 1941. At that time, it was a two-page form that also required supporting schedules listing employees paid a salary of $4,000 or more and a separate schedule listing donors who had contributed $4,000 or more. (In an attempt to protect against inappropriate inurement, compensation has been a continual focus of reporting.) since then, it has been revised multiple times in an effort to provide the public with broader, as well as more detailed, information.

For example, in 2007, Form 990 was revised to require information regarding corporate governance and board membership. In 2008, the IRS issued a comprehensive revision, requiring more information on finances, key employee compensation, and governance. In 2018, the IRS proposed a further change for 501(c)(3) organizations to require disclosure of donor names and addresses. (This change is controversial, and as of press time for this book, has not yet been implemented.)

Depending primarily on the financial size of the organization, different versions of Form 990 are used. Form 990-EZ can be used instead of the standard form for organizations with gross receipts of less than $200,000 and total assets of less than $500,000. Smaller organizations, those with annual gross revenues of $50,000 or less, can file a shorter electronic form (Form 990-N).**

Exhibit 13-A-1 is the cover page of the standard Form 990. The total form consists of 12 parts and 16 supporting schedules. Prior to submission, the form must be signed by a corporate officer and approved by the organizations' board. The latter provision is an attempt to force greater disclosure of corporate behavior in the belief that "sunlight" will help assure that nonprofit organizations perform appropriately. The requirement for information on compensation, board composition, governance, and policy information is required in the same belief. To further support this goal, the IRS requires that a filing organization provide copies of their three most recent filings to anyone who requests them or make the filings publicly available.

Exhibit 13-A-2 is the 990 EZ short form. This form is only four pages, requiring substantially less detailed information than the standard Form 990.

* The following appendix is a high-level overview of Form 990 reporting requirements. Further information can be found by going to the IRS website.

** Private foundations, including private operating foundations, use Form 990-PF.

Exhibit 13-A-1

Form **990**	**Return of Organization Exempt From Income Tax**	OMB No. 1545-0047

Under section 501(c), 527, or 4947(a)(1) of the Internal Revenue Code (except private foundations)

2020

Department of the Treasury
Internal Revenue Service

▶ Do not enter social security numbers on this form as it may be made public.
▶ Go to *www.irs.gov/Form990* for instructions and the latest information.

Open to Public Inspection

A For the 2020 calendar year, or tax year beginning _____ , 2020, and ending _____ , 20 ___

B Check if applicable:	**C** Name of organization		**D** Employer identification number
☐ Address change	Doing business as		
☐ Name change	Number and street (or P.O. box if mail is not delivered to street address)	Room/suite	**E** Telephone number
☐ Initial return			
☐ Final return/terminated	City or town, state or province, country, and ZIP or foreign postal code		
☐ Amended return			**G** Gross receipts $
☐ Application pending	**F** Name and address of principal officer:		

H(a) Is this a group return for subordinates? ☐ Yes ☐ No
H(b) Are all subordinates included? ☐ Yes ☐ No
If "No," attach a list. See instructions

I Tax-exempt status: ☐ 501(c)(3) ☐ 501(c) ( ) ◀ (insert no.) ☐ 4947(a)(1) or ☐ 527

H(c) Group exemption number ▶

J Website: ▶

K Form of organization: ☐ Corporation ☐ Trust ☐ Association ☐ Other ▶ **L** Year of formation: **M** State of legal domicile:

Part I Summary

Activities & Governance

1	Briefly describe the organization's mission or most significant activities:		
2	Check this box ▶ ☐ if the organization discontinued its operations or disposed of more than 25% of its net assets.		
3	Number of voting members of the governing body (Part VI, line 1a)	**3**	
4	Number of independent voting members of the governing body (Part VI, line 1b)	**4**	
5	Total number of individuals employed in calendar year 2020 (Part V, line 2a)	**5**	
6	Total number of volunteers (estimate if necessary)	**6**	
7a	Total unrelated business revenue from Part VIII, column (C), line 12	**7a**	
b	Net unrelated business taxable income from Form 990-T, Part I, line 11	**7b**	

		Prior Year	Current Year
Revenue			
8	Contributions and grants (Part VIII, line 1h)		
9	Program service revenue (Part VIII, line 2g)		
10	Investment income (Part VIII, column (A), lines 3, 4, and 7d)		
11	Other revenue (Part VIII, column (A), lines 5, 6d, 8c, 9c, 10c, and 11e) . . .		
12	Total revenue—add lines 8 through 11 (must equal Part VIII, column (A), line 12)		
Expenses			
13	Grants and similar amounts paid (Part IX, column (A), lines 1–3)		
14	Benefits paid to or for members (Part IX, column (A), line 4)		
15	Salaries, other compensation, employee benefits (Part IX, column (A), lines 5–10)		
16a	Professional fundraising fees (Part IX, column (A), line 11e)		
b	Total fundraising expenses (Part IX, column (D), line 25) ▶ _____		
17	Other expenses (Part IX, column (A), lines 11a–11d, 11f–24e)		
18	Total expenses. Add lines 13–17 (must equal Part IX, column (A), line 25) .		
19	Revenue less expenses. Subtract line 18 from line 12		

		Beginning of Current Year	End of Year
Net Assets or Fund Balances			
20	Total assets (Part X, line 16)		
21	Total liabilities (Part X, line 26)		
22	Net assets or fund balances. Subtract line 21 from line 20		

Part II Signature Block

Under penalties of perjury, I declare that I have examined this return, including accompanying schedules and statements, and to the best of my knowledge and belief, it is true, correct, and complete. Declaration of preparer (other than officer) is based on all information of which preparer has any knowledge.

Sign Here	▶ Signature of officer	Date
	▶ Type or print name and title	

Paid Preparer Use Only	Print/Type preparer's name	Preparer's signature	Date	Check ☐ if self-employed	PTIN
	Firm's name ▶			Firm's EIN ▶	
	Firm's address ▶			Phone no.	

May the IRS discuss this return with the preparer shown above? See instructions . . . . ☐ Yes ☐ No

For Paperwork Reduction Act Notice, see the separate instructions.   Cat. No. 11282Y   Form **990** (2020)

Exhibit 13-A-2

Click on the question-mark icons to display help windows.
The information provided will enable you to file a more complete return and reduce the chances the IRS will need to contact you.

Form **990-EZ**

Department of the Treasury
Internal Revenue Service

Short Form
Return of Organization Exempt From Income Tax

Under section 501(c), 527, or 4947(a)(1) of the Internal Revenue Code (except private foundations)

▶ Do not enter social security numbers on this form, as it may be made public.

▶ Go to *www.irs.gov/Form990EZ* for instructions and the latest information.

OMB No. 1545-0047

2020

Open to Public Inspection

A For the 2020 calendar year, or tax year beginning , 2020, and ending , 20

B Check if applicable:
☐ Address change
☐ Name change
☐ Initial return
☐ Final return/terminated
☐ Amended return
☐ Application pending

C Name of organization ?

Number and street (or P.O. box if mail is not delivered to street address) ? Room/suite

City or town, state or province, country, and ZIP or foreign postal code

D Employer identification number ?

E Telephone number

F Group Exemption Number ▶ ?

G Accounting Method: ☐ Cash ☐ Accrual Other (specify) ▶

H Check ▶ ☐ if the organization is not required to attach Schedule B ? (Form 990, 990-EZ, or 990-PF).

I Website: ▶

J Tax-exempt status (check only one) – ☐ 501(c)(3) ☐ 501(c) ( ) ◀ (insert no.) ☐ 4947(a)(1) or ☐ 527

K Form of organization: ☐ Corporation ☐ Trust ☐ Association ☐ Other

L Add lines 5b, 6c, and 7b to line 9 to determine gross receipts. If gross receipts are $200,000 or more, or if total assets (Part II, column (B)) are $500,000 or more, file Form 990 instead of Form 990-EZ . . . ▶ $

Part I **Revenue, Expenses, and Changes in Net Assets or Fund Balances** (see the instructions for Part I) ?

Check if the organization used Schedule O to respond to any question in this Part I . . . ☐

Section	Line	Description	Sub-line	Amount	Line	Amount
Revenue	1	? Contributions, gifts, grants, and similar amounts received . . .			1	
	2	? Program service revenue including government fees and contracts . . .			2	
	3	? Membership dues and assessments . . .			3	
	4	? Investment income . . .			4	
	5a	Gross amount from sale of assets other than inventory . . .	5a			
	b	Less: cost or other basis and sales expenses . . .	5b			
	c	Gain or (loss) from sale of assets other than inventory (subtract line 5b from line 5a) . . .			5c	
	6	Gaming and fundraising events:				
	a	Gross income from gaming (attach Schedule G if greater than $15,000) . . .	6a			
	b	Gross income from fundraising events (not including $ ____ of contributions from fundraising events reported on line 1) (attach Schedule G if the sum of such gross income and contributions exceeds $15,000) . .	6b			
	c	Less: direct expenses from gaming and fundraising events . . .	6c			
	d	Net income or (loss) from gaming and fundraising events (add lines 6a and 6b and subtract line 6c) . . .			6d	
	7a	Gross sales of inventory, less returns and allowances . . .	7a			
	b	Less: cost of goods sold . . .	7b			
	c	Gross profit or (loss) from sales of inventory (subtract line 7b from line 7a) . . .			7c	
	8	Other revenue (describe in Schedule O) . . .			8	
	9	**Total revenue.** Add lines 1, 2, 3, 4, 5c, 6d, 7c, and 8 . . . ▶			9	
Expenses	10	Grants and similar amounts paid (list in Schedule O) . . .			10	
	11	Benefits paid to or for members . . .			11	
	12	Salaries, other compensation, and employee benefits ? . . .			12	
	13	Professional fees and other payments to independent contractors ? . . .			13	
	14	Occupancy, rent, utilities, and maintenance . . .			14	
	15	Printing, publications, postage, and shipping . . .			15	
	16	Other expenses (describe in Schedule O) ? . . .			16	
	17	**Total expenses.** Add lines 10 through 16 . . . ▶			17	
Net Assets	18	Excess or (deficit) for the year (subtract line 17 from line 9) . . .			18	
	19	Net assets or fund balances at beginning of year (from line 27, column (A)) (must agree with end-of-year figure reported on prior year's return) . . .			19	
	20	Other changes in net assets or fund balances (explain in Schedule O) . . .			20	
	21	Net assets or fund balances at end of year. Combine lines 18 through 20 . . . ▶			21	

For Paperwork Reduction Act Notice, see the separate instructions. Cat. No. 10642I Form **990-EZ** (2020)

Exhibit 13-A-2, continued

Form 990-EZ (2020)   Page **2**

?	**Part II**	**Balance Sheets** (see the instructions for Part II)		

Check if the organization used Schedule O to respond to any question in this Part II . . . . ☐

		(A) Beginning of year		**(B)** End of year
22	Cash, savings, and investments		**22**	
23	Land and buildings		**23**	
24	Other assets (describe in Schedule O)		**24**	
25	**Total assets**		**25**	
26	**Total liabilities** (describe in Schedule O)		**26**	
27	**Net assets or fund balances** (line 27 of column (B) **must** agree with line 21) . .		**27**	

?	**Part III**	**Statement of Program Service Accomplishments** (see the instructions for Part III)	

Check if the organization used Schedule O to respond to any question in this Part III . . ☐

What is the organization's primary exempt purpose? _____

Describe the organization's program service accomplishments for each of its three largest program services, as measured by expenses. In a clear and concise manner, describe the services provided, the number of persons benefited, and other relevant information for each program title.

Expenses
(Required for section 501(c)(3) and 501(c)(4) organizations; optional for others.)

?	**28**	_____

(Grants $ _____) If this amount includes foreign grants, check here . . . . ▶ ☐ | **28a**

29 _____

(Grants $ _____) If this amount includes foreign grants, check here . . . . ▶ ☐ | **29a**

30 _____

(Grants $ _____) If this amount includes foreign grants, check here . . . . ▶ ☐ | **30a**

31 Other program services (describe in Schedule O) . . . .
(Grants $ _____) If this amount includes foreign grants, check here . . . . ▶ ☐ | **31a**

32 **Total program service expenses** (add lines 28a through 31a) . . . . ▶ | **32**

Part IV	List of Officers, Directors, Trustees, and Key Employees (list each one even if not compensated—see the instructions for Part IV)

Check if the organization used Schedule O to respond to any question in this Part IV . . . . ☐

? **(a)** Name and title	**(b)** Average hours per week devoted to position	**(c)** Reportable ? compensation (Forms W-2/1099-MISC) (if not paid, enter -0-)	**(d)** Health benefits, contributions to employee benefit plans, and deferred compensation	**(e)** Estimated amount of other compensation

Form **990-EZ** (2020)

Exhibit 13-A-2, continued

Form 990-EZ (2020) | | | | Page **3**

Part V	**Other Information** (Note the Schedule A and personal benefit contract statement requirements in the instructions for Part V.) Check if the organization used Schedule O to respond to any question in this Part V . ☐

			Yes	No
33	Did the organization engage in any significant activity not previously reported to the IRS? If "Yes," provide a detailed description of each activity in Schedule O	33		
34	Were any significant changes made to the organizing or governing documents? If "Yes," attach a conformed copy of the amended documents if they reflect a change to the organization's name. Otherwise, explain the change on Schedule O. See instructions	34		
35a	Did the organization have unrelated business gross income of $1,000 or more during the year from business activities (such as those reported on lines 2, 6a, and 7a, among others)?	35a		
b	If "Yes" to line 35a, has the organization filed a Form 990-T for the year? If "No," provide an explanation in Schedule O	35b		
c	Was the organization a section 501(c)(4), 501(c)(5), or 501(c)(6) organization subject to section 6033(e) notice, reporting, and proxy tax requirements during the year? If "Yes," complete Schedule C, Part III	35c		
36	Did the organization undergo a liquidation, dissolution, termination, or significant disposition of net assets during the year? If "Yes," complete applicable parts of Schedule N	36		
37a	Enter amount of political expenditures, direct or indirect, as described in the instructions ▶	37a		
b	Did the organization file **Form 1120-POL** for this year?	37b		
38a	Did the organization borrow from, or make any loans to, any officer, director, trustee, or key employee; or were any such loans made in a prior year and still outstanding at the end of the tax year covered by this return? .	38a		
b	If "Yes," complete Schedule L, Part II, and enter the total amount involved	38b		
39	Section 501(c)(7) organizations. Enter:			
a	Initiation fees and capital contributions included on line 9	39a		
b	Gross receipts, included on line 9, for public use of club facilities	39b		
40a	Section 501(c)(3) organizations. Enter amount of tax imposed on the organization during the year under: section 4911 ▶ ; section 4912 ▶ ; section 4955 ▶			
b	Section 501(c)(3), 501(c)(4), and 501(c)(29) organizations. Did the organization engage in any section 4958 excess benefit transaction during the year, or did it engage in an excess benefit transaction in a prior year that has not been reported on any of its prior Forms 990 or 990-EZ? If "Yes," complete Schedule L, Part I	40b		
c	Section 501(c)(3), 501(c)(4), and 501(c)(29) organizations. Enter amount of tax imposed on organization managers or disqualified persons during the year under sections 4912, 4955, and 4958 . . . . ▶			
d	Section 501(c)(3), 501(c)(4), and 501(c)(29) organizations. Enter amount of tax on line 40c reimbursed by the organization . . . . ▶			
e	All organizations. At any time during the tax year, was the organization a party to a prohibited tax shelter transaction? If "Yes," complete Form 8886-T	40e		
41	List the states with which a copy of this return is filed ▶			
42a	The organization's books are in care of ▶ _____ Telephone no. ▶ _____			
	Located at ▶ _____ ZIP + 4 ▶ _____		Yes	No
b	At any time during the calendar year, did the organization have an interest in or a signature or other authority over a financial account in a foreign country (such as a bank account, securities account, or other financial account)?	42b		
	If "Yes," enter the name of the foreign country ▶ _____			
	See the instructions for exceptions and filing requirements for FinCEN Form 114, Report of Foreign Bank and Financial Accounts (FBAR).			
c	At any time during the calendar year, did the organization maintain an office outside the United States? .	42c		
	If "Yes," enter the name of the foreign country ▶ _____			
43	Section 4947(a)(1) nonexempt charitable trusts filing Form 990-EZ in lieu of **Form 1041**—Check here . . . . ▶ ☐ and enter the amount of tax-exempt interest received or accrued during the tax year . . . . . ▶	43		
			Yes	No
44a	Did the organization maintain any donor advised funds during the year? If "Yes," Form 990 must be completed instead of Form 990-EZ	44a		
b	Did the organization operate one or more hospital facilities during the year? If "Yes," Form 990 must be completed instead of Form 990-EZ	44b		
c	Did the organization receive any payments for indoor tanning services during the year?	44c		
d	If "Yes" to line 44c, has the organization filed a Form 720 to report these payments? If "No," provide an explanation in Schedule O	44d		
45a	Did the organization have a controlled entity within the meaning of section 512(b)(13)?	45a		
b	Did the organization receive any payment from or engage in any transaction with a controlled entity within the meaning of section 512(b)(13)? If "Yes," Form 990 and Schedule R may need to be completed instead of Form 990-EZ. See instructions	45b		

Form **990-EZ** (2020)

Exhibit 13-A-2, continued

Form 990-EZ (2020)   Page **4**

			Yes	No
46	Did the organization engage, directly or indirectly, in political campaign activities on behalf of or in opposition to candidates for public office? If "Yes," complete Schedule C, Part I	**46**			

Part VI   **Section 501(c)(3) Organizations Only**

All section 501(c)(3) organizations must answer questions 47–49b and 52, and complete the tables for lines 50 and 51.

Check if the organization used Schedule O to respond to any question in this Part VI   . . . . ☐

			Yes	No
47	Did the organization engage in lobbying activities or have a section 501(h) election in effect during the tax year? If "Yes," complete Schedule C, Part II	**47**			
48	Is the organization a school as described in section 170(b)(1)(A)(ii)? If "Yes," complete Schedule E	**48**			
49a	Did the organization make any transfers to an exempt non-charitable related organization?	**49a**			
b	If "Yes," was the related organization a section 527 organization?	**49b**			
50	Complete this table for the organization's five highest compensated employees (other than officers, directors, trustees, and key employees) who each received more than $100,000 of compensation from the organization. If there is none, enter "None."				

(a) Name and title of each employee	**(b)** Average hours per week devoted to position	**(c)** Reportable compensation (Forms W-2/1099-MISC)	**(d)** Health benefits, contributions to employee benefit plans, and deferred compensation	**(e)** Estimated amount of other compensation

f   Total number of other employees paid over $100,000   . . . . ▶

51   Complete this table for the organization's five highest compensated independent contractors who each received more than $100,000 of compensation from the organization. If there is none, enter "None."

(a) Name and business address of each independent contractor	**(b)** Type of service	**(c)** Compensation

d   Total number of other independent contractors each receiving over $100,000   . . ▶

52   Did the organization complete Schedule A? **Note:** All section 501(c)(3) organizations must attach a completed Schedule A   . . . . ▶ ☐ Yes ☐ No

Under penalties of perjury, I declare that I have examined this return, including accompanying schedules and statements, and to the best of my knowledge and belief, it is true, correct, and complete. Declaration of preparer (other than officer) is based on all information of which preparer has any knowledge.

Sign Here	▶ Signature of officer		Date		
	▶ Type or print name and title				

Paid Preparer Use Only	Print/Type preparer's name	Preparer's signature	Date	Check ☐ if self-employed	PTIN
	Firm's name ▶			Firm's EIN ▶	
	Firm's address ▶			Phone no.	

May the IRS discuss this return with the preparer shown above? See instructions   . . . . ▶ ☐ Yes ☐ No

Form **990-EZ** (2020)

APPENDIX 14

Fundraising Resource Information*

Part 1

Planning For Fundraising

- In the Beginning
- Nonprofit Fundraising Demystified
- Don't Make Your Organization's Statement of Purpose a "Mission Impossible"
- Know Your Organization
- Greetings From America: How U.S.-Style Fundraising Can Work in Your Country
- Develop Your Fundraising Plan With Consensus
- Developing a Communications Strategy for the Development Operation
- Campaign Feasibility Studies: Taking the Time to Find Out Whether the Time is Right
- Check Out Your Organization's Fundraising Readiness and Learn the Secret of Fundraising Success
- Major Gifts Campaign Checklist
- Fitting Annual, Endowment, Capital, and Sponsorship & Underwriting Campaigns into Your Organization's Plans and Then Making Them "Sing"
- How Board Members Can Become Effective Fundraisers
- Building Donor Loyalty
- Annual Campaigns: Once a Year Every Year
- Sponsorships and Underwriting Campaigns: Would You Please Fund Our _____?
- Endowment Funds Go On Forever—An Endowment Campaign Should Not
- Capital Campaigns: Building for Now
- Fundraising with a Net—The Internet
- Should Your Organization Sell Products and Services to Raise Money?
- Cultivate a "Grass-Roots" Fundraising Campaign For Your Organization
- Your Organization's Next Special Event: "Fund-Raiser" or "Friend-Raiser?

* Tony Ponderis, Fund-Raising Forum Library, www.raise-funds.com.

Funding Sources and Prospects

- Tapping the Philanthropic Well
- In Search of the Elusive Major Giver
- Rating and Evaluating Prospects: Whom Do You Ask for How Much?
- Annual Fund Giving & "Getting" Guidelines for Your Organization's Board of Trustees

Organizing a Campaign

- A Campaign Deferred is a Campaign Defeated
- How To Recruit Your Volunteer Fundraising Team
- Twelve Things You Should Know about Setting a Capital Campaign Goal
- Campaign Solicitation Kits: "For Want of a Kit a Campaign Was Lost?"

Managing a Campaign

- Designing a Communications Plan to Enhance Your Fundraising Campaign
- Making the Development Office a Fundraising "Clearinghouse"
- The Name is the Game: Memberships and Named Gift Opportunities
- Asking For the Money: "If You Don't Ask You Don't Get"

Post Campaign Activity

- The Fallacy Of Financial Ratios: Why Outcome Evaluation is The Better Gauge of Grant Worthiness
- Campaign Assessment and Review: What Was Accomplished and What Was Learned

Developing the Development Team

- A Development Director Needs More than "A Smile And A Shoeshine," But It's a Good Start
- When Should a Nonprofit Organization Hire its First Development Director?
- What's a Good Director Of Development Worth?
- When the Development Officer is Obliged To Raise Her or His Salary
- Who Should Raise the Money from within Your Organization? The Executive Director and Development Director
- The Argument Against Paying Development Professionals Based upon the Amount of Funds Raised for Nonprofit Organizations
- Asking for the Money is the Job of the Leadership and Friends of a Nonprofit Organization: Never Hire Someone to Do What is Their Responsibility
- Wearing those Development and Marketing "Hats" at the Same Time: A Bad Fit and a Headache

- Positioning Grant Writers for Success
- To Consult, or Not to Consult—That is the Question
- Consulting Agreement for an Annual Fund Campaign
- Beginning a Career in Nonprofit Fundraising
- Sales Professional to Development Professional: A Workable Transition
- So, You Were Asked to Volunteer and to Work on a Fundraising Campaign

Part 2

Nonprofit Fundraising Demystified

When it comes to fundraising, there are truths and myths. The truths illuminate the path to success. The myths speak with the dark voice of "conventional wisdom" of what can't be done and won't work. Throughout my career I have had to overcome three myths of fundraising that would have me give up before I start. My tools have been The Nine Basic Truths of Fundraising.

Myth 1: Face it, fundraising is impossible and the process is a mystery. Anyone who has failed at it, or has managed to avoid being held accountable for that failure, knows this.

Myth 2: Everybody knows you need a proven track record if you are to raise money. If you doubt it, just look at all the help-wanted ads for development officers that list as a qualification "successful history of managing a major annual campaign or soliciting large donations."

Myth 3: It's common knowledge that corporations and foundations give most of the money. Just ask those who have never done any fundraising or who would find a contribution of $50 a strain on their budget.

Those three "beliefs" have helped doom many a fundraising campaign. On the other hand, there are some insights about fundraising that successful fundraisers have gained. These insights often fly in the face of the myths of conventional wisdom. They offer no shortcuts. They promise no instant results. However, they are not hard to understand, and nearly anyone can profit from them. They are The Nine Basic Truths Of Fundraising.

The Truths, The Whole Truths, And Nothing But The Truths

Sometimes in this world that showers us with new technology on what seems like an almost daily basis I think we can lose sight of the basics. It's easy to get caught up in the newest tools and the hottest theories. As concepts are wrapped in bright new language and claimed as fresh discoveries, it's easy to forget, that at its most basic, all fundraising is an endeavor of people, trust, and mission. By our actions, we earn from people the trust that the money they give will be wisely used to carry out a mission they support.

To be sure, there are refinements and tweaks to this business of development that help ease the job of assuring a steady source of contributed income for our organizations. And yes, some approaches that worked 10, or 20, or 30 years ago, don't deliver as well in the twenty-first century.

But the basics remain. Some things do not change. They are the bedrock upon which all fundraising efforts are anchored. They are the insights that have been gained through experience—through success and failure. These insights sometimes seem old fashioned to the gurus of leading-edge wisdom. They do not have the attractiveness of shortcuts and instant results. They do not offer a new paradigm. They are not the latest style. They are not quick fixes that can be employed to relieve the ever-increasing pressure to deliver more contributed income from fewer sources over shorter periods of time.

They are time-tested approaches. They are the basic truths that define successful fundraising. And they are basic, not simply because they work, but because their absence yields failure. A development effort that ignores the basics dooms its organization to missed goals, shrinking income, and a spiral of diminishing possibilities.

When I talk to groups, the most important things I have to share from my more than three decades of fundraising experience are The Nine Basic Truths of Fundraising. They come from hard-earned knowledge shared freely and enthusiastically with me by countless, gifted development professionals and volunteers over these many years.

Basic Truth 1: Organizations are not entitled to support; they must earn it.

No matter what an organization's good works, it must prove to those who support it the value of those works to the community and the efficiency with which the organization delivers them. The primary key to fundraising success is to have a first-class organization in every sense. There are no entitlements in the nonprofit world.

Basic Truth 2: Successful fundraising is not magic; it is simply hard work on the part of people who are thoroughly prepared.

There are no magic wands, spells, or incantations. Whenever you hear that someone has the magic fundraising touch, laugh. Otherwise, the joke is likely to be on you. No one pulls a rabbit—complete with its own lettuce farm—out of the fundraising hat. No one!

Fundraising is simple in design and concept, but it is very hard work! It is planning, executing, and assessing. It is paying attention to detail. It is knowing your organization and what it needs. It is knowing who has the money, and how much they can give.

Basic Truth 3: Fundraising is not raising money; it is raising friends.

People who don't like you don't give to you. People who know little about your organization give little at best. Only those people who know and like you will support you. Raise friends and you will raise money.

Basic Truth 4: You do not raise money by begging for it; you raise it by selling people on your organization.

No matter how good your organization, how valuable its services, how efficiently it delivers them, people will not give money unless they are convinced to do so. Fundraisers function much as sales and marketing people do in the commercial world. So, be ready, willing, and able to "sell" your organization and the programs for which you are raising money.

Basic Truth 5: People do not just reach for their checkbooks and give money to an organization; they have to be asked to give.

No matter how well you sell people on your organization, no matter how much money they have, no matter how capable they are of giving it, they have to be asked to give. There comes a point when you have to ask for the money. And by the way, make sure that you are asking for a specific amount. Don't leave it up to the donor to recommend how much to give. People with money to give are accustomed to being asked for it. The worst thing that will happen is that they will say no, and even then, they're likely to be supportive, even apologetic.

Basic Truth 6: You don't wait for the "right" moment to ask; you ask now.

If you are always looking for the right moment—the "perfect" time—to ask for the money, you will never find it. You have to be ready, willing, and able to close the solicitation at any time. You have to take the risk of hearing no.

If that happens, don't take the rejection personally. They are saying no to the organization, not you. Once you have presented your case, ask for the money. Don't wait. Either close the solicitation, find out what the objection to giving is and overcome it if possible, or get your turndown, and move on.

Basic Truth 7: Successful fundraising officers do not ask for the money; they get others to ask for it.

The professional fundraising officer is the last person who should ask prospects for money.

The request should come from someone within the prospect's peer group. It is the job of the professional development officer to design, put together, and manage the campaign. Volunteers who are themselves business executives, well-off individuals, community leaders, or board members, are the ones who should ask their counterparts for donations.

Basic Truth 8: You don't decide today to raise money and then ask for it tomorrow; It takes time, patience, and planning to raise money.

Make the decision to initiate a fundraising campaign before the need becomes dominant. It takes time to develop a campaign and its leadership. With each prospective donor the chances are you will get only one chance to present your case. Be prepared. If you present a poorly prepared case, you will be told no.

Basic Truth 9: Prospects and donors are not cash crops waiting to be harvested; treat them as you would customers in a business.

No successful businessperson deals with customers as if they had a responsibility to buy. Prospects and donors have to be courted as you would court a customer. They must be told how important they are, treated with courtesy and respect, and if you expect to do business with them again, thanked.

There are, of course, exceptions to each Basic Truth, but if you rely on the exceptions to support your organization, you will find them to be few and far between and dollars in short supply. In the end, we raise money from people who:

- Have it;

- Can afford to give;

- Are sold on the benefit of what we are doing;

- Wouldn't have given it to us unless we had asked;

- Receive appreciation and respect for their gifts.

It doesn't take a genius to raise money. The process is a combination of common sense, hard work, preparation, courtesy, commitment, enthusiasm, understanding, and a belief in what you are asking others to support.

APPENDIX 15A

Example
Board Policy: Volunteers

POLICY

The board of directors and senior management acknowledge and support the vital role of volunteers in achieving the organization's mission.

Operating policies and procedures are adopted by the organization to provide a framework that defines and supports the involvement of volunteers.

A qualified person is designated to be responsible for the volunteer program.

A clearly communicated recruiting, referencing, and matching process is consistently applied for all continuing volunteers and all volunteers who have individual contact with clients.

Volunteer assignments address the purpose of the organization and involve volunteers in meaningful ways—reflecting their backgrounds, abilities, and motivation for volunteering.

Volunteer recruitment and selection reaches out to diverse sources of volunteers.

Volunteers receive an orientation to the organization, its policies and procedures, and receive training for their volunteer assignment.

Volunteers receive appropriate levels of supervision according to their task and are given regular opportunities to receive and give feedback.

Volunteers are welcomed and treated as valuable and integral members of the organization's staff.

The contributions of volunteers are regularly acknowledged with formal and informal recognition methods.

*Adopted from: Welcome to the Volunteer Bureau of Leeds and Grenville-Volunteer Orientation Manual, 2004.

Rights and Responsibilities of Volunteers

A Volunteer has the right to be...	A Volunteer has the responsibility to...
... properly interviewed, selected, and provided with a position description	... choose an organization which he or she can respect
... given a position that is worthwhile and challenging	... be sincere in the offer of service
... provided information on the organization's mission, policies, structures, and funding	... only accept a position he or she feels will meet with his or her needs, skills, interest, and available time
... provided tasks and assignments that have been carefully considered and planned	... ensure he or she understands the organization's policies, structure, and mission
... provided an orientation and ongoing training	... prepare for work assignments, follow procedures, and utilize time wisely
... given support from a designated volunteer or staff person	... make and fulfill commitments
... treated as a co-worker	... acknowledge the need for training and participate fully
... given appropriate and timely recognition for services	... consult with supervisor when unclear on appropriate action or directions given
... involved in and informed of what is happening in the organization	... provide feedback that will improve effectiveness
... reimbursed for approved "out-of-pocket" expense where funds are available	... work as a team member, understand the role of paid staff, and stay within the bounds of the position description
... covered by organizational insurance while performing volunteer duties	... respect confidentiality

APPENDIX 15B

Volunteer: Supply, Demand, and Outcomes*

Volunteer Pool (Supply)
- size of population
- age of population
- income levels/need for paid employment
- community traditions

Individual Capacity
- skills
- time
- functionality: physical/cognitive
- knowledge/skills
- interest/need
- resources: money/transportation

Outcomes
- number of volunteers utilized
- volunteer tenure
- volunteer impact on enterprise performance
  - cost
  - results
  - fundraising
- volunteer satisfaction

Enterprise Needs

(Demand)
- programs
- resources

Enterprise Capacity
- policy decisions
- resources
- attitude
- flexibility
- management systems

* Adopted from: Song-Lee Hong, Nancy Morrow-Howell, Feng Yan Tang, and James Hinterlong, "Engaging Older Adults in Volunteering, Conceptualizing and Measuring Institutional Capacity," *Nonprofit and Voluntary Sector Quarterly*, Vol 38 No. 2, April 2009.

APPENDIX 16

Intermediate Sanctions: Excess Compensation*

Effective September 14, 1996, The Taxpayer Bill of Rights II (TBORII) increased the power of the Internal Revenue Service (IRS) to penalize tax exempt organizations' executives and board members who do not comply with the tax law regarding excess benefit, private inurement, and compensation.

TBORII authorizes the IRS to apply intermediate sanctions to any excess benefit transactions (compensation) involving disqualified persons.

- Compensation is defined as total compensation (i.e., base salaries, variable/at-risk compensation, benefits, perquisites, deferred compensation, and severance).

- A disqualified person is any person who is in a position to exercise substantial influence over the affairs of a tax-exempt organization.

Intermediate sanctions include taxes and penalties on individuals receiving excess benefits and anyone who knowingly approves any excess benefit transactions. Penalties include:

- If a disqualified person is engaged in an excess benefit transaction, that person must repay the excess benefit and can additionally be taxed an amount equal to 25% of the excess benefit.

- An organization official—trustee, director, or officer—who knowingly approves an excess benefit can be taxed an amount equal to 10% of the excess benefit (up to $20,000/transaction).

- If the disqualified person does not pay the tax and corrects the transaction within a specified time, an additional tax equal to 200% of the excess benefit can be assessed.

Intermediate sanctions enable the IRS to penalize those taking advantage of their relationship with a tax-exempt organization, without revoking the organization's exemption.

Excess benefits are payments or services provided by a tax-exempt organization, either directly or indirectly, to a disqualified person that are greater than the value received (i.e., paying more than "fair market" value).

*   This appendix is drawn from Clark Consulting, Health Care Group Presentation to the Alliance for Advancing Nonprofit Healthcare; D. Benson Tesdahl and Jodi Finder, "Don't Wait for Intermediate Sanctions Guidance," Nonprofit World, vol. 16, no.1, January/February 1998 and Sarah J. Schmidt and Sullivan Cotter and Associates, Inc., "New Regs Unravel Intermediate Sanctions Snares," Nonprofit World, vol. 19, no. 4, July/August 2001.

As noted above, a disqualified person is an individual who is in a position to influence the organization's decisions (i.e., someone who can essentially benefit from a decision which they have a substantial power to determine).

Intermediate sanctions apply only to tax-exempt organizations because non-exempt entities have no exemption to lose.

With regard to compensation issues, an exempt organization can create a rebuttable presumption of reasonableness, shifting the burden of proof of unreasonable compensation to the IRS by having a compensation committee composed entirely of independent, non-employee directors, which:

- utilizes appropriate comparability data in making decisions;

- meets in executive session for deliberations and vote;

- documents its processes, rationale, and decisions in contemporaneous minutes.

The IRS has not defined or established a "standard" for what is considered reasonable compensation. However, it has indicated the greater the amount by which pay exceeds market norms, the more it will scrutinize total compensation.

The following are "generally accepted" guidelines related to compensation at tax-exempt organizations.

- Pay levels at or below the 75th percentile generally are considered reasonable.

- Pay levels above the 75th percentile are considered the upper-end of market practice.

- Pay levels should not significantly exceed the 90th percentile of the market data, unless a leader's unique skills, performance, or market circumstances warrant compensation at this level.

APPENDIX 17

Selecting and Retaining a Consultant

At various points in the text the possibility of using consultants has been mentioned. These references have side-stepped the obvious question of how you find and then select a consultant.

The first step in hiring (retaining) a consultant is to understand what the organization needs or is trying to accomplish.

ROLES

In broad terms, consultants can play five basic roles.

Consultants can be used to provide specialized technical and subject matter expertise. From time to time, an organization will need advice or support in an area that is beyond the capability or availability of its staff. In these instances, it is more economical to engage a consultant than to hire additional permanent staff. Investment advisors are an example of this kind of consultative role. Other examples include data security specialists, executive recruiters, construction managers, compensation specialists, system installation specialists, process improvement advisors, etc.

A second role for which consultants are often used is to validate either what management wishes to do or has done. Examples are using a consultant to validate the benefits, costs, and savings that can be obtained through a proposed merger, the fairness of the price of an acquisition, or the reasonableness of compensation.[1] The enterprise's independent auditor is an example of a consultant who is used to validate what has been done.

Consultants can also be used to fill a short-term gap in the enterprise's staffing structure. An interim financial officer or interim chief executive is an example of this kind of role. Retaining a consultant on a long-term basis for carrying out core management activities is not recommended. In fact, it is probably an error in terms of both cost and overall operational performance.

As soon as practical the enterprise should replace the consultant with a full-time employee or retain the consultant as a full-time employee. Core management

1 In the same vein, a third party might want the enterprise to hire a consultant to provide an objective perspective. For example, a lender may want a third party to provide a going concern statement or a funder may want an assessment that the enterprise has the capacity and capability to carry out a proposed project.

functions simply cannot be delegated to external consultants. The enterprise's management staff must do them—otherwise the consultant is effectively the organization's management.

A fourth role for a consultant is a bit subtler. **Consultants can be used to present, particularly to boards, unpleasant realities.** These "messages" can run the gamut from operational performance matters to functional and/or interpersonal failures of governance. The consultant can serve as the messenger, who can be sacrificed for bringing bad news. However, with the bad news on the table, management can then go forward, with arguably "clean hands," to address the identified problem.

For this use of consultants to work, management and the consultant must hold the same views and interpret the objective data in the same way. The consultant must also understand what he or she is being asked to do and the potential consequences. In this context, the consultant is there to support a management initiative, not an independent agenda.

The last general role of a consultant is to serve as a catalyst and/or facilitator, enabling and if need be guiding the organization through a multi-step process. Examples of this are using consultants to lead an organizational development process or a personal leadership enhancement program. An even more common example is to involve consultants in designing and guiding an organization's business planning process. In this regard more than one consultant may be helpful. One consultant can be useful in guiding the overall process and another can be valuable as a technical or subject-matter expert in regard to such matters as the enterprise's environment, quality and process improvement, etc.

SOURCES

Potential public sources for finding a consultant for any of the above roles include:

- Institute of Management Consultants— www.imcusa.org
- BoardSource—www.boardsource.org
- Foundation Center— www.foundationcenter.org
- The Nonprofit Resource Center— www.not-for-profit.org
- The local United Way and community foundation
- Professional and trade associations
- Certification bodies
- Local colleges and universities.

In some communities large corporations may have community service programs that could provide consultant support. Also, the community may have an Executive Service Corps program that could be of help.

FINDING A CONSULTANT

Once management is clear as to what it wants to accomplish it can begin the consultant identification and hiring process. Finding and retaining a consultant is more of an interpersonal search process than an application of quantitative management formulae. The hiring party needs to reach out to various sources that maintain listings of consultants, who know of consultants, or have had personal experience with consultants.

Technical consultants (the above roles one, two, and three) can be found through professional associations, certification organizations, other consultants that the enterprise has worked with (e.g., lawyers can often suggest accountants and financial advisors, accountants can suggest investment managers, information technology vendors can suggest training consultants, etc.). Colleagues can also suggest consultants that they have used.

Frankly, finding a consultant is less difficult than finding the right consultant. To assure organizational and cultural fit, as well as interpersonal rapport, the hiring manager must personally interview the candidates and also check references, searching to find a past client who is professionally, and ideally personally, known so that a candid appraisal can be obtained of the consultant's work style and work product. This kind of reference resource can also provide information about the consultant's technical expertise and a frank appraisal of the fit between the organization and its culture, and the consultant's style.

If the fit is good, the consulting engagement can be productive. If not, no amount of technical and subject matter knowledge can rescue it.

FACILITATIVE CONSULTANTS

Finding and retaining a facilitative consultant (roles four and five) follows the same general pattern. Here though, personal contacts are more valuable, and the experiences of other organizations are both more important and more useful. The obvious requirement flowing from this is that more time must be spent on assuring rapport and establishing a clear understanding and agreement regarding what is to be done, how it is to be accomplished, and the consultant's explicit role and exit plan.

Because of the sensitivity of the tasks that facilitative consultants are being asked to undertake, the comfort level between management and the consultant, and if the board is to be involved, the board, management and the consultant, must be high. There must be a degree of trust that will allow probing and often difficult questions to be asked in an environment of psychological and emotional security.

CAUTION

Three final points should be noted: (1) consultants should be paid; (2) a written agreement should be signed by both parties; and (3) management should not become dependent on consultants.

First, unless they are volunteers or loaned executives being supported by another source, consultants will need to be paid. Consultants are in the personal service business and cannot give their services away and hope to stay in business. They may offer a discount, if the issue is particularly interesting or if they have a personal interest in the work of the enterprise. However, they will not and should not be expected to work for free.

Second, a written agreement should be drafted between the consultant and the enterprise so that there are no misunderstandings as to the scope of work, the cost, and the schedule. The starting point for this is asking all of the potential consultants for a written proposal.[2] A proposal provides the basis for assuring that an understanding exists as to the work to be done. It also provides a basis for negotiating price and the details of the work schedule and process. Handshakes and oral understandings only provide the foundation for ill will and possibly lawsuits.

Finally, management should neither become dependent on a consultant nor routinely outsource strategic decisions. Strategic decisions shape the future of the enterprise. Just as the management does not want the board to hand it a business plan, the enterprise does not want a consultant to do its business planning.

Consultants can help. Their help can be very valuable. However, if the enterprise must rely on consultants to determine where it should be going, how it should be getting there and then relying on the consultant to manage key elements of the implementation process, then the board and management should rethink either their approach or the enterprise's ability to continue as an independent entity.

---

2 Often a request for information begins this process and is then followed up with a request for proposals. The request for information enables the enterprise to better identify the consultants it may want to work with. The request for proposal provides the basis for the enterprise to specify the work it wants done. As in all purchasing situations, it is best to get multiple proposals and bids and to make the selection not just on the basis of price.

Chief Executive Officer Job Description: Examples*

The chief executive officer serves as the enterprise's principal management executive, responsible, within the policies and authorities established by the board, for the management of the enterprise. The position reports, for purposes of administrative clarity, to the chair of the board but is accountable to the full board, serving as the principal staff resource to the board.

The following are examples of chief executive officer position descriptions. The chief executive recruiting process will require a position description so that candidates (whether internal or external) will understand what is being sought and therefore be able to assess their interest.

For purposes of recruitment, the position description should also include information regarding:
- Qualifications
  - Education
  - Skills
  - Experience
- Compensation
  - Salary
  - Benefits
- Contact Instructions

Example 1

Nature of Position

Serves as the organization's chief executive officer. Reports directly to the board and is ultimately responsible for the operation of all programs, the management of all fiscal resources, the supervision of all staff, and the provision of quality services to the community.

Relationship to Other Administrative Staff

Supervises the activities of the staff. Final approval for employment, promotion, or termination of XYZ staff is the responsibility of the chief executive within the guidelines/policies set by the board.

*Excerpted from Barbara Lawrence and Outi Flynn, The Nonprofit Policy Sampler, Second Edition, a publication of BoardSource. For more information about BoardSource, visit www.boardsource.org. BoardSource ©2006.

Position Duties

- Plans, develops, and supervises programs.

- Evaluates program improvements and recommends policy to the board.

- Undertakes and oversees all employment actions for XYZ staff within guidelines/ policies set by the board.

- Serves as the primary organization planner, setting goals and objectives and developing projections of needs and funding.

- Seeks funding and/or resources from a broad range of sources.

- Develops and maintains records and reports on programs and services provided by the organization.

- Formulates budgets and maintains an accounting system that meets all federal, state, and local compliance standards.

- Prepares and submits regular operating (including financial) reports to the board.

- Acts as primary liaison with various governmental entities and community organizations.

- Serves as the chief spokesperson for XYZ and is responsible for all public relations.

- Performs other duties as directed by XYZ board.

Example 2

Function

- Serve as chief executive officer of the organization; report to the board of trustees; responsible for leading the organization's success.

- With the chair of the board, enable the board to fulfill its governance function and facilitate the optimum interaction between management and the board.

- Direct and formulate the plan for achieving the agency's mission.

Responsibilities to the board

- With the chair of the board, develop meeting agendas to ensure the opportunity for the board to fulfill all responsibilities effectively. Develop an annual calendar to include all critical issues in a timely manner.

- Keep the board and board chair fully informed on the condition of the organization and all important factors.

- Work with the board chair to ensure effective and efficient board committee structure.

- With the board chair, recommend the composition and commission of the board committees.

- Work with the board chair and full board to develop and implement appropriate business plans.

Responsibilities to the Organization's Personnel and Programs

- Assume responsibility for the organization's consistent achievement of its mission and financial objectives.

- Ensure the organization's philosophy and mission are practiced throughout the organization.

- Oversee the flow of funds to ensure steady progress toward goals, achievement of the mission, and that proper allocation reflects present and future potential.

- Hire and administer an effective management team with provision for succession.

- Implement appropriate personnel training and development that ensures qualified human resources necessary for the achievement of the organization's mission, goals, and objectives.

- Maintain a climate that attracts, keeps, and motivates top-quality people—both professional and volunteer.

- Formulate and administer all major policies and procedures.

- Serve as the chief spokesperson for the organization and ensure proper representation to its various constituencies.

Example 3

The chief executive works in partnership with the board and the staff to provide leadership, vision, and direction for the organization and to develop organizational business plans. The chief executive implements policies approved by the board, manages the organization's programs and operations, and represents the organization in the community. Specific responsibilities include:

- Overseeing the development, implementation, and evaluation of programs and services that support the mission.

- Leading the staff and board in developing realistic business plans, including annual financial, human resources, and operational plans.

- Developing a staffing structure that supports the efficient delivery of programs and services, and accomplishment of major goals identified in the business plan.

- Leading fundraising efforts.

- Providing regular, timely financial and operational reports to the board that compare performance to the plan.

- Complying with all local, state, and federal legal requirements.

- Building positive relationships with partner organizations, policymakers, media, and others.

- Representing the organization by participating in key associations and organizations, serving on committees and advisory groups, and speaking in public settings.

Example 4

Position Summary

The chief executive reports to the board and is responsible for the enterprise's achievement of its mission, goals, and objectives. Areas of responsibility include planning and evaluation, policy development and administration, personnel and fiscal management, fundraising and public relations. This position is hired by and is directly accountable to the board through its elected board chair.

Responsibilities

1. Management and Administration
   a. Develop and facilitate an active planning process.
   b. Oversee all programs, services, and activities to ensure that program objectives are met.
   c. Ensure compliance with funding sources and regulatory requirements.
   d. Provide information for evaluation of the organization's activities.

2. Fiscal
   a. Develop, recommend, and monitor annual and other budgets.
   b. Provide for proper fiscal record keeping and reporting.
   c. Submit monthly financial statements to the board.

3. Personnel
   a. Administer board-approved personnel policies.
   b. Ensure proper, legal, and board-approved hiring and termination procedures.
   c. Provide for adequate supervision and evaluation of all staff and volunteers.

4. Board Relations
   a. Assist the board chair in planning the agenda and materials for board meetings.
   b. Initiate and assist in developing policy recommendations and in setting priorities.
   c. Facilitate the orientation of new board members.
   d. Work with the board to raise funds from the community.
   e. Staff board committees as appropriate.

5. Public Relations
   a. Serve as chief liaison with specific community groups.
   b. Coordinate representation of XYZ to legislative bodies and other groups.

Example 5

Reports to: Board of Directors   **Exempt/Nonexempt:** Exempt
Salary Classification: Executive   **Date:**

I. Position Summary

The chief executive officer (CEO) is the top executive at ABC Inc. As an officer of the corporation, the CEO leads ABC Inc. in developing the knowledge infrastructure, culture, and competencies necessary to establish it as a nationally respected provider of resources and services.

The CEO ensures that the needs and interests of ABC Inc.'s stakeholders are served pursuant to its mission, strategic goals, and bylaws. The CEO is also responsible for programs, products, and services and ensures the smooth and efficient operation of the enterprise within the approved budget. The CEO is the spokesperson for the organization.

II. Major Responsibilities

1. Developing new initiatives and leading current activities.

2. Securing funding resources for new initiatives.

3. Developing personnel policies and procedures.

4. Liaising with the board of directors, including board meetings, budget review, and other communications.

5. Developing and implementing, as approved by the board, the annual and long-range strategic goals.

6. Assuring the compliance with the articles of incorporation and the bylaws of the organization.

7. Serving as the primary spokesperson for the organization.

8. Developing and maintaining relationships with other organizations and entities for joint product development and co-marketing activities.

9. Identifying grant opportunities and successfully winning grants.

III. Scope of Supervisory Responsibility

The CEO is responsible for the direct supervision of the chief operating officer (COO) and indirectly for all other staff.

IV. Revenue and Expenditure Responsibility

The CEO is responsible for the overall financial performance of the organization. The position also requires the development of new products and services that will generate revenue. The CEO is responsible for identifying new funding sources to support program development.

Example 6

Summary

The chief executive officer (CEO) serves as the leader of the organization and its primary public representative, reporting to the board of directors. The CEO works in partnership with the board to ensure that the organization fulfills its mission.

Functions

Planning

- Collaborates with the board to define and articulate the organization's vision and to develop, annually, business plans and strategies, and budgets for achieving that vision.
- Develops future leadership within the organization.

Management

- Oversees the operations of organization and manages its compliance with legal and regulatory requirements.
- Creates and maintains procedures for implementing plans approved by the board of directors.
- Promotes a culture that reflects the organization's values, encourages good performance, and rewards productivity.
- Ensures that staff and board have sufficient and up-to-date information.
- Evaluates the organization's and the staff's performance on a regular basis.

Financial Stewardship

- Prudently manages the organization's resources within budget guidelines according to current laws and regulations.
- Ensures that staff practices all appropriate accounting procedures in compliance with Generally Accepted Accounting Principles (GAAP).
- Provides prompt, thorough, and accurate information to keep the board appropriately informed of the organization's financial position.

Fundraising

- Develops fundraising initiatives with the board and supports the board in fundraising activities, as well as overseeing staff in the development and implementation of fundraising plans.
- Serves as a primary person in donor relationships and the person to make one-on-one fundraising solicitations.

Community Relationships

- Serves as the primary spokesperson and representative for the organization.
- Assures that the organization and its mission, programs, and services are consistently presented in a strong, positive image to all relevant stakeholders.
- Actively advocates for the organization.
- Builds relationships with peer organizations, when appropriate.

Programmatic Effectiveness

- Oversees design, delivery, and quality of programs and services.
- Stays abreast of current trends related to the organization's products and services and anticipates future trends likely to have an impact on its work.
- Collects and analyzes evaluation information that measures the success of the organization's program efforts; refines or changes programs in response to that information.

Board Support and Leadership

- Serves as a member of the board of directors and as an ex-officio member of all board committees.
- Advises the board in the development of policies and planning recommendations.
- Makes recommendations and supports the board during orientation and self-evaluation.

Example 7

Reports To

Board of Directors through its elected board president

Job Description

The chief executive officer is responsible for all financial, operational, administrative, and legal aspects of the daily organizational management of the enterprise, which includes but is not limited to annual fund development, public relations and marketing, sound management of all fiscal resources, supervision of an established program staff, and business operations in accordance with standard business practices. The incumbent will liaise effectively with national, state, regional, and local organizations, and coordinate the contributions of diverse groups of trustees, donors, staff, volunteers, and community groups. The chief executive officer works under authority granted by the board of directors to assist in defining priorities to build and develop teamwork between the enterprise and community volunteer leaders, to implement the board's strategic plan and ensure program and fiscal accountability.

Responsibilities

Organizational Development

- Work with the board of directors to develop the stakeholder base.
- Oversee and support current program staff and develop short- and long-term staff development plan.
- Oversee and support volunteer work force, appropriate volunteer activities and procedures, including recruitment, approval, confidentiality, retention and discharge, as appropriate.

Financial Management and Administration

- Implement the enterprise's board-approved strategic plan, and implement other board and enterprise plans in a timely way as they relate to the capital campaign, programs, annual fund development, communications, business development, and major gifts and endowment.
- Ensure legal compliance and program and fiscal accountability.
- Provide leadership in developing organizational and financial plans with the board of directors and other staff, and carry out plans and policies as authorized by the board.
- Maintain fiscal responsibility for the annual budget and report to the board regularly.

Program Development and Management

- Oversee the current programs of the enterprise and work with staff to develop programs to achieve objectives of the enterprise's strategic plan.
- Identify and cultivate partner organizations for mutual program benefit.

Fundraising

- Oversee and support fundraising efforts including appeal mailings, database management, capital campaign, special event, major gifts, and corporate and personal individual solicitations.
- Monitor grant opportunities and oversee the submission of grant applications.
- Provide support and work with the board in raising funds for the agency.

Board Relations and Communications

- Assist the board by maintaining and promoting the vision and mission of the enterprise and in achieving goals and objectives of the strategic plan.
- Initiate and assist in recommending and developing policies and setting priorities.
- Keep the board and board chair fully informed on the condition of the enterprise and other important factors affecting the health of the organization.
- Work with the board chair to ensure effective and efficient board committee structure and operation.
- Assist the chair in planning the agenda and materials for the board meetings and board strategic planning retreats.

Public Relations and Communications

- Implement marketing timeline and communications strategic plan approved by the board.
- Ensure appropriate representation, as a spokesperson, of the enterprise goals and objectives to community, corporate groups, and other stakeholders.

Personnel

- Develop and administer board-approved personnel policies.
- Ensure proper hiring and termination procedures as required by law.
- Provide for adequate supervision and evaluation of all staff and volunteers.
- Encourage staff and volunteer development and education.

Notes

CHAPTER 1

1. Katie L. Roeger, Amy S. Blackwood, and Sarah Pettijohn, *The Nonprofit Almanac 2012* (Washington, D.C.: The Urban Institute Press).

2. If the organizations are to succeed beyond the energies and commitments of the founder, they must either grow organically, through their own efforts, or through consolidation with other entities. Consolidation, however, does not simply mean organizational merger or acquisition. Certainly, these are forms of consolidations. Outsourcing, shared services, joint purchasing, etc., are also approaches to consolidation that can achieve a similar economic end with, perhaps, less disruption.

3. It is suggested that organizations can go through potentially seven life cycle strategies:

    - Concept
    - Startup
    - Growth
    - Maturity
    - Decline
    - Regeneration
    - Failure

Life cycle is not entirely a sequential process. An organization can go from "maturity" to "failure," without attempting to "regenerate" itself. Similarly, it can go from "growth" to "regeneration" without struggling through the "decline" phase. What actually happens is a function of the operating environment and management's leadership.

In the same vein, life cycle flow is not a direct function of organizational age or size. Even so, older enterprises are more likely to have faced the challenges of "maturity," "decline" and "regeneration" than newer organizations. In addition, size is not a defining characteristic, though large organizations have gone through, or may still be in, a "growth" stage.

In terms of target audience, it is assumed that organizations have at least reached the growth stage of their life cycle:
- focusing on mission, while simultaneously embracing change;
- formalizing organization structure, becoming position—not person—dependent, and
- transferring psychological ownership of the enterprise to an independent board.

  *Footnote drawn from presentation made by Anne Marie Kemp at the New York Spring Conference of the Association of Small Foundations.

4. David A. Freedman, *Corps Business* (New York: Harper Business, 2000), xvii–xx, 97–114.

5. As is discussed in the following chapters the planning process, and particularly the environmental assessment and ongoing performance reporting, provide tools for anticipating crises and developing "fail-safe" alternatives.

6.   William B. Werther and Evan M. Berman, *Third Sector Management* (Washington, DC: Georgetown University Press, 2000), 117–141.

CHAPTER 2

1.   Katie L. Roeger, Amy S. Blackwood, and Sarah L. Pettijohn. *The Nonprofit Almanac* 2012. (Washington, DC: The Urban Institute Press).

Data from the *Almanac* are used throughout this and subsequent chapters.

2.   Registered with the Internal Revenue Service (IRS) means that the organization has applied for and received tax-exempt recognition. Not included are religious organizations, their auxiliary groups, or small nonprofits earning less than $5,000 per year in revenues.

3.   Enterprises required to annually report to the IRS are registered organizations having annual gross revenue of $50,000 or more. As a result, not all registered enterprises are reporting entities.

4.   The Bureau of Economic Analysis staff suggests that the product value of nonprofit enterprises are difficult to quantify. A sounder comparison of economic sectors is the amount of wages and salaries paid by each. Based on this, the nonprofit sector accounts for about 9% of the economy. This approach, however, understates the employment in the sector by not recognizing the wage value of volunteers (equals almost 33% of total nonprofit wages) and, simultaneously, likely overstates the size of the sector by only considering the proportion of wage and salaries—not the other resources consumed (factors of production) which are higher in less labor-intensive enterprises.

5.   Burton A. Weisbrod, *The Nonprofit Economy* (Cambridge: Harvard University Press, 1988), 19.

6.   Lester M. Salamon, *America's Nonprofit Sector* (New York: The Foundation Center, 1999), 12.

7.   Burton A. Weisbrod, *The Nonprofit Economy* (Cambridge: Harvard University Press, 1988), 20.

8.   Harvey C. Mansfield and Delba Winthrop (ed.), *Democracy in America, Alexis de Tocqueville* (Chicago: University of Chicago Press, 2000), 489–493.

9.   The American democratic experiment is marked by a belief in a sense of egalitarianism. Without a ruling class, society needs to find another mechanism to champion community causes. This need is filled by the voluntary, collective association. Its development as the natural consequence of American democracy is clear. It provides the positive force for championing a cause. At the same time, it holds the potential of a threat to the incumbent government. Just as a voluntary, collective association can organize to promote interest in a charitable cause. It can do the same for a political position/interest. This was recognized by the early observers of American volunteerism. Although de Tocqueville is given much of the credit for documenting and promoting the American propensity to create voluntary organizations, in 1829 William Ellery Channing recognized America's vibrant civil associations. This was years before de Tocqueville did. Yet from Channing's perspective, voluntary associations posed a potential danger to society, representing a possible source of instability. He was not alone in this

perspective. The combination of the voluntary association and the corporation was viewed in some quarters as a potential threat to the power of government.*

*Peter Frumkin, *On Being Nonprofit* (Cambridge: Harvard University Press, 2002), 37-38.

10. Peter Frumkin and Jonathan B. Imber (ed.), *In Search of the Nonprofit Sector*, (Rutgers: Transaction Publishers, 2004). Steven Rathgeb Smith, "Government and Nonprofits in the Modern Age: Is Independence Possible?," *Society*, May, 2003, 36-45.

11. Others take a somewhat different perspective on de Tocqueville's observations and conclusions. For example, see Peter Dobkin Hall, *Inventing the Nonprofit Sector* (Baltimore: Johns Hopkins University Press, 1992).

12. The names of the sectors (i.e., private, public, community, also indicate to whom the sector's benefits inure). It should also be understood that all three sectors are heterogeneous in their composition.

13. Burton A. Weisbrod, *The Nonprofit Economy* (Boston: Harvard University Press, 1988), 4-5.

14. Legal Information Institute, Supreme Court Collection, Rehnquist, J. Dissenting Opinion, 464 U S 574, Bob Jones University v. United States.

15. Substantial nonprofit sectors also exist in other nations. In fact, as measured in terms of employment, looking at the percentage of total non-agricultural employment, the Netherlands, Ireland, Belgium and Israel all rank ahead of the United States.

16. Lester M. Salamon, *Holding the Center* (New York: The Nathan Cummings Center, 1997), 3.

17. Establishing a single name or label for this aspect of the economy has been a difficult task. The core of the problem lies in the diversity of the enterprises that have to be encompassed by a single, understandable label. Currently, nonprofit and voluntary sector are perhaps the most commonly used terms. At various times, and in some instances even today, the sector has been called the:

- Tax exempt sector
- Commons
- Third sector
- Civil society sector
- Nongovernmental sector
- Charitable sector
- Nonproprietary sector

Each of these terms has its advocates and critics, reflecting historical and operational circumstances, as well as political agendas. The notion of it even being a "sector" engenders debate in some quarters.*

For purposes of this discussion, the sector is identified as the community sector because the benefits flow back to the various stakeholder communities and the organizations that compose it have made the strategic decision to be nonprofit enterprises.

*Peter Frumkin, *On Being Nonprofit* (Cambridge: Harvard University Press, 2002), 10-16.

18. Stephanie Lowell, Les Silverman, and Lynn Taliento, *McKinsey Quarterly*, 2001, Number 1, 147-155.

19. Since 1980, the nonprofit sector (community sector) has been recognized in the National Income Accounts as a distinct institutional section.

20. Sectors can be defined by a major objective, and unalterable characteristic (e.g., ownership and beneficiary). For the community sector, ownership is private, but the beneficiary is public. By this measure the community sector is different from either the private or public sectors. Moreover, it possesses internal integrity, making it distinct, because its products and services are bound together by being collective goods, and are derived from private efforts yet yielding public benefits.

Taken together, these factors lead to the conclusion that the community sector is a distinct economic sector. They also reinforce the complexity of the sector (e.g., mixing private resources and public purposes), the simultaneous requirement for operational business rigor and social consciousness, and the economic necessity of addressing immediate needs while building for the future—and its unique role and place in contemporary society.

21. Retention of the personal income tax deductibility of contributions to 501(c)(3) organizations is a separate tax question, relating to capital generation—not income taxation. Charitable contribution deductibility should be maintained even if profits are taxed.

22. Each sector can also be thought of as having a different frame of reference. Competition drives the for-profit business sector as individual firms pursue self-interest goals. While not entirely free of competition, collaboration is more prevalent in the community sector as similar enterprises pursue common community interests. The common good arguably drives the public sector, over-arching self-interest and even community interest. As such, each is better structured than the other for particular goals.

CHAPTER 3

1.   Peter Dobkin Hall, *Inventing the Nonprofit Sector* (Baltimore: Johns Hopkins University Press, 1992), 13-114.

2.   Katie L. Roeger, Amy S. Blackwood, and Sarah L. Pettijohn, *The Nonprofit Almanac 2012* (Washington, D.C.: The Urban Institute Press).

3.   Lester M. Salamon, *Holding the Center* (New York: The Nathan Cummings Center, 1997), 11-47.

4.   Geraldine Fabrikant, "Tax Laws Popularize The Small Foundation," *The New York Times*, sec. B1 June 7, 2008 and The Nonprofit Almanac 2012.

5.   While the non-distribution requirement is probably the most widely recognized feature of nonprofit organizations, it is not the most important. For the non-distribution prohibition to be an issue, there must first not only be profits but also profits that are not needed for pursuing the enterprise's mission. Both for-profit and nonprofit organizations regularly demonstrate the ability to incur losses thereby making the non-distribution constraint at times moot. What is never moot, however, is their purpose. All nonprofit entities are created to serve a public purpose. The specifics of mission will obviously vary. Common to all, however, is the commitment to the achievement of a public purpose and to dedicate all of its efforts and resources to that end.

6.   The Internal Revenue Code establishes a fiduciary duty upon all officers and directors of exempt organizations. To satisfy this duty an organization must serve a public rather than a private interest. Practically there will be some serving of private interests in order to serve the public interest. However if this serving of the private interest is non-material or the vehicle for achieving the public interest then the organization's exemption can be maintained. In this same vein the Internal Revenue Code also requires that no part of the net earning of the organization inure to the benefit of any private shareholder or individual. The private shareholder or individual is in turn defined as a person having a personal and private interest in the activities of the organization. It is to these individuals that inurement is prohibited. Inurement, therefore, involves providing a benefit to an organizational insider i.e., employee, board member, contributor, etc. that furthers the private interest of that individual as opposed to the public interest of the enterprise. (Good Governance for Non-Profit HMOs: Best Practices and Cautionary Tales, Thomas K. Hyatt, Ober/Kaler).

7.   Paul Jansen and David Katz, "For Nonprofits, Time Is Money," *The McKinsey Quarterly*, January, 2005.

8.   Pitt County Memorial Hospital, Combined Financial Statements, 2004 and 2003, Note, Number 1, 11.

9.   Application is necessary to be approved for a 501(c)(3) exemption. Other nonprofit organizations are generally accepted as tax exempt without an Internal Revenue Service ruling.

10.   Just as the community sector is society's creative invention for addressing its human service, cultural, education, etc., needs, the social enterprise component of the sector is the pragmatic solution for the actual production and delivery of those services. Aside from the managerial aesthetics of demanding efficient and effective performance, social enterprises, because they both produce products and/or services and—often—compete in the intra and/or inter-sector marketplaces, have a clear incentive to be operationally efficient. At the same time, because they are created to fill a service and product need vacuum, they have a similarly clear incentive to make decisions that maximize community benefits, potentially at the expense of efficiency and almost always in preference to profitability.

11.   For reporting public charities in 2010, almost 75% of revenues were from fees, 8% from government grants and 13% from private contributions.

12.   The social enterprise is the organizational and managerial crucible for combining private resources and government program financing to solve societal problems and meet community needs. Social enterprises, while not fitting neatly into the operational behavior mold of either the public or private sectors, potentially incorporate both the best and worst elements of both sectors.

13.   Member-based enterprises provide services focused on the interests of an explicitly identified group, who have self-selected their affiliation with the organization. These members have voluntarily come together to seek and provide a specific collective benefit for themselves. Member-serving, provider organizations, though not charitable organizations, are essentially nothing more than social enterprises serving an explicitly known and self-identified group of stakeholders. In contrast, public-serving, provider organizations, while perhaps having members (i.e., public radio stations, museums,

zoos, etc.) focus on promoting the general welfare of a community/stakeholder group, regardless of the beneficiary's or potential beneficiary's personal membership status.

14. Private foundations, foundations created by individuals or their estates are required to make minimal payouts of 5% of net assets per year. Included in the 5% can be the non-investment operating costs of the foundation.

15. The skills involved in operating funding intermediaries are significant. This is reflected in the fact that there are graduate level courses and degrees focused on their management.

16. They are also tax exempt. However, tax exemption is a consequence of the Internal Revenue Code. Although tax exempt, these organizations do not have the deductible privilege related to contributions made to them. That is, individuals cannot deduct contributions to these organizations for purposes of determining their federal income tax liability.

17. Unlike the community sector where nonprofit-ness is a strategic decision, in the private sector, for-profit-ness is the goal.

18. A change in mission can be initiated by the organization. However, to actually change its mission the organization must obtain the approval of the court in the enterprise's state of incorporation. The state is typically represented in this action by its attorney general who acts to represent and protect the interests of the community (i.e., the organization's original stakeholders).

19. This also makes internal resource allocation decisions complicated due to the problems in reliably quantifying relative benefits and cost/benefit ratios.

20. In some jurisdictions, regulatory guidelines at least partially answer this question. For example, in San Francisco, California, nonprofit enterprises such as medical centers can secure a welfare exemption and be relieved of property tax payments if their annual net income does not exceed 10 percent. Rachel Gordon, "San Francisco Hospital May Owe Taxes," San Francisco Chronicle, July 25, 2005.

21. The interest paid on the debt of local and state government agencies is exempt from federal taxation. To the extent that governmental agencies use their debt issuing capacity to provide capital to nonprofit enterprises, the cost of capital to these enterprises is reduced. Such debt financing is generally labeled as tax exempt debt or tax exempt bonds.

22. As discussed, this action is encouraged, by the Internal Revenue Code allowing gifts to this classification of nonprofit organizations to be deducted, for purposes of calculating federal tax liability, from taxable income. The deductibility tax privilege is important. At the same time, it should be recognized that philanthropy represents only about 10% of total community sector revenues. Fees and service charges are the primary source of revenues, followed by grants and payments from government agencies and programs.

CHAPTER 4

1. In 17th and early 18th century England, corporations were used principally to promote royal goals as well as individual riches, and were invested in by the great

lords and merchants of the time. The corporations of the day, joint stock companies used to achieve these goals, included the East India Company, the Massachusetts Bay Company, and the Virginia Company. They possessed immense powers, including the ability to raise armies and dispense justice. (Those corporations that survived in America eventually became colonial governments and eventually were dissolved and converted into royal colonies, except Pennsylvania). The colonial fear of the corporate form of organization was rooted in this history. It was not clear what mischief a commercially conceived corporation could do, and there was no significant body of common law to offer guidance, so it was thought best to shun the form.

This is not to say that there was no familiarity with all corporate forms, only the business form. The corporate form had been used in the early national period for purposes tinged with a public interest or of an eleemosynary nature. Early at the national level, the First and Second Banks of the United States were created as corporations. By the 1820-1840s at the state level, this form of organization accompanied the creation of waterworks, canals, houses of refuge, orphan asylums and hospitals.

Eventually, necessity led to the wholehearted adoption of the corporation for business purposes. In a land rich in resources but poor in labor and capital, a mechanism was needed to enhance the kind of risk-taking necessary to develop the country. (Source: Observations of Irwin Flack, Ph.D., Retired Professor, State University of New York, Oswego.)

2.   To be created, corporations required state charters. State legislatures initially only gave those charters to people they trusted. Moreover, while the charters could be renewed, they were for fixed periods and corporate boards had a proportion of their members who were either elected or appointed by the legislature. State legislatures also held to themselves the right to alter, even once granted, corporate charters. This kind of uncertainty had a chilling effect on the potential of corporations.

3.   For most board members the corporation's charter typically is viewed as being little more than a historical artifact. This view, while common, is misguided. What the charter says—even in its intended legal generalities—should be understood. It is important because it is the contractual agreement of the corporation's creators, defining the common purpose and starting point from which all else is shaped and guided.

4.   "Corporate Social Responsibility: Lots of it About," *The Economist*, December 12, 2002.

5.   Limited liability is a big idea. Initially it was viewed as a form of subsidy, enabling joint stock companies to compete with owner-managed enterprises, and risk shifting.

Certainly, the possibility of unlimited gains, but the certainty of known maximum potential losses, is an intoxicating opportunity, reflecting the continuing saga of the triumph of hope over reality. It is also an ingenious mechanism for gathering the capital that society needed.

One can debate the philosophical and theoretical pros and cons of limited liability. However, when faced with the capital needs of building a railroad, a steel mill, an anti-missile assembly plant, etc., philosophy takes a backseat to pragmatism.

Limited liability, the guarantee that the most that can be lost is the amount that was invested, makes the raising of large sums of capital possible.

Limited losses and unlimited gains make the magic of the capital market possible.

6.   The origins of the board are thought to lie in the joint stock companies of the seventeenth century, particularly the English East India Company. After merging with another company the East India Company organized itself into a court of twenty-four directors elected by and reporting to a court of proprietors (i.e., shareholders).

7.   There are obviously a variety of nonprofit corporations: trade associations, universities, hospitals, health plans, condominium associations, social clubs and so on. From a legal perspective these various organizations are more alike than different. They are typically created and operate under the same state statute, each having a board of directors, empowered by statute to direct the organization's operations, regardless of size.

8.   A separate membership body, while offering the potential of checks and balances and grassroots democracy, also holds a risk. If the membership body is small and the cost (either in time or money) of becoming a member is low, then the enterprise runs the risk of a corporate takeover by a few individuals pursuing their own agenda. To safeguard against this, "membership" can be honorific (with no corporate authority), the cost of membership can be increased (thereby limiting the number of members), the size of the membership base can be expanded (to make it more difficult to get a majority) and/or scope majority votes can be required for certain specified actions.

9.   Bylaws are an internal document, approved by the corporation, providing the detailed rules by which the enterprise conducts itself. Bylaws will be discussed in greater depth later. At this point it is enough to recognize that they provide the ground rules for electing the nonprofit corporation's directors and the operation of the corporation's governance mechanism.

10. The Secretary of State's role is to be the custodian of records, issuing appropriate documents when all required conditions are met and approvals obtained.

11. The corporation is an organizational creation that has the ability to conduct business as if it were a person. Moreover, it has unlimited life and is also allowed to take advantage of the principles of limited liability, protecting those who invest in it from unlimited losses while simultaneously providing it with the opportunity to raise capital through the issuance of tradable securities, (i.e., equity in the form of shares (stock) in itself). This concept of tradable securities is itself another enabling technological innovation. Its importance to this discussion is its implications with respect to capital generation, giving the for-profit corporation the ability, to the extent it can sell its shares, to effectively print money.

The ability to generate capital through the sale of tradable securities is an important feature of the contemporary corporation. It is also a feature that pragmatically distinguishes the for-profit corporation from its nonprofit counterpart. Certainly, the nonprofit corporation could issue shares in itself. However, because of the strategic business decision requiring all resources be focused on pursuing the enterprise's mission, as well as the tax exemption prohibition concerning benefits inuring to investors—the market for such shares is thin.

There are examples of corporations selling stock and investors not expecting a direct financial return (i.e., the Green Bay Packers football team and the Rochester Red Wings baseball team). (See Chapter 12—Capital Formation). Such examples, however, highlight community spirit more than financial opportunity. They are fundamentally examples of community resources being dedicated to public purposes with the contribution being masked as an investment.

CHAPTER 5

1.   Ralf Caers, Cindy DuBois, Marc Jegers, Sara DeGieter, Catherine Schepers, and Roland Pepermans, "Principal–Agent Relationships on the Stewardship-Agency Axis," *Nonprofit Management & Leadership*, Vol. 17, No. 1, Fall 2006.

2.   Much can be said about the legal role of board members. Such pronouncements should be left to the attorneys and the courts, not managers. Therefore, no attempt is made to offer legal advice or opinion. The former should be sought from an attorney; the latter is the purview of the courts. The focus here is on a pragmatic, operational discussion of a corporate director's obligation.

3.   Directors are entitled to rely on the information provided by corporate officials and board committees as long as they keep themselves informed of the efforts, through reports and/or committee meeting minutes, of those providing the information.

4.   The business judgment rule is presumptive in that it assumes that in making a business decision the board acted on an informed basis, in good faith and in the honest belief that the actions taken were in the best interests of the company. The board's action must therefore be evaluated in light of the relevant circumstances. If no breach of duty is found, the board's actions are protected. Typically no breach will be found unless directors, individually and the board collectively, have failed to inform themselves fully and in a deliberate manner. Cede & Co. vs. Technicolor Inc. 634 A.2d 345, 368 (1994).

5.   Conflict of interest disclosure statements should be filed annually as well as whenever there is any material change in a director's circumstances that may generate a conflict. Key employees—individuals who can make purchasing or resource allocation decisions—should also submit conflict of interest statements.

6.   Included as a potential form of conflict is interlocking directorates, individuals serving on the boards of entities which do business with each other. Interlocking directorates carry the risk of self-dealing. Therefore, at a minimum, they must be disclosed.

7.   Boards may also have, due to either custom, common sense or regulatory or legal requirements, certain other legal responsibilities. For example, approval of retirement plans and plan amendments, approval of financial commitments and contracts in excess of certain amounts, appointment of medical staff members and independent auditors. These activities, while perhaps legally required, are not fundamental or basic duties that apply to all directors.

8.   Louis Lavelle, "Shhh! You'll Wake the Board," *Business Week*, March 5, 2001, 92.

9.   One of the common themes of board member satisfaction surveys is the desire of board members to be more involved in formulating the enterprise's strategy and plans. This is understandable given what board members bring to the table both in accomplishment and perspective. These insights can be valuable and the board should be actively engaged in supporting the planning process. The board's involvement must, however, be guided and shaped.

It is the board's purpose to govern, not manage. Therefore, while there must be a robust communication process, with give and take, proposal and revision, the board must play an oversight and guidance role, allowing/encouraging management to create and develop its strategy and plans.

The board, however, must ultimately also approve the plan. To fulfill its duty of care, the board must obviously be familiar with the strategy and plan. If for no other reason, this is why board involvement is necessary before the strategy and plan are presented for action.

Board review and approval is not a technical assignment. Rather, it is a policy action. The board should review the strategy and plan and approve it if it is consistent with:
• Mission,
• Financial capacity, and
• Human resources,
• and most importantly, makes common sense.

10.   There must be no ambiguity concerning this point. A director cannot ignore what he or she believes to be an unlawful activity or action on the part of the enterprise. If the matter in question cannot be resolved, then the director must formally note opposition and resign.

11.   Some believe that commitment to the enterprise's purpose is developed over time. This view holds that new board members cannot fully understand the role and complexity of the enterprise until they have experienced board service. As they serve on the board, their understanding of and commitment to the enterprise either grows— or they leave the board. For some board members this may be reality, and for some recruitment circumstances this risk may be acceptable. As the standard for recruitment and selection, it should not, however, be the standard.

12.   It is understood that risk is the probability of a hazard being incurred. Hazard is the loss or injury which may happen and which, in turn, has a cost attached to it. For simplicity, the term "risk" is used to combine both concepts.

13.   Of the tens of thousands of for-profit and nonprofit corporations in the country, it is estimated that between 1996 and 2000 fewer than three hundred lawsuits were filed against boards of directors. Recently, however, the number of lawsuits, while still proportionately small, has increased. See Healthcare Leadership and Management Report 10, Issue 6 (June 2002). For example, ten members of Allegheny Health, Education and Research Foundation's (AHERF) board of more than one hundred members ultimately became involved in a lawsuit relative to the enterprise's bankruptcy.

14.   Criminal prosecution stemming from misappropriation of assets or earnings is not included in this list of risks. Deliberate criminal actions are far different from the issues discussed here, which relate to a director's risk in trying to be an honest fiduciary.

15. Directors can be held personally liable if they concur in decisions resulting in the improper distributions of the corporation's assets in the form of payments, purchases or loans.

CHAPTER 6

1. Bylaws are the rules and regulations adopted by a corporation to govern its internal business affairs. They are intended to protect the corporation from arbitrary actions, as well as define issues of corporate structure and the entity's internal workings. See Watkins v. Clark, Misc. 2d 727, 380 N.Y.S. 3d 604 (Sup. Ct. Rockland County, 1976) and Vernon Manor Co-operative Apts. v. Salatino, 15 Misc. 2d 491, 179 N.Y.S. 2d 895 (Cty. Ct. Westchester County, 1958).

2. Most states have statutes specifying required officers, typically a chief executive or president, vice president, secretary and treasurer. An officer is a person holding a position of trust in a corporation. Since a corporation can only act through its agents, an officer is essentially an agent. These four are commonly considered the principal or executive officers of a corporation. Provisions allowing the board or stockholders to create other offices are common. In Delaware, for example, every corporation has officers with titles and duties as stated in the bylaws or by resolution of the board of directors not inconsistent with the bylaws.

3. Bylaws define how an enterprise and its board must act in their decision making processes. Bylaws, however, can be a double-edged sword. On the one hand, they can provide guidance and protection for board and management actions. On the other, if not followed, or if only followed when it is convenient or expedient, they can provide a "smoking gun" to critics of the enterprise's decision making and performance, in the extreme, providing the basis for invalidating board decisions and actions. Therefore, the content of the organization's bylaws and the standards that they set need to be understood by all members of both senior management and the board.

Recognizing the controlling influence of bylaws and the reality that the enterprise needs are continually changing, bylaws should be written to allow pragmatic operational flexibility. They should also be formally reviewed every several years and amended, as needed, to keep them from becoming a barrier to efficient and effective decision making.

4. There is no uniformity among the states as to the minimum number of directors. Many states require at least three. Others require only one. Some states have no minimum. For example, in New York State for-profit corporations are required to have at least one. In contrast, nonprofit corporations must have at least three members.

5. According to recent survey data, for-profit company boards average eight members, with only one percent having more than fifteen members. In contrast, limited data for health care organizations suggest board sizes that average in the mid-teens.

6. Bylaws should allow as much flexibility as possible with respect to the specifics of Board size. If possible, ranges should be used instead of specific numbers (i.e., "up to twenty-five members" as opposed to "a membership of twenty-five members").

7. The appropriateness and ultimate cost of using board seats in this way raises obvious questions about the possibility of alternatives. The unavoidable reality is that often there are no practical alternatives.

Regardless of the recognized merits of a merger or acquisition, it may not happen if it requires that some incumbent board members of the acquiring organization give up their seats or if the acquired organization gets no seats—or only token representation. Similarly, in a merger it is politically easier to add seats and accommodate everyone— or almost everyone—than to ask members in good standing to step aside.

8. The importance of a board member making the necessary time available to do the job cannot be overemphasized. Research, albeit limited, shows that organizations that emphasize willingness to give time in their board member selection process, typically have boards that are active in all aspects of board responsibilities and accountabilities.* The predicate for being willing to commit time is a potential board member's understanding of and belief in the enterprise's mission. Without that belief in mission, it is unlikely that either an individual member's or the full board's potential to contribute to the success of the enterprise can be realized.

In the same vein, board member commitment can only be maintained if they feel they are making a difference. This requires that they be able to contribute to shaping the content of the agenda and, as well, can be actively and meaningfully engaged in committee and board discussions.

*Francie Ostrower, "Boards of Midsize Nonprofits: Their Needs and Challenges, Center on Nonprofits and Philanthropy," (Washington, D.C.: The Urban Institute, May 2008).

9. Arguably, other skill sets could be listed. Additional detail, however, risks obscuring the core skills which members need if they are to serve effectively and grow individually—and which the enterprise needs in order to perform successfully.

10. General change in status can be thought of as change in employment or residence. However, it can also include legal matters, both criminal and civil, as well as matters of moral turpitude.

11. In the for-profit setting, term limits are also useful as an anti-takeover protection mechanism. If all terms expired simultaneously, it would be easier for a hostile party to gain control of the board. By only having a minority of seats open for election each year, a hostile takeover initiative has a more difficult task.

12. A note of caution is warranted. When directors are also employees of the enterprise a mandatory retirement age may be in conflict with the Age Discrimination in Employment Act (ADEA). While this reality does not negate the principle, it requires that counsel review mandatory retirement age provisions to assure that they meet the test of applying to directors who are not employees.

13. "Ten Questions to Ask before Joining a Board," *Black Enterprise*, June 1995.

CHAPTER 7

1. This approach may seem a bit clinical. It should be remembered, however, that candidates are being identified and recruited to meet the needs of the enterprise. Board membership, while potentially rewarding, is not a reward. Rather, it is an opportunity

to provide service for the public benefit. It is a high calling which should not be squandered.

2.   "Director Compensation, Report of the NACD Blue Ribbon Commission," National Association of Corporate Directors, 2001.

3.   If one director is paid, then generally all should be paid. There should not be two classes of directors—paid and unpaid. Paid directors who do not feel that compensation is necessary, can either return their fees to the corporation or contribute them to a charity of their choosing. An exception to this egalitarian rule, however, can be made for the chairman. It is generally the recognized reality that the chairman must devote more time to the enterprise and that, as a consequence, some stipend may be both appropriate and necessary.

4.   See Chapter 6 for more on how to keep non-board members engaged on an ongoing basis with the enterprise. This is particularly an issue for public benefit corporations, such as hospitals and nursing homes. These organizations make extensive use of volunteers, advisory boards, and auxiliary organizations as a means of involving and keeping people involved in their work.

5.   Regardless of the specifics of the bylaws, the full board should always be informed when a special committee is created and be advised as to its charge, duration and membership. In fact, regardless of the bylaws, prudence and discretion suggest that the creation of a special committee and its charge, etc., always be discussed with the board before the chair acts.

6.   If committee chairs are not specified in the bylaws, it is a useful practice to rotate chairs every two to three years. This will protect against the inadvertent concentration of power. Similarly, committee members should be rotated. The latter will both avoid concentration of influence and expand board member knowledge of the enterprise and its workings. Finally, to the extent possible, all board members should serve on at least one committee.

7.   For publicly traded companies, the Sarbanes-Oxley Act of 2002 (Public Law No. 107-204 [July 30, 2002]) specifies actions that corporations must adopt in order to strengthen public confidence in their financial integrity. The Act does not directly apply to nonprofit, tax-exempt organizations. Even so, the principles and goals do apply. Therefore, to the extent possible, the provisions of the Act should be voluntarily adopted.

8.   The audit committee is generally called the audit committee. The compensation committee might also be called the personnel committee, the committee on management, the management development committee or the compensation and management development committee. The committee on governance might also be named the nominating committee or the committee on directors.

9. "Auditing the Audit Committee," *The Wall Street Journal*, December 9, 2002.

10. In the post-Enron, Global Crossing, Waste Management era, and as a result of the Sarbanes-Oxley Act, the question of auditor independence is drawing more attention. The issue centers on the risks of the audit findings being compromised due to the auditor wanting to protect/sustain current business relationships and profits or gain future ones. To avoid even the appearance of this, some are suggesting that auditors

have no business relationship with their clients other than the audit. Others suggest, with the exception of consulting services, a less draconian approach, emphasizing disclosure and judgment over absolutely "bright line" prohibitions.

11. Brian E. Pastuszenski and Inez H. Friedman-Boyce, "The New Governance Reforms: Best Practices for a Riskier World," *The Corporate Board*, November/December 2002.

12. In a small enterprise, the compensation committee, like all other committees, may have to take a more active role providing technical expertise as well as governance oversight. This is one of the operational realities continually confronting small enterprises. Recognizing this functional need, small enterprises must adjust their board member recruitment strategy to attract members having the necessary technical skills.

13. In some enterprises the past chair may leave the board at the end of his or her term as chair in order to provide a smooth governance leadership transition and to avoid any sense of conflict between current and past board leadership. The past chair can still stay involved with the enterprise through an advisory committee or special projects role and after a reasonable break be invited to again serve as a board member.

CHAPTER 8

1. The words chair and chairman are used interchangeably in the text. Chairman has its origins in 10th century Kingdom of England, when the king or his spokesman sat alone in a chair before the group, who sat on benches. Manus is Latin for "hand," so the chairman is one who sits in the chair and handles the meeting. The term has nothing to do with gender, which is designated by addressing the official as "Mister Chairman" or "Madam Chairman." In spite of this, chairwoman and chairperson are sometimes used in place of chairman. Chair is used to avoid the awkwardness and perceived sexism of the other terms. The National Association of Parliamentarians does not approve using "chairperson."

2. As part of its accountability the board ratifies the organization's basic policy directions. Operational policy decisions, set by management, flow from these. The board also approves the enterprise's strategy and operating plan and monitors performance against that plan. Within the policy parameters approved by the board, the chief executive makes operational policy decisions, as well as manages both current operations and plans for the future. To accomplish this, the chief executive both implements the board's policies and brings to the board policy, strategy and operating recommendations. This dual role of being a leader (bringing recommendations to the board) and simultaneously a follower (implementing the decisions that the board makes) is part of the alchemy and difficulty of the chief executive position.

3. Ram Charan, "Getting Structure Out of the Way," *Boards at Work* (San Francisco: Jossey-Bass, 1998).

4. "G.E. Is Set to Appoint Two New Outside Directors," *The Wall Street Journal*, October 25, 2002; Jeffrey E. Garten, "Don't Let the Chief Executive Run the Board, Too," *Business Week*, November 11, 2002.

5. J. Larry Tyler and Errol Biggs, *Practical Governance* (Chicago: Health Administration Press, 2001); Jeffrey E. Garten and Ellen Cochran Hirzy, *The Chair's Role in Leading the Nonprofit Board, Governance Series*, no. 4 (Washington, DC: National Center for Nonprofit Boards, 1998).

6.   Maureen K. Robinson, *The Chief Executive's Role in Developing the Nonprofit Board*, Governance Series, no. 2 (Washington, DC: National Center for Nonprofit Boards, 1998).

7.   Sana Siwolop, "When Deadwood Doesn't Refer to the Table," *The New York Times*, October 17, 1999.

8.   The example survey questionnaires presented in Appendix 10 give form to the data-gathering component of the assessment process. They reflect a middle ground in terms of rigor. Organizations just beginning an assessment program would likely take a more simplified approach. Others having more experience and success to build upon could pursue various questions or aspects of assessment in more detail and depth.

9.   These are all examples of items which would normally appear on either the board's or a committee's forward agenda.

10.   Richard Leblanc, "Assessing Board Performance: 10 Key Factors," *The Corporate Board*, January/February 2002.

11.   Committee chairs also need to be groomed. While an individual may not be interested in being or suited to be the chair of the board, he or she may have the skill and ability to be a committee chair. This distinction should not be overlooked. Moreover, it should be exploited with specific member development plans.

CHAPTER 9

1.   Leadership is about creating an understanding of the direction in which the organization should be heading. Leaders create an inspiring story (describing that direction), one that others will commit to and follow. From this story come the roots of the enterprise's energy to achieve its mission.

2.   Peggy M. Jackson, *Nonprofit Strategic Planning* (Hoboken: John Wiley & Sons, 2007).

3.   The fundamental perspective of this text is that of a social enterprise operating manager. In particular, this and the following chapters take this view. Obviously, it is not the only perspective for creating an enterprise's strategy.

Consultants, for example, take a different approach, focusing more on an exercise in "guided discovery." That is, through data, perhaps presentations and designed questions focusing on "how and why," leading the group—both management and the board—to recognize certain realities, their implications and the resulting actions that the enterprise might consider.

For organizations that are relatively new to comprehensive business planning, this kind of approach can be not only non-threatening, but also quite productive, allowing difficult issues to be raised and addressed at little risk to management. However, as the enterprise matures, management must increasingly assert itself, both putting more of its visionary stamp on the work product and actively guiding the board to resolve thorny issues.

Even in the mature organization's business planning efforts, consultants and facilitators can still play a role. However, as the organization evolves, their role must also change, shifting from leading the process to "staffing" it.

4.   Peggy M. Jackson, *Nonprofit Strategic Planning* (Hoboken: John Wiley & Sons, 2007).

5.   Robert S. Kaplan and David P. Norton, "The Office of Strategy Management," *Harvard Business Review*, October 2005.

6.   James, A. Phills Jr., "The Sound of Music," *Stanford Social Innovation Review*, Fall 2004.

7.   Smith, Bucklin & Associates, Inc., *The Complete Guide to Nonprofit Management: Second Edition* (New York: John Wiley & Sons, 2000), 3-26.

8.   William B. Werther Jr., and Evan M. Berman, *Third Sector Management* (Georgetown: Georgetown University Press, 2001), 28-50.

9.   Strategy is many things: plan, pattern, position, ploy perspective, etc.

As a plan, strategy relates how we intend to realize our goal(s). As pattern, strategy is the "rhyme and reason" that emerges in the course of making the endless decisions that reconcile the reality we encounter with the ends we seek. As a position, strategy is the stance we take. As a ploy, it is a ruse. As perspective, strategy is part vantage point and part the view from that vantage point.

Strategy is all of these. It is the bridge between the philosophy of mission and the concrete actions of operations. Strategy is the framework that steers the actions that the enterprises will take to achieve its understood purpose.

At the enterprise-wide level, strategy is an overarching concept. It is the organization's comprehensive planning statement, reaching from the board to the smallest functional work unit, in sum, defining what the enterprise will do and the specifics of how it will do it.

Strategy, as used here, is a big concept and a significant resultant work product.

However, strategy is also used as a term to describe particular managerial or problem solving actions. At the functional work unit, project level or even specific issue levels, managers often speak of their "strategy" for achieving a particular "end." In this context, strategy is a small concept. It may reflect all of the components of the enterprise level perspective and therefore look like a strategy, but it should be more accurately thought of as tactics, the means by which resources are to be deployed and actions taken to achieve an understood "end"—not strategy.

Understanding this, it is more important to appreciate that a work unit's strategy may accurately be that unit's tactical element of the enterprise-wide strategy. Fred Nickols, 2000.

10. For purposes of understanding the planning process, it is useful to conceptualize an enterprise's business plan as consisting of two major components that can be expressed in two ways. The two components are the strategic and operating plans. Taken together they sum to represent the enterprise's strategy. That is, how the organization is going to move from the philosophy of mission to the achievement of mission—from what the enterprise hopes to accomplish, to measurable targets of what is expected to be achieved.

They differ from one another, not in terms of direction, but rather with respect to time frame and detail. The strategic plan has a macro level perspective and is not as subject to dramatic change as the operating plan. Operating plans are continuously being refined—in response to changing performance realities.

Strategy can be expressed in the prose and numbers of the strategic and operating plans, or it can be expressed in the financial quantification of the operating and capital budgets. If the organization's strategy is not just rhetoric, then the strategic and operating plans rhetoric should match the resources of the operating and capital budgets. The budgets should simply be the enterprise's strategy expressed in monetary terms.

11. Arguably an organization can have static or dynamic contingency plans. Static plans are plans that try to anticipate all events and hence, an anticipated response "on the shelf" ready to be used. Dynamic contingency plan is really continuous planning where plans and tactics are continually being reviewed and modified, as a consequence of changes in the environment and actual performance results. Since all contingencies cannot be anticipated with certainty, making continuous planning part of the management culture and style is a better approach.

12. Tony Poderis, Fund-Raising Forum, "Don't Make Your Organization's Statement of Purpose a 'Mission Impossible,'" http://www.raise-funds.com.

13. Idealist FAQ, "What Should Our Mission Statement Say?" http://www.nonprofit-info.org.

14. As noted earlier, to substantively alter the enterprise's mission, the approval of the corporation's state of legal domicile must be obtained.

15. The mission statement declares why an organization exists. It is the foundation on which strategy must be built.

The mission statement should be clear and relatively concise. It should identify those whom the enterprise hopes to serve and the difference(s) it hopes to make to them. It should do this in as few words as possible, focusing on:
- ends not means;
- management results not efforts, and
- uniqueness of the enterprise.

In terms of language, it should avoid weak words, (try, seek, encourage) and utilize active verbs, (cure, increase, eliminate).

The mission statement should leave no doubt about who the enterprise serves and what difference it will make to them, without being either too broad (e.g., being all things to all people), or too narrow (e.g., preventing growth and expansion).

Structurally it should be composed of a purpose clause having two components:
- an infinitive that indicates a change in status (e.g., to increase, to decrease, to prevent)
- an identification of the problem or condition to be changed.
  Examples: To eliminate homelessness or to improve the quality of life.
- a business statement that outlines the business the enterprises choose to pursue in order to achieve its purpose
  Example: To construct housing for homeless individuals to provide job training to homeless individuals.
  Combined, the two can, for example, be expressed as:
- to eliminate homelessness by providing job training to homeless individuals.

In addition, the mission statement can include a statement of the values that will guide the enterprise in pursuing its mission (e.g., transparency, continuous improvement, diversity, respect, etc.).

16. Mission identifies the enterprise's reasons for being. It is expressed in ideally an emotionally and psychologically soaring statement that establishes the enterprise's general direction.

Goals specify how the general direction is to be carried out. They are a limited number of statements that translate an enterprise's mission into major areas of attention.

CHAPTER 10

1. Jim Collins, *Good To Great and the Social Sectors* (New York: Harper Collins Publishers, 2005).

2. Innovation Network Inc., *Logic Model Workbook*, 2005.

3. Laura Silverstein and Erin J. Maher, "Evaluation Blues," *Stanford Social Innovation Review*, Winter 2008, 23-24.

4. Thomas A. McLaughlin, "Let's Study That: The Real Cost of Cost-Benefit Studies." *The Nonprofit Times.* July 1, 2007.

5. A more complex variation on the same process is the MacMillan Matrix.*

MacMillan Matrix* Several Orgs. Offer Similar Programs		Program is Very Attractive to Funders and/or Community Participants		Program is Not Attractive to Funders and/or Community Participants	
		Few/No Orgs. Offer Similar Programs	Several Orgs. Offer Similar Programs	Few/No Orgs. Offer Similar Programs	
G O O D **F I T**	High Org. Capacity and Credibility	Keep and Compete	Keep and Grow	Keep and Collaborate	Keep and Subsidize
	Weak Org. Capacity and Credibility	Give Away to Other Orgs.	Grow Your Capacity or Give Away	Give Away to Other Orgs.	Collaborate or Stop
POOR FIT		Give Away		Give Away	

The MacMillan Matrix is a management tool intended to assist nonprofit enterprises in determining operational activities. It is built on the notion that:
- resources are finite and limited
- duplication of services/programs is unwarranted
- low quality to large numbers is less desirable than high quality to fewer people
- the demand for resources is competitive

Current and potential services/programs are assigned to the square in the matrix with the best fit. Activities that fall into the top row should be kept. Initiatives in the top right-most squares are a "good" organizational fit—but, are difficult to finance and may require cross-subsidization. Activities in the bottom row should, as a general rule, either not be undertaken or done in collaboration.

* MacMillan Matrix is a management decision-making tool developed by Dr. Ian MacMillan.

6. Examples of process improvement literature include:
   - Charles G. Cobb, *From Quality to Business Excellence*
   - Ralph Smith, *Business Process Management and the Balanced Scorecard*
   - Praveeen Gupta, *Six Sigma Business Scorecard*
   - Michael L. George, *Lean Six Sigma for Service*
   - Stanley Marash, *Fusion Management: Power of Six Sigma, ISO, 9001:20000, Malcom Baldrige, TQM, and Other Quality Breakthroughs of the Past Century*
   - W. Edwards Deming, *The New Economics for Industry, Government, Education, 2nd Edition*

7. Burton A. Weisbrod, "Why Nonprofits Should Get Out of Commercial Ventures," *Stanford Social Innovation Review*, Winter 2004.

8. Examples of process budget literature include:
   - Murray Drapkin and Bill La Touche, *The Budget Building Book for Nonprofits: A Step by Step Guide for Managers and Boards*
   - T. Raiser, *ROI For Nonprofits: The New Key To Sustainability*
   - David C. Maddox, *Budgeting for Non-For-Profit Organizations*
   - John Zeitlow, Jo Ann Hankin and Alan G. Seidmen, *Financial Management for Nonprofit Organizations: Policies and Practices*

9. Operational responsibility for the budget process generally falls to the organization's finance function. While finance may have responsibility for putting all the budget components together and may be the "score keeper" in terms of numbers and balance, the accountability for constructing work unit budgets should never be simply delegated to finance. If work units give up this management opportunity, the enterprise risks the budget becoming an end to itself, separated from the organization's strategy.

CHAPTER 11

1. Michael C. Mankins and Richard Steele, "Turning Great Strategy into Great Performance," *Harvard Business Review*, July-August 2005.

2. At times management must even get its "hands dirty" doing the actual work and/or experiencing what the enterprise's clients are experiencing in order to understand the processes and actions involved and steps necessary to achieve the desired results.

3. Knowledge of the business, at both the strategic and tactical levels, is necessary so that one knows what must be done to achieve both performance improvement and overall success.

4. Mark Gottfredson, Steve Schubert, and Elisabeth Babcock, "Achieving Breakthrough Performance," *Stanford Social Innovation Review*, Vol. 6, No. 5, Summer 2008, 32-39.

5. Daniel Tinkelman and Bairj Donabedian, "Street Lamps, Alleys, Ratio Analysis, and Nonprofit Organizations." *Nonprofit Management and Leadership*, Volume 18, Number 1, Fall 2007.

6.   Judith M. Gueron, "Throwing Good Money After Bad," *Stanford Social Innovation Review*, Volume 3, Number, 3, Fall 2005.

7.   Jed Emerson, "But Does It Work?," *Stanford Social Innovation Review*, Vol. 7, No. 1, Winter 2009, 29–30.

8.   Innovation Network, *Evaluation Plan Workbook*, 2005 and Innovation Network, *Logic Model Workbook*, 2005.

9.   Jeff Cook, "Driving Change," *Board Member*, May/June 2007.

10.   Potential references to consider:
   • Thomas R. Ittelson, Financial Statements: *A Step-By-Step Guide to Understanding and Creating Financial Reports*, 2009.
   • Ray H. Garrison, Eric Noreen, and Peter C. Brewer, *Managerial Accounting*, 2014 (15th edition).
   • Steve Albrecht, Earl K. Stice, and James Stice, *Financial Accounting Concepts and Applications*, 2010.
   • Scott Besley and Eugene F. Brigham, *Essentials of Managerial Finance*, 2007 (14th edition).
   • Stephen P. Baginski and John M. Hassell, *Management Decisions and Financial Accounting*, 2004.

11.   Additional information about Form 990 can be found at the IRS web site—http://www.irs.gov.

CHAPTER 12

1.   Recall the earlier discussion of the Corporation and its ability to issue stock having limited liability to the investor.

2.   Francie Ostrower, "Boards of Midsize Nonprofits: Their Needs and Challenges," (Washington, D.C.: The Urban Institute, 2008).

3.   A quick look at the *Chronicle of Philanthropy, Nonprofit News* or any other nonprofit publication targeted at practitioners, makes clear that fundraisers are in a special class. They are, based on the recruitment and consultant ads and the products and services offerings, the superstars of the nonprofit management world. Effective fundraising leaders must have substantial subject matter expertise. However, they cannot function successfully on their own. They are part of the enterprise's senior management team and can only achieve sustainable success with the support of others.

4.   *The Chronicle of Philanthropy*, May 15, 2008, 32.

5.   Responsible management and governance requires that reasonable and equitable charges be established wherever possible. People with resources will likely pay less if the opportunity is there and pay more if expected to do so. People without resources or with only limited resources—are obviously not a source of, or opportunity for, revenue growth.

6.   John Zietlow D.B.A., CTP, John, "Step By Step," *Exempt*, May/June, 2007, 8–11.

7.   William B. Werther Jr. and Evan M. Berman, "Third Sector Management," *Fund Raising*, 185–203.

8. For example, see Web Site for Seton Hall University, Nonprofit Management Education, Current Offerings in University Based Programs and Web Site for Indiana University-Purdue University Indianapolis, Degree Information, Philanthropic Studies.

9. Smith, Bucklin and Associates Inc., *Complete Guide To Nonprofit Management*, 2nd ed., (New York: John Wiley & Sons, 2000), 97–122.

10. Like the data describing the sector, the data detailing charitable giving is derived from multiple sources using different databases and time period. Therefore, the reader should consider all data as best estimates and approximation, designed to paint a broad picture rather than precise detail.

11. Katie L. Roeger, Amy S. Blackwood, and Sarah L. Pettijohn. *The Nonprofit Almanac 2012.* Washington DC: The Urban Institute Press, 2012.

12. Alex Daniels, *The Chronicle of Philanthropy*, December 12, 2013.

13. Collective fundraising organizations obviously are the exception to this point, having fundraising as their mission—see Chapter 3.

14. Large institutions taking on multi-million and even billion plus dollar campaigns require dedicated staff, systems and a great deal of behind the scenes work, securing pre-announcement commitments. The latter is particularly important to creating a sense of confidence that an aggressive goal is achievable.

15. The enterprise's development staff must also be well versed in the legal and tax rules relating to the deferred gifts. This is necessary both for the obvious reason of not wanting to provide misleading information, but also to demonstrate competence as a well run enterprise.

16. Obviously, the organization must also have a plan specifying what it wishes to do (i.e., newsletters and reports to keep the donor base informed), annual membership solicitations and renewals, annual events major giving and special project campaigns, etc. The plan must also use research to determine who should be asked for what, and when. For example, a major gift opportunity does not want to be lost because the donor is only asked for a membership renewal.

17. There is no getting away from the importance of the board to any nonprofit organization's fundraising efforts. An organization will never achieve its full potential without the board. But this does not mean that the only criteria for board membership should be the ability to give or get large sums of money. An organization needs a good mix of skills on a board which is responsible for guiding its overall policies and maintaining its fiscal health." Bonnie Osinski, "Effective Fund Raising For Human Service Organizations," *Journal for Nonprofit Management*, Summer 1997, Vol. 1, No. 1.

18. Whether through a formal annual report, a special letter from the chairman and/or chief executive that is sent to the enterprise's donor and friends mailing list, an event (e.g. a recognition luncheon or dinner), or some other mechanism, the enterprise must publically recognize and thank its donors. This public recognition is simultaneously the closing step in one fundraising cycle and the opening initiative in the next.

19. Harvey Berger and Gregg Ichel, "Tax Exempt Bonds," *The Nonprofit Times*, August 1, 2006, 16–18.

20. Perpetual bonds (i.e., bonds with a steady flow of interest payments but, no redemption obligation), are more theoretical than practical. The most notable example of perpetual bonds are the consols issued by the British government to finance the Napoleonic wars (1814). Since then others have issued bonds, including foreign governments. Use of perpetual bonds, however, is uncommon in the United States and unusual in other economies.

CHAPTER 13

1. Femida Handy and Laurie Mook, "The Interchangeability of Paid Staff and Volunteers in Nonprofit Organizations," *Nonprofit and Voluntary Sector Quarterly*, vol. 37, no. 1, March 2008, 76–92.

2. The data estimates are the best available. However, as noted earlier, there are difficulties with the data that make the specific number imprecise. In this context, however, a sense of size relative to the volunteer workforce, not precision, is the goal.

3. This and the following data are obtained from The Nonprofit Almanac 2012, Published by The Urban Institute Press.

4. See the Mayor's Office of Volunteerism & Engagement in Albuquerque, New Mexico; Office of Volunteerism, City of Fall River, Massachusetts; Serve LA, Los Angeles, California; Minnesota Department of Health, Community Engagement.

5. Katie L. Roeger, Amy S. Blackwood, and Sarah L. Pettijohn. *The Nonprofit Quarterly 2012*, Washington DC: The Urban Institute Press.

6. 2008 data estimates 26.4% of Americans volunteered. Interestingly, as a result of the recession more enterprises used volunteers as a coping strategy (i.e., 33%.)*

   Corporation for National and Community Service and *The Chronicle of Philanthropy*, August 20, 2009.

7. Christopher J. Einolf, "Will the Boomers Volunteer During Retirement? Comparing the Baby Boom, Silent and Long Civic Cohorts," *Nonprofit and Voluntary Sector Quarterly*, Vol. 38, No. 2, April 1990, 181–199.

8. The focus of this discussion is on volunteers providing services to the organization. Board and advisory committee members are also volunteers. The role and management of these volunteers is discussed in Part II. Service providing volunteers are workers who are doing things—either for the organization or its beneficiaries—that otherwise would not have been done or would have to be provided through paid workers.

9. Recruiting volunteers is a task that begins with a focus first on making organizational friends, who then can be asked to volunteer. Friends of the organization can be both groups and individuals. For event-based activities that require large numbers of short-term volunteers, groups may be the most useful source of volunteers. Long-term volunteers are most likely found on an individual basis. In either event, volunteers also hold the potential to complement their time and work contribution with financial support.

10. Matthew A. Liao-Troth and Craig P. Dunn, "Managerial Sensemaking of Volunteer Motivation: Do Managers See Things the Volunteer Way?," *Journal for Nonprofit Management*, Vol. 3, No. 1, Summer, 1999.

11. Marc Freedman, "Prime Time," *Public Affairs*, 1999.

12. David Eisner, Robert T. Grimm. Jr., Shannon Maynard, and Susannah Washburn, "The New Volunteer Workforce," *Stanford Social Innovation Review*, Vol. 7, No. 1, Winter 2009, 32-37.

13. While the bulk of volunteers indicate that they leave because of poor volunteer management, 9% say that they leave because they are not thanked for their efforts.

14. Compensation involves more than just current salary or wages. It also includes current and future benefits—both monetary and non-monetary. In administering compensation, the total package must be equitable. The fact, however, that it is a package of components means that tradeoffs can also be made—by either management and/or employees without impairing equity or defensibility.

15. Stinson Morrison Hecker LLP, *Self Assessment Guide for Tax-Exempt Hospitals*, 42-55, 95-105, 137-140.

16. Section 4958 involves more than just compensation. See Appendix 16.

17. In addition to the chief executive, the committee can also be accountable for the oversight of other highly compensated employees. This oversight may be active—involving the actual determination of pay and benefits, or passive—simply reviewing the actions that the chief executive is going to take with respect to his or her direct reports. If the committee is going to take an active role in non-chief executive compensation matters, it must be careful not to undermine the authority of the chief executive. Therefore, while actual practice will vary with the enterprise's circumstances and traditions, an active review role is preferable.

18. Ian Wilhelm and Grant William, "Salary Under Scrutiny," *The Chronicle of Philanthropy*, February 26, 2008.

19. If perquisites are to be eliminated and replaced by providing increases in current cash compensation, it is important to remember that since cash compensation is taxed, the amount of increase has to be "grossed up" so that the after tax, not pre-tax, the amount is sufficient enough to compensate for the loss of the perquisite.

20. In simplified form, there are two general types of pension plans: defined benefit and defined contribution. There are also hybrid plans, which are a combination of the two. Hybrids basically combine the certainty to the employer of a fixed dollar contribution (defined contribution plan), but also leaves with the employer the investment return risk (as in a defined benefit plan).

Defined contribution plans are retirement benefit plans where, on a predetermined schedule, an employer makes a fixed dollar contribution to the employee's retirement benefit account (i.e., depending on tax status, 401(k), 403(b), 457(b), or 457(f)). Because the contribution is a known amount and is made on a scheduled basis, defined contribution plans are fully funded. In contrast, defined benefit plans promise a fixed dollar benefit, usually based on years of service and some average of salary, on retirement. The risk of assuring that sufficient funds have been set aside to fulfill this promise falls to the employer. To ameliorate this risk to employees, pension plans can be guaranteed, by the Pension Benefit Guarantee Corporation (a Federal government corporation). The Pension Guarantee Corporation in effect insures the pension benefit. However, to be eligible for this "insurance" the pension plan must meet certain funding standards. Also, the guarantee only applies to a maximum level of annual earned income. Income above this amount is outside of the "qualified" plan. This creates the need for a supplemental plan to, in effect, fit on top of the qualified plan, continuing its benefits, albeit non-guaranteed, regardless of income level.

21. TIAA-CREF, the Teachers Insurance and Annuity Association and the College Retirement Equities Fund, is a $400 billion nonprofit financial services group dedicated to serving the retirement needs of those in the academic, medical, cultural and research fields.

22. Supplemental retirement benefits to be secure must be funded with the monies being held in a "rabbi trust." The term rabbi trust takes its name from the IRS case involving a rabbi that determined that funds held by the congregation in a properly structured trust, for the rabbi's retirement, were protected. The rabbi trust protects the funds within it from changes in the corporation's decisions, regarding supplemental retirement benefits, without giving constructive receipt of those funds, and thereby creating a taxable event, to the beneficiary.

23. Until thirty years ago, few tax-exempt organizations used variable compensation. Many still don't out of a sense that they are inappropriate for many types of tax-exempt organizations.

The IRS settled the question of the permissibility of variable incentive compensation in a series of private letter rulings in the 1970s and 1980s. Some of these pertain to use of all-employee incentives in the form of profit-sharing plans or gain sharing plans. Others pertain explicitly to use of incentive plans for executives.

The IRS said that it is permissible for tax-exempt charities to use profit-sharing or incentive compensation plans, so long as the plans are designed to support the organization's tax-exempt mission, so long as they are administered by a disinterested third party, so long as the size of awards paid is reasonable, and so long as payment of awards does not result in unreasonable compensation. It has indicated in public forums that it would regard a cap on the size of incentive awards as evidence that incentive awards are likely to be reasonable.

24. If an opportunity is provided to improve performance, then a decision must be made concerning any compensation adjustment for the remedial period. The choices are limited, either compensation is held constant, or if because of salary range adjustments the incumbent would be below the minimum, compensation is adjusted to match the minimum—with the understanding that this adjustment is a mechanical policy driven change, not a reward.

CHAPTER 14

1. The same challenge also plays out at the personal level. The question becomes one of building a legacy. While most people may downplay the matter of legacy, the reality is that it is a powerful motivational force. Everyone wants to be remembered well, and also wants to be well remembered. To achieve this, a career marked by success and accomplishment cannot be followed by a series of shortfalls and failures. While some chief executives view the failure of a successor as evidence of their own superior abilities, in reality it only demonstrates flawed governance and a triumph of short term ego over long run organizational needs.

2.   The cost of investing in enhancing personal skills can be thought of as part of total compensation as some employees will view educational financial support, due to its favorable personal income tax treatment, as a legitimate salary tradeoff.

3.   The IDP can also be used, if it is within the enterprise's human resources policies, to identify the support that can be provided to enable the employee to satisfy his or her personal needs to grow and achieve their potential.

4.   The succession management plan can be thought of as the human resources equivalent of the financial budget, providing the means for making decisions as to how human resources will be developed and deployed—and the road map for implementing those decisions. Like a financial budget, the succession plan also provides the board with the information to use in carrying out its oversight responsibilities.

5.   The succession management process can be thought of as consisting of a succession plan and the implementation of that plan.

The succession plan is the specific identification of backups for each key position.

Implementation of the plan involves both the identification of the skills and competencies that individuals need to develop and/or enhance in order to be able to be ready to succeed an identified incumbent and the actions being taken in pursuit of those competencies.

The litmus test of the plan and its implementation asks the following: are people moving from secondary to primary successor and are primary successors being selected to actually fill vacancies as they occur?

6.   An integral part of succession management is determining if the succession management program is being implemented. Specifically, are IDPs being developed and pursued, and are those who are identified as being primary successors being offered the opportunity to fill vacancies as they emerge?

The review should be done annually by the chief executive for all key positions—and by the board or the assigned board committee for the chief executive and all of his or her operational direct reports.

7.   It is estimated that up to 70% of chief executives will leave their positions within the next 5 years and that the Community Sector will be confronted with the need to attract or develop new senior mangers equal to two and a half times the number currently employed. See, Thomas J. Tierney, "The Leadership Deficit," *Stanford Social Innovation Review*, Summer 2006; Marla Cornelius, et al. "Ready to Lead: The Next Generation Speaks Out," *CompassPoint*, 2008; and, Grantmakers for Effective Organizations, "Supporting Next-Generation Leadership," February 2008.

8.   Thomas F. Toole, "CEO Succession: An Urgent Challenge for Nonprofits," Center for Community Engagement at St. John Fisher College, 2008.

9.   Evidence of this is most easily found by just looking at board meeting discussion items and comparing how often financial performance and investment matters are discussed as compared to the time spent on human resources performance.

CHAPTER 15

1. Thomas A. McLaughlin, "Leaderless," *The NonProfit Times*, August 1, 2008, 23- 26.

2. It should be recognized that for some community sector enterprises, consolidation becomes the corporation's succession plan. Enterprises with good succession management processes are, therefore, in a better position to be able to pursue consolidations, if for no other reason than their "bench strength" gives them flexibility to maneuver management attractiveness to others.

3. Thomas A. McLaughlin, "Tying The Knot," *The NonProfit Times*, October 1, 2008, 13.

4. Martha Golensky, "Board Governance," *Nonprofit Health*, Vol. 26, No. 2, March/April 2008, 8-9.

5. Previously the importance of personnel development was discussed. Depending on the size of the enterprise, the chief executive should ideally have an heir and a spare groomed for the board's consideration. In smaller enterprises this is obviously not possible. In these instances the chief executive should try to have at least one internal candidate for the board to consider. If this is not pragmatic, then the chief executive, during the prelude phase of transition, should introduce to the board potential external candidates by, for example, inviting those candidates to make presentations to the board of work that they are doing. If this is done on a planned and systematic basis, the board will have a sense of the direction it wishes to pursue in its search for a successor.

6. The incumbent chief executive should be interested in providing this support because a good successor is measured by how well he or she protects their accomplishments and protects their legacy.

7. The interviews also provide an opportunity, if the candidate is going to have to relocate, to see the community and look at potential housing, schools, etc.

8. The economics are the same whether the candidate is internal or external. That said, an internal candidate might cost less, in effect providing a "home town discount" because they do not have to relocate.

9. The outgoing chief executive might be given a non-specific consulting retainer to ease the economics of the transition. Also, on either a paid or voluntary basis, he or she should be available to advise the new chief executive or carry out some task on behalf of the new chief executive—if asked to do so, by the chief executive.

CHAPTER 16

1. Small community sector organizations that survive and function through the continuing commitment of their volunteers and patrons also need to maintain trust and confidence of their constituents. In these instances, however, the constituents are their community. Moreover, because of the limited size of their operations, the questions of tax exemption, community benefit, compensation, etc. are not central issues to their continuing success.

2. "Independent Sector, Obedience to the Unenforceable," *Independent Sector*, 2002.

3.   Regina E. Herzlinger, "Can Public Trust in Nonprofits and Governments Be Restored?," *Harvard Business Review*, March–April, 1996.

4.   While it may be speculative as to how the public will use the more extensive data provided by the new Form 990, it can be expected with a great degree of certainty that the legislatures and regulators are going to use it to push, particularly large, community sector enterprises, to do more for their communities—as both the price of remaining tax-exempt and as a way of reducing the operating burden on government and the tax burden on the public.

5.   Thomas A. McLaughlin, "Streetsmart Nonprofit Manager," *The NonProfit Times*, July 1, 2008.

6.   Jed Emerson, "But Does It Work?" *Stanford Social Innovation Review*, Vol. 7, No. 1, Winter 2009, 29–30.

7.   NPQ Editors, "Working: Nonprofit-Style," *The Nonprofit Quarterly*, Vol. 15, Issue 3, Fall 2008, 10–22.

8.   Profits from unrelated (to mission) business activities are taxed at the normal corporate tax rates. Such income does not jeopardize the enterprise's tax exempt status as long as it continues to meet all of the requirements for maintaining its tax exemption.

9.   "Nonprofit Healthcare Organizations and the Public Trust," *Inquiry*, Fall 2006.

10.   Emily Friedman, "Hospitals and Health Networks," *H & HN Online* (http://www.hhnmage.com), December 2, 2008.

INDEX